Terror and Taboo

Terror and Taboo

THE FOLLIES, FABLES, AND FACES OF TERRORISM

Joseba Zulaika

and

William A. Douglass

Routledge
New York and London

Published in 1996 by
Routledge
29 West 35th Street
New York, NY 10001

Published in Great Britain by
Routledge
11 New Fetter Lane
London EC4P 4EE

Copyright © 1996 by Routledge

Printed in the United States of America on acid-free paper.

Library of Congress Cataloging-in-Publication Data

Zulaika, Joseba.
    Terror and taboo: the follies, fables, and faces of terrorism / by
Joseba Zulaika and William A. Douglass.
        p.   cm.
    Includes bibliographical references.
    ISBN 0-415-91758-1 (cl: alk. paper).
    ISBN 0-415-91759-X (pb: alk. paper).
    1. Terrorism. 2. Terrorism—Government policy. 3. Terrorism in the
media.   4. Discourse analysis.   I. Douglass, William A.   II. Title.
HV6431.Z85   1996
303.6'25—dc20   95-46989
                                                              CIP

Contents

Acknowledgments

Joseba Zulaika wishes to acknowledge the Harry Frank Guggenheim Foundation for its generous support of his research on the ritual bases of Basque political violence. William Douglass expresses his gratitude to the National Institute of Mental Health for a Research Scientist Career Development award.

We wish to thank David Brent, Karen Colvard, Ana Douglass, James Fernandez, F. Allan Hanson, Carolyn Nordstrom, and our anonymous readers for their insightful suggestions and comments on earlier drafts. We are, of course, responsible for the opinions expressed herein.

Parts of this argument were presented at the universities of Zagreb, Princeton, Nevada-Reno, Chicago, Newfoundland, Compostela, Santander, San Sebastián, Amsterdam, and at several conferences organized by the H. F. Guggenheim Foundation. We benefited greatly from the reactions of the various audiences.

Preface

In the aftermath of the World Trade Center and Oklahoma City explosions, terrorism is at the center stage of American political discourse. Unlike the Reagan years' "international terrorism"—a distant arena with its phantomlike characters engaged in a largely fictional war—the shock of "terror in the heartland" has finally slammed home awareness of the monster in our midst. Terrorism is no longer just about fanatical Muslims or European crazies; America is now proclaimed the future promised land of terrorism. On any given day the *New York Times* may carry several stories in which "terrorism" is the central theme.[1]

Even Clinton's embattled presidency received a much needed public-opinion boost after Oklahoma City. After barricading the White House and closing Pennsylvania Avenue to potential terrorists, the President was quick to remind us that such a measure was unnecessary throughout two centuries of civil war, world wars, and the Cold War. Pennsylvania Avenue, also called "America's Main Street" and "a symbol of national openness,"[2] is the President's front yard. Its closure speaks volumes about his new relationship with the American people.

We are baffled by the use and abuse of terrorism discourse; we voice our skepticism. After many years of writing on the issues of political violence, our misgivings about the intellectual and moral values of the concept of terrorism have only increased. We are bothered by the referential invalidity, the rhetorical circularity that is all too characteristic of much that goes on under the rubric of "terrorism." It is the reality-making power of the discourse itself that most concerns us—its capacity to blend the media's sensational stories, old mythical stereotypes, and a burning sense of moral wrath. Once something that is called "terrorism"—no matter how loosely it is defined—becomes established in the public mind, "counterterrorism" is seemingly the only prudent course of action. Indeed, at present there is a veritable counterterrorism industry that encompasses the media, the arts, academia, and, to be sure, the policy makers of most of the world's governments. There is now, in fact, an "official" line acknowledging that terrorism poses a global threat to world security, which in turn justifies the expenditure of billions of dollars on counterterrorism measures.

So is it not prudent to install metal detectors in airports to try to prevent Lockerbies and Oklahoma Cities? Of course. Metal detectors are necessary with or without terrorism discourse; our concern is whether the promotion of terrorism itself as a quintessential threat is necessary and useful. While we can all agree that we must try to prevent bombings, what is lacking is a serious investigation of the extent to which the discourse itself might be partly responsible for them.

It is one of the tenets of counterterrorism that any interaction with the terrorist "Other" is violation of a taboo. Terrorists are kooks, crazies, demented, or at best misguided. Contact with them is polluting; dialogue is pointless since terrorists are, by definition, outside the pale of reason. Yet as anthropologists working in the field, we have lived many years in communities that have produced "terrorists." As a practical matter, we could not simply demonize and then shut them out of our awareness. We know that this personal experience with violent political activists makes us vulnerable to various criticisms. Yet it is the very strategy of "tabooing" subjects one has never spoken with or contemplated face-to-face that we will question on both intellectual and moral grounds.

Besides, if talking to a terrorist is so contaminating, how is it that governments readily do so? What can we make of the fact that terrorism has become such a shifty category that yesterday's terrorists are today's Nobel Peace Prize winners? Sean McBride, Menachem Begin, Yassir Arafat, and Nelson Mandela have all been so honored; Gerry Adams would appear to be a likely candidate. How do we manage to produce apocalyptic madmen who are later considered to be paragons of peace and virtue? How did terrorism become the dominant political concern during the Reagan era? What rhetorical power did terrorism discourse possess to bring such a sideshow to center stage? With the political conflict in South Africa resolved and the situations in Israel and Northern Ireland in a state of flux, the three most reputed terrorist hotspots with vested western interests are trending towards resolution. Has terrorism lost its momentum?

The grounds for new reasons to dread the unknown appear boundless. We are seemingly beset with the rampant proliferation of violence—an atomic genie out of its bottle, invisible viruses, sinister foreigners, vague plots. The explosion in Oklahoma City and the toxic gassing of the Tokyo subway are, in their apparent meaninglessness, chilling reminders of just how reasonable it is to be fearful. A glance at the movie ratings and lists of best-selling books reveals how fixated we have become upon contagious disease, murder, and terrorism.

Our text is a mythography of Terror, particularly as experienced by the American and European publics through images of both near and distant terrorists. We treat this terrorism discourse as an enabling fiction—the monster is there, but what are its features?

We write not as terrorism experts producing a "study," but rather as essayists perplexed by the terrorist phantasmagoria. We have elsewhere described the evolution of "terrorism" within the specific political context of Basque society.[3] Although our *locus standi* is the ethnographic encounter, this essay is not intended as an ethnography. Rather, it deals centrally with the academic fashioning, media consumption, and political manipulation of terrorism discourse.

Do we perhaps, beyond its fables and follies, pretend to *know* what terrorism *is*? No. Indeed, we question the very possibility of defining, and thereby giving a satisfactory account of, the facts categorized as terrorism. Our goal is not to elaborate yet another typology, but rather to redirect the study of terrorism into an examination of the very discourse in which it is couched. As is the case with other discourses of the postmodern world we inhabit, the terrorist signifiers are free-floating, and their meanings derive from language itself. The connections between discourse and reality therefore become open to question. The challenge is not to learn the ultimate "truth" about terrorism, but to delve into the rhetorical bases of its powerful representations; not to insist that myths are often used to "fool" audiences, but rather to scrutinize the concrete discursive practices whereby this transpires.

In a field of research animated by life-and-death concerns, anything that smacks of an exercise in discourse analysis might appear frivolous. Yet we believe that its implications for public policy are profound. Our conceptual strategy is to dissolve the phenomenon into its ritual and imaginative bases, which are poles apart from the ongoing academic and governmental efforts to constitute it further. In our view, nothing feeds the growth of the phenomenon itself more than the inability of terrorism discourse to distinguish actual combat from ritual bluff, real violence from imaginary terror. By questioning the conceptual grounds of the discourse of "terrorism" itself and neutralizing the taboo surrounding it, we seek to gain ironic distance. Instead of staging a frontal campaign against the mills of terrorism, it is our purpose, by concentrating on what has been labeled "the politics of epistemic murk and the fiction of the real,"[4] to subvert terrorism discourse by undermining its credibility and efficacy for actors, victims, and witnesses alike. Our text is therefore intended as exorcism. We further demand, by questioning not only others but ourselves, that it have a redemptive quality.

part one

FASHIONING
TERRORISM
DISCOURSE

1 | WAITING FOR TERROR

Thriller writers, who are ever searching for plots of intrigue and characters worthy of the trumpeted New World Order, increasingly invoke terrorism as a substitute for espionage. The evil other of the Cold War being moribund, we will no longer be taken to Checkpoint Charlie or be presented with a cast of KGB villains. Now we must visit terrorist haunts and contemplate desperate madmen from the beleaguered corners of the earth or the estranged sectors of society, their hands holding not just guns or conventional bombs but nuclear devices and biological weapons as well. Thus, we confront the new exemplar of inscrutable wickedness, the latest perpetrator of ultraviolent gore. This is all fiction, we know, but what about that other discourse on terrorism, the starkly factual one, the one invoked by politicians, journalists, and scholars, the one we hear and read about daily in the media?

The credibility of the political thriller would imply that the nonfictional discourse must be deadly real. The definitive evidence of its truth has been presumably provided by the World Trade Center and the Oklahoma City explosions; terrorism experts have never been so firmly on the side of seemingly unquestionable "reality."

There is no need to deny or diminish by one iota the atrociousness of these chilling events. What we call into question here, however, is the apocalyptic and absolutist framework within which terrorism discourse casts its characters and networks, i.e., its assumptions of all-encompassing discursive coherence. The exaggerated and conspiratorial style of terrorism rhetoric itself should be a warning that we are dealing with political pathology. As Richard Hofstadter noted, "What distinguishes the paranoid style is not...the absence of verifiable facts...but rather the curious leap in imagination that is always made at some critical point in the recital of events."[1] We believe that regarding terrorism, the brandishing of stark facts goes hand in hand with great leaps into discursive fantasy. The present intellectual world is, after all, one of self-referential illusions and postmodern self-parodies, of crimes perpetrated in real life whose public significance is far greater in terms of their commercial value for increasing TV ratings, a world in which the boundaries between the real and the make-believe are increasingly blurred. We therefore question to what extent all discourse on terrorism must conform to and borrow from some form of fictionalization.

By "fictional" we "do not mean their feigned elements, but rather, using the other and broader sense of the root word *fingere*, their forming, shaping, and molding elements: the crafting of a narrative."[2] Doesn't terrorism provide the arena for a chamber of horrors in which imagined events are as possible as factual ones, and the latter are frequently perceived, in their senseless atrocity, as a kind of fictional reality? Indeed, it is often argued that the news media, the terrorism specialists, and the terrorists themselves require one another in order to thrive. This relationship is quite complex, however, and warrants much more consideration than a mere indictment of journalistic and academic opportunism.[3] Yet their interests coincide in that the more dramatic the account, the more mysterious, threatening, and incomprehensible the terror, the greater its public impact and enhanced audience appeal—aspirations shared by all three.

Rhetoric thus becomes quintessential to the phenomenon in the sense that the actions themselves are related to their goals "only through the ways in which the terrorist strategy is interpreted by those responding to it. It is the response which becomes the primary persuasive vehicle for the terrorists."[4] We begin by underscoring the inescapable complicity between fact and fiction in terrorism discourse.

I

*Overall, the volume of terrorist activity has grown at an annual rate
of about 12–15 percent. If the rate of increase continues, we could
see a doubling of terrorism by the end of the decade—not an incon-
ceivable prospect.*

> —B. Jenkins, "Future Trends in International Terrorism"

"The 'real' is supposed to be self-sufficient."

> —R. Barthes, "The Reality Effect"[5]

Brute facts in their speechless horror are the very substance of serious
terrorism discourse. Examples include the downing of Pan Am flight
103 over Lockerbie, Scotland, with the deaths of 270 innocent travelers; the World Trade Center bombing, which killed six people and
injured more than one thousand; and the Oklahoma City explosion,
which killed 167. Then there are the 3,100 deaths in Northern Ireland,
the 4,500 people murdered by the Tamil bloodshed in Sri Lanka, the
23,000 people assassinated by the Shining Path in Peru, and so on. As
if to dispel any doubts regarding terrorism's compelling reality, it is
routine for writers to begin their journalistic reports or scholarly
papers with such dreadful statistics about the innocent victims. These
are indeed the hardest of facts, and who can doubt their validity?

It is difficult to transcend the initial shock over such numbers in
order to contemplate the reality behind them. The reporting of innocent travelers killed in the bombing of an airplane is so brutally factual that no possible explanation makes sense; indeed it is so "real"
that it requires no frame, so "true" that no interpretation is necessary,
so "concrete" that no meaning need be inferred. Its reality appears to
belong more to nature than to society. This is discourse so over-
whelmed by the "reality effect" of the facts that the very suggestion
that it authenticate itself appears ridiculous. Potentially anybody and
concretely almost nobody, everything possible and nothing predictable—this is how the randomness of the terrorist threat denotes
little yet turns that very absence into a situation that connotes terror.

Yet the play with the shock value of statistics can also be turned
against terrorism discourse itself. Sociologist William Catton studied
the approximately 800 deaths attributable to terrorism worldwide
between 1968 and 1975 and noted that "The annual death toll from
influenza in the United States is almost ten times the seven or eight
year global toll from terrorism, yet people tend to think of flu as more
of a nuisance than a dire peril."[6] The period 1980–1985 was the peak of

the counterterrorist campaign during which the Reagan administration had labeled terrorism its major international problem; at times
over 80 percent of Americans regarded it as an "extreme" danger,[7]
although only seventeen people were killed by acts of terrorism in the
United States.[8] In 1985, one of the worst years in terrorism history, in
the 812 incidents of terrorism worldwide, 23 Americans were killed, or
"about one-fourth the number who die each year as a result of being
struck by lightning."[9] In April of 1986, a national survey showed that
terrorism was the most frequently mentioned problem facing the
country, "the number one concern."[10] Between 1974 and 1994—two
decades in which terrorism loomed large as a threat—more people
died in the United States of bee stings.[11] Jenkins's prediction that by
the end of the 1980s terrorism incidents might double is in fact belied
by the fact that in the United States between 1989 and 1992 there was
not a single fatality from terrorism.[12] During this same four-year period, the United States reported approximately 100,000 homicides.

What is the mystique of something that, while statistically less fatal
than choking to death on one's lunch,[13] has been perceived as one of
the greatest public threats? What are the cultural premises and discursive strategies that provide terrorism with its rhetorical power?[14]
Why do America's few domestic "terrorist" murders annually arouse a
fear that, annually, 25,000 "ordinary" murders cannot? As in the "referential illusion" of the realist aesthetic of modern literature, "the very
absence of the signified…becomes the very signifier of realism."[15]

At a primal level, terrorism is set apart from any other form of
struggle. The terrorist becomes the paradigm of inhuman bestiality, the quintessential proscribed or tabooed figure of our times. In
contrast, despite its toll in millions of lives, the discourse concerning
conventional warfare neither taboos the soldier nor defines and
defiles war as an incomprehensible aberration. There are even military conventions that distinguish between licit and illicit warfare. War,
then, does not pose the perplexities of a Lockerbie, which is perceived
of as entirely arbitrary. As spectators and lectors we can project ourselves aboard Pan Am flight 103 much more readily and vividly than
into the trenches of the Bosnian conflict; the injustice perpetrated
upon innocent passengers is much more personalized for each of us
than are the deaths of civilians in the former Yugoslavia. The one is
terrorism; the other is war.

Furthermore, the terrorist has a far greater capacity to garner
public attention than does the soldier. It is a particularly salient con-
firmation of the common perception in postmodern discourse that

reality is being shattered into images and that everyday life is becoming confused with TV's hyperreal world. For example, the spectacular case of the TWA hostage crisis in the summer of 1985 received massive media attention: for two weeks, the three major TV networks devoted 65 percent of their news coverage to the incident and the most prestigious newspapers 30 percent of their A sections.[16] The media's decisions regarding what constitutes news determine to a great extent the public's perception of the facts and the threat they pose. CBS provided as much coverage to the fifty hostages held in the Teheran embassy as it did to the 150,000 American soldiers overseas during the peak of the Vietnam War in 1972.[17] ABC's Ted Koppel, himself a product of terrorism news, summed up the situation nicely:

> Without television, terrorism becomes rather like the philosopher's hypothetical tree falling in the forest: no one hears it fall and therefore it has no reason for being. And television, without terrorism, while not deprived of all interesting things in the world, is nonetheless deprived of one of the most interesting.[18]

At the same time, the media's depictions can have "important, even fatal, consequences" for the affected communities, as Sluka found in Belfast.[19]

The present media paradigm for treating terrorism emerged during the early 1970s and, once in place, acquired a life of its own. It both established the parameters of further terrorism reporting and provided the exemplar of how aspiring terrorists should look and act. Scholarly paradigms form no exception to it. It is not surprising, therefore, that more than one author has concluded that terrorism is essentially a media creation.

There is no question that journalism as storytelling has benefited from terrorism. For example, consider the feature article, "The Capture of a Terrorist: The Hunter and Her Witness," by Steven Emerson in a Sunday *New York Times Magazine*.[20] Its subtitle proclaims that "After a decade of mayhem, Iraq's top bomb courier awaits trial in a Greek jail." It portrays the mastermind of an underground terrorist organization supported by Saddam Hussein, located in Baghdad during the 1980s, responsible for dozens of terrorist attacks in at least thirteen countries, and in possession of technological advances such as "invisible" bombs. The organization had tried to kill more than 1,000 people by planting as many as 15 high-powered bombs on American airplanes and in Western embassies. The terrorist was finally brought to justice thanks to the perseverance of a woman in the U.S.

Department of Justice. She had pursued the vicious murderer despite the stated policies of the Reagan administration, which had removed Iraq from the list of countries supporting terrorism, and against the explicit wishes of Oliver North's National Security Council during the Iran-Contra affair.

As visual support of the story about "perhaps the most dangerous terrorist in custody today,"[21] an adjoining inset sums up a long list of his numerous terrorist actions. Examined more closely, however, the total count of casualties and damages is seven people killed, sixteen injured, and six buildings damaged. Without dismissing its victims and the destruction, one still wonders how such an apocalyptic organization, with an international base and the support of (who else but) Saddam Hussein, throughout a decade of unbridled activism and in possession of "high-powered bombs," could be so impotent? It makes for a great story, but it can also be taken as evidence of terrorism discourse's penchant for ominous representations. Furthermore, it is the story of an "expert," Emerson, who later became notorious for his preposterous speculations regarding the World Trade Center and Oklahoma City bombings.

The consequences of the terrorism scare are enormous. Consider its effects during the recent Persian Gulf War. After daily TV warnings of massive terrorist threats—which were reinforced by sinister appeals from Baghdad, many interviews with experts, and implementation of strict safety measures—during January 1991 alone, an estimated 10 million people were dissuaded from taking an international flight.[22] And yet nothing happened. The proponents of the measures aver that they deterred the potential terrorists—a contention that, conveniently, can be neither proved nor disproved.[23]

Still, was the post-Gulf War terrorist threat real or hocus-pocus? That we cannot know; that is the very essence of the phenomenon, call it threat, play, bluff, or terrorism. It is, of course, in the very nature of such behavior that one wishes to keep one's opponent guessing and that success in doing so translates into leverage/power. The perception of threat, in particular, is notoriously subjective. Once again, the very absence of concrete denotation turns into the most doom-ridden foreboding—if we at least knew their intentions; if there was perhaps an explanation for their villainy, a clear grievance that could be redressed; if they would show themselves and fight face-to-face, if only…. There is the news—later proven to be false—that terrorists have placed a bomb somewhere. This time, but only this time, the public is spared the burden of contemplating an orchestrated atrocity. However, the reasons for being terrified were, after all, "real." Furthermore, rather than being sanitized or vaccinated against further fear we have been predisposed for it. Fear breeds fear in the certain expectation that the bomb will, in fact, go off eventually. The lack of certainty regarding when and where simply raises the level of terror.

It is worth noting that the reality effect in terms of terrorism's costs has been staggering to the American taxpayer. By 1985 the U.S. government was spending $2 billion a year and employing 18,000 people to deal with terrorism; the outlays of Special Operation Forces grew from $441 million to $1.7 billion in 1987. In February of 1985, U.S. Secretary of State Schultz announced the creation of the Overseas Security Advisory Council, composed of twenty-two members, and the government asked Congress to authorize a $4.2 billion budget to fund a ten-year project on counterterrorism.[24] Yet when Trans World Airlines' flight 847 was skyjacked, "none of the organizations—the Terrorist Incident Working Group, the Joint Special Operations Command—the bureaucracy had created to fight terrorism was of any use in the TWA crisis."[25] The economic costs of the fear of flying were estimated for 1985 alone at $7.3 billion. Terrorism has bolstered a thriving security industry; the Rand Corporation estimated that in 1986 U.S. businesses were spending $21 billion annually on security, largely to combat terrorism; the equipment market of the security industry, according to Terrell Arnold's estimate, is headed toward $50 billion by the turn of the century.[26] Yet such expenditures failed to prevent either the World Trade Center or the Oklahoma City bombing.

II

The first science to be learned should be mythology or the interpretation of fables.

—G. Vico, *New Science*

To appreciate the extent to which terrorism discourse is closely associated with fiction, we need only examine the backgrounds of the violent actors themselves. The Oklahoma City explosion, for example, took place on April 19, 1995, the second anniversary of the Waco catastrophe, an event that became a cause célèbre for paramilitary militias across the country. By all accounts, the Waco incident was paramount in the antigovernment ire of the army veteran Timothy McVeigh, accused of the Oklahoma City bombing. Full of rage,

Livingston has aptly termed "The Terrorism Spectacle."[34] By now we have been sensitized by the media to accept the existence of a bizarre club of nations, the so-called sponsors of terrorism. What is most striking about the blacklisted is not their sinister vocation but rather the shiftiness in club membership. A country which is today an "evil empire" tomorrow becomes a close partner, or a ruler with whom we have been doing business as usual commits an act of bloody aggression and is suddenly a new Hitler, a nation such as Syria, catalogued for years as a supporter of terrorism, becomes a friendly ally by siding with the West against Iraq, which in turn had been removed from the blacklist for fighting against Iran. The slipperiness of definition of membership is indeed exemplified by Iran, seemingly the firmest of candidates for permanent membership; yet by not siding with Iraq in the Gulf War, and its overtures to the West, it seemed for a while to be in the process of becoming a friend; yet under the Clinton administration it is now singled out again as the principal sponsor of terrorism. A cursory look at the ways that Iraq, Iran, and Syria were dropped from or included in the State Department's list of terrorism's sponsors (depending on the U.S. Administration's policy interests) demonstrates the extent to which blacklisting is indeed a "terrorism spectacle."[35]

Debating the dozens of definitions and typologies of terrorism is a staple of the literature. Yet in the United States there is one definition that carries particular weight and that influences all others: after hearing the recommendations of the Office for Counterterrorism, the Secretary of State decides which groups and countries are "terrorists."[36] Academics may object to the erratic changes and other inconsistencies, but they do so in vain since once the Secretary of State decides who is or is not a "terrorist," that becomes an established fact in the U.S. media and its political discourse. Thus, a Pentagon report in 1988 listed Mandela's African National Congress as one of the world's "more notorious terrorist groups," whereas pro-South African government RENAMO, which the same report admits killed over 100,000 civilians in Mozambique between 1986 and 1988, is identified merely as an "indigenous insurgent group."[37]

Regarding definitions of terrorism—and still setting aside the scholarly efforts of academics and experts—there is a particularly memorable moment in which the CIA's director William Casey decided that the 109 different definitions given between 1936 and 1981 were too narrow, for they ruled out "many cases where the Soviets might be actively involved." He ordered a new draft that "went whole hog, took every kind of national liberation movement, every left-wing movement that used violence, and called them terrorists."[38] Dr. Wynfred Joshua, "known throughout the intelligence community for her virulently anti-Soviet views," wrote a draft that was protested by independent advisers and State Department officials. They complained that under her definitions George Washington and Simon Bolivar would be terrorists and asked "to call the effort off."[39] Casey ignored the protests. The following year the incidents of international terrorism doubled.

The media followed suit.[40] When Alexander Haig began claiming that terrorism was America's deadliest enemy, between 1981 and 1985 the *New York Times* increased by 60 percent its coverage of terrorism; by 1986 it was running on average four terrorism stories daily. Small wonder that by then a large majority of the public considered the frightening phenomenon—yet one that had produced but seventeen fatalities in the United States between 1980 and 1985—to be the gravest threat to America.

Terrorism news is framed according to a definite world view that opposes countries and cultures within a hierarchy of values in which "we" are at the top and the practitioners of terrorism at the bottom. Thomas Cooper calls this "adversarial perspectivism"[41] (in which there is not simply a relativity of perspectives, but rather *apex* ones that are superior to all others). As a premise, terrorism tends to be about the Other; i.e., one's country, one's class, one's creed, one's president, oneself can hardly be a terrorist. Can we even conceive of American "terrorists" trying to protect our American values? "If our president ordered it, then it is not terrorism," one read in the letters-to-the-editor section of American newspapers during the Iran-Contra affair.[42] However, apparently the answer to the dreaded question is yes. The real shocker regarding Oklahoma City was that, after two days of finger pointing at Muslims as the "natural" suspects, it was a white American who was ultimately detained.

Accordingly, a cursory examination of how news is produced reveals the decisive import of one's own government's perspective in journalistic reporting. The example Cooper adduces is the bombing of La Belle Disco Club in West Berlin on April 5, 1986, which Soviet media described as engineered by the CIA and the Mossad, whereas the U.S. media attributed it to Libyan-sponsored terrorists. The counterposed stories ignored the other side's version, did not grant equal time to neutral spokepersons, and failed to reveal their sources. Rather, they constituted mutually irreconcilable "accounts" of the same events.

"Terrorism" has therefore acquired such a slippery/phantom quality that it readily becomes a parody of accusation and counteraccusation. A paradigmatic example of such irony is the Iran-Contra affair, in which the Reagan administration was secretly trading arms for hostages with Iran while proclaiming a highly publicized policy of no negotiations whatsoever with states sponsoring terrorism. But instances of the burlesque use of terrorism abound in the daily news, as when (in November of 1991) delegations from Israel and the Arab nations convened in Madrid for an historic peace conference on the Middle East. Tensions peaked when Israel's Prime Minister Shamir accused Syria of being a leading terrorist nation, prompting Syria's foreign minister to display a 1940s' "wanted" poster issued for the "terrorist Shamir" by the British. Terrorism, then, is first and foremost discourse. There is a sense in which the terrorist event must be reported by the media in order for it to have transpired at all.

Fictionalization, far from being limited to terrorism news and the plotting of stories, is also inevitably a component of the serious scholarship on terrorism and, more critically, of governmental policy at the highest levels. One only has to read Gary Sick's[43] and Martin and Walcott's[44] insider accounts of the Carter and Reagan White Houses' respective wars on terrorism to realize the extent to which the decisions of top public officials may be based upon the perception of threats that are essentially fictional. Whenever policy mistakes are made, the tendency is always to blame them on "intelligence failures"; but there is something else at play that is far harder to correct and that was detected by Gary Sick when describing the Carter administration's myopia regarding Iran: "[it] was not so much a failure of sources or observation of data as a structural inadequacy of the system itself to make a conceptual leap from chessboard to hurricane."[45] During the Iran crisis, the journalist Robert Moss had an enormous influence upon Secretary of State Zbigniew Brzezinski and top U.S. policy makers. At a decisive moment Moss wrote a piece stating what many in the administration feared, namely, that the Soviets must have been guiding the events of the Iranian hostage crisis. Although Moss lacked hard evidence and had no qualifications as a specialist on Iran, his view prevailed and influenced U.S. policy disastrously.[46]

And it is no secret that, during the initial period of their mandate, Ronald Reagan, Alexander Haig, William Casey, and other high officials read and praised Claire Sterling's book *The Terror Network*, only to later discover to their embarrassment that it was based essentially on CIA disinformation "blown back."[47]

General Haig's strong views about terrorism were shaped by the failed attempt on his life days before he was to retire as NATO commander. No one was ever apprehended, and several groups claimed responsibility, but Haig was told privately by a German intelligence officer that the Soviets had directed the attack. European officials, such as Hans Josef Horchem, head of West Germany's Office for the Defense of the Constitution, were convinced in 1979 that "The KGB is engineering international terrorism."[48] There was no evidence to support the charge, but Haig became convinced that the Soviet Union was the mastermind. It is not surprising, therefore, to read about an exchange between him and Ronald Spiers, the head of the State Department's Bureau of Intelligence Research, in which the secretary "believed that Moscow controlled the terrorist *apparat*" and that the intelligence officer "thought he was kidding."[49] Despite reports to the contrary, "the Reagan administration would continue to confuse terrorism with communism"[50] and hold unsubstantiated assumptions, such as the alleged Moscow-based plot to kill the pope.

After the departure of Haig, who embarrassed the CIA by espousing Sterling's book, George Shultz continued to accuse the Soviets of complicity in supporting terrorism. Comments by well-informed commentators such as Eugene Rostow read today as fiction. Rostow wrote, "The United States has finally begun to supplement the Truman Doctrine of containment by undertaking a policy of more active defense against the process of Soviet expansion. In this context, the bombing of Libya is a breakthrough of incalculable psychological and political importance."[51] In general, during the 1980s, counterterrorism became a surrogate for earlier efforts to fight Communist subversion abroad, whereas at home it became "the talisman" the FBI needed "to conduct investigations of those in opposition to the Reagan administration's policies in Central America."[52]

While not exclusively an American phenomenon, international counterterrorism is primarily American in that it rests upon premises informing American *realpolitik* throughout the post-Second World War period. These include: American assumptions regarding the inviolability of the nation-state; assumptions about the efficacy of change within liberal democracies as the highest and most acceptable expression of political behavior; a Middle East policy clearly skewed in favor of Israel; and the recently culminated Cold War confrontation. The disastrous results of the entire terrorism discourse for the administrations of Carter, Reagan, and Bush are in the public domain. The monster they created—the demonic Terrorist so inhuman that its annihiliation was the only acceptable policy—came back to haunt them in the forms of hostage taking, secret accords with the loathsome enemy, and denials that they had any knowledge of such deals. Nor has the Clinton administration learned from its predecessors' mistakes. Scarcely a day goes by without its making a reference to the threat of terrorism in justification of its policy.

Even if it is obvious that U.S. administrations have "played politics with the fight against terrorism,"[53] ideology and politics per se are not our main concerns but rather what Hayden White has labeled the "fictions of factual representation."[54] When we examine the epistemic status of the category itself and the shifting meanings that it holds for various audiences, we realize the radical extent to which terrorism discourse constitutes its object. This is also true of the position of some critics who, on the basis of the obvious double standard concerning the definitions and rhetorics of terrorism, simply redirect the term to argue that Washington inflicts a deliberate policy of wholesale terrorism on Third World countries, which are subsequently demonized for their own retail brand.[55] There is certainly ample evidence of terror inflicted by Washington, but we object to rendering it as discourse that further recreates and reifies the terrorism paradigm instead of undermining its fictions.

In today's world, political violence triggers within the global village a debate over which narrative plot best captures its true essence: Romance? Tragedy? Farce? Crime? Insanity? Terrorism? Far from being a benign or gratuitous labeling exercise, the stark issue of who has the power to define another as terrorist has obvious moral and political implications. Yet we are also concerned with something prior—the very conceptual formation of "the terrorist." In the beginning was the *word*…terrorism. The various types of fictionalization—representation by the media, political manipulation, academic definitions, the imaginary archetype informing the thriller—find their genesis and nourishment in the play with meaning and confusion of contexts inherent in the word "terrorism."

Since we are intent upon disaggregating terrorism discourse, it is legitimate to question *our* epistemic stand. Are we maintaining that terrorism is simply "fictional"? Has it no "real" substance? Conversely, do we claim there is some underlying "cause" beyond all the images? By underscoring the narrative dimension of terrorism, we are not so much opposing the real and the fictional as questioning the status of reality within *terrorism discourse*. In our view, terrorism's "reality" is intrinsic to certain kinds of behavior—play, threat, ritual, dreaming, art—characterized by a radical semantic gap between concrete action and that which it would ordinarily denote. It therefore becomes more relevant to examine the nature of the behavior labeled "terrorism," as well as the labeling process itself, rather than to focus upon the ostensible "face value" of particular terrorist events and episodes. Moreover, the capacity of terroristic activities to have an impact is largely contingent upon their being played out on the hyperreal screens of the electronic mass media. Hence, the quest for some definitive distinction between the real and the unreal is futile.

In the mid-1970s, terrorism strikes everywhere and is mushrooming at an alarming rate. On its own terms, terrorism has literally been a smash hit.... The little guys and the little groups make the big difference.
—F. J. Hacker, Crusaders, Criminals, Crazies

In 1933, Jacob Hardman published an article on terrorism in *The Encyclopedia of the Social Sciences.* He argued that terrorism was for years an accepted tenet of anarchism, and its fullest expression was to be found in the Russian revolutionary movement of late last century.[56] There was an attempt to revive terrorism at the beginning of the present one, but various factors "made terrorism appear outmoded as a revolutionary method…. The rising mass movement and the spread of nation-wide economic and political strikes made terror irrelevant and unnecessary."[57] Apart from brief episodes, terrorism was simply an antiquated mode of struggle that had ceased to exist. But after World War II it again became fashionable (due to the political struggles of Israel, Kenya, Vietnam, Algeria, etc.). There is no small irony in this brief history of terrorism, in that those decades blessed with the interlude witnessed the emergence of Stalin and Hitler and experienced the two World Wars that resulted in some 70 million fatalities. Seemingly, when there is unbridled real combat, there is less need for a ritual surrogate.

There are several interrelated factors that contributed to the emergence of terrorism in its modern guise. All were set in motion by certain events and developments of World War II and its immediate aftermath, but the mix of elements required about two decades of fermentation before attaining full strength as terrorist brew by the late 1960s and early 1970s.

First, there was the process of decolonization, which created a plethora of new states around the globe. The seemingly enlightened leadership of each promised to guide an independent "people" to either democratic paradise or socialist utopia. The initial euphoria of national liberation obfuscated or trivialized such fundamental problems as the dangers of internal ethnic and sectarian divisions, economic underdevelopment, and the authoritarian traditions characteristic of most of the new countries. Inevitably, over time euphoria gave way to cynicism as the failures became increasingly obvious and as self-serving ruling elites became ever more entrenched.

Second, in the postwar period the world became polarized into two spheres of influence, each dominated by mutually antagonistic superpowers. The Cold War confrontation quickly lapsed into gridlock sustained by the balance of nuclear threat. The fear of escalation into nuclear annihilation all but ruled out conventional warfare, at least on a major scale. Consequently, the real struggle was fought over "the hearts and minds" of the uncommitted (the shrewdest of whom became adept at playing one side off against the other). Both superpowers encouraged foreign students by the tens of thousands to attend their universities in the hope of inculcating future generations of world leaders with their respective political philosophies. Both launched outreach programs designed to help underdeveloped countries to modernize, which thereby enmeshed them within the transnational economy dominated by the benefactor. On occasion each probed the limits of the other's power by sponsoring military insurrections, the dirty little wars of the guerrilla variety so characteristic of the last fifty years. In their relentless pursuit of client-states, both superpowers developed a clear double standard in which the gap between the propaganda and actions within their domestic versus their foreign policies became patently apparent.

Third, the postwar world experienced a variety of demographic and socioeconomic developments that exacerbated its difficulties. A population explosion negated many of the efforts to improve living standards. At the same time, the spread of the commitment to mass education and communication led to the creation of the "global village," in which everyone's frame of reference was expanded enormously. In the process most of the citizens of the planet bought into modern consumerism as *the* desired life style against which to measure one's personal success. Even the more developed societies, with their modest population growths, struggled to meet the rising expectations and absorb the capacities of an increasingly trained and educated work force. The enhanced efficiency of modernized agriculture displaced huge segments of the rural populace; developments in heavy industry likewise made redundant many of the heirs of the industrial revolution. The resulting postindustrial, urban society has become fraught with uncertainty regarding the capacity to meet human needs and aspirations without destroying the ecological balance of the planet in the process.

With all of the foregoing factors put in motion, by the late 1960s and early 1970s there was ample reason for any citizen of Planet Earth to feel a degree of personal alienation. We all seemed to be caught up in a web of forces far beyond our control. The political leadership of every country appeared incapable of dealing with the plethora of social, economic, and ecological issues of an increasingly complicated world. Expansion of every individual's personal frame of reference seemed to shrivel and undermine the intimate web of traditional values as articulated through family and neighborhood, church and community. Interaction between human beings became increasingly electronical and technological rather than of the face-to-face variety. Works like Phillip Slater's *The Pursuit of Loneliness* captured the essence of the combination of alienation and anomie seemingly inherent in the modern condition.

By the late 1960s, then, for idealists (the most notoriously unrelenting of whom are the young) there was much cause for cynicism. The euphoria of victory in the aftermath of World War II, which even affected the vanquished through programs such as the Marshall Plan and the reconstruction of Japan, evaporated in the wake of failed economic recoveries, subverted independence movements, and the Cold War stalemate. Within the dominant superpowers themselves and their client states, the capacity of the individual citizen to influence the course of events had seemingly shriveled to the vanishing point. Rather, political life appeared dominated by the remote, impersonal state and economic life by the multinational firm. Philosophers such as Marcuse and Habermas described the resulting human dilemmas.

It is against this backdrop that we can understand the appeal of many of the social and political developments of the second half of the twentieth century. The civil rights and countercultural movements, the concern with environmentalism, perestroika, religious fundamentalism, and the recrudescence of ethnonationalism on a near planetary scale may all be interpreted as the search for a meaningful cause. It is even possible to regard the recent Yuppie movement as the reverse side of the same coin, in which the individual elevates a concern with self to the status of cause.

The nemesis, the ready foil that catalyzed such reactions, was the faceless, impersonal, and ultimately sinister forces represented by distant and insensitive elites protected by operatives identified by such acronyms as FBI, CIA, KGB. The central morality play informing twentieth-century artistic expression has been the individual's struggle within an alien world that is designed specifically to suppress self-expression. Whether described in Kafkaesque or Orwellian terms, painted by postexpressionists or portrayed by *Apocalypse Now*, the plot is essentially the same—individual survival within an alien environment.

Dropping out, affiliation with a social or religious movement, and fixation upon oneself are alternate ways of coping with the dilemmas of the late twentieth-century condition. Each is a means of humanizing a dehumanized world, at least in terms of one's own circumstances. Each has the potential of creating individuals so alienated that they become prone to antisocial violent behavior. In the cases of the pathological dropout and violent egomaniac there is the consensus that their violent acts are deranged behavior. Thus, as horrible as may be the wanton shootings of children in a California schoolyard, or John W. Hinckley Jr.'s attack on President Reagan in order to impress the actress Jodie Foster, each perpetrator was acting out a personal agenda whose implications for the rest of us (excluding the immediate victims) was but minimal. The same may not be said for persons prepared to employ violence in the name of a social or political cause. It is at this point that we are dealing with behavior that is often labeled "terrorist."

In this regard terrorism assumes several guises. There is the ecoterrorism of persons defending old-growth forests by driving spikes into trees in order to intimidate the sawmill workers who can be injured when processing them. There are the kidnappings and assassinations in defense of the working class by groups such as Italy's Brigata Rossa and Germany's Baader Meinhof activists. There are the Muslim fundamentalists in North Africa and parts of the Middle East employing violence in pursuit of sectarian goals. But by far the most salient form, the one that has demonstrated the greatest staying power to date, is the political violence of ethnonationalists, the self-styled guardians and avenging angels of ethnic homelands real and imagined. In Europe the two most prominent, though far from exclusive, recent examples would be the Irish Republican Army (IRA) and the Basques' ETA or Euzkadi ta Alkartasuna (Basque Country and Freedom).

In short, twentieth-century developments have created a climate favoring the resort to violence by a variety of politically alienated indi-

viduals and groups. At the same time we believe that there was one catalyst that provided the paradigm for modern terrorism: the events and
developments regarding the creation of the State of Israel and its subsequent history. For it is within the context of the conundrum presented by Israel that the occident has clashed with the orient, the
superpowers have contested global hegemony, and the world's need
to assuage its guilt over the Holocaust has been counterbalanced by
its self-interest in continued easy access to major petroleum reserves. It
is also an arena in which the fundamentalist zealots of three of the
world's major religions—Judaism, Islam, and Christianity—contest for
control of the Holy Land alongside Zionists and Palestinians with their
mutually antagonistic agendas for an ethnic Home Land. The Israel
conundrum has served as the prime seedbed of accusations and coun-
teraccusations of terrorism, and therefore provides the textbook for
the study of terrorism discourse as labeling exercise.[58]

Finally, as Ted Koppel has told us, since terrorism must be perceived in order to exist at all, in its modern guise it is a discourse
unique to the western democracies and the dictatorships within their
spheres of interest. Unreported bombings, kidnappings, skyjackings,
etc., do not qualify. Prior to the collapse of the Soviet Union, systematic
censorship of the news in the Eastern Bloc countries made it impossible to create the synergism between perpetrator, victim, and audience
that produces the phenomenon we are calling terrorism discourse.
The adage regarding "the people's right to know" is clearly operative
at some level in the western press. This is even evident in the case of
the dictatorships within the western sphere, which would clearly prefer
less scrutiny but which must endure at least a modicum of journalistic
probing. Indeed, they have had a vested interest in managing the
impression that a challenge to existing authority is a terrorist/
Communist plot. Success in putting such a spin upon domestic events
has easily translated into enhanced aid from a nervous international
community, at least prior to the end of the Cold War. It may have also
engendered greater tolerance of repressive policies in the belief that
the known quantity was better than the likely chaotic alternatives. If
the dictator was a beast, he was our beast on our leash and with little
potential for contaminating his neighbors, whereas the political
metaphor regarding the terrorist/Communist possibility was the
feared "domino effect."

IV

The irony is that this particular fantasy of the revolutionary Left [such as Marighella's catechism on terrorism] has been accepted by everyone else.
                    —T. Gurr, *Handbook of Political Conflict*

John le Carré's words about "espionage" after the collapse of the Soviet Union (who should know better than he?)—that it always was "a sideshow got up as major theater"—seem applicable to the history of "counterterrorism" since the 1970s as well. It is only in the wake of major geopolitical changes that we are struck by such disclosures. It is then that we learn that "the failure of common sense is absolutely weird in its stupidity," and that "it is the very nature of the life you lead as an intelligence officer in a secret room that the ordinary winds of common sense don't blow through it."[59] Nor is the problem limited to "weird stupidity" and self-delusion, for we are also told that during the Cold War the CIA systematically and purposefully overestimated the strength of the Soviet Union in order to justify its own agenda and budget—"the Soviet economy was thought to be three times as large as it turned out to be."[60] The sideshow of terrorism was put center stage during the Reagan period, when it played as "major theater" to an uncritical audience. Yet the Oklahoma City explosion on the second anniversary of Waco seemed to finally lend some justification to the prophets of pending disaster.

Ironies abound in anything related to terrorism. Tragically, peoples and governments resort, at the end of the twentieth-century, to methods of terror that other able politicians found "irrelevant and unnecessary" at its beginning. On the academic front, the increase in "expert" knowledge about acts of terror has not yielded any definitive advance in our understanding of terrorist behavior. In fact, a case could be made that Hardman's views are conceptually clearer and politically sounder than most of what has been written subsequently on the topic. Characteristically, terrorism discourse singles out and removes from the larger historical and political context a psychological trait (terror), an organizational structure (the terrorist network), and a category (terrorism) in order to invent an autonomous and aberrant realm of gratuitous evil that defies any understanding. The ironic dimension of terrorism discourse derives from its furthering the very thing it abominates.

Even if it is openly admitted in the literature that terrorism discourse lacks a working definition (a typical rejoinder is that terrorism is like pornography—you know it when you see it), the reader is provided a panoply of visual aids such as numbers, data, organizations and acronyms, charts, inserts, and other quantificational devices as writing ploy and authentication that its conclusions are not inherently flawed. Lacking not only definition but also even a general framework, it is scarcely surprising that the conceptual problems behind the statistical samples become glaring. We are told, for example, that "the figures produced by the best-known databases on international terrorism vary considerably. This is due mainly to differences in definition and categorization—as regards what constitutes not only an act of terrorism, but also an 'incident'."[61] Statistical manipulation is therefore unavoidable. Yet such statistics are the backbone of the entire discourse.

Not surprisingly, many acts that previously would have been labeled "assassination," "kidnapping," "threat," "bombing," etc., are nowadays classed and written about as "terrorism." A notable instance taken from the CIA's reports illustrates this point well: its 1979 report claimed there had been 3,336 terrorist incidents since 1968, whereas its 1980 report claimed that there were 6,714 over the same period. The reasons for the dramatic increase in just one year were definitional. It was decided, retrospectively, to include in the statistics "threats" and "hoaxes." Depending on how acts are characterized, terrorism multiplies.

The political costs that derived from terrorism discourse during the 1980s received much more publicity than its economic ones. The whole fiasco of the Iran-Contra arms-for-hostages deal epitomizes the parody of U.S. terrorism policy. All too often, in the U.S. as well as in Europe, the counterterrorism crusade has ended up devouring its promoters. Yet, as anthropologists, we are more concerned with the intellectual and cultural disasters inherent in terrorism discourse. The media's homogenization and trivialization of vastly different social realities under the buzzword "terrorism"—the nerve gas attack in the Tokyo subway, the latest mail bomb of the Unabomber, the Oklahoma City explosion, the violence in Northern Ireland, Muslim fundamentalism, Iranian foreign policy—are reproduced and granted respectability through a rapidly proliferating scholarly literature. A word that has been defined in literally hundreds of different ways, depending on the immediate purpose of a text, and which therefore has essentially a different or nuanced meaning for each writer, has become a subject in its own right. It now spawns academic curricula and think tanks. The political mockery of dismissing entire countries as "terrorists" or "terrorist sympathizers"—by abolishing their long and rich histories, by debasing their languages, by stigmatizing their representatives, by sheer self-deception—is premised on the intellectual banality of constructing a discourse around a word that inevitably imposes conceptual reification within a tabooed context.

Additionally, criticisms can be made of analyses of terrorist groups based on either their organizational properties and activities (internal structure, recruitment, membership profile, ideology, and tactics) or the extent of their support (through examination of electoral results and public opinion polls). Such treatments tend to reify the organizational structure of the group as if it were a regular army unit or political party. In our experience, if one examines the organizational properties of groups such as the Basques' ETA, they appear to be as much a concept as a structure and, as concept, they transcend any particular political organization.[62] In time such organizations have martyrs and legends, an entire liturgy of anniversaries and gatherings in honor of the fallen, as well as a rich iconography of tortured bodies, pictures of dead friends, and tombstones. Such violently radical groups tend to become alternative realities playing a decisive role in the calculations of political parties. They also have the capacity to rise out of their own ashes insofar as the concept retains its efficacy, a fact which makes them particularly impervious to ordinary police measures.

There is one crucial element required for the "terrorism" of small militant groups to make miracles, an element that is entirely beyond their very limited strength—namely, that the collective imagination of whole countries empowers them beyond their wildest dreams into a finely honed international network capable of engaging the entire spectrum of world governments in instrumental combat. For this, ironically, the terrorists count on an army of experts, academics, and journalists whose role it is to convince the general public that, indeed, Terrorism is a world-threatening force. Thus, terrorists have a common bond, i.e., share a common interest, with counterterrorists.

The terrorism writer's ironic dilemmas are matched by those of the terrorists. Like their inquisitors, some of the witches themselves believed that they flew to the Sabbaths and had intercourse with the Devil. Like his frightened audience, the terrorist himself may end up assuming the great powers of his art. Such belief epitomizes the ironic obsolescence of postmodern militarism. Only the magic of an exorcist or the midwifery of an ironist can alleviate it. As Barthes remarked, "The disintegration of the sign—which seems indeed to be modernity's grand affair—is of course present in the realistic enterprise, but in a somewhat regressive manner, since it occurs in the name of referential plenitude, whereas the goal today is to empty the sign and infinitely to postpone its object so as to challenge, in a radical fashion, the age-old aesthetic of 'representation'."[63] As writers of terrorism discourse, we must learn from such instances of "epistemic murk"[64] in history and ethnography.

It is our purpose, then, to question the conceptual, imaginative, and textual components of terrorism discourse itself. Now that the Cold War is over and the specters of the nuclear holocaust are subsiding, the tasks are to examine closely and to exorcise the political culture of the past two decades that have framed contemporary terrorism discourse. To accomplish this we must examine its cultural bases and take seriously the proposition that terrorism is primarily a rhetorical product, i.e., quintessential to its strategy and efficacy are the anticipated reactions to, and interpretations of, certain concrete acts of political violence.

In ritual combat the link between actions and goals transcends mechanical instrumentality, and the value of performances and texts is measured by the public outcry they provoke. In the end, terrorism becomes that heart of darkness in which, by virtue of the referential circularity between threat and reaction, a concrete act echoes in the collective imagination, actors discover their true significance in media reports, and audiences recreate the thing itself—usually set in a distant, dehumanized world that has lost all touch with reason and morality. The writer's task is to question this complicity.

We are no longer alone, waiting for the night, waiting for Godot, waiting for...waiting.

—S. Beckett, *Waiting for Godot*

Finally and shockingly, the long-awaited bomb explodes in the World Trade Center. "Is this a new day in American politics?" Dan Rather asks the politician. Suddenly we hear from public officials that "until now we haven't had any terrorism in the United States" and that "for the first time we are vulnerable to foreign terrorists." No terrorism until then? But what of the earlier campaign that convinced a majority of Americans that terrorism was a paramount threat? So we are permitted to realize that *nothing happened* during those former scare years now that we have the real thing. Furthermore, after Oklahoma City, we are also allowed to conceive of terrorists as other than swarthy Mediterraneans. At last the folly of fearing fictions for decades becomes the wisdom of having long anticipated and experienced such a vision of hell.

The most typical mode of terrorism discourse in the United States has been, indeed, one of Waiting for Terror. From presidents to government officials to the general public, from the media's constant bombardment of emotional warnings to the intellectualized ones of the academic industry, from the lofty level of American policies to counterterrorism's billions spent on prevention, "terrorism" emerged during the late seventies as a hydra-headed monster capable of fixating our imaginations and provoking intense fear. Now that we are told "nothing happened" during the period, Beckett's drama of aborted metaphysics and absurdity, with its intolerable emphasis on waiting turned into a kind of art, becomes an apt parable. That which captivates every mind is something so meaningless that it may never happen, yet we are forced to compulsively talk about it while awaiting its arrival. In the theater of the absurd, "nonsignificance" becomes the only significance. Such nonsignificance is also dear to a terrorism discourse that for years has envisioned and feared myriads of conspiratorial plots being prepared in the utter danger of an invisible underground. When something does happen, after decades during which the absent horror has been omnipresent through the theater of waiting, the event becomes anecdotal evidence to corroborate what was intuited all along—the by-now permanent catastrophe of autonomous Terror consisting of the waiting for terror.

But what are we to make of the facts once the long anticipated horror finally becomes a reality? In February of 1993 the World Trade Center in New York City was bombed. We are told that the act was the work of amateurs using only a few hundred dollars worth of chemicals that are available to the public.[65] But, more importantly, the arrested suspects had been under close police surveillance since 1989, when they were photographed by the FBI on four successive weekends on Long Island while taking target practice.[66] Sheik Omar Abdul Rahman, their reputed leader, was charged with the conspiracy. As with Qaddafi, Noriega, and Saddam Hussein, the blind sheik is but another instance of yesterday's friend turned into today's archterrorist enemy. For it is no secret that the sheik was initially recruited by the CIA to rally support for Islamic guerrillas in Afghanistan.

As extensively documented by Robert Friedman in his article "The CIA's *Jihad*," the CIA's involvement with the World Trade Bombers "is far greater than previously known."[67] The CIA campaigned to set up several jihad (holy war) offices across the United States. The most important was called Alkifah—Arabic for "the struggle"—and was established in Brooklyn where the sheik had settled. One of the visitors to Alkifah was a Green Beret from the U.S. Special Forces at Fort Bragg, Ali Mohammed. He came regularly from North Carolina to train the sheik's followers in the use of weapons, as well as tactical, reconnaissance, and survival techniques. The sheik's followers fought in a war that cost the United States $10 billion.

After examining the evidence it is hard not to conclude that "the CIA has inadvertently managed to do something that America's enemies have been unable to: give terrorism a foothold in the United States."[68]

Were thousands of counterterrorism agents and massive funding needed for this? The bombing of the World Trade Center had to share media attention with the events at Waco, Texas, which began to unfold two days later. In the aftermath of the fifty-one day siege and botched assault, there was scathing criticism of the actions of the government's agents. Subsequent reports by the Treasury and Justice Departments underscored the fundamental mistakes of the authorities. Two years later, on the anniversary of the Waco tragedy, the bombing of the federal building in Oklahoma City again challenged the government's capacity to deal with "terrorism." We will examine this connection between Waco and Oklahoma City, reactive law enforcement and counterterrorism's agenda, in subsequent chapters.

If we postulate as polar opposites "natural horror" (earthquakes, ecological disaster, death by prolonged illness) and "art horror" (the genre that includes *Dracula* and Stephen King thrillers, as well as Artaud and Beckett), terrorism would lie somewhere in between. We are prompted to invoke "art," or some form of cultural fabrication, rather than "nature" to account for the various devices (assumptions, rhetorics, representations) by which a single terrorist killing is perceived as far more dangerous than the corresponding thousands of "ordinary" fatalities. But it is the terrorist killing's similarities with the "art-terror" form that are the most intriguing. The Waco tragedy, for example, was not a natural disaster but rather the product of carefully staged actions by the Bureau of Alchohol, Tobacco, and Firearms (ATF). Reports of illicit sex and child abuse, which in any event fall outside the agency's purview, and possession of illegal weapons by the Branch Davidians, had been investigated on several occasions by local child welfare agencies and the sheriff. No substantiating evidence was found. The ATF manufactured the story that the Davidians had a drug lab. The assault begins to make sense when we are told that, "The ATF was in a severe time bind. Rumors were flying that they were headed for a budget cut, and there were a number of proposals that the ATF be dissolved and its duties reassigned to the FBI and other law enforcement structures. They had a budget review hearing coming up in March. They needed something impressive to take to that hearing. They selected the Branch Davidians."[69]

When, on the morning of February 28, the ATF acted, the press was already at the site with live coverage, thereby eliminating the crucial element of surprise and hopelessly compromising the entire operation. The previous day Sharon Wheeler, a secretary working for the ATF, had called various news media, "some from as far away as Oklahoma," asking them whether they would be interested in reporting a raid against a local "cult."[70] Each side accused the other of firing first. If the goal of the raid had been to detain Branch Davidian leader David Koresh, it could have been accomplished quietly in one of his frequent visits to the city. There was simply no good explanation for the ATF's initial raid, other than the need for action in front of TV camera crews. The intended audience appeared to be the budget cutters in Washington, DC; in this sense the whole affair was primarily "art horror."

Philosophers of the aesthetics of horror find themselves invoking the notion of "make-believe" to refer to the mental state whereby a fictional form of art may arouse such emotional states as "fear" or "pity." In his paper "Fearing Fictions", Kendall Walton proposes the notion of "quasi-fear" for that fright experienced when contemplating on a movie or TV screen agents (such as a terrible green slime or the creature from the Black Lagoon) that the viewer knows for certain are only fictional. Then there is the fear of a person afraid of a nonexistent ghost or burglar who are nonetheless "real" since the person *believes* that they are present. Fear of terrorism is never solely fictional, as in the first case, but is rather of the second type. Still, faced with the extraordinary fact that during one single month 10 million Americans decided to stay at home rather than take an airplane reportedly because of a terrorist threat issued several thousands miles away by a beleaguered dictator, one questions whether they were dissuaded by real feelings of terror or were engaging in some sort of make-believe in which they acted "as if" the threats posed real danger to their lives.

As reader-oriented literary critics have reminded us, "meaning should no longer be viewed as an immutable property of a text but must be considered as the result of the confrontation between reading act and textual structure."[71] Similarly, its readers' assessment of the "terrorist" text must be taken into account. Fundamentally, the reading becomes a media-driven social process in which the interpreter of the discourse also becomes "a social construct whose operations are delimited by the systems of intelligibility that inform it."[72] Terrorism, as we shall consider in the next chapter, provides an excellent example of the extent to which both the "text" and its writer/reader/viewer are produced simultaneously.

Terrorism discourse is characterized by the confusion of sign and context provoked by the deadly atrocity of apparently random acts, the impossibility of discriminating reality from make-believe, and text from reader. These strange processes and their mix make terrorism a queer phenomenon. Emptying the sign of its deadly messages seems to be, following Barthes's advice, the best antidote to the experience of terror. And nothing appears to be more damaging to the ghosts and myths of terrorism (for audience and actors alike) than fictionalizing them further to the point that fear dissolves into "as-if" terror.

The discourse's victory, then, derives from imposing a literal frame of "this *is* real war", "this *is* global threat", "this *is* total terror." Its defeat derives from writing "this is an *as-if* war," "this is an *as-if* global threat," "this is *make-believe* total terror."

Terrorism discourse stems from such play with sign and context, actors and audiences. While it refers to violent events and seeks to interpret them, the text itself is actually more about threat, ritual bluff, deception, and stratagem. In semiotic terms, the sign of terror may not necessarily refer to something signified, but all distance between the act and its meaning gets erased in the bombastic context. The confusion may be deliberate, yet its play embraces agents and audiences of terrorism discourse far more than they consciously realize.

The experience of real terror is intimately tied to the breakdown of all norms (moral, legal, military) epitomized by the specter of terrorism and the utmost confusion of contexts invoked by it. It is by abandoning a reified, near-magical notion of uniform terror extending its tentacles through the hidden networks of "international terrorism" that we begin to see its play with blurred contexts and ritual premises—deceptive posturing, the psychology of threat, a logic of chance, the shock of innocent victimology. The grip that terrorism discourse holds upon the collective imagination is far beyond what the phenomenon would merit in strictly military or destructive terms; the subjectively experienced potential terror becomes "real" independent of the actual violence.

The power of threat, even when hollow, is not to be taken lightly. Even if hypothetical, terror and its deterrence evoke intense fear. The manipulation of frames for purposes of creating collective terror has to be directed to the imagination. There is no sense of the "untrue" or "unreal" when one is submerged in dream or fantasy—no clear metastatement as to their "only" being a dream or fantasy. Even a self-contradictory tendency may develop, consisting of substituting the fictional reality for the actual one, as when a society is unable to find a solution to the actual violence in its streets but consumes vast amounts of gory make-believe violence in literature and film, or when a puritanical public is exposed to ample doses of TV pseudosexual fantasy that would not be tolerated in real life. If one analyzes closely the frequent reports on terrorism, it is hard to avoid discerning a similar sense of unreality.

From this perspective, what is noteworthy about terrorism as a contemporary phenomenon is that, while manipulating the referential circularity between media stories and violent actions, it has succeeded in imposing an apocalyptic frame in which suspension of disbelief appears to be the rational course and no commentary as to its discursive configuration seems relevant. No text on *meta*terrorism is conceivable, because we remain trapped by a perspective that is "*internal* to the game"[73] of terrorism discourse. As in Beckett's play, we get the interaction: "Let's go. We can't. Why not? We're waiting for Godot."

2
WRITING TERRORISM

During the four years 1989–1992 in which there was not a single fatality caused by terrorism in the United States, and in which thirty-four Americans were killed worldwide, American libraries catalogued 1,322 new book titles under the rubric "terrorism" and 121 under "terrorist."[1] The careers of thousands of experts, consultants, journalists, and scholars (ourselves included) have benefited substantially from this production. The question is: How, in the absence of a significant number of fatalities, can a discursive machine provide sufficient ammunition to sustain the plethora of texts, expertise, and conferences that will depict the phenomenon as the ultimate threat to civilization?

Whatever else it might be, "terrorism" is printed text. Initially it is a pamphlet prescribing action, the militant's personal document, his manual—a shabby text, in essence a catechism, replete with directives, stuffed with morality, and bursting with urgency. Then it is the daily journalistic report, sometimes as front-page news, more frequently as a formulaic note on a bombing or a killing, usually accompanied by a gruesome photograph. Occasionally it is the proscribed text outlining a government's policy of *not* reporting the phenomenon. Such policy

may become a topic of debate, as in Great Britain, and then much is
stated about the wisdom of not writing about, interviewing, or visually
presenting terrorists.

Terrorism has become a major theme in the thriller literature.
Needless to say, it is also examined by a myriad of political scientists
and other experts in what has turned out to be a major growth industry in academia, with its literally hundreds of publications annually.
Even we ethnographers can scarcely describe our changing societies
without paying some attention to it—a focus that is also capable of
adding market value to our arid monographs. We are all writing "terror." We are asked, commanded, paid to do so; we are intrigued and
fascinated by it; the challenge is professional and intellectual; at times
even our very souls seem to be at stake. These various types of writing
terrorism—the radically different descriptive realities they constitute;
their very complicity in terrorism discourse—are examined in this
chapter.

Leaving aside the absurdist tension between fact and fiction considered earlier, we now focus upon terrorism discourse per se. Prior to
considering discourse-as-ideology and discourse-as-subjectivity, we
must examine discourse-as-language—and particularly the perspective
that writing (in the narrow sense and as an entire structure of investigation) is evidence of the reification intrinsic to language.[2] For example, as argued by well-informed former police officers and criminal
investigators, labeling Waco's Branch Davidians as a "cult" was crucial
to criminalizing them and thereby making the violence almost
inevitable.[3] Waco subsequently became "a dark and violent text for
right-wing militants"[4] and played a key rhetorical role in the framing
of the Oklahoma City tragedy.

Further typical examples from the various kinds of terrorism
texts—from the pamphlet to the novel, from the witness to the expert,
from the actor to the newsman—demonstrate the extent to which the
whole phenomenon hinges upon writing. Let us examine how the various types of terrorism writing function within the same political/cul-
tural situation—the Basque Country of Northern Spain, a classical case
of a "terrorism" venue in all of the literature.

We have both worked in Basque contexts and have therefore dealt
with types of violence that fall clearly under the "terrorism" rubric. We
coauthored a piece on how to interpret terrorist violence[5] and collab-
orated on the publication of a long ethnography of Basque political
violence.[6] Therefore, it is not only in our reading of the terrorism literature but also in our own ethnographic writings that we find plenty

of material for a critique of the writer's rhetorical ploys and the fictions of factual representations. We bring to the present task our personal and professional biographies. We have both conducted anthropological field research in the Basque area of Spain, although at different times. We both were exposed directly to operatives of ETA, the most radical and violence-prone force within the Basque ethnonationalist movement. Douglass, an American, conducted his field research in the early 1960s, or during the depths of the Franco dictatorship. Zulaika, a Basque, worked in his natal village of Itziar between 1979 and 1981, after Franco's death.

Yet if we thought that we could leave terrorism behind in the field when finally returning to the placid life of American academia, we were wrong. Here, too, we are constantly bombarded by the ubiquitous interest in terrorism, and sixty miles from where we sit writing this essay, in Fallon, Nevada, there is a military base that is a key training ground for America's counterterrorist operatives,[7] while a few hundred miles to the south Nellis Air Force Base houses NEST, or the nuclear device detection team. If, as ethnographers curious about all aspects of human behavior, we ended up in the field meeting the "terrorist" brutes, now we are neighbors to the "counterterrorist" eagles and jaguars who are preparing the nation's defenses against the presumably impending invasion of those we came to know in the field. We cannot take lightly the fact that counterterrorism writers here are dealing with our ethnographic protagonists there. Writing about the varieties of terrorism discourse, and the diverse forms of consciousness they subsequently create, is our only catharsis. We begin by looking at the texts produced by the violent actors themselves.

I

Iraultza ala Hil (Revolution or Death)

—An ETA slogan

"Propaganda by deed"—is, in a nutshell, the epigraph that sums up the main argument of most books on terrorism. Gramsci's words best capture the youthful enthusiasm of the ETA operatives we came to know personally: "Who were we? What did we represent? Of what new ideas were we the heralds?... We wanted to act, act, act."[8] They must have read, one suspects, since in Franco's Spain there were no TV sets until the late sixties, and then "Bonanza" became the most popular program. There were books of course, but given the dictator's cen-

sorship the public was more disposed to ascribe real truth to the photocopied pamphlet written and circulated clandestinely than to the
printed word. Least credible of all were the officially sanctioned daily
press reports and national news broadcasts.

Act, act, act meant that inaction was at best wasteful, and more
likely escapism, cowardice, or perhaps even treachery. There were
those, pitifully, who were given to, of all things, theorizing. They were
the readers and the debaters—those addicted to endless meetings
until the wee hours of the morning. They brandished words such as
"organization of the masses" and established arcane distinctions
between "tactics" and "strategy," while positing long-term dialectical
processes and large-scale transformations. The action people knew, of
course, it was hot air, summed up best by "It is all literature."

Writing was miles apart from real action. But one morning,
already months into the confusion which made fieldwork become
almost impossible, the Basque ethnographer (Zulaika) was startled by
an unexpected event: a book salesman knocking at his door with merchandise relevant to his own work. The sales brochure displayed pictures of eighteen large volumes of writing, entitled *Documentos,* consisting of the publications and internal documents produced
throughout its twenty-year history (1960–1980) by ETA! The action
people also wrote? The extensive volumes contained 10,000 pages and
weighed ninety pounds!

Eighteen volumes by the people espousing nothing but action.
Eighteen volumes by the people who had misspelled the simplest graf-
fiti on a village wall (*Es* instead of *Ez,* or "No", the most cryptic and
overpowering word in the lexicon of Basque resistance). The wisdom
of ETA offered door-to-door by a book salesman. One should know
the facts; this was a fact.

The ethnographer wasn't going to be fooled, of course. Writing
was what *he* was doing. The ninety pounds of ETA's literature could
only be, at best, a footnote to his own work. Yet here were the nettle-
some many thousands of pages, too many to be simply finessed.
Indeed, for most readers of the Basque political violence scene the
ethnography was the footnote.

As we revisit the impressive corpus of beautifully produced volumes, replete with texts written by ETA activists, it is hard for us to
avoid a sense of unease. One imagines the pen that wrote some of
those pages close to bursting into flames. The text is so charged with
fate and passion that it makes a mockery of the academician's bour-
geois rhetorical stance. More than one of those authors was consumed

by the logic of what his/her text commanded and demanded. One also imagines the frightened yet outraged readers of the photocopied original. They were texts to be read with one's entire being, letters etched in fire and blood. A writer willing to explode taboos and myths is one thing; one willing to sacrifice life, his/her own included, is another.

One approaches the first volume with a sense of risk. After a few pages of introduction and interviews with some of the founders of ETA, as well as photographs illustrating Basque human geography, on page 49 we are transposed to 1959, the year in which ETA was officially constituted as an organization. The text reproduces the world news that appeared in the bulletin of the PNV, the Basque Nationalist Party, which had been in exile since the Spanish Civil War. The first three items are about the USSR's launching of a satellite to the moon, the *Corriere della Sera*'s article about the five levels of censorship that any news item had to undergo before appearing in Spain, and General Franco's declaration in his year's-end message to his people that Spain's only assistance had come from the Almighty when, according to the *New York Times*, he had received from the United States, since 1953, $350 million for the army as well as $894 million in other forms of American aid. There then follow short items by EKIN, a study group formed by a handful of Basque students in Bilbao during the early 1950s, and out of which ETA was born. These initial pages, significantly, offer a synopsis of Basque ancient laws, deal with the European federation of nations (which they strongly favor for cultural, political and economic reasons), provide general self-defense procedures in the event of arrest taken from a Sinn Fein manual, and present a basic outline of Basque political history. Perhaps most relevantly, there is a text on patriotism in which it is stated categorically that independence of the Basque Country is the only way to ensure the survival of its ancestral language, then in imminent danger of extinction. "A Basque for whom the problem of the Basque language is not DECISIVE is a traitor."[9] The seeds had been planted.

Use of "original" or baseline Basque prehistory and history, laws, and institutions is obviously far from accidental. It is a deliberate attempt at what Tololyan has lucidly described regarding Armenian "terrorism" as "the social construction of individual motivation through narrative."[10] Rather than looking at the rebellion as generating just "political" facts, there is mediation through past events experienced "as narratives that transcribe historical facts into moral or immoral acts, vehicles of social values."[11] Thus, the rebel may recognize a cultural idiom that has its roots in prehistoric archaeology, popular and learned discourse, and in living song. Through the use of continuous quotation and allusion in the writings of the university-students-turned-underground-militants, the canonical legends of the Basque past become intertextual. Narratives of ancient victories, whose historical accuracy is beside the point, "are projected upon both the present and the future as morally privileged patterns for action and for interpretation of that action."[12] Writing is indispensable to the process of shaping such projective narratives into historical record, legendary epic, the scientific interest in archaeology and lifestyles, and, of course, the political charter for revolutionary action.

For terrorism discourse, these eighteen volumes yield ninety pounds of "terrorism" texts. This is a typical sample from one of the editorials of ETA's main organ *Zutik*: "Violence is necessary. A violence that will strike and demolish, that will turn our struggle into the good, profitable violence that the Jews, the Congolese and the Algerians have created; that will place in our hands a substantial counterweight in the confrontation between our will for liberty against theirs for tyranny."[13] ETA, its acronym typically encircled by the slogan *Iraultza ala Hil*, "Revolution or Death," defines itself as the "Basque Revolutionary Movement for National Liberation." From Indochina to Tunisia, from Cuba to Algeria, there are models of glorious national liberation struggles, but one was particularly dear to ETA: "The case that is most similar to our own is Israel. For ETA...revolutionary war is feasible and it has real chances of success in Euzkadi."[14]

On closer examination, and still in the first volume, on page 111 and now in the year 1960, one finds an unexpected text, a six-page letter of strong denunciations of Spain's totalitarian regime signed by 339 Basque priests and addressed to their bishops. Two lines in the text are capitalized: "EUSKERA [Basque language], THE NECESSARY INSTRUMENT FOR THE EVANGELIZATION AND CULTURE OF THE BASQUE COUNTRY, has a right, before the Church and before civilization, to survive and to be cultivated, obliviousness to which would signal within the Church an absurd and glaring contradiction, and in society reactionary and inhuman politics bordering upon genocide."[15] The rest of the volume reproduces a book on insurgent movements around the world and, beginning in April of 1961, copies of ETA's official publication *Zutik* (mere possession of which at the time could entail up to seven years in prison).

Three of the signatories of the priests' letter were stationed in a village called Itziar on the Gipuzkoan coast, later the field site for

Zulaika's ethnography. As punishment for the priests having collected signatures, the bishop transferred one of them to a new destination. The priests' letter was, of course, anathema to the regime and was excluded from the state-controlled media. Two of Itziar's youth took part in an underground operation to circulate it during the annual pilgrimage to the religious sanctuary of Aranzazu. The mission failed, and they were caught with the compromising text in their possession. One of them was arrested and brutally tortured.[16] Thus "terror" began to be written by both sides. The official media characterized ETA and its underground activities as subversive "terrorism"; a frequent and key expression in ETA's publications became "police terror." By this time, then, the "terrorist text" was being transformed radically and inscribed indelibly on the printed page, the slogans on blank walls and the bodies of suspects.

He was at once a priest and a murderer.

—J. G. Frazer, The Golden Bough

Who were these priests? An undisputed tenet in the history of ETA's formative years is that priests and seminarians constituted the main recruitment base. ETA's initial assemblies, for example, took place for the most part in church buildings in rural areas. Who, if not the anthropologist, could be interested in Basque rural society and its traditional forms of religiosity? By then the American ethnographer, Douglass, had left the University of Chicago's department of anthropology and was at work among Basque peasants and, inevitably, Basque priests. Nothing was further than "terrorism" from his interest in funerary rituals,[17] yet at times it would seem that nothing was closer to the celebrants of them. What follows is a first person testimony of the ethnographer as witness. We present it as *ethnographic writing* regarding the people and circumstances leading to the violence, one of the various modes in which, with its own brand of the participant observer's "realism," terrorism can be written.

At the time of my fieldwork (1962–1963) ETA was in its formative stage and its future direction was far from clear. The subject of my investigation was twentieth-century rural depopulation in two small villages. Ethnonationalist politics were not directly relevant to my concern and, in any event, impacted the two settings differently. In Murelaga

(Bizkaia) it was a pervasive issue, in Echalar (Navarra) ethnonationalism was perfunctory. In both it was illegal and essentially off-limits. Indeed, the willingness of an informant to even discuss Basque nationalism, let alone candidly, was one measure of his/her trust in me and, particularly, my discretion. There was an unspoken assumption that such confidence implied and imposed a burden of confidentiality.[18]

For me the issue of Basque nationalism is ineluctably intertwined with a strong personal friendship. Don Emilio Kortabitarte was the parish priest in Murelaga. It was he who convinced me to settle upon his village as the venue for my comparative study after I had completed a year of field research in Echalar. He found us (my wife and infant son were with me) lodgings, opened many doors of suspicious villagers, and served as my key informant. He taught me Basque and about Basques. He eventually taught me to play the card game *mus* and to appreciate the soccer matches that we watched on his kitchen television set, and which always took precedence over mere mortal matters. He showed me his secret fishing spot and his special technique for catching wary, trophy trout when all others failed. Together we traveled as tourists to other places in Spain.

In short, Don Emilio and I became the best of friends. In my many return trips to the Basque Country over the years, which ranged from two-day frantic visits to full summer stays, the parish house in Murelaga was *the* obligatory stop and, as often as not, my base of operation. It became my surrogate home and its housekeeper, Balentina, my surrogate mother.

Don Emilio was in his last year of seminary when the Spanish Civil War broke out. Upon ordination he enlisted immediately as a chaplain in the Basque army. He retreated with it into Santander and, when all was lost, was among the contingent that surrendered to the Italian forces at Santoña. The prisoners' hope of receiving better treatment from the Italians was dashed immediately when they were turned over to the insurgents. Don Emilio was tried as an ordinary soldier by a military court, which refused to recognize his clerical credentials. He was sent to a concentration camp where the authorities prohibited him from saying mass. For two years he ministered to others as a kind of male nurse and shared their fears of being singled out for the periodic executions.

Upon his release he returned briefly to his coastal hometown of Lekeitio. The mayor spotted the young man on the street, denounced him as a "red separatist" and gave him a few days to leave. Don Emilio went to the bishopric and was informed that he could be transferred to Andalusia (at the time most known or suspected Basque nationalist priests were denied appointments within the Basque Country). Dismayed at the prospect he was able, through the intervention of friends, to secure a notoriously difficult parish in a remote part of the Araba province. He would later laughingly equate it to Andalusia when recounting his experiences. It seems that his youthful religious zeal and his career expectations (coming from a part of the Basque Country where priests were respected, at times, revered, authority figures) failed to square with the reality of the remote Alavese valley. It was an area periodically without religious ministration of any kind. After delivering one fiery sermon on the immorality of premarital sex Don Emilio had to run a gauntlet of young men who waited in ambush to assault him!

Barely tolerated by the parishioners, time weighed heavily upon him. He passed it by reading voraciously, particularly novels by writers such as Sinclair Lewis. In this fashion he became influenced by social criticism without, however, making the transition to a full-blown leftist viewpoint. For the rest of his life, his thought and actions were informed by total commitment to both the Basque nationalist cause and social justice.

After a few years in Araba, and his many petitions, Don Emilio was transferred to the tiny parish of Gizaburuaga, which was a few kilometers inland from Lekeitio. A short time later he was given the church in the somewhat larger nearby village of Aulestia (also called Murelaga), a post he held until retirement.

Among the priests of the area Don Emilio was sometimes referred to as the "bishop of Aulestia," in recognition of his leadership qualities. There was also the implication that had he not had the checkered background of a Basque nationalist political activist his evident intelligence and religious zeal would likely have translated into a brilliant career within the church. As it was, he was essentially marginalized and aware of it, a fate which he accepted without obvious bitterness.

When we first met in 1962 Don Emilio was a staunch supporter of the Basque Nationalist Party, which represented the moderate mainstream within Basque nationalist politics. Indeed, at the time it was essentially the only stream, since ETA was as much a shadowy rumor as a reality. His kitchen was the informal meeting place for a large number of priests from throughout the region. Most were young, newly ordained, and recipients of a tiny rural parish as their first assignment. In Don Emilio they found a mentor willing to school them in the practicalities of parish administration and the psychology of spiritual coun-

seling. They also found a man whose interpretation of Basque nationalism and social justice were completely intertwined and summed up
in the divine right of a people to exist.

In 1960 Don Emilio was one of the 339 Basque priests who signed
the petition denouncing Basque cultural genocide under the existing
regime. The document was sent directly to the pope, an obvious infer-
ence that the Spanish and Bizkaian church hierarchies were in collusion with Franco. Like the other signatories, he was fined and his pass-
port rescinded. While Don Emilio did not restrict his circle of friends
and acquaintances to Basque nationalists (indeed he enjoyed debating the skeptics), his kitchen was the venue of an open-ended political
seminar. It was there that a score or more of young Basque priests, as
well as a young anthropologist, were steeped in the history and
polemics of Basque nationalism.

By the time I left the field in late 1963, the stakes had been raised
and the kitchen klatch was abuzz with the unfolding developments
surrounding one of its members—Father Alberto Gabikagojeaskoa.
When a member of his parish was detained and beaten by the police
for nationalist activity, he denounced the action from the pulpit.
When the bishop failed to defend him (without quite endorsing the
police), Alberto publicly denounced that timidity as well.

The impasse lasted for several months and became the latest
expression and escalation of the long-simmering confrontation
between the Bizkaian church hierarchy and the regime, on the one
hand, and the rural Basque clergy on the other. At that time the civil
authorities nominated the candidates for important church positions
and paid the salaries of the Spanish clergy. In the Basque area this
close working relationship between state and church was being challenged by the lower clergy of Bizkaia and Gipuzkoa. Much of Alberto's
strategy was formulated in Don Emilio's kitchen.

The confrontation posed dilemmas for both sides. For the authorities, incarceration seemed out of the question, at least initially.
Neither the state nor the church was quite prepared to explore the
unknown consequences of jailing a priest. Alberto was fined on several occasions and refused to pay. In the courtroom he refused to testify
in Spanish, thereby converting the proceedings into a symbolic statement regarding Basque culture and its imperiled language. Faced with
Alberto's intransigence and the emulation of his actions by others, the
regime ultimately decided to build a wing for clerics onto the prison at
Zamora.

For the rural priests, who were increasingly prone to sermonize against the events as they unfolded, the issue became one of respect for ecclesiastical authority. The bishop began sending out orders for them to desist. Some of the firebrands were prepared to denounce them publicly and thereby challenge the bishop's authority. Don Emilio was not quite willing to go that far, since he had taken a vow of obedience to the church. He therefore suggested the subterfuge that the priests should simply stop opening any letter received from the bishop!

During the late sixties I returned to the Basque Country nearly every summer. In 1965 I met (in Don Emilio's kitchen) the newly appointed pastor of Gizaburuaga—Xabier Amuriza. He was an accomplished *bertsolari*, or versifier, and was already traveling throughout Bizkaia performing at village festivals. This represented a departure from the reserve and aloofness of the Basque parish priest, and even made Don Emilio, who was scarcely a traditionalist, somewhat uncomfortable. Yet it was consonant with the emerging new generation of Basque priests imbued with the ecumenicalism and social thought of Pope John XXIII, a philosophy that encouraged the clergy to become more directly involved in society.

Xabier, like many new-guard priests, required no schooling in Basque nationalism. He and Alberto became fast friends, and both were openly sympathetic to the radical or hard-line view espoused by ETA. By then, ETA's challenge to the regime was increasingly more serious. The organization was regularly bombing symbolic targets and conducting robberies to finance its activities. It had also declared that force would be met with force, so, while no one had died as yet, it seemed to be only a matter of time.

One rainy night I clasped Xabier's waist while riding on his Vespa to a meeting that he had arranged at my request. In a rural tavern I met with two young men from ETA. They insisted upon anonymity and were prepared to discuss, or rather debate, the issues. At the time ETA was undergoing a schism over the question of whether the primary goal was the triumph of Basque nationalism or the creation of a marxist state in the Basque Country. I was face to face with "terrorists."

I recall the tone rather than the detail of our conversation. I had no particular agenda, which was fortunate since it would have been impossible to pursue. For their part, they seemed intent upon converting me regarding the ills of capitalism. I do remember questioning whether a marxist message would have much appeal to the quintessentially capitalistic Basque farming population that I knew best. It didn't really matter since the exchange scarcely transcended the repetition of slogans. To this day, ETA is characterized more by activism than by political sophistication. It was a long evening and one that I feel certain left both sides dissatisfied. I am unsure to this day why I initiated the contact. I suspect it was more or less in the spirit of the vacuum cleaner approach that permeates anthropological field work, i.e., ETA existed within the milieu that I was studying, and hence I should learn something about it.

In the summer of 1969 I was in the Basque Country for a brief visit and was dining with Don Emilio in his kitchen while catching up on the previous year's news when Alberto and Xabier arrived. They animatedly outlined their latest plan. The next morning they intended to begin a hunger strike on the bishop's doorstep in protest over his unwillingness to protect his priests in their escalating confrontation with the civil authorities. We spent most of the night together in a near festive atmosphere that, however, had some of the overtones of a wake. The hunger strike lasted for a few days before the bishop consented to their arrest; they were sentenced to twelve years in the Zamora prison.

By the time Alberto and Xabier were released from prison several years later (after rejecting compromises that would have facilitated early parole), they were folk heroes to Basque nationalists of all stripes. In the interim, the struggle between ETA and the police had turned quite deadly. The Basque clergy faced a moral dilemma and generational schism. Whether to condone the bloodshed distinguished the old guard, moderate Basque nationalists, from the firebrand younger clergy. For the former it was impossible to rationalize the killings on any grounds, for the latter there were the issues of legitimate individual and collective self-defense. Indeed, some in their ranks were arrested and tried as either harborers of ETA activists or members themselves.

These were difficult times for Don Emilio. At first his kitchen served as a common ground where members of both generations debated the issues. As the division grew, boiling over into animosity in some cases, the venue became less a forum than a place where at different times either the old guard or the new enjoyed Don Emilio's coffee and company. For his part, he was postured impossibly somewhere between the radical wing of the moderates and the conservative one of the radicals. The violence never ceased to bother him, but neither did I ever hear him condemn it categorically. He was truly a man cursed with the ability to see both sides of the argument.

Meanwhile, Don Emilio was enduring other minor psychological wounds. Upon their release, both Alberto and Xabier left the priesthood. Again, Don Emilio was supportive once their decision was made, but his understanding of it was strictly intellectual. It pained him to see the church lose two of its best and brightest. The greatest hurt of all, however, was the growing division within the ranks of the nationalists.

Don Emilio never wavered in his support of the cause, and he never turned one of its activists away from his door. Indeed, within at least certain ETA circles this must have been understood. On one of my visits I found both Don Emilio and Balentina in a highly agitated state. If I was looking for "ethnographic realism," the events they recounted filled my cup to the brim. A few nights earlier two ETA operatives had arrived in Murelaga with the police in hot pursuit. Just before dawn they were eating a meal in Don Emilio's kitchen when there was a knock at the door. While Balentina cleared the dishes Don Emilio showed the two fugitives to an inconspicuous water closet located off the kitchen balcony. For several anxious minutes the police searched the house. It never occurred to them to go outside onto the balcony and then into the hideaway where the two youths awaited with pistols drawn.

After the police left, the ETA operatives knew that their only chance was to separate and try to slip through the cordon. One man handed Don Emilio a belt with plastic explosives, since, were he detained with it, he would lose all deniability. At that moment the church bell rang, summoning the priest to mass. Fearful that the police might return to resume the search in his absence, he strapped the belt around his waist and covered it with his cassock. After saying mass, and not knowing how else to dispose of the explosive, with trembling hands he pulled the plastique apart and flushed the small pieces down his toilet.

As they recounted the night Balentina wrapped herself tightly in her shawl, and rocked back and forth while exclaiming over and over "Jesus! Jesus!" A short time later she had a stroke. Don Emilio ministered to his paralyzed housekeeper until her death. At her funeral he, too, suffered a partial stroke. He told me that he was overcome with emotion and blamed himself for Balentina's collapse. He retired shortly thereafter and moved to Lekeitio, where his sister cared for him.

The last time we were together he recounted with tears in his eyes the day of tribute that the youth of Aulestia had organized in his honor. Xabier Amuriza, by then a champion *bertsolari*, served as moderator. As we walked along the seawall in Lekeitio we passed another retired priest who averted his eyes. Don Emilio said sadly, "He never

greets me, he thinks I am a red separatist." A few months later Don
Emilio died.

As his disciple I have long shared Don Emilio's dilemma regarding Basque nationalism. While an evident outsider, I am just as surely a
fellow traveler. From the perspective of terrorism discourse, my con-
tacts with ETA operatives at the time, and, particularly, my close relationship with Basque nationalist priests, could be construed as unmistakable sympathy, and even collaboration with, "terrorism."

*The priest of the Bizkaian town...has been found guilty once again...for
justifying terrorist means of extremist groups.*

—*El Diario Vasco,* July 31, 1968

In order to discover that the Basque priests were committing, or at
least fostering, terrorism, one had only to read the Spanish media of
the time, which accused them of "justifying" it. Items of the following
sort occasionally appeared in the press: "The priest X, charged with
presumed assistance to an armed terrorist group...is summoned by
the military judge Y to appear in front of him within a period of five
days."[19] This purported interplay between religion and terrorism is
scarcely limited to the Basque case. Recall the sectarianism of Ulster
with its incendiary figures such as the Reverend Ian Paisley. Rabbi
Kahane lived and died by the sword in the highly charged arena of
Middle Eastern politics. According to several governments and much
of the media, the new terrorist threat in that region comes from
Muslim fundamentalism.

Then there is the recent bombing of the World Trade Center.
There were a few arrested suspects, but one man unequivocally bears
the brunt of the responsibility for the bizarre act: the Muslim cleric
Sheik Omar Abdel Rahman. A key charge against the arrested suspects
was that, allegedly, they attended the mosque in which the blind cleric preached. In media reports, any speculation of dark conspiratorial
intrigue regarding the action became justifiable if links could be
established with him. Will Omar Abdel Rahman turn out to be his
community's Don Emilio or the mastermind (or at least guiding influence) of a terrorist organization? We cannot say.

Some will regard the description of Don Emilio as hopelessly vitiated by "sympathy." The ethnographer wishes to neither elude nor
deny such implication in his account. Indeed, willingness to listen,

understand, and even empathize with one's informants is distinctive of ethnographic writing. Fieldwork often requires a significant investment of one's lifetime in the field experience and forces such challenges as learning a difficult language precisely in order to achieve the level of understanding that permits informed empathy. It was not the ethnographer's role to contest the historical validity of Basque nationalist claims made around Don Emilio's kitchen table, but rather to attempt to comprehend *in their terms* their capacity to inform a world view and motivate behavior. In short, success in anthropological fieldwork is predicated upon what the masterful ethnographer Evans-Pritchard called "the capacity to think and feel alternatively as a savage and as a European.... To succeed in this feat a man must be able to abandon himself without reserve."[20] At the same time, empathy is not to be confused with sympathy.

Journalistic knowledge is both gleaned and presented in quite different fashion. Normally, the reporter writes his story from secondary sources (the wire service) or after a brief visit to the scene of an action. He conducts an interview or two, takes some photographs, and then writes a story under the pressure of a strict deadline. Developing a personal relationship with the subjects and learning their language is usually out of the question; indeed, the former activity may be suspect. The final account is subject to severe space restrictions and even censorship in accord with the particular newspaper's editorial policy.

There is also a sense in which the framing of the journalistic report is beyond the individual reporter's control. Public officials and government policy set the parameters. "The State Department stated today that terrorists kidnapped an American professor in Beirut" can be modified slightly by the skeptical journalist, e.g., "The State Department *alleged* today," but only within strict limits. It is therefore virtually impossible for the journalistic account to begin "The State Department's questionable [or deceptive or false] claim today...."

The media did not generally frame political violence as terrorism until the early 1970s. Ronald Crelinsten analyzed the coverage of what was deemed to constitute terrorism by two newspaper indexes, the *New York Times Index* and the *London Times Index*, and two periodical ones, the *Reader's Guide to Periodical Literature* and the *British Humanities Index* from 1966 to 1985. Only the *RGPL* included the heading TERRORISM before 1970. The *NYTI* incorporated it for the first time in 1970, and listed only four entries. In 1971 TERRORISM recurs as a heading in the *NYTI* but without citations; the reader is simply referred to *Subjects, e.g., Bombs and Bomb Plots.* Only in 1972 did all four indexes include the main heading TERRORISM. The *NYTI* referenced 64 articles for that year.

Crelinsten's data suggest that 1970 marks a turning point in the media's perception of terrorism, the year in which "Indexers began to struggle with how to classify this phenomenon and where to place the various articles."[21] According to the title of Sterling's first chapter, there is a baseline for terrorism—"1968, When It Began." "The Terrorists we are talking about," she tells us, belong "to the emerging forces of the radical left, in Africa, Asia, South and North America, Europe, the Middle East. They come from the generation of 1968, an amazing year."[22] There was a time lag until the major newapapers picked up on the new label.

The year 1972 marked a major transition in the framing of the media's treatment of political violence. Events that previously were covered under the rubrics of assassination, bombing, torture, repression, massacre, etc., were now classified as "terrorism." The word (and hence the concept) was catching on.[23] Ever since terrorism became equated to drama, it has ranked high, at times even at the top, of the media's list of priority topics. The obvious question is: What suddenly made terrorism a major discourse in the narrative of world affairs? One key factor appears to be that every reporter, every anchorman, and every pundit began utilizing "terrorism" as a key term that captured the essence and the intrigue of violent responses to nationally and internationally intractable political problems. There was the added advantage that, the terrorist being always the evil other, any exercise in moral indignation was most edifying for both writer and audience.

At this stage what interests us is that terrorism's capacity to intimidate rests wholly upon credibility, which in turn derives from writing and publicity. Thus, we should not be surprised to learn that *mafiosi* welcome and exploit their negative image, while their Japanese equivalent, the *yakuza*, even finance films about themselves in order to propagate their slick and dangerous stereotype.[24] In similar fashion we might speculate that, were Hollywood to ignore them, terrorists would require their own film companies!

IV

Diamond possessed the most extensive computer system in the world; Hel had some file cards. Diamond had all the governments of the industrialized West in his pocket; Hel had some Basque friends. Diamond represented atomic energy, the earth's oil supply, the military/industrial symbiosis, the corrupt and

> *corrupting governments established by the Wad to shield itself from responsi-*
> *bility; Hel represented* shibumi, *a faded concept of reluctant beauty. And yet,*
> *it was obvious that Hel had a considerable advantage in any battle that might*
> *be joined.*
>
>   —Trevanian, *Shibumi*

If the television or newspaper reporter must, after all, derive situations, characters, and quotes from real people and real stories, the
novelist or screenwriter is under no such restraint in the world of literary and visual pleasure domes. Terrorism is the sizzle in many a plot
of intrigue, as any moviegoer or reader of the best-seller list knows.
Nor is the appeal strictly contemporary, since novelistic terrorism has
exerted its spell over readers at least since the publication of Joseph
Conrad's *The Secret Agent* in 1907. Of the various ways of "writing" terrorism reviewed in this chapter, this is perhaps the dominant and the
most emblematic.

The novel *Shibumi* is protagonized by Hel, the perfect assassin for
our times, one who consorts with Basque terrorists. He is a professional exterminator of international agents, from the PLO to the CIA.
The plot commences with the Munich killings of Israeli athletes, and
includes the Septembrists, the Japanese Red Army, the IRA, and the
Moluccan terrorists, as well as unexpected conspiratorial networking
among them (the PLO with the CIA, prominently). The superhero
moves freely between Washington, Shanghai, Japan, and Europe,
but lately we find him retired to the seventeenth-century Chateau
d'Etxebar in the French Basque countryside, the only remaining
redoubt not infected by western values. Here he maintains his superhuman *shibumi* charisma by practicing four stages of lovemaking with
his concubine and exploring caves with his ETA friends. The element
that makes the hero/antihero invulnerable is his uncanny "proximity
sense." Learning Basque with the help of a dictionary compiled by a
priest is his cryptographic pastime. The superhero relishes the company of his "Neanderthal" friends, Basques who choose romantic danger over boring security, and whose cuckoo-land dream of a Basque
nation is represented by fairyland caves that are all but inaccessible.
The thriller is peppered with accurate references to local folklore and
mythology, as well as shrewd observations of Basque character.

Trevanian, like the ethnographer, also found a priest, "Father
Xavier," for his plot, but gave him a far different role. Although he
never faces danger personally, Father Xavier preaches revolution in an
attempt to subordinate Basque independence to the Church. The ETA

cavers are his adversaries. If the ethnographer's ex-Father Xabier is the consumate *bertsolaria*, or improvisational poet, the novelist's is the treacherous informer who causes the death of our hero's loyal friend, an ETA poet who personifies the "mythical Basque" as scholar, cave explorer, and patriotic versifier of folk legend.

The novel is saturated with reality vertigo. In Hel's supreme devotion to superior cause and his virtuoso perfectionism as an exterminator of terrorists, he disdains the "thrill-seeking, middle-class muffins tickling themselves with the thrill of terror and revolution"[25]—a characterization perhaps best applicable to the novel's audience. The hero's combination of Zen-like philosophy, aesthetic elitism, paranormal mental powers, and the comforts of retirement invoke literary transcendence of the terrorist thrill; but ultimately it is to brutal killing that Hel must return in order to avenge unpardonable injustice. The reader is told of the omnipresence, banality, and evilness of terror, while reminded that at times anyone might be forced to face it and act accordingly in a superhuman manner.

Shibumi headed the best-seller lists for weeks. The readership knew it was literature, but perhaps nothing better captured the *reality* of the terrorism discourse of the times. Cooperation between the Septembrists and the CIA must surely be pure fiction, and yet not entirely far-fetched for anyone reading the newspapers. Remember that the case of the bombing of La Belle Disco Club in West Berlin in April of 1986 would be attributed by the U.S. media to Libyan-sponsored terrorists, whereas the Soviet media described it as engineered by the CIA and the Mossad.[26]

In such fashion there is blurring of the line between fact and fiction in ostensibly objective journalistic reporting, particularly since it is the very nature of covert operations and intergovernmental confidentiality to place a premium more upon "deniability"—a fancy expression for mendacity—than upon veracity. Hence the novel's plot of intrigue and the journalist's political discourse collapse into the monolithic frame that we have labeled contemporary terrorism discourse.

This blurring of genres is further exacerbated by the propensity of some journalists and counterterrorism specialists to author terrorism novels (e.g., Robert Moss, Arnaud de Borchgrave, William Buckley Jr., Brian Crozier). Thus, at terrorism conferences it is not uncommon for the experts to discuss their next fiction project!

V

Such research will enable action to combat terrorism, particularly in the social,
cultural, educational and legal fields, to be progressively refined and focused,
thus becoming increasingly more effective as knowledge about the phenome-
non of terrorism in the Basque country is improved.

—*Report of the International Commission*
on Violence in the Basque Country

Texts by "terrorism experts" supply a critical subgenre of the various
modes of terrorism writing. Thus, in 1985, the autonomous Basque
government commissioned international experts on terrorism to
determine the causes and consequences of Basque violence. The
panel was comprised of foreign scholars with only the remotest knowledge of Basque society, history, and culture.[27] Their efforts, announced
with considerable media fanfare, raised the hopes of policy makers
that a definitive solution to the political violence was at hand. The
experts were never seen in public, did not interview the people, made
no presentations of their results during or after the research, and consulted no Basque scholar or political activist. Yet, in the name of social
science, they sat in a hotel in London and wrote that the "Basque
problem" *is* terrorism. They even provided an account, to everybody's
amazement, of a previously unknown Basque terrorist group in
Southern France—a blunder that was subsequently discarded.

The approach of the panel of experts to the phenomenon obviously entailed none of the ethnographer's reserve. They—all authorities of international reputation—purported to bring "scientific"
knowledge to bear on the issues and, by treating the issues in strictly
instrumental terms, seemed confident that the challenges to public
policy posed by the violence could be resolved once and for all. Their
expediency made a mockery of the ethnographer's work; their surety
underscored his equivocation. It was obvious that the representational modes of the ethnographer and the panel of experts had ended up
producing altogether different realities.

Two-thirds of the text of the expert report is devoted to describing other European terrorist groups. One might question whether the
specifics of Italy, Germany, or the South Tyrol are crucial for understanding what is happening among Basques, but for the experts there
is no doubt. The reason is simple: their fundamental assumption
about Basque violence is that it *is* terrorism and therefore belongs to a
particularly heinous category of behavior. Once established, it is the
paradigm itself that defines the Basque problem. ETA *is* IRA *is* Baader-

Meinhof *is* Brigata Rossa *is....*

If most of the report was about the "is" of European terrorism, the remainder was framed in the "ought" mode. That is, the panel advocated an antiterrorism crusade that included legal and juridical measures, socioeconomic policies, security provisions, intelligence gathering, and a "Plan for Consciousness-Raising" of the Basque population. It declared the pivotal role of the social sciences in determining the

> aims, membership, personalities and methods of ETA. This information should be sought in parallel with the implementation of the counter-measures recommended later in this report, which should not await the outcome of the research studies indicated below.[28]

Social science was needed, the experts contended frankly, because "such research will enable action to combat terrorism."[29] The consciousness-raising was premised on clearly stated ideological and moral imperatives that included an active use of media exposure of the plan; detailed indoctrination against radical nationalist values at all educational levels, from primary school to the university; and advice to political parties regarding the role they should play in combatting terrorism. Thus, the ethnographer is exhorted to participate in the antiterrorism campaign; in fact the results of our own work, whatever its assumptions and our intentions, were to be co-opted into the effort.

These measures were not propounded by members of the community concerned with political reform or tormented by the moral paradoxes of the ongoing violence; they were recommended in the name of scientific expertise by international scholars who claimed the high ground of impartiality and universal ethical standards regarding a local conflict. As noted by Nordstrom and Martin, "The process legitimates a way of thinking about violence and conflict that emanates from a position of power."[30] The question is not whether politicians, police officers and moral advocates should exert control and urge value transformations within their societies, but rather, from a social scientific viewpoint, how an expert *knows* what a society's public school curriculum, political orientation, and ethical consensus ought to be. The assumption is, of course, that we all know that terrorism is bad and that anything that contributes to preventing it should be considered positive.

The reader might be misled into thinking that the Basque case is highly localized and even marginal to global terrorism discourse. We would argue the opposite. The more we examine the scholarly and media representations of it in the United States, and compare them to the ethnographic reality we experienced in the Spanish Basque Country, the more we realize the extent to which stark incongruities that are seemingly poles apart may be subsumed within the same political discourse. In this regard the arguments become both incestuous and circular. Some of the very same experts instrumental in diagnosing and framing the Basque case have also been influential in U.S. counterterrorism policy. Sterling's book was read not only in the White House and in the State Department, where Haig distributed copies, but also in Spanish government ministries. In fact ETA was a prime example of her claim that Moscow was behind the entire international terror network. Basque politicians, although long opposed to ETA's tactics, were utterly skeptical, and their hiring of a panel of international experts on terrorism was in part to counterbalance the impact of the book. Horchem, the best-known German expert when Haig was attacked in Germany, was also a prominent counterterrorism adviser to the Spanish government who played a key role on the Basque terrorism panel. He was one of the sources quoted by Sterling for her tale of an international terrorist network masterminded by Moscow, although the panel of experts, of which he was a member, did not support Sterling's allegations regarding Basque terrorism.

Paul Wilkinson, another academic doyen of terrorism discourse, is also attentive to the Basques, although his counterterrorist zeal makes it difficult for him to grasp the bare facts of the case. Thus he states that "the electoral support that the pro-terrorist political party, Herri Batasuna, achieved in the 1984 autonomous elections was only one in ten of the Basque adult population. It has now (1989) dropped still further."[31] Wilkinson cites a paper by Pollack and Hunter, but the actual numbers provided by them state, "HB obtained 16.5% of the votes cast, and thus remains the second most important party in the Basque country."[32] It is by factoring in the 31.5 percent of abstentions, without informing the reader, that Wilkinson reduces HB's "electoral support" to 10 percent. As for the 1989 election, contrary to Wilkinson's claims, Herri Batasuna's electorate did not diminish compared to 1984. In 1984 it received 185,444 votes, whereas in the European and legislative elections of 1989 it got 215,878 and 217,278 votes, respectively. Any neutral observer might conclude, as do Pollack and Hunter, that HB's vote total, representing open support for a "terrorist" organization, is simply "too significant a figure to be ignored." Yet Wilkinson, after reworking the data, argues that "the claim of the terrorists that they are a legitimate national liberation movement can be shown to be entirely spurious."[33] After examining Wilkinson's main work, *Political Terrorism*, Philip Schlesinger concluded that, rather than the theoretical essay it purports to be, it is "an undeclared counter-insurgency text," and that, "Wilkinson is in fact working with the concept of a militarized 'democracy,' and it is the logic of counter-insurgency thought which leads him there."[34]

The "factual" and "fictional" literatures on terrorism share rhetorical strategies. There is stark similarity in their narrative plots between two of the best-known books on terrorism, Trevanian's novel *Shibumi* and Sterling's allegedly factual report *The Terror Network*. In Sterling's prologue we encounter a Trevanian roster of events and cast of characters: the Munich Olympic Games, Black September, the PLO, radical groups from Arab terrorist countries, OPEC, the Red Army, and, very prominently, the CIA. Trevanian's charismatic hero, Nicholai Hel, is replaced in Sterling's plot by "Carlos the Jackal" as "the Man on the international scene." Sterling adds historical depth to her story: 1968 was the year in which, from Berkeley to Paris to Frankfurt to the Basque Country to Beirut to Tokyo, "The colossal force released by a bunch of beatnik kids once dismissed as a lunatic fringe knocked the breath out of the world's various Establishments."[35] If the Trevanian novel mobilizes all sorts of ploys to add suspense and near ethnographic narratives for realism, the reporter creates her own reality effect by advising the reader that, "This is not a book of fiction. It deals with facts."[36] The facts supporting the first chapter, "1968, When It Began" are the assassinations of Robert Kennedy and Martin Luther King Jr., the ousting of Presidents Lyndon Johnson and Charles de Gaulle, the Vietnam offensive, a sudden flare of violence in the Basque provinces.... "There is nothing random in this concentrated assault on the shrinking area of the world still under democratic rule."[37]

Sterling's text, which became the catechism of the Reagan White House and State Department, exudes factualism. A closer look at the chapter "Terror in Basqueland" reveals, however, a very flawed grasp of the facts. When she openly refers to her sources as Spanish Secret Service reports or various European governments, there is simply no way for the reader to verify them; at other times she draws her crucial support from authors notoriously committed to the counterterrorism campaign, authors such as Horchem, Moss, and Semprun. For anyone sensitized to Basque reality, there is glaring disparity regarding such basics as population numbers and the ratio of Basque speakers—statistics that are routinely presented in any study of the Basques—and which are simply wrong in Sterling's book.[38] While it is common knowledge that in the noted Burgos trial six activists were given nine death sentences, for Sterling there were nine activists condemned to death. She declares that the Basque language is dead and that it does not even have a written alphabet; in fact there are 600,000 Basque speakers, their number is growing, and there is an active Basque-language press that publishes dozens of magazines and newspapers as well as about a thousand books annually. At one point Sterling quotes the Spanish name of a dish and achieves the difficult feat of committing five orthographic errors.[39]

Turning to her contentions regarding terrorism, one of the major proofs of critical international links between the various terrorist groups regards the connection between ETA and the IRA. However, one becomes suspicious of Sterling's information, ostensibly provided by secret police sources, when the very activist constituting the link, "Iñaki," is in fact misidentified.[40] She reports that 143 ETA members of the military branch were being trained in Algeria "for a doctorate in guerrilla warfare" in 1975 and that by 1977 ETA "had a couple of hundred finely honed and superbly armed *pistoleros*"; whereas our fieldwork, which is described at length in an ethnographic study, determined that as much as 80–90 percent of all ETA actions carried out during 1975 and early 1976 were executed by four rural teenagers, each with one pistol and no special training whatsoever.[41] Sterling states twice, in order to underscore its special significance, that ETA activists approached the IRA with fifty revolvers in return for training in the use of explosives. This is her telling revelation in support of the view that there exist "colossal supplies of weapons employed by the terrorists of four Continents in Fright Decade I."[42] Her hyperbole knows no bounds when we are told that a transaction involving fifty revolvers signals "an inexorably advancing enemy" against

> the industrialized democracies of North America and Western Europe. The most deadly have come in a strategic crescent from the Black Sea to the Atlantic—Turkey, Italy, Spain, Great Britain, Federal Germany—half encircling the European continent. The terrorists are the first to say that they hope someday to close the circle.[43]

It is hard to imagine a better and more widespread example of what Richard Hofstadter labeled "the paranoid style in American politics" than the rhetoric of experts such as Claire Sterling. She replicates, almost literally, the fears of other alleged grand world conspiracies, such as the panic that broke out at the end of the eighteenth century in New England against the Bavarian Illuminati, and which merited a leap into fantasy by the well-known author John Robison when he charged that the association had been formed "for the express purpose of...OVERTURNING ALL THE EXISTING GOVERNMENTS OF EUROPE."[44] Soon the Illuminati were held to be the Antichrist and denounced from the pulpits of New England, even though it is uncertain whether any of them ever came to the United States from Germany. The anti-Masonic movement of the 1820s and 1830s reflects the same obsession with conspiracy, thus illustrating the essence of the paranoid style, which posits "the existence of a vast, insidious, preternaturally effective international conspiratorial network designed to perpetrate acts of the most fiendish character."[45] Such an apocalyptic framework is quite characteristic of terrorism discourse.

Another example that illustrates the extent to which a single terrorism discourse covers situations worlds apart, as well as the thin line between counterterrorism reality and the fabrication of facts, is provided by Jerrold Post. He is a familiar figure to those who watch major TV network news shows such as CNN or ABC's *Prime-Time Live.* Whether it is the question of "what makes Saddam Hussein tick" or "the paranoid personality" of the Branch Davidians or the "terrorist mind-set," Post is the expert political psychologist repeatedly called upon to explain the workings of the mind behind the bizarre actions. Based on his writings, it appears that much of what he knows about terrorism he has learned from studying the literature on Basque political violence.

Post's standard explanation of terrorist behavior is that the establishment and perpetuation of terrorist groups result from their members' psychic states regarding commitment, revenge, guilt, risk-taking, and so on. Terrorists are recruited, he tells us based on his understanding of ETA, from among "marginal, isolated, and inadequate individuals from troubled family backgrounds"[46] who typically suffer from various personality disorders. He therefore argues that terrorists are "psychologically compelled to commit acts of violence." What the undiscriminating reader is unlikely to discern is the extent to which Post distorts and manufactures "facts" by removing them from their contexts or simply misinterpreting the analyses of their authors. His basic contention is that, while only 8 percent of Basques are of mixed Basque-Spanish heritage, 40 percent of ETA members belong to this category; hence ETA activists are "marginal" people, "outcasts" attempting to "out-Basque the Basques."[47] He bases this conclusion upon data presented by the political scientist Robert Clark.[48] Yet, leaving aside the erroneous premise of identifying Basqueness solely by surname, Clark's data are far different: for 51 percent of the population of the Basque Country, both parents have an identifiable Basque surname; 40 percent have neither parent with a Basque surname; and for 8 percent only their father or mother has a Basque surname. What Post does not tell the reader is the 40 percent figure, nor that this corresponds largely to the migrants from other parts of Spain living in the Basque Country. That is, these are the really "marginal" persons; Clark notes that only "in a few cases" have their children joined ETA. According to Post's theory of "out-Basqueing the Basques," the children of the migrants should constitute the majority within ETA's ranks. In fact, Clark's paper, with its profusion of evidence, argues forcefully the very opposite of what Post posits.[49] Even after the foregoing critique Post has continued to espouse the same blatant distortion of Clark's data.[50] Since everything written on Basque political violence contradicts Post's theory of marginality and genetic predisposition to violence, he must skew the data or have no explanation at all.

Once published by an "expert," such findings become part of the scientific discourse and recur throughout the terrorism literature.[51] Nor are such conclusions devoid of political significance when they are recycled as unquestionable dogma by counterterrorism officials. This was the case with Paul Bremer III, Ambassador at Large for Counterterrorism, who recapitulated Post's skewed data about the Basques before the Norwegian Atlantic Committee in Oslo, Norway, February 4, 1988.[52] Thus, the highest-ranking U.S. counterterrorism official, in an address ironically entitled "Terrorism: Myths and Reality," employed data that anyone familiar with the Basque case knew to be utterly erroneous. Such a deceptive metaterrorism game, by which experts are allegedly capable of sorting out "reality" from "myth," is an integral part of the entire discourse's strategy of self-authorization.

Experts such as Steven Emerson, a regular fixture on TV when terrorism requires commentary, may in fact turn out to be dead wrong in their analyses. After the World Trade Center explosion, for example, Emerson, an investigative reporter for CNN, announced that the attack had been carried out by a Serb terrorist group. Undeterred by his earlier lapse, on the night of the bombing in Oklahoma City he attributed it to Arabs by saying on *CBS Evening News*, "This was done with the intent to inflict as many casualties as possible. That is a Mideastern trait."[53] Even after the FBI announced it had arrested two white males as key suspects, Emerson maintained on *Crossfire*: "The FBI considers radical Islamic extremists on American soil to be the number-one domestic national security threat, period."[54] He believes that the planned bombings by Islamic terrorists would have killed 50,000 people.[55] Citing Emerson's December 1994 PBS documentary, *Jihad in America*, which shows Muslims meeting in Oklahoma City, former Oklahoma U.S. Congressman Dave McCurdy concluded likewise that Islamic terrorist groups were involved in the explosion.

Terrorists and counterterrorists share the same culture of secrecy. Espionage and other intelligence-gathering agencies want us to believe that only they can penetrate the veil of secrecy and thereby foil the plots that threaten our safety. Ostensible breaching of the adversary's secrecy while speaking in vague, i.e., secretive, terms about their own agendas are key to the efficacy of the security agencies' messages. With the Cold War over, and the public increasingly questioning the relevance of organizations like the CIA, KGB, FBI, etc., counterterrorism grants new legitimacy to secret sources and conspiratorial theories.

VI

Should we qualify ETA as a manifestation of revolutionary nationalism, or rather as a terrorist group? Is it possible to link, in a single action, a social focus, a revolutionary vision, and a fight for national liberation, without sliding into acts of violence destined to issue, sooner or later, into terrorism? Such will be our basic question.

—M. Wieviorka, *The Making of Terrorism*

Not all scholarship is of the prescriptive sort. Some political scientists, sociologists, psychologists and historians are engaged in writing about political violence, bringing to bear the best that their disciplines have to offer while being committed to the values of objective research. Wieviorka's interventionist sociology and comparative analysis of various "terrorist" movements is an exemplary study devoid of tabooing prejudices. He personally engages his informants in earnest, forces his subjects to confront their enemies, and allows the outcomes of fieldwork to determine the validity of his research hypotheses. Yet Wieviorka is captive to terrorism discourse.

Wieviorka begins his analysis of ETA by providing the recent history of armed struggle in the Basque Country: the birth of ETA within the broader context of Basque nationalism; its formative years as a student group; the early schisms between its class-struggle-oriented and more national-liberation-prone factions; the ethical debates over the use of deadly force; the tensions between the various "assemblies" that were to effect ETA's official line; the Burgos trial of 1970, which first brought ETA to international attention; the endemic internal struggles during the 1970s; the death of the leader Pertur, most probably at the hands of his armed comrades; and the transition to democracy and the political explosion of the post-Franco era. The recurring theme in this historical reconstruction is ETA's claim to speak in the name of all Basques, despite the impossibility of unifying their diverse social and nationalist aspirations under a single banner.

The three main components "of the myth of an all-Basque movement" examined by Wieviorka are: the struggle for statehood, social protest, and organized political action of an either "revolutionary" or "reformist" nature. For a short period, during the disintegration of the Franco regime (1974–1975), the three forces appeared capable of forming a united front. ETA's significance can only be understood in light of its self-image as a revolutionary movement capable of embracing simultaneously these three concerns. ETA "was the arena in which the myth played itself out, first on a symbolic and later on an increasingly violent level."[56]

Wieviorka's main hypothesis regards the "inversion process" suffered by an armed insurgency when it degenerates into meaningless violence that is antithetical to the ideals that it originally professed. Thus, revolutionary nationalism is supplanted by terrorism's indiscriminate violence. He convened two groups of informants. One, the veterans, was composed mostly of ex-ETA militants who became politically committed to the post-Franco democratic process, members of *Euskadiko Ezkerra*, a political party fiercely critical of ETA after their own politico-military branch of it renounced violence in 1981. The other group consisted of the independentists, who placed greater faith in the efficacy of political violence than in political process.

In interviewing the veterans, Wieviorka's methodology was to let his informants speak initially of ETA's irrational and terroristic nature, thus lending credence to the hypothesis of the inversion process. But then he challenged them to describe what course of action is capable of unifying the national and sociopolitical agendas. He forced them to contemplate themselves as actors and, after a charged moment in which two participants equated Basque patriotism to Naziism, Wieviorka engaged them in an analysis of armed insurgency. The debate provoked self-criticism by former insurgents now incapable of formulating their own efficacious course of action. Unexpectedly, in their frustration, the notion of ETA's complete inversion was then attacked by those who had defended it with the greatest ardor. Wieviorka concluded that "today, it is impossible to develop a visionary program of action or to support, by linking them together, the principal ideals of an all-Basque movement, without resorting to armed struggle."[57]

The results of the sociological enquiry with the independentist group of informants were no less interesting. The discussion focused upon issues of nationalism and totalitarianism. The informants questioned the blessings of democracy and professed that there is state terrorism. The hypothesis that "violence is inseparable from a universalizing definition of the categories of action"[58] was confirmed. Their rationale for political separatism operated on the three levels of conviction (violence is the unavoidable and necessary condition for the movement), intimidation (the necessity to silence the individual at odds with the group), and denunciation (as when the mothers of jailed ETA members protest their incarceration). The notion that the armed struggle should unify the various nationalist and social fronts was rejected. The group refused to accommodate or entertain any deconstruction of its modes of action.

Paradoxically, even though the two groups are in total disagreement, they "converge and complement one another." Both regard violence as constituting the only possible means for unifying the various sociopolitical and national struggles, their only difference being that such an approach strikes the independentists as a real solution, whereas the veterans regard it as an unrealistic tactic. Asserting that "ETA's power base extends well beyond the quite considerable 15 or 20 percent of the electorate of the [pro-ETA] HB," Wieviorka stresses the conclusion that "sociologically speaking, ETA violence is, on the whole, not terrorist."[59]

Wieviorka's treatment of recent Basque political violence could hardly be more factual, lucid, and honest. We agree with his final assessment that "ETA violence is primarily the result of the increasingly difficult task of simultaneously speaking in the name of the suppressed nation, social movements, and the revolution. It is aggravated by the fact that the meanings of each of these three components have themselves become diminished or deconstructed."[60] Yet we are poles apart from his uncritical appropriation of terrorism discourse as the foundation of his analytical edifice.

At the outset Wieviorka confronts the reader with "the essential problem" of his work on Basque violence:

> Does revolutionary nationalism not find its necessary…conditions in the most extreme forms of violence imaginable, a violence that therefore extends into terrorism? Or is it more accurate to say, on the contrary, that the most profound meanings of revolutionary nationalism are subverted, perverted, and inverted as soon as groups who claim to be fighting in its name sink into terrorism?[61]

The strength of Wieviorka's analysis derives from the fact that, contrary to most of the terrorism literature, "the answer is not an obvious one." Yet what makes "terrorism" a pristine a priori category against which all types of violent action should be measured? Why should a sociological study subordinate its analytical agenda to whether certain nationalist forms of violence are "terrorism"? Does this imply that reaching such a final verdict invests the research findings, thus canonized by it, with some ultimate theoretical efficacy? The unexorcized assumption is that terrorism is a kind of pathological disease, a cancerous thing in itself, a litmus test of political aberration.

The contradiction between the analytical premises and the actual results of Wieviorka's work is nowhere more evident than in the general conclusion of the book. The very author who admits that "a rather limited body of research has brought us to reject the systematic use of the notion of terrorism"[62] curiously does not question its discursive basis but rather provides his own typological distinctions between domestic versus international terrorism, broad-based totalitarianism versus demobilized terrorism, delinquency versus political terrorism, right-wing versus left-wing terrorism, and so on. Above all, there is an unquestioning "terrorist inversion," a "downward spiral that leads into terrorism" that proceeds from the "loss of meaning."

In the concluding pages, in order to restore the reader's faith in the entire terrorism discourse so badly battered by his own sociological findings, Wieviorka repeatedly defends the conceptual and political "unity of terrorism" as the final underpinning of his analytical edifice. He is aware that "every instance of terrorism is unique," that its constituencies are "highly diversified," and that a terrorist process requires "a great number of conditions." Yet we are told in the final words of the book,

> this phenomenon finds its sociological unity, on a global level, in that to which it most often gives voice. This is the reshaping…of the final convulsions of a now moribund and decaying collective action or, less often, a unilateral transposition of itself into an action in search of itself.[62]

Despite such obfuscating sociological metaphysics, so necessary if the author is to salvage terrorism discourse, we find Wieviorka's work courageous and engaging. In the chapters that follow we will present our own arguments as to why "terrorism" is analytically far more of a hindrance than an aid to understanding political violence, and why there is no need to posit such a discursive first premise for writing about it.

It is because writing is inaugural, in the fresh sense of the word, that it is dangerous and anguishing. It does not know where it is going, no knowledge can keep it from the essential precipitation toward the meaning that it constitutes and that is, primarily, its future.

—J. Derrida, *Writing and Difference*

As evidenced by the foregoing examples, it is the "inaugural" aspect of writing that most characterizes terrorism discourse. Far from being a passive medium incidental to the essence of language, writing is central to the very structure of the discourse. Writing operates in the absence of both the writer and the reader as a "sort of machine";[64] the written sign can be reproduced apart from its original context, this material operation being intrinsic to language in general, of which writing is but one expression. Every sign, merely by being cited or put between quotation marks, can break with its original context and access a multiplicity of potential new ones. As a consequence, the text means for its readers something other than what it meant for its author. The writer's intention cannot govern the text's reception. In Derrida's view, all language is characterized by such inevitable reification.

Terrorism discourse provides a grand example of the primacy and centrality of writing in both its literal and "grammatological" senses. Accordingly, we must grant precedence to the signifier rather than the signified, and focus our attention at the level of discourse rather than upon a single text. In this chapter we have considered various ways of writing "Basque terrorism"—whether as "patriotic cause" (ETA's *Documentos*), "ethnography" (Douglass), "entertainment" (Shedd and Trevanian), "news" (the Basque and Spanish presses), counterterrorist "intelligence" and "expertise" (Sterling, Post, the panel of international specialists), and "sociology" (Wieviorka). Each, as we have seen, is more than simply a different perspective of the same reality; rather, each *produces* its own separate reality. Terrorism writing aims at constituting these various texts into a single field of discourse.

As we know from personal experience, "terrorism" possesses such great power that the terrorism writer must be prepared to "be written" by the discourse. Any claim of neutrality for one's own writing appears most illusory when dealing with a topic that evokes such apocalyptic fears. The author's original context cannot be but a distant reference lost within the discourse's own phantasmagoria.

The very act of describing in any fashion those communities plagued with "terrorism," or writing about events that can be construed in "terrorist" terms, runs the risks of intellectual and moral contamination.[65] Far from being a passive agent, terrorism discourse casts its powerful rhetoric of "contagion" over those who get too close to it.[66] Its mutational powers transform academicians and journalists into experts, experts into novelists, and novelists into journalists.

We would illustrate the above points with our own professional careers. In 1967, Douglass was hired by the University of Nevada System to start a Basque Studies Program. Nevada's interest was more in the history of Basque immigrants, who had served as the state's and region's sheepherders over the past century, an interest that could scarcely compete with the contemporary world's fascination with "Basque terrorism." As the only one of its kind, the Basque Studies Program nationally attracted the attention of journalists seeking a facile quote in response to the latest ETA bombing. Douglass learned the bitter lesson that reporters from the *New York Times* or the *Village Voice*, faced with tomorrow's deadline and space limitations, were scarcely interested in the complexities of labyrinthine Spanish/Basque politics. He came to dread their calls.

Then there was the visit from the novelist seeking material. For hours, Douglass spoke with her about life histories and the communal relations he observed during two years of living in rural Basque society. The ethnographer's staple of structural issues and social changes was of secondary interest to her. What she wanted to capture, of course, was the burning, turbulent reality far different from the ordinary flow of daily life. She wanted to know about the meeting with the ETA operatives, about Don Emilio saying mass with plastic explosives strapped around his waist, the details about the Burgos trial in which ETA members, including two priests, were tried and condemned by a military tribunal, causing an international uproar.[67]

Who, then, becomes the main protagonist of her novel?[68] A tall, bespectacled American student interested in Basque history and folklore, who has studied the *Chanson de Roland* for two years, and then finds himself in the midst of Basque terrorists pursued by the Spanish police. He falls in love with a jailed girl from ETA. The tall, bespectacled ethnographer's thinly disguised personal experience is thereby turned into literary heroism in a novel about terrorism. There are, of course, other protagonists such as the Monsignor-protecting priests, who were "Virgin-fucking terrorists."

Nor were the protagonists in the Basque political opposition immune from using the ethnographer's thoughts and person. Douglass coauthored an article on Basque nationalism. [69] A short time later it appeared in Spanish translation under the title "Soy Vasco" ("I am a Basque"). It was produced in Venezuela in pocket-sized pamphlet form for easier clandestine introduction into Franco's Spain. The ethnographer's "authorial authority" was thereby co-opted by the cause without his permission or knowledge.

Nor has Douglass, as head of the Basque Studies Program (BSP), been immune to the calls of the counterterrorism campaign. In the early 1980s he was approached by an agent of the CIA who spent the afternoon trying to convince him that the BSP should analyze the Basque language press and send reports to the agency. The agent later returned with a colleague based in Madrid. They wished to place a "student" in the BSP's study-abroad program held in the Basque Country, who would then try to penetrate ETA. Douglass's refusal to collaborate led to a lengthy debate that left him shaken. That evening he watched a television newscast in which its director testified before the U.S. Congress that the CIA never uses journalists or academics as a cover!

Zulaika, too, has experienced the trip through the looking glass. His book, an ethnography of Basque political violence, elicited in both the Spanish progovernmental newspaper *El País* and the pro-ETA *Egin* the identical charges of cultural relativism, moral ambiguity, and the playing of superfluous rhetorical games. He was accused of contributing to terrorism with his moral and intellectual depravity, while the subjects of his book were charged with mad criminality and repugnant delinquency.[70] An ethnographic approach to political terrorism implied such a violation of narrative convention and the politically admissible in Spain that an anthropologist colleague charged that privileging ethnography was tantamount to an "anthropological imposture."[71] In short, the very act of writing an ethnography of political violence outside of conventional terrorism discourse can become in itself a major act of transgression of the policy of tabooing the violent actors.[72]

The following incident encapsulates the extent to which the writer of "terrorism" can fall under the spell of its all-encompassing international discourse. One morning in early August of 1991 Zulaika visited the cemetery of Itziar accompanied by TV cameramen from NBC and Basque Television. The NBC men spoke of their visit to Moscow earlier that week and were unsure of why they were filming in Itziar. They speculated that the images might be for a program on Basque terrorism should ETA strike against the Barcelona Olympics. The ethnographer was in the dark as well, for all he had been told was that NBC was interested in an interview about Basque political violence. When Basque Television learned of NBC's visit, a crew was dispatched to the cemetery to film Americans filming Itziar, much to the chagrin of the NBC team. Zulaika was caught somewhere in the morass constituted by the curious villagers, the Americans reporting on the villagers, and the Basques reporting on the Americans reporting on the villagers. He attempted to mediate the parodic encounter by telling the Basque reporters that the Americans did not want to blow their story by constituting news themselves, telling the American reporters that the villagers were real people who would resent being portrayed unfairly as "terrorists," and telling the villagers that the Americans were just interested in a story about Itziar and that the Basque TV people wanted a story about Americans interested in a story about Itziar.

Fortunately, NBC did not air its story, and Zulaika never heard a word from them again. Unfortunately, he agreed to assist Basque TV in filming a documentary based on his book, but conditioned it upon the villagers' prior approval. When Itziar rejected the project, the television journalists went ahead anyway, while ignoring Zulaika's protests that they were violating their pledge to ensure the villagers' anonymity. Such, then, are the perils of ethnographic writing on political violence, whether one is subsumed as protagonist into the vortex of a sensationalized novel or co-opted to lend authenticity to a television docudrama; it is a ruthless world, where marketing terrorism discourse is big business.

There is a point at which the lives of madmen and murderers become so bizarre that we question whether the discourse about them "starts to function in a field where it qualifies as literature."[73] Oedipus with his crimes or Faust with his devilish pact remain as emblematic literary figures of their times; "The Terrorist" and his apocalyptic threat might perhaps endure as an archetype of the late twentieth century's postmodern military simulacrum.

3

TROPICS OF TERROR
Plots and Performances

In topics such as these, there are always legitimate grounds for differences of opinion as to what they are, how they should be spoken about, and the kinds of knowledge we can have of them....

This is specially the case when it is a matter of trying to mark out what appears to be a new area of human experience for preliminary analysis, define its contours, identify the elements in its field, and discern the kinds of relationships that obtain among them...discourse effects this adequation by a prefigurative move that is more tropical than logical....

Tropic is the shadow from which all realistic discourse tries to flee. This flight, however, is futile; for tropics is the process by which all discourse constitutes the objects which it pretends only to describe realistically and to analyze objectively.

—H. White, *Tropics of Discourse*

Terrorism is an event, a news story, a social drama, a narrative. It is a genre of "emplotted" action in which narrative sequence is a moral and discursive construct, and in which "the event is not what happens. The event is that which can be narrated."[1] The initial problem that the writer must confront, as is the case with any storyteller or historian, is selection of the narrative form in which to plot the events and the arguments. Whether searching for the *longue durée* of historical "causes" or seeking explanation within the more immediate realities of a personal biography, whether viewing terrorism as a recent form of warfare or as a type of ritual action, such "emplotments" are intimately connected with "tropes." Metaphor, metonym, synecdoche, and irony are the ultimate keys, the master tropes of distinctive narrative modes as well as their associated types of consciousness. How such tropes function in the various arguments and performances of terrorism discourse is the subject of this chapter.

"Type of warfare," "ritual," "pathology," "social drama," and so on, are some scholarly categories and poetic strategies—each equipped with its disciplinary literature and prominent authors—commonly applied to the study of terrorism. These are for the most part self-enclosed genres in which each author refuses to relinquish or transcend the vocabulary and premises of his/her discipline. "Ritual," for example, is high on the list of anthropological preferences, for that omnivorous concept sums up much of what is distinctive about anthropological understanding; yet such preference does not preclude that "theater" might serve equally well. Wagner-Pacifici's work on the kidnapping of Aldo Moro, with its concluding argument for "the victory of melodrama over tragedy in the Moro social drama,"[2] brings the self-conscious competition over narrative genre to the center stage of terrorism analysis.

Our preferred view, the plot we borrow from cultural anthropology to make sense of "terrorism," is to regard terrorism as ritual behavior. Were we to further terrorism discourse, our basic tenet would read something like "terrorism is ritual." In our view, much of what passes for terrorism can best be typified as ritual expediency and bluff within a highly symbolic context, rather than as something that functions in strict means-ends terms. It has to do more with personal initiation, ritual sacrifice, the play with chance, and the imposition of an either/or logic, than with instrumental causality, military organization, or well-planned strategy. It is the performative plenitude, the culturally embedded premises of a magical sort of activism, the presence of nonverbal and primordial components, the nonreferential semantics of threat, and, in general, the ritualization that is all-pervasive in preindustrial types of warfare and responses to them, that we find most helpful in examining "terrorist" behavior. In light of anthropological theories, ritual becomes an incisive paradigm to sharpen our focus on the tension between ambiguous form and purposeful indeterminacy that is so typical of terrorism.

Yet, if anthropology teaches us that ritual can be fundamental social reality, we also learn about the futility of imposing *a* conclusive explanation of historical events. Calling something "ritual" is only the beginning of explanation. This is our preferred rhetorical ploy because it underscores the incongruity of causal models and narrative closures. We observe that, besides providing a new sense of order, ritual can also produce its own dilemmas and chaos. At the same time, terrorism discourse itself challenges anthropology's attempts at totalizing theories. We find such core anthropological notions as "ritual," "taboo," "symbolism," "body," "writing," "fiction," "experience," "theater," "face," to be particularly useful for our analysis; yet at the same time we believe that terrorism discourse reveals their limitations.

Thus our primary concern in this chapter is not whether terrorism stories are true or false nor whether rituals and symbols explain or exculpate violence. Rather, our inquiry regards the nature of various types of narratives and performances—each with its corresponding "illusion of sequence"—employed in terrorism discourse. Narrations purport to be mediators between fact and fiction; ritual performances would mediate between history and myth. Given the many disparities and conflicting claims upon reality that we have already considered in the first two chapters, here we question the value of narrativity as a device for making sense of events labeled "terrorism."

The explanation of "why terrorism" has so far eluded scholars and political scientists, and the research studies suggested above should aim to find the answer to this question.

C. Rose, et.al, *Report of the International Commission on Violence in the Basque Country*

Among the various possible modes of formal argumentation within terrorism texts there is one that, for its very prevalence, deserves primary attention. This is the causal argument. It takes the form of the simple question: "What are the *causes* of terrorism?" Most conferences and texts regarding it are framed in such terms. The very query creates the mirage that the bizarre phenomenon may finally be reduced to a formulaic question the answer to which holds out the prospect of resolving the riddle. This seemingly innocuous and even most scientific of questions gets formulated over and over again as a mantra, the quintessential research issue, the key point of reference against which any analysis of terrorism must be measured.

Given the long history of disputes within the social sciences regarding the plausibility of such alleged laws of social causation, it is most surprising that a causal agenda is pursued so uncritically within terrorism studies. In a sense, the entire discourse rests upon such argumentation because there is no dispute at all over the value of causal explanations regarding terrorism. There is nowhere in the literature a hint that causal analysis might be just *one kind of explanation*, and that such discourse has to be tied to metaterrorism premises.

The "world hypothesis"[3] underlying such causal discourse is mechanistic and far removed from contending ones such as the dispersive strategy of Formism, the abstract ideas of Organicism, or the relative functional integration of Contextualism. Causes deal with the real and the true, or so goes the assumption; unlike interpretations, causal analysis need not justify its method or theory. Hence, one must examine the unquestioning historical/structural causes, the willingness to give one's life for "the cause," the authorial insistence upon the social/psychological causes, the pervasive metaphors of violence being "a chain" and "a spiral" of causal actions and reactions. The prospect of a Foucaultian inquiry for the *genealogy* of the entire discourse as linked to power and situated in formations of bodily violence is simply beyond such causal investigation. Yet, paradoxically, the causal perspective is employed to examine a phenomenon that is ideal—typically portrayed as "random" and "indiscriminate" violence. Thus, the discursive emplotment is buttressed with arguments full of causes in order to deal, ironically, with aspects of behavior that are notoriously *non*causal—chance, ritual, play.

The research question of "why terrorism" is thus readily presented as the best ploy for getting at the heart of the matter; there is no consideration that it might be a mandate for intellectual obsolescence. The literature is therefore beset with the definitional issues, which amount to the difficulties in differentiating between legitimate and illegitimate causes, as well as the relationship between means and ends. The shock caused by seemingly nonrational terroristic behavior can only be mitigated by the exclamation of a "Why?" The puzzlement seems to demand a causal search, when the exclamation may in fact be recognition of a lack of cause and purpose inherent in the very "absurdity" of the action.

Military thinking, in particular, is conspicuously causal, as necessary or sufficient causes are adduced to justify going to war, and final causes are elaborated by politicians to create an ends-means perspective. The arguments about what causes the violence reproduces the same kind of thinking in which the encounter between the contending parties is a functional, nonprobabilistic, causal relationship. Devoid of feedback and different orders of prediction, in the causal approach all creativity is reduced to the purposive means-ends syndrome. The shift from the physical event to its symbolism, from function to meaning, is conspicuous by its absence.

Predictably, conferences on terrorism are invariably "concerned with the causes and consequences" of the phenomenon in direct terms. For example, there was the one organized by Rand in 1980, which gathered together 144 officials and investigators from 13 countries. The causal quest informed the agenda, even though its director was well aware that "discussion of the causes of terrorism or the conditions that are propitious to terrorism are invariably frustrating.... [We] do not know what causes terrorism to flourish in one society and to be absent in another."[4] This conference concluded that "no single factor could be identified as a universal cause or even as a universal precipitator of terrorism."[5]

This is not to say that the causal search has not produced positive results. A lucid summary of "the causes of terrorism" is provided by Crenshaw,[6] who distinguishes between preconditions (modernization, urbanization, social facilitation, and a government's inability to prevent it) and direct precipitants (presence of a discriminated ethnic minority, lack of opportunity for political participation, the disaffection of an elite, some event that precedes the outbreak), as well as the group's reasons for resorting to terrorism (revolutionary, reformist, or reactionary; advertisement of the cause; provocation of a counterreaction from the government; the needs of internal organizational functions) and individual motivation and participation.

The significance of such analyses is not to be denied, yet attention should be called to the dangers inherent in the uncritical belief in "cause" that ignores categorical differences in various kinds of causation. Bateson[7], for example, counterposes "cybernetic explanation" to "causal explanation" on the grounds that what matters in the former are not causally positive connections but rather the alternatives that could have occurred but did not because of restraints; in such cases the argument is a kind of *reductio ad absurdum* in which all but one of the possible propositions are proven invalid.[8]

Most significantly, ritual situations are typically not governed by intrinsic or instrumental means-ends connections. Such ritual contexts are particularly decisive for the anthropologist, who is trained to distinguish schematically between a "rational" type of behavior aiming at specific ends in strictly mechanical fashion and a "ritual" one in which there is no mechanical link between means and ends but rather only culturally defined connections. As is most obvious with magic and religious sacrifice, ritual is only efficient in terms of the cultural conventions of the actors, or not what we might understand by strictly rational goals.[9] The narrow search for causal explanation reduces the perception and analysis of violent processes to an essentially rational type of behavior alone, whereas from a global communicative perspective, ritual aspects are at least as essential to much of human behavior. In fact, if chance is what best typifies terrorism, as the literature tells us, then its true logic is one of "objective causelessness."

The genetic and etiological approaches to social institutions were fashionable in anthropology at the turn of the century, when the most pressing intellectual problems were thought to be the discovery of the "origins" of religion, law, family, and so on. The obsession with the origins, sources, or rationales of an institution, however, has long since disappeared from the social science agenda. Evans-Pritchard could write in 1951: "We would, I think unanimously, hold today that an institution is not to be understood, far less explained, in terms of its origins, whether these origins are conceived of as beginnings, causes, or merely, in a logical sense, its simplest forms."[10] Any undergraduate becomes aware that "why magic" or "why ritual" or "why religious belief" are rather misplaced questions. Yet this is exactly the vital "question" the experts urge in the name of science, "why terrorism," with the demand that scholars "find the answer."

There is a long-standing discussion on the desirability of causal explanations in social science that finds a *locus classicus* in the methodological essays of Max Weber. He does not deny such desirability, but he thinks there is not one cause or a definite set of causes that can present a complete explanation of what he calls an "historical individual" ("terrorist" is a good candidate for one such historical individual): "an exhaustive causal investigation of any concrete phenomena in its full reality is not only practically impossible—it is simply nonsense."[11] All is a matter of causal imputation, which will depend totally upon assumptions. The Weberian tradition is firmly established in cultural anthropology, one of whose leading exponents finds that discerning what is really going on in society "is more like interpreting a constellation of symptoms than tracing a chain of causes."[12]

Try, as an exercise, to explain "causally" the bombing of Oklahoma City. The most notorious attribute of the man charged with the explosion is his antigovernment obsession; reportedly, both the Waco events and the legislation banning assault weapons figured prominently in his aversion. Yet what instrumental *cause* might one propose for the widespread assumption of linkage between Waco and Oklahoma City? If one exists at all, it could only result from a wild interpretive leap into fantasy by the bomber, never the instrumental causality postulated by terrorism discourse. In examining the Rambo type of avenging hero in the paramilitary culture of post-Vietnam and the crackpot conspiracy theories of the post-Waco militias, one gets a sense of a constellation of symptoms rather than a causal chain. The connections can only be bridged with narrative and ritual symbolism, not rational instrumentality.[13] The most ominous aspect of the paranoid style is that its "fundamental paradox… is the imitation of the enemy."[14] Thus the horror attributed to Waco had to be ritually reenacted in Oklahoma City. These are pivotal associations at the level of narrative mythology, yet terrorism discourse's uncritical attribution of "causation" to such highly rhetorical linkages can only lead to categorical confusion. Ironically, the Koreshes and McVeighs, on the one hand, and the terrorism experts and law enforcement officers, on the other, echo one another in the rhetorical style of a common paranoid discourse.

While alleged conspiracies usually smack of crackpot theories and intellectual obfuscation, it is noteworthy that terrorism is the exception that allows governments wide use of conspiratorial plots against terrorist suspects. The trial against Sheik Omar Abdel Rahman and his followers is an excellent illustration. In no other area of the law can we imagine people being punished to life imprisonment under conspiracy charges which "only required [the Government] to prove *the intention* to wage a terror campaign."[15] The defendants were found guilty despite, according to a *New York Times* editorial, "only the sketchiest connections [being] established between Sheik Abdel Rahman and the alleged mastermind of that crime, Ramzi Ahmed Yousef."[16]

If anything, it is this very lack of connectivity—the conspicuous absurdity in terrorism discourse's play with chance, the apparent indeterminacy of any choice—that cries out against any narrative's "illusion of sequence." But "sequence goes nowhere without his doppelganger or shadow, causality."[17] Rather than springing from the inquisitive "why?," terrorism's rationale and efficacy derive from the very absence of a reasonable "why?" and a satisfactory "because." What the acts loudly repudiate—the narrative continuity of cause/effect connections—is ironically the very thing that turns into the cornerstone of the entire discourse.

II

No laymen could say how big a part emotional deformities played in drawing Feltrinelli toward political violence, whether Black or Red. His troubles in that connection were all too plain. Fatherless and oppressively mothered, unbearably lonely and starved for affection, he was also born with a shriveled penis. Not for all the Feltrinelli money could he purchase the normal sexual pleasures enjoyed, say, by his stepfather or the gardener. He ran through four wives in a rising frenzy of frustration.

—C. Sterling, *The Terror Network*

If, according to Sterling, the seeds of the "planetary fashion" in terrorism were all planted in the events of 1968, the more immediate
causes were to be found in the personal biography of people such
as Giangiacomo Feltrinelli, Henri Curiel, Petra Krause, Gabriele
Krocher-Tiedemann, Nicholas Ishutin, Muammar Qaddafi, and Ilich
Ramírez Sánchez "Carlos"—each of whom receives an entire chapter
in her book. Employing this powerful rhetorical ploy, the search for
the evidence of narrative sequence is thereby concentrated upon the
history—full of chronology, development, and closure—of a person's
character. If we imagine the lone terrorist as an underground soul
overburdened with secrecy, the narration suddenly makes everything
crystal clear through its personal and organizational account. By their
very nature, "secrets...are at odds with sequence."[18] Not any longer,
since the passion for sequence triumphs by unveiling terrorist conspiracies for the reader!

The personal narrative of one individual is made to capture the
essence of an entire people or period of violence. Feltrinelli, for
instance, despite all his pathological neurosis, "was nevertheless the
first to put together a fully operational terrorist network in Europe,
the first to get it moving across national frontiers, the first to set the
scene and provide the props for the glittering cast of international
killers soon to burst upon the worldwide stage."[19] In his role as director
of international terrorism, he is credited with "shaping the history of a
decade."[20] Thus, according to Sterling, ETA is one of the many organizations under his influence in the early 1970s; yet no student of it
has ever mentioned such a tie. In our many hours of conversations
with ex-activists of the period, his name was never mentioned. — *destruction*

Such thinking easily leads to the pernicious assumption that, say,
Arab and Irish "characters" have explanatory value at some level
for understanding the PLO and the IRA. In this way, a whole people
is tar-brushed as criminal terrorists. Ancestors are made to share
posthumously in the negative imagery of a race imputed to be less
than "civilized" due to the actions of one segment as it confronts contemporary problems. Never mind that terrorism-prone activists are
likely to constitute a tiny minority even within the ranks of the politically disaffected. Indeed, when this ceases to be the case, terrorism
shades into full-blown guerrilla warfare. At that juncture the combat
becomes more conventional than ritualistic, and the society in question may be regarded as in a state of civil war.

"The psychology of terrorism" is one of the thriving subfields.
Needless to say, there is a political imperative for the students of ter-

rorism to define it in pathological terms. As recognized by Hill, "there is a broad level of agreement on essentials: namely, that we cannot risk legitimizing terrorism (difficult cases like the African National Congress are generally avoided), and that the phenomenon has therefore to be defined as a form of pathology."[21] Others emphasize the influence of terrorist ideologies and false beliefs in urging revolutionary terrorism. It is symptomatic of terrorism studies that a phenomenon purported to be "the new challenge to the West" should be reduced in the work of leading authors to personal psychological attributes deprived of collective political commitments, or to logical errors and ideological aberrations.

Since Aron defined terrorism as an action whose "psychological effects are out of proportion to its purely physical result,"[22] it is common to characterize it fundamentally as a manipulation of the psychology of violence through the fear aroused in potential victims. This is a major tropic strategy in the entire discourse. "How does one know whether a person experiences awe or thrill or whatever it may be?" "How does one recognize it, and how does one measure it?"[23] Such critical questions applied to obsolete emotionalist theories of religion are certainly applicable to the theories of political terror.

A most elementary methodological point, which is but the *pons asinorum* in the study of society, is that the study of social institutions and individual psychology must be approached with different methods and with different goals. There is a danger of overvaluing their organizational structure, but the view that an understanding of armed groups such as the ETA, the IRA, or the PLO should turn primarily on the study of life histories and psychological shortcomings of individuals, rather than on an understanding of social and political context, is like arguing that whatever is transpiring in a courtroom or church has to do primarily with the personal mood of the judge or priest. Authors such as Durkheim and Weber oppose this view out of hand. Thus the social scientific axiom that "impulses and emotions explain nothing: they are always *results*"[24] fails to inform the literature on terrorism.

III

Man lives by those propositions whose validity is a function of his belief in them.

—G. Bateson, "Conventions of Communication"

If there are not global or psychological causes of terrorism, what then? The social sciences prefer descriptions based on the concept of socio-cultural context—that is, attentiveness to communal intersubjectivities, sensitivity to political metaphor, and awareness of the logic of ritual performance. The contextual argument is another fundamental rhetorical strategy or trope for establishing what constitutes terrorism, how we should communicate about it, the kinds of knowledge we can have regarding it. Seemingly, there must be some logical explanation of the madness.

Terms such as "personality," "competition," "war," "play," "aggression," "pretending," and the like refer not to single actions but to *classes* of action. The very same behavior will have different meanings depending on context: aggressive words and acts are not threatening in a playful context; conversely, joking relationships convey serious messages when situated in structural imbalance. An example closer to our concern would be that homicide in time of peace is a crime, while in time of war it is a duty. Is there a class of action that can be labeled "terrorism"? Until we first describe the context that frames the "terrorist acts," we are simply ignorant of the basics regarding such behavior. This contextual argument, typical of the "play of tropes in culture,"[25] is far removed from the causal ones considered earlier, yet it cannot avoid its own illusions of meaningful coherence or sequence.

As an instance, when confronted with the Oklahoma City explosion and the warrior fantasies of the paramilitary culture of those charged with it, there is a temptation to place the blame of such terrorism squarely on the far-right movement. There is ample evidence of such links, if one wishes to press the contextualist argument; headlines such as "GOP Friendly to Militias" were not infrequent after Oklahoma City. The links established by such fallacious thinking are in a way reminiscent of the conspiratorial connections between Ruby Ridge, Waco, the Brady Bill, and the ban on assault weapons. Yet it is one thing to trace mythological ties and cultural connivances between groups and violent individuals, and quite another to closely link them within a heavily tabooed terrorism discourse. America's "bomb culture," for example, in 1993 produced 1,880 bombings that killed 43 and injured 281. Oklahoma City's explosion might be construed as a mere extension and expansion of that culture. Yet such a discursive ploy would miss entirely the specifity of the Oklahoma City explosion.

A sensitivity to various kinds of context makes the writer aware of the habitual error of postulating substantive factors whose internal logic then determines the character of the actors. This consists of "drawing a generalization from the world of external observation, giving it a fancy name, and then asserting that this named abstraction exists *inside* the organism as an explanatory principle. Instinct theory commonly takes this monstrous form."[26] The current explanation of political violence as the result of "ethnicity" is a good example; it is a generalization of facts observable in the external world that, when turned into an explanatory abstract category, works in a fashion similar to the explanation of aggression on the basis of instinct. The thing itself, be it aggression or ethnic terrorism, appears to rest more upon biology than society, more on instinct than learning; it is linked to behavior causally, not contextually. Classification and learning are instruments to avoid bringing such quasi-instinctivist premises into the study of human behavior.

Any terrorist narrative that posits full contextual consistency must be suspect. As Edward Sapir warned decades ago, cultural overdetermination "can be made to assume the appearance of a closed system of behavior."[27] The value of such a reified construct is likely to arise "out of a desire to have real events display the coherence, integrity, fullness, and closure of an image of life that can only be imaginary."[28] Every description leaves out a set of events that might have been included. The assertion of realistic objectivity in representing human agents has to be challenged by the frequent unpredictability of their acts. Terrorist "actions" in particular display an intrinsic discontinuity that no sequential narrative can properly capture. To these we now turn.

IV

In the Beginning was the Act.

—J. W. Goethe, *Faust*

A major narrative plot in descriptions of terrorism is that *activism* is quintessential to small militant groups. Action for action's sake becomes a credo. Not words, not nice theories, not paper programs, but rather it is the doing that matters. Action is positive, nothing is of value unless it is done. Within such a mentality of obsessive insistence upon the deed, action acquires a momentous efficacy that far surpasses its own instrumentality. As if by magic, each action appears to impose a new qualitative baseline, thereby setting in motion a revolutionary process that aims at transforming everything. However, the actions are in no way sustained and cumulative activities such as are, say, political debate in a town council, teaching at school, studying for a university degree, or taking territory through conventional military operations. In terrorism, an "action" is rather a thoroughly discontinuous act governed by the ritual premise of marking a qualitative transition to a new order. "Something big is going to happen," McVeigh warned Terry Nichols before the Oklahoma City explosion; he was not just going to rant against the government, like so many others, he was going to *do* something about it.

The history of any armed militant group illustrates well the action mentality. "Doing acts was the *real* thing," stated one ETA ex-activist. And he offered this definition: "Action is the ordeal by fire in which you test your personality." There is nothing worse for the activist than having to wait without performing an action. The "ordeal by fire" can be likened to an initiation ritual in which the young boy obtains his warrior identity. Such an action mentality substantiates perfectly Nietzsche's contention that agency is the result of doing, that no agent exists apart from the acting out itself, that the doing is everything. Action having a semantic autonomy of its own, power is embedded in situated practices and there is no other legitimation but performative contingency.[29]

The narrative gains depth if such actions are situated in their cultural semantics. As an instance, they can be perhaps modeled after a game in which the cumulative point-by-point progression is coopted by an all-or-nothing game point; such an outcome creates an either/or disjunctive context, an on/off alternative of qualitative change.[30] The premise taught by such a game would be that progression as the result of a gradual process can always be offset by the economy of an all-or-nothing decisive discontinuity through sudden, partial, arbitrary acts. These transitions are typically accompanied by rites of passage. An "action" would thus resemble ritual performance in that it is a discrete unit of behavior that signals discontinuity in the ordinary flow of events while attempting to make a transition to an altogether new state.

If anything, "terrorism" is a succession of actions; its real efficacy lies in its power to provoke, through sudden actions, disruptions of the existing order. Its purpose is to switch the entire game to a different plane by arbitrarily postulating its resolution on the basis of a single symbolic point. In terrorism, as in ritual, the means-ends relationship between action and effect is closer to the symbolic logic of magic than to the rational logic of mechanical linkages.

According to such rhetorics of action, the all-or-nothing nature of the terrorist game plays with the logic of random events; chance and bluff are consubstantial with it. This is again a key ritual component that breaks down cause-and-effect instrumental connections. Election by chance guarantees not only the innocence of the victim in ritual sacrifice, but also the perpetrators' personal irresponsibility for the outcome of an action that is being decided by luck. As in poker and other games, bluffing is also a strategic component in certain kinds of activism, particularly those in which very scarce technical and organizational means are required in order to mount enormous threats to society. The actual magnitude of such threats in military terms can never be known quantitatively but can only be guessed. Indeed, could they be assessed by one's opponent, by definition they would lose their efficacy. Such types of action, although ultimately governed by rational calculation, in themselves do not respond to technical-instrumental linkages between means and ends; rather, the preference for the quick-acting resolutions would respond to cultural premises of efficacy, which are based on the ritualization of performance.

In this regard the underground militant coopts the capacity to initiate the action. He or she chooses the venue, the time, and the content of it. Thus, despite the obvious disparity in the "real" power of the activist and his or her target (the government and its representatives), he or she retains considerable control over the risks attending action. The odds of apprehending, maiming, or killing the militant in any particular action are slight, though cumulatively they certainly favor the victim. Over time there is a considerable casualty rate among activists, since they can only afford one mistake, as it were.

The difference marked by the alleged terrorists' unforeseen "action," then, consists in depriving the system of its feedback devices of gradual process.[31] Such a strategy is typical of ritual combat, in which the all-or-nothing alternative that admits no correction is always at hand. "Terrorism" would systematically play with that premise as the ultimate weapon against the controlling mechanisms of political and military institutions; what would distinguish terrorism as a pure type is that it purports to abandon the progression through gradual to final points by turning them all into totalized end games. This "strategy" seeks to deprive the system of its ordinary feedback mechanisms—the bases for refining strategy—and thereby works to vitiate the rules of the game. This dissolution or deterioration of the rules through "terrorism" is precisely what exasperates the professional military establishment. It no longer makes sense to talk of strategy when the whole affair seems to be reduced to a game of chance; there is no longer any distinction between military and civilian targets, and the ordinary rules of war are so vitiated that there is not even a clear way of ending the fighting and proclaiming victory.

Lacking narrative coherence, terrorist actions are by their very nature unpredictable. Thus, when dealing with the internal logic of the momentous "action," we seem to have approached a field of rare "objectivity." We ourselves have written many pages under the spell of *ekintza*, "ritual action," "cultural performance," and the like.[32] The danger consists, once again, in narrativizing discourse—the illusion that "the events seem to tell themselves."[33] But real events, as White notes, should not speak but simply be; they "can be spoken about, but they should not pose as the *tellers* of a narrative," for "narrative becomes a *problem* only when we wish to give to *real* events the *form* of a story."[34] When a bizarre terrorist act has taken place—the outcome of so many possible factors, from chance to tactics, from revenge to accident, from despair to madness—the author borrows from narrative its authority in order to turn the event into the fiction of a story.

V

Violence in the international system will increasingly take the form of guerrilla warfare and terrorism.

> —P. Wilkinson, *Terrorism and the Liberal State*

Terrorism is a type of warfare—this is the favorite and most convincing argumentative plot of the best-informed students of terrorism. It is the preferred perspective of the activists themselves ("we are soldiers and this is a war"). The alleged terrorists contend that they are simply refusing to grant the state the monopoly of violence, while state officials may retort that terrorism is indeed a specific mode of struggle that is available to the state as well.[35] The view that terrorism is "a surrogate form of warfare" is also predominant in the literature.[36] Within military stratagems, terrorism is part of so-called low-intensity warfare, defined as a form of conflict that does not include protracted engagements of opposing regular forces but rather a limited use of power for political purposes. However, what *type of war* is terrorism?

Once again, the term "war" would seem to refer to a universal and univocal category of behavior. Such categorical validity is far from certain if we look at the three basic types of warfare coexisting in the present world: conventional, nuclear, and low intensity. Resorting to regular motorized armies was, until World War II, practically the only way of waging a successful campaign. However, conventional warfare has become increasingly obsolete in the face of nuclear arms, on the one hand, and low-intensity-level conflict on the other. According to one analyst, "all the conventional forces...are about as relevant to war in our age as Don Quixote was in his."[37] The Persian Gulf War demonstrated that conventional wars are not extinct; still, both sides feared the possible use of terrorism and nuclear power by the other, which suggests that "limiting" one's capability to conventional forces alone will be an increasingly difficult option.

Even granting that these various modes of struggle—from nuclear missiles to the underground cell's Molotov cocktails, from the army numbering in the millions to the lone terrorist, from the Hiroshima bomb to the guerrilla ambush—might be seen as variants of the same military phenomenon, still we would be left with the task of delineating their vast differences in organization, technology, social legitimation, and so on. In particular, we would need to sort out types of warfare that are based on actual combat (those that we might term *functional*, in the sense applied by ethologists to most of animal behavior) from those that are essentially nonpractical and that hence simulate rather than practice combat (those that ethologists label *ritual*).[38] Admittedly, any war strategy will attempt to mobilize both kinds of combat, yet warfare that by necessity must restrict itself to the ritual kind is a fight that is altogether different from conventional battle.

We begin with a simple fact. Contrary to what happened in the aftermath of Nobel's invention of dynamite in 1867, which made it possible for bombings to become a most effective terrorist tactic, no generalized use of nuclear power is viable. Its very technological condition makes nuclear warfare an all-or-nothing option that is practically useless for the purposes of fighting limited wars. Such functional impracticality calls for its ritualization—since we cannot fight with it, let us turn it into potency displays and messages. Thus, far from being excluded with modernity, *ritual behavior* appears to play a necessarily fundamental, even enhanced, role in the new types of warfare. Deterrence works by "hypothesized effects," not functional ones; its basic presupposition is that the *threat* it poses is sufficiently large as to exclude armed aggression as policy alternative. Guerrilla and terrorist warfare also play with stratagem, unpredictability, and threat.

In Aron's opinion, "in the treatise of a twentieth-century Clausewitz...revolutionary warfare would figure just as prominently as the theory of nuclear weapons."[39] Yet from the conventional military perspective, both of these new types are largely dysfunctional, impractical, "symbolic." They recall the situations of ritual warfare described by anthropologists: a war dance or the taking of an enemy head can temporarily deter the enemy from aggression. It is well known that in the past, too, warfare was highly ritualized, the polite wars of the eighteenth century being a classical example;[40] still the nuclear reality forces a qualitative change, one which compels military thinking to substitute ritual for actual combat. "Terrorism" and "nuclear deterrence" both underscore the necessity for greater ritualization of contemporary warfare. Setting aside obvious differences in scale and technology, as well as the fact that intimidation through nuclear deterrence is thought to be based on retaliatory anticipation alone, whereas the intimidation of terrorism springs from concrete acts of terror, it is the presence of similar premises in both kinds of terror (threat, simulation, bluffing, symbolic posturing) that is most instructive.

Despite solemn declarations by public officials that "terrorism" presents a direct threat to the strategic interests and moral values of western democratic society, it is well recognized in the literature that the upsurge in international terrorism is due to political and strategic factors. Since there is grave risk that a limited war might escalate into nuclear conflagration, international war is perforce a less attractive option and, according to political scientists such as Wilkinson and Jenkins, international violence is likely to take the form of guerrilla warfare and terrorism.[41]

If one reviews the recent and ongoing conflicts in various parts of the world, it is difficult not to conclude that, paradoxically, governments have already accepted enemies' behavior that they conveniently label as terrorism as a useful way of pursuing their own military agendas. This willingness is particularly apparent in the policies of countries most beset by terrorist challenges. For example, Spain implemented a counterterrorist policy of pursuing and killing ETA operatives in southern France.[42] There would also appear to be little that Israel's Mossad was unwilling to do to challenge its PLO adversaries world-wide. The history of the South African government's dealings with the ANC clearly entailed paramilitary force. The British government instituted a secret shoot-to-kill policy for dealing with its IRA foes.[43] The United States has resorted to kidnapping its adversaries on foreign soil, a practice defended by the American legal system.

Conventional war imposes a frame of strict literalness; if a simulation of combat is ritual play, combat that cannot be simulated is war but such "truthful" literalness contains its own paradox of deception that pervades war in every aspect. For example, the repeal of a state of law by war is in itself "a legal condition"; individual states are the

legitimate guarantors of positive law in times of peace and of its abrogation in times of war, but no law can place limits upon the power of
the state to declare war. One obvious example of such contradiction
is, as Arblaster points out,[44] that "terrorism" plays a part in creating
states that, when accepted as legitimate, must then turn around and
condemn and repress terrorism; prime examples would be Ireland
and Israel. It is not surprising, therefore, that discussions on disarmament and conflict resolution are forced to consider the following paradoxes:[45] (1) The major powers justify nuclear weapons as a factor in
promoting peace, so how can the minor powers be prevented from
possessing them?; (2) When governments perpetrate "acts of terrorism," by what logic can the tactic be denied to their opponents?; (3)
The goal of peace is framed and enforced through the rhetoric threatening a resort to violence in order to "maintain the peace" and the
use of "peace force" as a metaphor for standing armies.

Such paradoxes are revelatory of the war frame in various ways;
they show that technological disparity may effect a hierarchical grad-
ing among nations without resorting to actual war. Nonnuclear nations
partially lose their sovereignty vis-à-vis the nuclear ones by being incapable of waging a victorious war against them; such forced subordination promotes "peace"; conversely, technological parity fosters the possibility of war. Hence, superpowers have access to acts of military
domination justified as the ordinary functioning of the hierarchical
structure and that are therefore not categorized as "war," whereas military acts by the nonnuclear states can only mean war. Similar manipulations of what constitutes war apply to "terrorism": if practiced by a
lawful state it is legitimate self-defense, if practiced by a substate group
it is terrorism. Again, we are obviously dealing as much with who has
the power to *label* as to *level* their adversaries.

Asymmetries of power determine the convenience of imposing or
not the message "This is war." The superior power can trivialize the
threat posed by a minor one and decide that it is more advantageous
to carry out combat actions against it without a formal declaration of
war. The U.S. raid on Libya in April of 1986 illustrates this point. The
basic message of such attacks can be read as not only "we can impose
war on you whereas you cannot impose it upon us," but also "the war
we force upon you cannot be accepted as war by you," and "all your
potential for war is only a simulacrum, not a real war threat to us."
Such attacks, then, are and are not acts of war, just as the threats of
war by minor powers are and are not real threats—if for no other reason than that there is a qualitative difference between nuclear and

nonnuclear nations. The obvious conclusion is that the deadly literalness of the war frame ("this is all true") can be manipulated as a tactical ploy or simply ignored. That is, military powers can lie about the very rules of war and disagree about what constitutes it. Asymmetries of power determine who has the capacity to issue the message "this is war" and "this is peace." The alleged literalness of the war frame becomes in itself an instrument of tactical and political deception.

"There is no substitute for victory," General McArthur claimed in a lapidary synthesis of the conventional military mentality. Traditionally, the necessary goal of any military venture has been victory, understood in exclusive and totalistic terms as the triumph of one side over the other. Yet which types of war are those based on "terror" and "deterrence" in which, as is commonly stated, military victory loses its traditional meaning? The concept of "war" itself is no longer the same when deprived of the goal of military victory; the traditional meaning of war is being replaced by *terrorism* (defined as "surrogate war") and *deterrence* (defined as "mutual balance of terror").

Deterrence theory developed as a result of the basic premise that "nuclear war is not winnable." Thus, with nuclear technology it is no longer "either you or me" but "either both of us or neither of us." The disjunction is situated at a higher logical level, not aiming at the exclusion of one of the individual contending parties but the exclusion (or not) of both—the alternative is no longer victory or defeat in war, but war or its absence. Thus the traditional recourse to all-out military action is out of the question. This is also the first lesson one learns from terrorism and counterterrorism, that it is hardly possible to devise a strategy for winning a clear victory. As the head of the U.S. Crisis Management Team commented in his summation of a three-day counterterrorism exercise, "Once a terrorist incident has taken place, you have already lost something: the possibility of a clear-cut victory for one side or the other."[46] Most public officials and experts choose to ignore this basic condition of terrorist violence.[47]

The emplotment of warfare—with its polarities, its tension between tactics and strategy, its rules of engagement, its goal orientation and ideology, its endemic history, its roles and expectations—provides a powerful source of narrativity for terrorism. Nonetheless, terrorist activity breaks down all such traditional rules of warfare. What would characterize "terrorism" quintessentially are its unpredictability, anomie, invisibility, impermanence, improvisation, and accident—elements antithetical to any fixed pattern and facile illusion of military sequence. By casting terrorism in the guise of warfare, these unruly elements can

be converted into the work of a full-fledged army against which an
organized counteraction can be mounted.

VI

*This kind of ritualism makes some of the warfare of primitive human soci-
eties comparable not only to such ceremonialized aspects of the threat
behavior of modern states as war games and May Day parades but also to
the threat behavior of infrahuman animals, which, at times, fulfills the
same functions as actual fighting but does so without a maladaptive loss
of life.*

—A. P. Vayda, "Primitive Warfare"

In this section we explore the argument that "terrorism" is ritual
behavior. By bringing to bear the body of theory developed by cultural anthropology, it is possible to argue that terrorism is indeed ritual
bluff. Yet does the thesis "terrorism is ritual" warrant turning it into a
separate field of knowledge, the foundation of an entire discourse pur-
porting to deal with a major international problem embedded in the
culture of the last three decades? We don't believe so.

A common anthropological definition of ritual used to be: "A category of standardized behavior (custom) in which the relationship
between means and ends is not 'intrinsic,' i.e. is either irrational or
nonrational."[48] Among the many tropic oppositions of cultural anthropologists, "ritual" versus "rational/instrumental" behavior has been a
major one. If we situate political violence within the domain of ritual
action and compare it with other similar cultural realities, it loses the
strangeness it displays when treated within the "rational" frame alone.
In this manner the powerful rhetoric of "ritual," founded on the
meticulous work of generations of ethnographers, can be brought to
bear on the terrorist phenomenon. Ritual is a useful paradigm with
which to apprehend terrorism, because it deals centrally with disorder and because it mediates between form and formlessness; as stated
by Moore and Myerhoff, "ritual is a declaration of form *against* indeterminacy, therefore indeterminacy is always present in the background of any analysis of ritual."[49]The very absence of logic, sense,
causality, and purpose, which seems to characterize terrorism's indeterminacy, are thus narrativized and turned into explanation.

Far from being odd and marginal, for anthropologists ritual is frequently *the* basic social act, one that is fundamental for obtaining and
expressing a sense of reality.[50] In technical terms, ritualization denotes

"the adaptive formalization and canalization of motivated human activities so as to secure more effective communicatory ('signalling') function, reduction of intra-group damage, or better intra-group bonding."[51] Ethologists have reached the conclusion that most animal behavior patterns entail a process of ritualization. That is, there is a qualitative difference between behaviors that are functional (set functions such as eating, flying, mating, walking, and so on—i.e., related to specific anatomical organs) and behaviors that are ritual (displays, courtship, bird songs, bee dances, and the like). Animals and humans, however, differ radically in that the ritual behavior of the former derives from genetically determined instinct, while for the latter it is transmitted in nongenetically based symbolic codes of culture. Rigidification and unambiguity of form become essential for animal communication in stressful situations,[52] whereas "We suspect that in man the *overcoming of ambivalence* as well as of ambiguity is one of the prime functions of ritualization."[53]

In sharp contrast to the politician, who thrives upon ambiguity, the military mind feels compelled to rescue political discourse by forcing upon it the unambiguous either/or logic of warfare. Politics has to rely primarily on verbal communication, which is plagued with the problems of deceit and lying, and which leads to the deep-seated mistrust of the politician's mere talk.[54] Ritual, which mobilizes nonverbal as well as verbal elements, is a partial solution to the arbitrariness of the verbal sign. When something more than words is needed, such as a readiness to die for one's own political ideals, then only ritual action can communicate such totally uncompromising behavior. Consequently, the appropriate way of getting at the nonverbal components of violence is to study its ritual aspects, for there is a "performative plenitude" and even an internal "abyss" in ritual.[55]

Rituals are identified by their repetitive and stereotyped forms, which transpire at special places and within specified circumstances; invariant formality can be observed particularly in fixed ritual sequences such as initiation ceremonies or rites of passage.[56] Performance is the other necessary condition for ritual; the "doing" itself becomes an essential aspect of its efficacy. Despite their similarities, the significant difference between ritual and theater is that in a play or drama the audience knows that this is "only acting," whereas with ritual the congregation is in earnest. Rituals and ceremonies are magico-religious in origin; military rituals are no exception. Obviously, "to speak of such actions as the Terror of the French Revolution as ritual is not to deny the reality of their effects."[57] Regicides provide clear instances of such ritual institutions, not only in the ethnographic literature but in European history as well.

Regarding both terrorism and nuclear warfare, the two military taboos of the present period, the very impossibility of fighting a victorious war according to the conventional rules of warfare calls for ritual simulation. Preparing for nuclear war in order to avoid it is reminiscent of the recourse to the economy of ritual found among animals who engage in simulated combats in order to convey the message "let's not fight." Such ritualization of aggression is not an accidental outcome of the armaments race, but rather a vitally necessary survival strategy; the nuclear predicament forces us to "ask about the conditions of ritualization of violence."[58] Public officials frequently boast that nuclear deterrence is already responsible for fifty years of peace among the superpowers; "terrorists" likewise argue that theirs is a very economical way of fighting a war by producing only a few symbolic casualties. To deter and to terrorize—both partake fundamentally of the capacity to impose the frame of ritual threat.

If there is a functional imperative to ritualize warfare, so there is a necessity to move away from a military culture of literal reference. With bluffing, pretending, playing, and the like, it is easy to realize that a distinction has to be drawn between the action itself and that which is denoted by it. Yet it is much harder to realize that military rituals, too, partake of such nonliteral context. Threats are particularly susceptible to deception; they are statements of purpose, not empirical facts—a threat of murder and an actual homicide are two divergent phenomena. Since threats refer to subjective intentions, their very objectivity rests on the interpretation given to them—one never knows for certain in advance whether the threat was intended seriously or not. The manipulation of purpose by the use of threats is quintessential to "terrorism," as we shall see in chapter 5; in fact, by playing on the abysmal separation between the actual action (a mere threat) and the denoted action (annihilating unwanted enemies), in terms of propaganda and public intimidation, "terrorism" achieves extraordinary results.

This is not to say that terrorist violence is nothing but intimidation, a Trotskyan view that Hardman opposes on the basis that "the terrorist does not threaten; death or destruction is part of his programme of action."[59] Still, mere threats *per se* constitute "terrorist incidents." Indeed a key definitional criterion of what constitutes terrorism has to do simply with "intention." Schmid sums it up: "The nature of terrorism is not inherent in the violent act itself. One and the same act...can be terrorist or not, depending on intention and circumstance."[60] Intention is a very subjective thing and open to interpretation. In ritual behavior, too, there is actual biting during the playful fights of animals and real blows in peacemaking ceremonies, yet their intention is not functional but ritual—they are make-believe bites and blows, but they might be misinterpreted and thereby turned into real ones.

From the viewpoint of military theory, terrorism can be included within the ancient concept of stratagem, which commonly encompasses trickery, deception, surprise, ambush, feigned retreat, reversal of an expected pattern of behavior, disinformation, betrayal, sophistic interpretation of treaties, technological surprise through new weapons, and various other ploys. Such strategems characterize not only primitive warfare but also nuclear deterrence. We might conclude that "indeed the second half of the twentieth century could be characterized as an age of stratagem, in which theories of deterrence exploit the idea of bluff, intelligence agencies have become masters of deceit, and guerrilla warfare and terrorism consistently employ surprise, psychological tactics, and avoidance of battle."[61] As noted earlier, all of this is well known to anthropologists aware that primitive warfare is intimately related to ritual functions. Far from being extinguished by modernity, then, ritualization appears to play an enhanced role in the new types of warfare. Rather than the quantitative, mechanical, and literal aspects of conventional war, the prevalence of stratagem and threat imply for the most part "as if" forms of struggle and imaginative deception.

As anthropologists, dissolving "terrorism" into *ritual* violence is our preferred rhetorical ploy. Yet labeling something as "ritual" is not the end but rather the beginning of explaining a kind of behavior. Any type of militarism resorts to ritualization. If there is nothing more significant about "terrorism" than its use of ritual elements, we must conclude that there is nothing startlingly original enough about it as to deserve new interdisciplinary discourse.

VII

Every effort to understand destroys the object studied in favor of another object of a different nature; this second object requires from us a new effort which destroys it in favor of a third, and so on and so forth until we reach the one lasting presence, the point at which the distinction between meaning and the absence of meaning disappears: the same point from which we began.

—C. Lévi-Strauss, *Tristes Tropiques*

In the village cemetery of Itziar, there is a tragic juxtapositioning that captures the grotesque incongruities of the Basque political struggle: a funerary monument honors an ETA activist killed in combat, while next to him lies a slain Castilian civil guard. Villagers who idolized their native son hate such intimacy between their hero and the enemy. Not even death should reconcile them. That eternal companionship on a peaceful plot of land overlooking the Cantabrian Sea (the land whose sovereignty the fallen warriors had contested unto death) gives overwhelmingly graphic testimony of a blending of meaning and non-sense—the political drama has been settled for them in the shared destiny of forced fellowship, neighbors forever in their adjacent plots.

In fact, as ethnographers we can easily frame patriotic struggles, such as the Basque one, through the rhetorical lens of a Homeric tragedy—a tragic plot in the Aristotelian sense that the typical hero is a good man who falls into vice and error; the dramatic cycle redeems itself by returning to the zero starting point. A Homeric tragedy! But is this not in itself literary obfuscation of what, for all legal purposes, is ordinary murder? Tragedy is surely about crime, yet the protagonist commits the fateful error "under conditions so adverse that we watch him with compassion…the sort of error a good man would make,"[62] even ourselves. *response to a specified stimulus*

Yet we are playing with the tropics of discourse, and the essential point one should learn from such rhetorical exercises is not the ultimate truth of a given plot but precisely the awareness that any narrative can be plotted in alternative modes and still be valid. The competition among plots is, in fact, fierce in terrorism discourse, unless, of course, there is simple recourse to the blatant criminality trope, which denies the need for any narrative strategy. For those disposed to probe further, however, Romance, Tragedy, Comedy, Farce, Melodrama, Warfare, Fantasy—all compete with their individual historical and narrative powers to capture the essence of terror. The same writer may discover by reading, say, Northrop Frye, that the Romance of his central story (the triumph of courage and transcendence) can be made to fit exactly a Homeric Tragedy (a crime that is all too human and that arouses pity); but then he might note that the story is best cast in the Ironic mode as a repetitious Farce and be tempted to distance himself from it all with the burlesque gaze of Satire (the resolutions expected by human consciousness are always frustrated by failure and death). Then, too, while attempting an overview, he may even stumble upon Kenneth Burke's comic principle of tragedy (the awareness that the inalterably opposed elements in the world can be comically reconciled). Whether the story commands the somber resignation of Tragedy or hopeful reconciliation through Comedy, whether it searches for the redemption of Romance or declares the ultimate inadequacy of any representation with Satire, the very archetypal structure of the plot determines the historian's knowledge and judgement of "what is *really* happening." Such precritical selection of genres is obviously "constitutive of the *concepts* he will use to *identify the objects* that inhabit that domain and *to characterize the kinds of relationships* they can sustain with one another."[63] In terrorism discourse, what is termed "the definitional problem" (an endemic issue that we will analyze in chapter 4) is in fact a prior one of narrative style whereby the modes of ideological implication are *pre*figured through specific genres of plotting and argument.

A critical case is the Romantic mode, which obtains among the sympathizers of the violent process who are prone to view their political activists as heroes battling the enemies of their country. The ethnographer, for one, must pay attention to the true believer's emplotment—neither to uphold and promote nor to caricature and criminalize it, but simply to understand the internal logic of the perspective. We believe that the task of an ethnographically informed writer is not to impose a given form of consciousness upon the reader but rather to help "dissolve" the puzzlements of the human experience by demonstrating their inherent relativity. In this fashion, the ethnographer underscores the validity of alternative perspectives considered in their own terms (i.e., as perceived by their proponents) without endorsing any particular one.

If a writer finds himself compelled to go astray in such a rhetorical quest, it is because these are narratives in which, as Girard has put it, "it becomes impossible to distinguish history from ritual."[64] The very categories of "history" and "ritual" as apt representations of the events become problematic. An ethnographer is bound to consider whether the classic Frazerian question of murder that is also simultaneously ritual sacrifice does not obtain among present-day terrorists. But it is far from certain that ritual achieves social integration; as Fernandez argued, symbolic consensus and social consensus are of a different order;[65] and, as Geertz found in Java, in an equivocal cultural setting "the rituals themselves become matters of political conflict."[66] In the case of the beleaguered terrorist one can also observe a process of ritual deterioration; the purposeful tendency is to break down any formal structure for the sake of playing with chance and context, thereby flirting with the extraordinary dangers of anomaly and taboo.

Terrorist acts, in their pure form, tend to be seen as the result of this process of ritual aberration in which meaninglessness itself is turned into the ultimate message.[67]

A holistic perspective on human communication, such as we have been taught by psychoanalysis and anthropology, seeks to integrate both conscious and unconscious thought. If we may describe the true believers as engaged in ritual action, so can we perceive, as does Wagner-Pacifici, the profoundly theatrical nature of an entire sequence of violence. We are not engaged in singling out a triumphant genre among the contending plot structures. Rather, we view terror as a shifting representation that commands diverse perceptions from different actors and audiences in separate situations. What is happening is simultaneously *struggle* for the supporters of the violence, *crime* for its detractors, *error* for those who know the actors too well, *stupidity* for those maintaining satirical distance. It is by rescuing history from the violence of a totalizing discourse (be it Romance, Tragedy, or Criminality) that new forms of representation and changes in modes of consciousness are possible.

Needless to say, the underground militants themselves—either by reacting to "the lies" of the media or by deliberately manipulating their sensationalism, either by mocking the incongruities of the status quo or by persuading their audience of the truth inherent in the struggle—actively resort to the various rhetorics of violence. While action is the quintessential message, the activist needs to mobilize other forms of programmatic, hortatory, and excusatory persuasion as well. To this end, the stigmatized actor is likely to resort self-servingly to the same arguments of "causes," "war," "martyrdom," "economy of ritual action," etc., developed by terrorism discourse.

Rejections of ambiguity and contradiction are inherent in a totalizing discourse—no trace of division, no disjointed linkage, no double bind. Such discourse presumes that truth can never be allegory, fact is poles apart from fiction, essential evil merits no interpretation, the documents of civilization have nothing in common with those of barbarism. Far from questioning the bag of tricks of its own assumptions, terrorism discourse gains respectability by representing itself as the factually true one. No paradox of reflexivity, no soldierly dilemma, no initiatory ordeal has the power to intrude into the closed dichotomy of world order versus world chaos. The premise underlying such a notion of reality is that, far from ironic eclecticism, truth corresponds to narrative closure. Out of a need for positive moral resolution, the discourse creates a drama in which ultimate good confronts supreme evil, and the battlefield is populated with angels and devils rather than mere mortals struggling with the dilemmas of their common human condition. As a further step in unveiling such narrative closures, we must consider the ways in which the "thing itself" of terrorism plays with its own definitions and categorical constructs, a point to which we now turn our attention.

4

CATEGORIES AND ALLEGORIES

[handwritten: theory of the nature of knowledge]

An "episteme," according to Foucault, is "an epistemological space specific to a particular period," a general form of thinking that determines "what ideas can appear, what sciences can be constituted, what experiences can be reflected in philosophies, what rationalities can be formed, only, perhaps, to dissolve and vanish soon afterwards."[1] Terrorism—as a global idea, as a scientific object, as a daily experience, as a military rationale—is such an épistémè. That it should be constituted at the end of the twentieth century is, to our minds, a major element for understanding the political and intellectual world in which we live. In this chapter we concentrate on the analytical fashioning of "terrorism," the "thing itself," into a category of discourse with its own academic pedigree. This will entail consideration of its powerful allegorical resonances as well.

[handwritten right margin: Knowledge]

[handwritten left margin: symbolic excitation]

Treatises on terrorism regularly ask: what *is* it? The ontological question is implied by the very search for its "causes and consequences." There is no such *ding an sich*. The quest for quintessential distillation by which "terror" could be encapsulated, diagnosed under laboratory conditions, defined in precise terms, and finally be con-

quered and extinguished for the benefit of mankind, is an academic
illusion. As noted previously, regarding terrorism the "real" is to a
great extent "narrative." Such "unreality" derives from the very logic of
terror, its semantics of play and threat, its deceptive use of sign and
symbol, its enormous power for collective representation.

"You couldn't figure me out then, and you can't figure me out now."

The Unabomber[2]

To illustrate how such definitional quandaries are not at the borderline of terrorism discourse, but rather concern its paradigmatic
essence, we may consider the case of the Unabomber. His career as a
terrorist trickster is a good instance of the irrelevance and opportunism of terrorism discourse in grappling with the issues. For most
of the past seventeen years he had been a perplexing "bomber" who
targeted professors and, on one occasion, an airliner. His "embarrass-
ingly ineffectual"[3] letter bombs had caused three deaths and 23 victims over nearly two decades of activity. While hardly a laughing matter, the Unabomber's record of violence scarcely transcends that which
transpires in, say, the hold-up of a bank or a convenience store on any
given day in violent America. Certainly the countermeasures taken
against the Unabomber are incommensurate with the resources
expended on other crimes and criminals. By one estimate, the FBI
alone has spent over $50,000,000 in pursuit of him.

After the 1993 World Trade Center explosion, when terrorism
captured public attention and the first demands for major antiterrorism legislation were heard, the Unabomber became the prime example of the domestic terrorist. But it was not until after the bombing in
Oklahoma City, which made Timothy McVeigh the ultimate American
terrorist, that news about the Unabomber began to be framed in
terms of competition between two rivals for the top ranking in domestic terrorism. The Unabomber was thought to have "an epic case of
envy."[4]

The Unabomber had his summer of glory in 1995, when he
informed the *San Francisco Chronicle* that within the week he would
blow up an airliner over Los Angeles, while simultaneously sending a
letter to the *New York Times* declaring the threat to be a "prank." It all
worked beautifully, since officials regarded the threat to be "most credible." Transportation Secretary Federico Peña and Los Angeles Mayor

Richard Riordan warned that "every person should exercise their own individual judgment" regarding the wisdom of flying.[5] Peña blamed an emerging new order: "With the New York Trade Center bombing and the Oklahoma City bombing—and now this threat—we realize that our lives are being inconvenienced because of the changing nature of the world."[6] The disruptions in air travel were enormous and the Unabomber was front-page news for weeks. A university professor and the editor of *Penthouse* magazine urged him through open letters in the media to publicize his manifesto instead of killing people. The Unabomber supplied a 35,000-word manuscript and the demand that it be published in the *Washington Post* and the *New York Times*. After deliberations, the press complied. The experts concluded that he didn't need to be envious of McVeigh any longer.

The Unabomber's manuscript was hailed by the intelligence community as a great potential source of new clues regarding his identity and whereabouts. For several months it was subjected to intense scrutiny by dozens of agents and academics. Some were convinced that the text "was the work of a frustrated social scientist," others found his "scholarly credentials...uncertain," while still others thought it "improbable" that a serious scholar would address the dislocating influences of industrial society without quoting Durkheim or Weber. To his credit, the Unabomber had used "Latin phrases like modus operandi with ease;" one professor thought it relevant that "You never see two independent clauses that aren't connected by a comma."[7] The manifesto helped to develop an "increasingly elaborate psychological and physical profile of a white man in his mid-40s, who is probably reclusive and has difficulty relating to women."[8] Other agents applied "computer techniques developed for market research...to cross-check vast lists of people living in Northern California."[9] The press reported that "The publication of the manifesto in the Unabomber case has produced no breakthrough at least in terms of detention of a suspect."[10] However, the exercise was not entirely barren because the experts had concluded that, lo and behold, even if they had "previously thought the suspect might be a terrorist with a political agenda,"[11] it was now clear that he was "a serial murderer who kills to satisfy an inner psychological need."[12] Only three months earlier the same sources had told *Newsweek* that, "he does not appear to be a serial killer in the mold of Ted Bundy, John Wayne Gacy or Jeffrey Dahmer. He is not, from the available evidence, a sexually driven psychopath."[13] The writing style of the manifesto had apparently forced a change in their expert convictions.

For our purposes, the real story has less to do with the violence itself but rather regards the sleight-of-hand definitional changes whereby the Unabomber is couched in one discourse or another depending on the current strategic needs of the law-enforcement community. Initially, he was depicted as "an amateur" whose first bombs were "crude devices whose explosive material consisted of match-heads."[14] Match-heads scarcely count as an ultra-dangerous terrorist weapon, yet increasingly the Unabomber became more sophisticated and deadly. Then, during the antiterrorist frenzy of the mid-90s, with its active campaign for new counterterrorism legislation, he was made to epitomize the domestic terrorist, and by the summer of 1995 the Unabomber had thereby been so empowered that he could literally bring a major airport to a standstill. His ability to capture public attention and to dictate to two of the world's most important newspapers must have transcended his wildest dreams.

Finally law-enforcement officials realized that it was they and the media that had made the Unabomber omnipotent. At the same time, the ostensible terrorist was openly scornful of the attempts to capture him. This was, indeed, a dangerous game, for it could easily escalate and jeopardize the billions of dollars expended annually to counter terrorism. If you can't capture an exhibitionist terrorist then how can you hope to deter a furtive one? So finally the frustrated forces of counterterrorism took their only possible revenge on the Unabomber: "We made you a 'terrorist' and now we are making you a '*non*-terrorist'!" The Unabomber had been downgraded to a mere serial killer and sacred budgets, if not necessarily their taxpayers, remain secure.

In order to be efficient, the politics of labeling requires minimally stable categorical constructs. The problem with terrorism is that its basic categories are so devoid of conceptual fixity and moral consensus that the entire discourse turns on *ad hoc* definitions framed as mere appendages to whatever international and national policy is at hand. Such questioning of categorial fabrications is starkly reminiscent of similar debates in the social sciences.

II

Totemism is like hysteria, in that once we are persuaded to doubt that it is possible arbitrarily to isolate certain phenomena and to group them together as diagnostic signs of an illness, or of an objective institution, the symptoms themselves vanish or appear refractory to any unifying interpretation.... But the comparison with totemism suggests a relation of another order between scientific theories and culture, one in which the mind of the scholar himself plays as large a part as the minds of the people studied; it is as though he were seeking, consciously or unconsciously, and under the guise of scientific objectivity, to make the latter—whether mental patients or so-called "primitives"— more different than they really are.

—C. Lévi-Strauss, *Totemism*

The anthropological treatment of totemism illustrates well the point about conceptual reification while suggesting ways of deciphering it. Its theoretical framer, McLennan, characterized totemism as fetishism combined with exogamy and matrilineal descent.[15] In 1914, W.H.R. Rivers defined it as a combination of (1) a social element (connection of an animal or plant with, typically, an exogamous group or clan); (2) a psychological element (belief in a kinship relation between members of the group and the animal, plant, or thing); and (3) a ritual element (taboos on eating the totem).[16] By 1920, Van Gennep had identified no fewer than forty-one theories of totemism. Yet, as early as 1916, Boas had charged that totemism was an artificial entity existing nowhere but in the mind of the anthropologist; his own suggestion was that totemism is about the metaphorical formation of society.[17] To the question of why the animal and vegetable domains offer a nomenclature for denoting a social system, and what relations exist logically between the system of denotation and social reality, Lévi-Strauss postulated an homology, not so much within the system of denotation, as Boas contended, but between differential features existing between two given species, on the one hand, and between two clans, on the other;

> The totemic illusion is thus the result, in the first place, of a distortion of a semantic field to which belong phenomena of the same type. Certain aspects of this field have been singled out at the expense of others, giving them an originality and a strangeness which they do not really possess; for they are made to appear mysterious by the very fact of abstracting them from the system of which, as transformations, they formed an integral part.[18]

There is no doubt that totemic groups are exogamous, but is not exogamy *per se* a more basic feature than totemism itself in marking social groups? Totemism establishes relationships between human groups and objects of the natural environment, but does that make it a phenomenon *sui generis,* or is it just one more specific instance of the general relationship? Totem and mana have been intimately associated by the students of totemism, but is it not a crass confusion to equate both notions? A.P. Elkin, after defining totemism according to the three criteria of form, meaning, and function, tried to salvage the reality of the phenomenon by reducing it to a multiplicity of forms; he differentiated between "individual" totemism, "sexual" totemism, "clan" totemism, and "dream" totemism. Still, the one thing that does not occur to the analyst is that it is "the very idea of totemism that is illusory, not just its unity."[19]

Historians, likewise, are baffled by the existence of pervasive social phenomena that, on close inspection, appear to be nothing but imaginary constructs deeply embedded in the culture of the times. European witchcraft immediately comes to mind; Hugh Trevor-Roper ponders over how such a "grotesque mental construction" could rivet the attention of entire countries for extended periods without being "dissolved." However, dissolution would require the undoing of an entire cosmology rooted in deeply held social attitudes: "If men were to revise their views on witchcraft, the whole context of those views had to be revised. Then, and then only, this extension—the weakest part of it, but theoretically essential to it—would dissolve."[20] This conclusion by anthropologists and historians—that the theoretical and public policy issues posed by faulty conceptual formations such as totemism and witchcraft are best served by "dissolving" the categories in question—might come as a surprise, but the dissolution of semantic nonsense turns out to be an analytical as well as a political necessity.

The analytical dissolution of fake categories is in fact a prominent task in social science. As did Lévi-Strauss concerning totemism, Crick has proposed that "our understanding will advance when 'witchcraft' is analytically dissolved into a larger frame of reference."[21] It can be argued that witchcraft may have become a separate topic in anthropology simply because of its significance in Europe's history during the sixteenth and seventeenth centuries. In this view it had very little to do with practices in primitive cultures. If the notion of witchcraft in Europe was interrelated with other Occidental categories such as natural philosophy and theology, the conceptual domain among, say, the Azande is quite another category, and no easy equation or translation is possible between the two worlds.

And what about the category of terrorism? The following words by one of the major authorities in the field, Bower Bell, perhaps best reflects the situation:

> No one had a definition of terrorism. In academia, the various concerned disciplines could not even define "terror." There was no

agreement as to the effectiveness of "terror," or the basic causes of
the phenomenon, or the barest means of approach to analyze it. The
lawyers sought recourse in law, the psychologists in the personality,
the historians in the slow unwinding of the past. Some applied the
frustration-aggression thesis, and others the tools of quantitative
social science. With some exceptions, most did so at a distance—
except for those who interviewed the victims of the prisoners. There
were really no general experts in the analysis of terror, only those
with special academic skills.[22]

For anyone familiar with the literature on terrorism it is not difficult to
agree with this diagnosis. The frustration is enhanced by considering
such literature reviews as Schmid's *Political Terrorism: A Research Guide to
Concepts, Theories, Data Bases, and Literature.* Almost every page reflects
the conceptual disarray by pointing out the basic lack of agreement
on the most elementary concepts of "violence," "political," "power,"
"aggression," "force," and so on—notions that are in turn used to
define "terrorism."[23] Schmid examined 109 definitions of terrorism in
1983; five years later, in a revised edition of the book,[24] the definitional quandary had actually worsened through proliferation.[25] The problems inherent in the project are perhaps best reflected in Schmid's
own sprawling definition.[26]

"Terrorism: A Cliché in Search of a Meaning" is the apt title of a
Christopher Hitchens's article.[27] He relates his debate on C-SPAN with
Terrell E. Arnold—a consultant to the State Department, executive
director of the Institute on Terrorism and Subnational Conflict, and
coeditor of an important book on terrorism.[28] Hitchens asked Arnold
whether, since it is an issue that might lead to war, he could offer a definition of "terrorism" that was not: tautological or vacuous ("the use of
violence for political ends") and that would apply to any state, party,
or movement not committed to pacifism; a cliché ("an attack on innocent men, women, and children") employed by all warring states and
parties in denouncing their enemy; or a synonym for "swarthy opponent of United States foreign policy." Arnold admitted there is no uni-
versally accepted definition.

Yet how could "a word with no meaning and no definition…have
become the political and media buzzword of the eighties? How can it
have become a course credit at colleges, an engine of pelf in the
think tanks, and a subject in its own right in the press, on television,
and at the movies?"[29] Thus, Ted Koppel devoted half an hour to
"Is Syria *terrorist*?"—the sort of question that insults the audience

as much as the presumed victim or target. Terrorism discourse also leads world-class newspapers such as the *New York Times* or the *Los Angeles Times* to equate Chechnyan fighters holding hostages with McVeigh in Oklahoma City. Then there is terrorism's manipulation by governments following a logic whereby, say, the 297 Israelis killed by Palestinians between the beginning of the *intifada* in December 1987 and its end in July in 1995 were due to "terrorism," whereas the 1,418 Palestinians who died during the same period as a result of Israeli repression, including 260 under the age of sixteen,[30] were not. It is not simply that, like "Communist" or "fascist," the word "terrorist" is being abused; rather the word is itself an abuse, a banality that disguises reality while impoverishing language and thought by obliterating distinctions.

The consensus among the various authors seems to be that there is no adequate definition of terrorism; indeed there is argument over even the wisdom of defining it, some taking the position that it is better not to do so.[31] The definitional conundrum does not consist in disagreement regarding some details or partial approaches; rather it is the very "general framework [that] is chosen for definition"[32] that is the primary issue. The atrocious facts are there, the horrible images are indelible, yet we cannot agree upon the cultural, political, or tactical contexts in which they are embedded.

In such a world of control, clarity itself was deceptive, and attempts to explain terror could barely be distinguished from the stories contained in those explanations—as if terror provided only inexplicable explanations of itself and thrived by so doing.

—M. Taussig, *Shamanism, Colonialism, and the Wild Man*

It is standard procedure for a terrorism writer to begin by protesting the glaring flaws in the literature (the more than one hundred definitions, the absence of a basic perspective, the political biases, and the taxonomic inaccuracies) and then to proceed to add his or her own definition, classification, perspective, or theory of the phenomenon. It is therefore with certain trepidation that we contemplate joining this group of writers who are so skeptical of terrorism discourse yet end up engaging in the self-parody of furthering it.

We have noted that "totemism" and "witchcraft" afford emblematic cases of problematic categories that can be taken as analogues of "terrorism." This does not imply that such terms should be rejected out of hand; rather, it is a warning to the analyst not to assume the obviousness of the category in question.

In Beidelman's words;

> Taxonomic preoccupation may sometimes distract us from recognizing ambiguities inherent in social beliefs and acts. When applied on a cross-cultural, comparative level, such labels may conceal problematical interdependences. We feel we have explained matters away through having imposed some nominal category.[33]

Typically, an anthropological monograph begins by questioning the semantic content of the key terms used in the analysis.[34] For instance, "the category of *trickster* may be merely the product of a series of false translations, much as terms such as *family* and *witchcraft* seem incomparable cross-culturally when taken out of context."[35] If anthropologists, who have carried out intensive studies of witchcraft and sorcery in many societies, can be criticized in this manner, the criticism is even more applicable to the field of terrorism studies, which possesses scant ethnographic knowledge regarding terrorist groups,[36] but prefers instead to concentrate on "international terrorism" in the most general manner, as if it were dealing with "the thing" itself.

The foregoing discussion echoes the current situation in the study of terrorism, which—like totemism and witchcraft, and despite its many theories—resists a unifying perspective. It is also a discourse in which the scholar plays a crucial role in making the subjects more different than they really are. In the field of terrorism, too, the category rests on the obvious existence of a social system, comprised of persons and groups ostracized for the breach of certain norms, a transgression that is tantamount to the fearsome violation of a taboo. The best-informed writers on terrorism are well aware that "in reality there are many terrorisms, each calling for different theories, models, and approaches from the scholar seeking to relate these phenomena to other dimensions of political change."[37] They understand that no amount of expertise has produced a final solution to the unpredictable facts of terrorism. "I simply cannot give you answers. There aren't answers," was Brian Jenkins's reply when, in 1974, the House Subcommittee on the Near East and South Asia held hearings on international terrorism. Yet not all experts are so resigned and therefore premise their investigations on the assertion that there are answers that might lead to a solution if their recommendations are followed. This is reminiscent of the eighteenth century's rationalistic optimism that, whatever else it accomplished, "*obstructed* the discovery of the *problematic* character" of social reality.[38]

The most common terrorism typology includes "nationalist," "ideological," "religious fanatical," "single issue," and "state-sponsored";[39] other varieties of terror encompass the "psychotic," "criminal," "endemic," "authorized," "vigilante," and "revolutionary."[40] The objection that terrorism may be a fake category is in fact mentioned and then quickly dismissed in the literature.[41] That wars, killings, and violence of various kinds are endemic to the human condition is obvious; the real issue concerns the wisdom of describing all (or many) such events as the work of "terrorism." Does this concept better clarify the facts, or is it, as with so many other historical constructs, a hypostatized creation of learned and lay people alike that is a certain path to self-deception?

The apotheosis of writing terrorism, we would reemphasize, encompasses a deeply ironic project: it creates the very thing it abominates. Hardman found in 1933 that terrorism is an "outmoded" and "irrelevant" method;[42] in the 1990s it is driving a growth industry in academia. The various academic disciplines are even now in the process of recognizing terrorism as a subject worthy of scholarly consideration. For example, it was as recently as 1982 that *Psychological Abstracts*, the authoritative compendium of publications in academic psychology, listed for the first time references to terrorism or related terms.[43] Should this process of constituting "terrorism" as a valid field of scholarly investigation be encouraged? Do we really better understand the behavior called terrorism by piling up new definitions and theories and by reifying the phenomenon within its broadest framework of international and cross-cultural comparison?

As with the categories of totem and taboo, the demons of terror are awaiting their analytical dissolution. But into what? Into categories of persons, social contexts, cultural norms, ritual warfare, a logic of chance, a staging of innocence. When we contemplate terrorism as the ironic formation of playing with sign and representation, its categorical discourse begins to dissolve into the allegories of writing.

What confers this [criminal] character upon them is not the intrinsic quality of a given act but that definition which the collective conscience lends them.
　　　　　　　—E. Durkheim, *The Rules of Sociological Method*

Which attributes would we ascribe to a "terrorist"? In an ethnographic approach, the classification and powers attributed to each of the person categories ("witch," "sorcerer," "diviner," "prophet," "priest," and the like) must be culture specific, i.e., dependent on the intersubjective definitions of their communities. Not only do these categories differ from society to society; within each society the semantic domain of a particular category is defined in relation to the rest, the "person field" being structured as if it were a chess board. The value of a given piece, say the "bishop," derives from the attributes of the others (those which the bishop is not).[44] This one classification is interdependent with other cultural domains such as behavioral categories, belief systems, and value orientations. Just as one cannot understand chess through knowing about only one of the pieces of the game, the meaning and functions of, say, "the witch" cannot be understood without the broader context provided by the entire set of person categories within which the identity is defined in a specific culture. It is by virtue of the entire system of definitions and rules that a pawn—or witch or terrorist—exists.

The label "terrorist," rather than referring to a type of person situated in a particular society's political space and cultural domains, exudes generic or universal overtones. To the extent that it acquires social and cultural specificity, it does so (as we have seen) within an implicit hierarchy of world cultures in which the definer of terrorism occupies the apex and Arabs, Basques, Irish, or Sri Lankans are subordinated. By relying upon such taxonomic labels as "ethnic" or "ideological" terrorism, by focusing generally on "the international terrorist," and by abstracting some feature of the universal terrorist such as "mindset," "goals," or "personality," the intimate relationship between the actor and his immediate audience is trivialized or concealed; the drama and dialectics of their mutual recreation is denied meaning. If close scrutiny reveals that a person category, such as "the witch," does not stand the test of cross-cultural comparison unless its various components are dissolved in a person field, similarly we should be compelled to dissolve the general category of "the terrorist" into its constituent elements. Rather than assuming the "pathology" of the fictionalized terrorist, the analyst must specify the set of person alternatives available within the society in question. Furthermore, this context is likely to change over time.

As one example, in the Basque case there have been significant shifts in the person category of activist during the years of ETA's existence. The political alternatives that rivaled ETA activism changed over the decades of the sixties, seventies, and eighties; consequently,

becoming a member of the organization had markedly different connotations in each: in the early sixties during the depth of the dictatorship, it was the project of a small group of students with no other
weapon than the myth of revolutionary freedom; in the seventies it
became the main political outlet for rebellious youths; in the eighties,
Spain had solidified its democratic reform. The person field intersects
with the ideological system, which also changed from the late fifties to
the present.

Similarly, an understanding of ETA's internal history of ideological and organizational subdivisions is essential to contextualize different personal options: being either an *españolista* ("pro-Spain") or
abertzale ("Basque patriot") in the mid-sixties, supporting the Fifth or
Sixth Assembly in the early seventies (the former gave priority to the
nationalist goal, the latter to working-class issues), or belonging to the
ETA military or ETA politico-military branches in the late seventies
(the former espoused violent activism, the latter political dialogue as
well), are all instances of ideological and strategic alternatives that
were fundamental for defining the person category that the prospective activist might embrace. As a consequence, individuals who fought
for the ETA in different periods of its history, and who consider themselves products and representatives of its political goals, disagree radically over what ought to be the organization's present agenda.

Similar arguments as to how to cut the Gordian knot of definitional problems and historical markers have been made regarding the
mafia. The source of the term is most likely fictional, taken from an
1863 play by Placido Rizzotto. According to Gambetta, "in at least two
ways the word can be said to have *created* the phenomenon: firstly, and
most obviously, it supplied outsiders with a label to identify a blurred
conglomerate.... More importantly, the word began to bounce back
on the very agents to whom it referred."[45] As the *capo* Lucky Luciano
observed of his *Union Siciliana*, "You've got to give the new setup a
name; after all, what the fuck is any business or company without a
name?"[46] Thus, in Gambetta's view, the initial label is crucial in creating and sustaining the phenomenon. This conforms to the view of dis-
course-oriented analysts, who hold that "myth essences are created by
the metadiscursive practice of naming."[47]

In short, by applying the scientific rule of parsimony, also known
as *Occam's razor*—whereby one must privilege the simplest assumptions
and eliminate unneeded theoretical constructs—a skeptical question
emerges: If all sorts of murders, kidnappings, threats, civil wars, government crimes, killings by secret or underground organizations,

paramilitary executions, and so on, were simply called by those names without ever using the word "terrorism," would there be something missing in the description of the real world?

Cults don't exist.

—J. Gordon Melton, "A Fiery Ending"

As an instance of the fateful consequences of such metadiscursive naming, there is a poignant argument about the role of labels in the Waco disaster. Well-informed analysts concluded that the "cult" label itself was decisive in making the violence almost inevitable. Noting that the ATF offered no explanation for the raid other than "suspecting" violations of firearms laws, former police officer Robert Hicks stated: "The strongest hint of the ATF's rationale lies in their language—labeling the Branch Davidians as a 'cult' and their leader David Koresh as a 'self-proclaimed messiah.'"[48] Having specialized in uncovering phony international satanic conspiracies, Hicks concluded that the "cult" label forced upon the Branch Davidians by the ATF and the media "branded the group's motivations as criminal and even evil."[49] Moorman Oliver, who specializes in gangs and cults, concurred that the Davidians "were ultimately accused of being a 'cult.'"[50] He charged that the fiasco had its roots in the labeling of them as "cultists" by "a group of self-appointed religion police that goes by the name of 'Cult Awareness Network' (CAN)."[51]

What is the actual descriptive value of the pejorative term "cult," as applied to religious groups? Gordon Melton, a leading authority on nonmainstream religions, ends his reassessment of the Waco tragedy by underscoring: "Cults don't exist; and therefore, anyone who would pass himself or herself off as a 'cult expert' is an expert about nothing!"[52] Similarly, Michael Barkun declares: "The term 'cult' is virtually meaningless."[53] In the 1940s, for instance, books on cults regularly applied the term to Christian Scientists, Mormons, Jehovah's Witnesses, and Seventh-Day Adventists; they would most likely not be referred to as cultists today. There are some 900 Christian churches and another 600 religious groups from other traditions;[54] who decides, and on the basis of what criteria, which ones are stigmatized "cults" and which are rightful churches?

"Cult," then, is obviously a residual category applied to marginal, powerless, amorphous religious groups. In the public's perception it connotes dubious, secretive, mindless, potentially criminal outcasts. Far from being a mere descriptive term, the label itself is a stigma that invites law enforcement intervention. As their discursive goal, the architects of the Waco spectacle seemed intent on achieving an advanced form of villainous reification—the creation of a loathsome new public enemy named "the cult."

Such conceptual errors and enterprises are far from inconsequential at the level of public discourse and policy. In the case of Waco, they produced both an action and a reaction. Waco became a rallying point for antigovernment militia groups around the country. The suspects in the Oklahoma City bombing were immersed in such paramilitary culture. Ranting about Waco was crucial to their new antinomian education. The Washington political establishment, which unanimously applauded Janet Reno's handling of Waco, was later haunted by the explosion in Oklahoma City and its connections with the Texas events.

$\overline{VI}$

The use of the undifferentiated collective concepts of everyday speech is always a cloak for confusion of thought and action. It is, indeed, very often an instrument of specious and fraudulent procedures. It is, in brief, always a means of obstructing the proper formulation of the problem.

—M. Weber, *The Methodology of Social Sciences*

Max Weber was concerned with the logical status and analytical efficacy of holistic concepts. He reminded us that categories such as "state," "society," and "institution" are necessary in social science; but he warned in unequivocal fashion that they are "solely the resultants and modes of organization of the specific acts of *individual* men."[55] Weber subscribed to Kantian epistemology in which concepts are nothing more than analytical instruments for intellectually mastering empirical reality. Weber thought that the primary task of social science was the construction of ideal types specifically formulated for the analysis of concrete individual phenomena, constructs that must then be confronted with empirical reality in order to make explicit their heuristic value.

The notion of "ethnos" is a case in point, since "ethnic terrorism" (versus "ideological terrorism") is widely employed in the literature as a major typological category. Thus, according to a panel of international experts, "the basis of the Basque problem is ethnicity, which…means the feeling of shared identity and unity which comes from being Basque."[56] Other factors contribute as well, but "ethnos," configured by unabashedly juxtaposing such disparate phenomena as historical origins, family surname, marriage, religion, philosophy, dress fashion, voluntary association, psychological attributes, etc., is the root cause.

That Basques support terrorism, which is of an ethnic nature because they are "ethnocentric," is the kind of argument that parallels the explanation that opium puts people to sleep because it has a "dormitive principle."

Similar ethnic clichés are also operative in other arenas, such as when Arab "volatility," Serbian "intransigence," or Asian "low regard for human life" are invoked for explaining contemporary conflicts. In fact Weber observed many decades ago that as a concept "ethnic…is unsuitable for a really rigorous analysis" and that it "dissolves if we define our terms exactly."[57] By adopting ethnos as the cornerstone of their analytical edifice, the terrorism experts seem to be intent upon doing obsolete social science. Such naturalistic premises are surely far removed from considering the phenomenon as a set of relations,[58] as the product of the imagination,[59] or as a social drama.[60]

What is wrong with these reifications? They ignore the old truism extant since Durkheim and Mauss that, classification being a necessary condition for social existence, "it is the *marking* of relations—of identities in opposition to one another—that is 'primordial,' not the substance of those identities."[61] Hence, "ethnicity, like totemism, exists above all else as a set of relations. In this respect, they are formally similar."[62] Far from such classificatory perspective, in former times "the Devil" was deemed to empower the witches' flight and other bizarre metamorphoses, phenomena that were utterly impossible within the Christian worldview. Such conceptual hypostatization of evil prevented the medieval theologian from focusing on the contradictions inherent in the witchcraft perspective, while precluding questioning the very reality of the phenomenon. He could not examine it in its own terms. Such error is as habitual with us as with medieval thinkers. The ploy consists, in the words of Gregory Bateson, in "drawing a generalization from the world of external observation, giving it a fancy name, and then asserting that this named abstraction exists *inside* the organism as an explanatory principle. Instinct theory commonly takes this monstrous form."[63] Nothing else needs to be examined if someone's actions (indeed the collective actions of entire societies) can be explained as the result of an inherent force called "the Devil," "instinct," "race," or "ethnos."

VII

We approach the id with analogies.
    —Freud, *New Introductory Lectures on Psychoanalysis*

In the final analysis, the difficult and risky task of writing about the "thing itself" of terrorism forces one to face Freud's dilemma: he noted that we can talk about the unconscious only through allegories and in negative terms. Ours is a fragile text regarding a proscribed topic. The precariousness of our position is underscored by our conscious eschewing of most of the expertise on the subject. Rather than searching for precise conceptual and explanatory categories, we end up resting our arguments upon ethnographic allegories, historical analogies, and even biblical parables. *C'est la guerre!*

The current concept of "the terrorist" is a relatively recent phenomenon but one with ancient roots in human affairs. The word was coined during the French Revolution, Robespierre being the figure most associated with it. A harbinger of ambiguities in future terrorism discourse, this Man of Terror was also the leader of the Jacobins, proponents of the Cult of the Supreme Being who saw themselves as apostles of a new religion. He wrote: "In revolution it [the principle of popular government] is simultaneously virtue and terror: virtue, without which terror is fatal, and terror, without which virtue is powerless."[64] If we examine his spirited speeches, we are surprised to find that he opposed war and capital punishment. Instead of shocking harangues inciting bloody terrorism, we are regaled with impassioned pleas for personal virtue, public morality, and civil liberty. By most accounts, Robespierre, whose very name evokes horror and contempt, enjoyed the greatest of followings in his time and was perceived as a "virtuous man." The justification that he and his followers gave for revolutionary terror was their belief that they were founding a whole new society of virtue. Nor is this penchant for morality in the original and quintessential "terrorist" foreign to the thinking of present-day ones, as attested to by many writers. The collusion between morality and violence, religion and revolution, self-transcendence and terrorism— starkly antinomian realities at first blush—turns out on closer inspection to be obvious.[65]

Was "terrorism" unknown before Robespierre? Hardly. Prior to its recent secular uses, religion was the golden field of naked terror within the annals of history. Several writers insist on the ancient religious genealogy of modern terrorism[66] based on the premise that, "before the nineteenth century, religion provided the only acceptable justification for terror."[67] In David Rapoport's classic paper "Fear and Trembling," the Thugs, the Assassins, and the Zealots-Sicarii all provide stunning instances in which the religious traditions of Hinduism, Islam, and Judaism legitimated terror.

The Thugs, for example, strangled and deliberately prolonged their victims' agony in order to provide Kali, the Hindu goddess of destruction, more time to enjoy their expressions of terror:

> The reinterpretation of a cardinal Hindu myth and theme provided the Thugs with their peculiar purpose and method.... The Thug understood that he was obliged to supply the blood that Kali, his creator, required to keep the world in equilibrium. His responsibility was to keep himself alive as long as possible so that he could keep killing.[68]

According to one estimate, incorporated into the title of J. L. Sleeman's book *Thugs: Or a Million Murders*, during just the last three centuries of their existence (they had been active since at least the seventh century) the Thugs assassinated one million people. Rapoport regards that figure to be inflated, "but half that number may be warranted."[69] Then the British came and, lo and behold, a small group of "thirty to forty" relatively unprotected administrators "exterminated...some 10,000 Thugs."[70] Whether there were half a million or one million murders ("every estimate flounders"), whether they had been operating since the seventh century or were actually, as some believe, the same group as the ancient Sagartians—the stranglers described by Herodotus some 2,500 years ago—the important message is the baffling, utterly impenetrable cruelty of people demented by religious belief.

This tale of Terror, Taboo, and White Liberation is the kind of plot that can be turned into a literary blockbuster and, not surprisingly, the British officer W. H. Sleeman, the slayer of the Thuggee Monster, was accompanied by the novelist Meadows Taylor who wrote a best-selling novel on the bizarre killers. In this regard our modern terrorism experts/novelists of chapter 2 are but the most recent representatives of a literary tradition. Once again, we are forced to ask what is the narrative status of the nonfictional reports themselves when turned into a paradigm of "holy terror"? How do we draw the line between history and mythology?

All these murders, we are told, have a religious origin and purpose: the delectation of the goddess Kali through the prolonged terror of the victims. Yet nothing is said of the social structure, the economy, the caste system in which the killings are situated; there is no political rationale, no cultural context, no discernible boundary markers (the victims were travelers) that might shed some light on the horrible tradition. Should not social science be skeptical of claims that a society can preserve for centuries such a sacrificial institution that produces victims on such a massive scale simply because of a foible in religious belief? It is not our intent to defend or deny the reality of the murders; we simply question to what extent such narratives operate as fictional allegories within terrorism discourse.

European witchcraft provides another instance of historical analogy with which to illustrate some of the flaws in contemporary terrorism discourse. No one will deny the paramount importance of the witchcraft "craze" in sixteenth- and seventeenth-century Europe, during which many thousands of accused persons were burned in inquisitorial flames. Clearly, whether labeled as such, the inquisitorial proceedings and the resulting *autos-da-fé* qualify as holy terror. Yet from the outset, even a cursory examination of the literature challenges the reader with the truly perplexing question: did witchcraft exist or was it simply imagined? This was the decisive question that confronted theologians, lawyers, and inquisitors over the centuries, yet, until quite recently, witchcraft remained a litmus test of European mores and laws. Far from being a rhetorical issue, men of great learning struggled with the intellectual and moral dilemmas posed by the sinister, sacrilegious, flying human beings that they regularly condemned to the pyre.

The Catholic inquisition brought its witches under control "by the device of an extended definition of heresy."[71] The inquisitors were also called "definers"; their role was to *define* the essence of witchcraft and who qualified as a witch. It made a world of difference whether one abided by the Church's definition and actually *believed* in the powers of witchcraft. Some inquisitors, like Pierre de Lancre, accepted as readily as the witches themselves the portentous reality of magical metamorphoses; others, like Alonso de Salazar, remained skeptical. For the de Lancres, intellectual definitions and the police function were, in practice, inextricable.

Whether believing or disbelieving in magical flights and secret sabbaths, the inquisitor projected a deeply ironic figure. Were he credulously to accept at face value the confessions of his tortured suspects, then he shared their superstitious and demonological worldview that was proscribed by the Church; if he disbelieved their testimony, then he was judging the accused for confessions that he knew to be untrue.

Since the Church's inquisitorial system required a single, uncontestable verdict, the inquisitors confronted not only the "facts" of the matter but also their own belief systems. In the final analysis, we are left to wonder how the Holy Inquisition fell into grand delusion, with the institution itself and most of its functionaries coming to accept the extramundane reality inherent in the confessions of the alleged "witches." That which was "real," the inquisitors' ontologies, depended to a startling degree on what they believed, their epistemologies.

Does the terrorism expert have anything to learn from such instances of "epistemic murk,"[72] and particularly from the essential ironies of the inquisitor? The ironic mode is involuntary, yet also absolutely deliberate and conscious.[73] This antinomy is readily applicable to inquisitors and terrorism experts alike. Both involuntarily become ironic figures by themselves imagining, believing, and thereby constituting the very unthinkable reality against which they struggle. However, once having adopted the substantive form of intractable evil, they engage in discourse that even they suspect is intellectually and morally ironic—yet still preferable to relativism and inaction.

Quite aside from denying or confirming the facts of their historical reality, in terrorism discourse, stories have an essentially moral and figurative content; their narrative goal is to provide a context (religious, cultural, national) in which to situate terrorist behavior. In a narrower sense, the factually intended descriptions provide historical sequences that typify "terrorism." They are not intended as exemplars but rather as examples of the real thing—of "holy terror." The foregoing interpretation of a million murders caused by a Hindu myth is not simply meaning added to the "factual" narrative, but rather the very "condition of its meaningfulness."[74] The Thugs, Assassins, and Zealots provide morally charged stories about terrorism, which may then be perceived as a fable of the sinister times in which we live.

Violence and the sacred are inseparable.

—R. Girard, *Violence and the Sacred*

So the search for terrorism throughout history often leads to religion. Yet "religion" itself is an excellent example of what we mean by categorical reification. It is not the purpose of this essay to attempt yet another redrawing of the boundaries between revolt, rebellion, revolution, guerrilla warfare, terrorism, etc.; but the quest for greater understanding requires that we continuously challenge categorical reifications—the all-too-frequent assumption that categories such as "economy," "social structure," "religion," "family," "psychology," etc., describe and explain altogether autonomous areas of behavior. "Religion" is increasingly selected as an indispensable component for explaining terrorism, both in the scholarly literature[75] as well as in journalistic reporting—witness the interpretation of the World Trade Center events.

The view of religion as some sort of invariant cultural universal in all societies over long periods is not supported by empirical evidence.[76] Any ethnographer is likely to find, as did Jorgensen among Shoshones,[77] that during the short span of a century the very substance of a people's "religion" might change drastically from the transformative movement of the Ghost Dance ritual in 1869, to its subsequent millenarian interpretation and conversion to Mormonism, to a second version of the Ghost Dance in 1889 calling for an accomodation of the whites, to revival of the precontact Bear Dance around 1892 for the purpose of promoting health, to the redemptive Sun Dance religion in response to misery and repression, to the rebelliousness of the 1960s and 1970s against the federal administration, to the latest shift in belief from Christian redemption to forms of spiritual power deriving from various Native American religious practices. If "religion" in a single cultural tradition can transform itself in such chameleonlike fashion from one generation to the next, how can we invoke the reality of universal religion cross-culturally? How can social science postulate, as has been done, the religious reality throughout a millenium of a country as vast and varied as India as the single explanation for violent terror?

Religion within the Occidental tradition may be submitted to a similar exercise in categorical deconstruction. During the Enlightenment, when the belief was paramount that revelatory religion was the major impediment to rational thought, there were at least four distinct ideal-typical positions (represented by Rousseau, Condorcet, Robespierre, and Montesquieu) concerning the extent to which traditional religion, and the counter-call for a substitute secularized version, were necessary. These debates continued during the nineteenth century, mostly through the work of Hegel (who argued that modern societies need both types: the new forms of the State as the spiritual realization of the religious ideal; and the conventional personal forms), Marx and Engels (who provided an updated version of the straightforward, antireligious attitude of the previous century), Comte

(who saw religion as cognitively redundant but simultaneously necessary for societal cohesion), and de Tocqueville (who advocated the
promotion of religion as conducive to moral discipline and the viabil-
ity of democracy). Then there were the founders of the modern sociology of religion, Durkheim and Weber, whose interest in it grew in
tandem with the notion of revolution in European societies, and who
attempted to show that what the Enlightenment had heralded as ratio-
nality was not the antithesis of religion but derived largely from
Occidental religious-ethical foundations. Weber insisted on the connection between Protestant ethics and capitalism, and he emphasized
the quasi-religious dimension of the French Revolution as the culmi-
nation of charisma. Likewise, Durkheim discovered the quintessential
character of Society in the study of religion.[78]

If religion is, indistinctly, what the various authors claim ("Supreme
Being" for Robespierre, "State" for Hegel, "Morality" for de Tocqueville,
"Alienation" for Marx, "Charisma" for Weber, "Society" for Durkheim,
"Illusion" for Freud, and so on), then it is hard to imagine how any sort
of violence can lack being "religious." We cannot do without general
categories, but "fake categories" of the sort criticized by Kroeber[79]
become insurmountable obstacles to understanding. If religion is virtually everything, then in stating that terroristic violence *is* religious,
are we really referring to anything other than a distant allegory?

IX

*Be on your guard for morality and thus the well-known immorality of many
moralisms.*

    —J. Derrida, "Like the Sound of the Sea Deep within a Shell"

Conceptual and moral hypostatizations feed into one another. If religion is considered to be the thing itself, the motivations of the holy
terrorist become a complete enigma that we can only regard as both
senseless and unnatural: "the act of terror is holy because one is acting
against his natural impulses," for "the people attracted to it may be so
intrigued by the experience of perpetrating terror that everything else
is incidental."[80] The process of understanding is ordinarily assumed to
be one of rendering the unfamiliar and exotic into the more familiar;
in much of the terrorism discourse we read in the press, it would seem
that the ideal explanation flows in the opposite direction: the more
absurd, aberrant, and decontextualized the portrayal of the behavior
the better the description of true "terrorism."

One must resist the pretense and temptation of providing a final interpretation of political violence. Nevertheless, social science attempts to understand familiar reality by analyzing the interplay of concrete narratives within their various contexts. Anthropology has long taken for granted the Weberian postulate that the social sciences "are the least fitted to presume to save the individual the difficulty of making a choice";[81] should an anthropologist start indoctrinating the natives in matters regarding ritual practice and belief, we would consider him a missionary rather than a social scientist. Still, the leap from the "is" to the "ought" has very different implications for a scientist, an expert, a storyteller, or a philosopher.

For Weber, in the final analysis the very objectivity of empirical social knowledge must take into account the ordering of reality according to the agent's "subjective" categories, for these "present the *presuppositions* of our knowledge and are based on the presupposition of the *value* of those *truths*."[82] It is the awareness of the relativity of these presuppositions that converts our inquiries into scientific methodology, "the hair-line which separates science from faith."[83] Such awareness starts with the realization that scientific truth is but one more cultural product. It has no universal value and therefore offers nothing to those persons for whom the particular truth has no meaning. The objectivity of our research is always related to our own evaluative assumptions, but Weber finds no disharmony between "the incessant changefulness of the concrete viewpoints" and "the belief which we all have in some form or other, in the meta-empirical validity of ultimate and final values."[84]

Since the points of contention regarding political violence so readily become matters of life or death, the counterterrorism specialist, in a fit of moral outrage, might as well write a political bible for each country, outline the democratic methods it should follow, and list the causes for which a citizen should be willing to fight and die. In fact, much of the literature on terrorism approximates such an approach. The writer might as well conclude that the activist has committed a technical, not to mention tactical, error once having decided to surrender his or her life for a cause.

And thus we come full circle. By claiming the moral high ground in the name of scientific objectivity and universal ethics, the terrorism expert in effect is close to proclaiming the political status quo to be sacrosanct. Violence in its defense is "natural"; the resort to violence in the furtherance of alternative political agendas is "unnatural." Persons engaged in unnatural acts are easily demonized, dehumanized, and, consequently, targeted. There is also a sense in which their agenda is trivialized and thereby dismissed as absurd, except insofar as they serve the practical purpose of providing credible, larger-than-life, and, hence, terrifying, foils for the counterterrorism industry and its budget.

But even on the facts available to them it is astounding that so much could have been written which appears to be contrary to common sense. Yet these men were scholars and of great learning and ability.
        —E. E. Evans-Pritchard, *Theories of Primitive Religion*

If much of the literature "explains" the phenomenon in terms of "ethnic terror" and "holy terror," what of its practitioner? In chapter 3 we considered Sterling's tropical ploy of presenting her narrative in the form of exemplary biography. In fact, her tactic is emblematic of a much broader psychological school that locates the "essence" of terrorism in the terrorist "personality" or "mindset." Yet once again anthropology provides a cautionary note.

At the turn of the century, armchair anthropologists were busy gathering data from all over the world on religion, magic, witchcraft, taboo, and other social institutions without respecting the cultural contexts from which they were drawn. The tendency was to explain everything in terms of emotional states. The concepts of fear, terror, awe, fanatic belief, evil projections, and the like were employed profusely to account for a variety of recently "discovered" institutions. Much as anthropologists once relied on emotionalist explanations, students of the recent terrorism plague have tended to assume that by pointing out the psychological stresses, the political frustrations, and the self-transcending components leading to terrorism, we are describing the causes of otherwise inexplicable behavior. Subsequently, social anthropologists have denounced "the psychological fallacy" of confusing the study of individual behavior with that of social life. It is also known as the "If I were horse" argument, whereby one projects one's own emotions and attitudes onto the subjects under study and judges them in terms of how one would react were s/he to be in the same situation.

A fine example of this approach is found in Herbert Spencer's treatment of primitive religion as originating in dreams and belief in ghosts, his conclusion being that ancestor worship is at the root of every religion. In Edward Tylor's work, Spencer's ghosts evolved into the notion of *anima* (soul) which Tylor employed for his theory of "animism." With such "dream theories" of religion, the scholar imputes his own logical construct to primitive man as the "explanation" of primitive belief. Writers who explain violent nationalist movements as products of mere "millenarian dreams" or terror as the result of "messianism" can be considered heirs to such theories.

The animistic theory remained unchallenged for many years, or until advances in associationist psychology and ethnography provided new insights. Marett, in particular, challenged it on methodological grounds and claimed that, with primitive man, action takes precedence over ideas. In the preanimistic stage, religion cannot be separated from magic, and he spoke of both as mana. However, for Marett religion still had psychological causation, being based on primitive feelings of awe, fear, admiration, and love. Other psychological theories of religion were propounded by Freud,[85] Lowie,[86] Radin,[87] and Malinowski.[88] Common to them all is the notion that magic and religion are reduceable to psychological states; that is, they result from frustrations, sentiments, or delusions of some sort. Since then, this kind of psychological explanation of social facts has been strongly contested by anthropologists and sociologists on reductionist grounds.[89]

Tylor, Frazer, and Lévi-Bruhl also assumed that a certain rational thought process underlies all magical and religious ritual. Intrinsically, then, the priest and magician are comparable to the scientist. Where religious and magical thought err is in postulating that because two things are alike there is some sort of mystical link between them; the magician and the shaman impute a causal relationship to nature, when the connection is only analogous and subjective. Frazer classified these associational relationships into the law of similarity (homeopathic magic) and the law of contagion (contagious magic); the savage thinks that when he acts in a certain way, certain consequences will inevitably follow in virtue of these laws.

Characteristically, another major approach to the study of terrorism concentrates on logical processes—the so-called paleologic of the terrorist, who is frequently depicted with clichés like "the terrorist is at war with society or with civilization." Since there must be some logic even to this madness, the student of terrorism seems to be in a position similar to that of the turn-of-the-century anthropologist who had to explicate how the savage could mistake fable with reality while engaged in ritual magic. The terrorist, too, must be making some logical error by confusing, say, real and fantasy warfare (law of similarity), or by mistaking an innocent civilian target for a military one (law of contagion).

On the basis of psychological concepts such as soul, ghost, dream, and mana—all of which have an ancient tradition in the imagination of many cultures—categorical concepts were coined and fostered as explanatory theories that were later found wanting and therefore were abandoned. That alone ought to sound a cautionary note regarding the category of terrorism. Whatever else it might be, this "new plague" that has captured world attention during the last two decades is one more example of conceptually objectifying a psychic state of sudden and momentary fright. Anthropologists regularly equate emotional states to ritual situations and question which come first. Not even such an elementary distinction between the structure of the action and its emotional outcome, however, is posited in most of the literature on terrorism. It is odd that a discipline that purports to address some of the thorniest contemporary issues in the politico-military domain should ground its conceptual foundation in that most impermanent state of sudden terror.

A relevant aspect of the psychological interpretations of religion, as well as of terrorism, is the long-standing comparison between the savage mentality and the mentally ill within our own society. Thus Freud compared primitives to neurotics in that both are characterized by the omnipotence of their thoughts, although anthropologists have insisted all along that they have not encountered primitives who believed they could change the external world through mere wishful thinking. In similar fashion, the comparison of terrorists to the mentally disturbed is almost irresistible to students of terrorism, despite the fact that the best informed are well aware that most terrorists are "normal."[90] In classic "If I were a horse" fashion, it is easy to regard seemingly vicious murderers as insane or at least overburdened with guilt.

There is an echo of Freud's ideas in *Totem and Taboo* in writers who propound that the establishment and perpetuation of terrorist groups rests on their members' psychic states regarding commitment, revenge, guilt, risk taking, and so on. In chapter 2 we examined how Post employs (erroneously) the case of ETA to argue that terrorists are recruited among "marginal, isolated, and inadequate individuals from troubled family backgrounds."[91] Typically, in this view, terrorists are the product of an incomplete family structure, the loss of the father being particularly negative; they suffer from the mechanism of "splitting" as the result of narcissistic wounds incurred during childhood; they share many features of the paranoid personality; they display unconscious patricidal impulses; or there is in terrorism a regression to what Freud called the "oceanic feeling" common to mysticism and the infantile state. Hence, it is not surprising that major conferences on terrorism may arrive at the conclusion that "the road to terrorism usually begins with some form of alienation, sometimes mixed with boredom."[92] Some advocates of the "terrorist personality" theory even argue, quite seriously, that terrorists suffer from faulty vestibular functions in the middle ear or from dysphoria resulting from inconsistent mothering.[93]

The boundaries between science and fiction are difficult to maintain in such arguments. If *Totem and Taboo* is a work notorious for its confusing blend of historical fable and emotional reality, contemporary psychologists echoing it as a paradigm with which to elucidate modern terrorism can hardly be more discriminating between the factual and the allegorical. Of course, a realist reading of Freud's parables (he replied to his critics that they were not "just so" stories) misses the point altogether—as does a similar reading of the arguments regarding dysphoria and a faulty vestibule, not to mention "If I were a horse" analogues and stories of holy terror. These, too, are fables.

If ideas such as "hysteria" (Freud), "madness" (Deleuze), "totemism" (Lévi-Strauss), and "witchcraft" (Evans-Pritchard) could not withstand the scrutiny of historical or cross-cultural examination—just as after studying the archaeology of the human sciences (nineteenth-century linguistics, economics, zoology examined as types of fiction) Foucault could conclude that they had "a poisoned foundation"[94]—should we be surprised that "terrorism" and "terrorism studies" might deserve similar exorcism?

X̄I

But why should it not really be (partly, anyway) just the idea *that makes the impression on me. Aren't ideas frightening? Can I not feel horror from the thought that the cake with the knobs once served to select by lot the victim to be sacrificed? Hasn't the* thought *something terrible?—Yes, but that which I see in those stories is something they acquire, after all, from the evidence, including such evidence as does not seem directly connected with them—from the thought of man and his past, from the strangeness of what I see in myself and in others, what I have seen and have heard.*

—L. Wittgenstein, *Remarks on Frazer's "Golden Bough"*

Terror is my constant emotion. I deal in terror. I buy it, sell it, and make a profit.

—Bob Dylan

Anthropologists have long taken issue with the view that belief takes precedence over ritual action. Wittgenstein's remarks on reading Frazer's account of the rituals and magic of primitive peoples are perhaps as relevant as the thoughts of any other influential thinker: "where that practice [the killing of a king] and these views go together, the practice does not spring from the view, but both of them are there."[95] Religious notions cannot be "mistakes" unless they are put forward as a theory, he contended; error goes with opinion, and religious symbols are not based on opinion. The philosopher is not here concerned primarily with religion or anthropology, but with the "mythology in our language." Instances of that mythology would be expressions such as, "for the holy terrorist, the primary audience is the deity."

Wittgenstein chastised Frazer for using familiar terms such as "ghost," "soul," "spirit," and "deity," all of which are imbued with a sense of "superstition," in order to describe primitive behavior. Interestingly, he insisted that there is a close kinship between the ritual beliefs of primitives and the metaphysical problems of the modern interpreter (faced with "the limits of language"). Wittgenstein believed that we can tackle such issues, which are anything but trivial, only with mythical language. And if primitive practices seem so shocking, it must be partly because "there is something in us too that speaks in support of those observances by the savages."[96]

Such inevitable presence of mythology in our own thinking is what begs for an increased awareness of the allegory in our discourse. We should be suspicious of reified notions in the name of science, as well as of the depiction of the violent actor as wholly unlike ourselves in the name of morality. Yet allegorical imagination should not be understood as a concept or image that merely refers to something else, but rather it should be evaluated on its own terms and as the manifestation of an original power. We are led here to Vico's conception according to which experience is ordered by "imaginative universals" (*universali fantastici*) and culture works metaphorically. This is a philosophy that privileges image over concept and mythic elaboration over fact. It is concerned, most crucially, with the connection of form of thought with form of symbolism; hence, such imaginative ideal portraits "gave the fables univocal rather than analogous meanings."[97] The allegorical reality *is* the true one, in such a world view.

One of the three functions ascribed by Vico to the imagination is precisely that of causing mankind to be seized by fear and terror when faced with things that have no direct meaning. "Thus it was fear which created gods in the world; not fear awakened in men by other men, but fear awakened in men by themselves"[98] and, according to such "imaginative metaphysics," "man becomes all things by *not* understanding them"—that is, on the basis of the primordial analogies created by the imagination, "when he does not understand he makes the things out of himself and becomes them by transforming himself into them."[99] The imaginative fable or poetic character thereby becomes the condition of reality in mythic thought. The power of such thought is the assertion of identities, not similarities. This univocal predication is achieved by linking fable and allegory.

Such forms of predication by the mythic mind invoke the theories of metaphor developed by authors such as Black in philosophy and Fernandez in anthropology.[100] The important thing about metaphor is not whether it is true or real, but rather the system of commonplace meanings and evocations associated with it. When we say "man is a wolf," we do not invoke the dictionary reference of "wolf" but rather expressive associations. Thus something entirely different is created in metaphor, something that is essential to a new cognitive content.

Metaphors, cultural models, and ethnographic allegories are not epiphenomenal to explaining terrorism. As Black contends, metaphors and models are an irreplaceable part of scientific research; they are explanations not only "*by* analogy, but *through* an underlying analogy."[101] This echoes Weber's methodological point that "the comparison of `analogous' events is to be considered as *a* means of this imputation of causal agency, and indeed, in my view, one of the most important means and one which is not used to anywhere near the proper extent."[102]

Unless we want to assume that "terrorism" is a new cultural product created *ex nihilo*, we must start by asking which old bottles best contain such unexpected vintage. The nature of such models is "ideal typical." Although offered primarily as heuristic devices, they reflect significant cultural isomorphism with the violent processes, since they are grounded in ethnographic evidence. Cultural models have a dual "of" and "for" sense by which "they give meaning...to social and psychological reality both by shaping themselves to it and by shaping it to themselves."[103] The ethnographic perspective assumes that the basic culture of the actors and the spectators conditions decisively the selection of certain performative elements for mobilizing violence. In times of critical social transformation with attendant violence, the return to the cultural unconscious is partly expressed by tacitly assuming modes of performance long sanctioned by tradition.

The existence of major social phenomena grounded in some doubtful image or concept is, as we have seen in this chapter, nothing new in history. Additional religious movements, millenarian cults, ritual revolts, and inquisitorial practices could be invoked. Critical aspects of such "unreality"—the ones that concern us primarily—derive from misconstrued categories and objectified images that, in their delusional nature, have critical implications for the culture and politics of a period.

Lest we be admonished that a cavalier reading of "terrorism" as an essentially allegorical rather than categorical construct ignores the stated platforms and stated agendas of militant groups prescribing terrorism,[104] we should hasten to add that, indeed, "the terrorist" tends to actually coopt the discourse imposed on him or her. The activist might thereby seek to turn to his or her own advantage the very capacity of the discourse to terrify, despite the fatal consequences it can have for the proscribed actors and their communities. Depriving terrorism of the magic it derives from a categorical essence hurts no one so much as its apostle.

It is within the power of the analyst either further to reinforce or to unravel (and thereby dissolve) the phenomenon under study; the descriptive language we use configures its essence. An integral part of the skeptical inquisitor's task consisted in convincing the witches that their portentous powers were sheer fantasy and trickery. The implications of uncovering the semantic nonsense behind witchcraft accusations could hardly have been more relevant for ecclesiastical policy then; comparable inquisitorial delusions concerning "terrorism" are equally significant for public policy now. Rather than reinforcing an extreme sense of danger by taking any potential threat literally, we believe that exorcism is the best antidote to a public opinion fallen under the spell of Terror. Redemption "the terrorists" might need, but one that derives from skepticism and irony.[105] To taboo and demonize them further accomplishes little and is indeed counterproductive, since such imagination confers upon the violent actors the mythical power of fabled martyrs or monsters.

part two

THE CULTURES
OF TERROR

5

FATEFUL PURPOSE, FEARFUL INNOCENCE

It is the play with chance and innocence, the frightening dance with risk and cruelty, that best typifies the work of a terrorist. In this chapter we focus upon the fault lines within the totalizing arguments of this discourse in order to reveal their concealed paradoxes, their double-binding dilemmas, their absurd transcendencies. This is the Blakean world of "The Marriage of Heaven and Hell." Blake's genius intoned the "Songs of Innocence and of Experience." He envisioned "A Divine Image" even in the midst of the horrors of inhumanity.

> Cruelty has a Human Heart,
> And Jealousy a Human Face;
> Terror the Human Form Divine,
> And Secrecy the Human Dress.[1]

Here we enter the realm of Abraham, Hiroshima, and the Innocent Killer.

I

And God tempted Abraham and said unto him, Take Isaac, thine only son, whom thou lovest, and get thee into the land of Moriah, and offer him there for a burnt offering upon the mountain which I will show thee.

—Genesis 22: 1-2

Terrorism discourse not only evokes a Beckettian theater of the absurd (the frightening and costly Waiting for Terror), it also confronts us with what appears to be the actor's impenetrable enigma, the tale behind the commitment and the atrocity—the Kierkegaardian *credo quia absurdum* that sustains a belief to the point of absurdity and murder. Compliant with Freud's counsel, we turn once again to an allegory to frame such experiential absurdities of faith and obedience, innocence and cruelty.

The biblical theme of the sacrifice of the chosen son turns upon the parable of Isaac. God commands Abraham to sacrifice the innocent boy as a sign of faith. In supreme obedience to God's will, Abraham prepares to comply. The father having passed the ultimate test, God rescinds the order and Abraham sacrifices a ram in his son's stead. The story anticipates the Jewish Passover, in which the blood of the lamb prevents the death of the Israelites' first-born sons, as well as the Christian Crucifixion of Jesus, the *victima paschalis*.

Abraham's unique parable has captivated the imagination of religious thinkers for centuries. In his essay *Fear and Trembling*, Soren Kierkegaard turned the story into a paradigm of transcendent faith; for him such absurdity is the quintessence of religious belief. "That man [Abraham] was not a thinker, he felt no need of getting beyond faith,"[3] writes Kierkegaard in a panegyric of the story according to which "Isaac could not understand him." The look upon Abraham's face is horrific and he deliberately frightens his son by telling him that the sacrificial killing is not divine will but, out of idolatry, his own, so that Isaac would retain his faith in God by believing his father to be the monster.

What happened on the mountain is unforgettable: "from that time on Abraham became old, he could not forget that God had required this of him";[4] he even "prayed God to forgive him his sin, that he had been willing to offer Isaac that the father had forgotten his duty toward the son";[5] and, above all, "he could not comprehend that it was a sin to be willing to offer to God the best thing he possessed, that for which he would many times have given his life; and if it was a sin, if he had not loved Isaac as he did, then he could not understand that it might be forgiven. For what sin could be more dreadful?"[6] The biblical story condenses the paradoxical absurdity of transcendent belief, be it religious or patriotic, which demands the suspension of ethics. Occasionally, Abraham's willingness to sacrifice Isaac has been construed by artists and writers as an allegory of the fatherland's readiness to sacrifice its sons for the greater cause of the country. What could be a less comprehensible act of faith, a more dreadful and unforgivable sin?

Kierkegaard turned a fictional tale into the paradigm of the absurdities of transcendent faith; a different perspective might consider religiously motivated terror to be almost equatable to mere deviant violence (either in terms of pathological drive or as an act contrary to the perpetrator's natural impulses). Both extremes harbor their own kind of closure: the Kierkegaardian "leap," in building a whole theology out of an anecdotal tale, transforms "finite species into the currency of the infinite,"[7] and ends up providing theological luster to the tribal morality of the killing cult; the causal reduction, by equating science with nature, transforms human behavior into basic instinctive reactions, and ends up explaining the same cult as alien to ourselves while privy to others.

An analysis which seeks to avoid both types of closure must observe attentively the lives of the actors. In our own personal experience with Basque violence, we have been struck by the agonizing political uncertainty and the almost unbearable sense of moral dilemma pervading it. Thus the Kierkegaardian view that transcendent faith, be it religious or patriotic, is fraught with excruciating cognitive and ethical paradoxes appears to us to be very much to the point. And if there is play, as we shall argue below, it is not trivial amusement, but rather the deep play of risking one's life for a questionable purpose. We find Kierkegaard's argument, with all its blindness and horror, particularly revelatory of the underground rebel's play with purpose. The greatness of the tragic hero consists in his or her moral virtue, in that he or she abandons one expression of the ethical in order to seek a higher form. This is not the case in the biblical story, Kierkegaard argues, for in Abraham we observe the "teleological suspension of the ethical"[8]—the ethical is overridden altogether by a higher telos. For Abraham, despairing yet obedient to superior orders, and with a knife in his hand poised over his son, the ethical is the temptation not to fulfill God's will. "Abraham is therefore at no instant a tragic hero but something quite different, either a murderer or a believer."[9] The ethical "temptation" is also what the modern "terrorist" must overcome, as when the future prime minister Isaac Shamir stated in 1943: "Neither Jewish ethics nor Jewish tradition can disqualify terrorism as a means of combat."[10] Such lack of ethics led Shamir to execute his comrade and competitor Eliahu Giladi, the coleader of Lehi.[11] An Abraham provokes a *horror religiosus*, and so does a Shamir. Abraham's existence is sinful yet, Kierkegaard contends, he is not a sinner because of his unconsciousness. Thus we are taken back to the closed discourse in which violence flourishes.

But in the last attempt to portray what happened that ominous morning on Mount Moriah, Kierkegaard introduces a chilling new element into the story: "Then they returned again home, and Sarah hastened to meet them, but Isaac had lost his faith. No word of this had ever been spoken in the world, and Isaac never talked to anyone about what he had seen, and Abraham did not suspect that anyone had seen it."[12] Abraham's supreme act of faith results in Isaac's loss of faith! The father's idolatry opens the eyes of the son; the absurdity of transcendence rules itself out and turns into the unforgettable burden of a traumatically ignoble experience. Finally, paradox breaks down the closed discourse of the morality of killing; we learn that ultimate surrender to religious belief may lead to the ultimate barbarism of repudiating humanity; reflexive self-transcendence comes full circle with the revelation that morality must be an autonomous domain of purpose inherent in the human condition. At last Isaac is freed from Abraham's teleology and imagery, and the birth of a new culture is possible.

The military cultures of all nations play with a similar transcendence. In his powerful novel, *Sacrifice of Isaac*, Neil Gordon has applied this parable to the Israeli military. It is the son who is reflecting on his father, Yossef Benami, a professor and general who is an Israeli national hero and whose other son, Danni, had defected during the 1982 invasion of Lebanon. We are told:

> From far in his memory came the sounds of a fight about the central idea of his father's most famous book. For a moment his mind blanked; then the title came: *Sacrifice and Symbolism*. They had argued, bitterly, about Benami's reading of a biblical story—the sacrifice of Isaac—and clear in his ear he heard his mother's full-throated voice sounding: "Ach, Yossi, how can you be such a fool?", her Yiddish filling the kitchen, reaching up the stairs to his attic room, where he slept next to his brother's abandoned one. "Your own son has left you, and you think it's a story about the Jews. Your son is gone. Your son is gone. Where is the fucking symbolism?"[13]

Later in the novel "Your son is gone" becomes: "You've killed your son."[14] In the end, Benami, for whom "not wanting to die for Israel… was unthinkable,"[15] had sacrificed his father, his wife, and his sons not to a God sending angels, as depicted in Caravaggio's Isaac, "but worse: to an idea, to a country, a country of soldiers."[16] Like Kierkegaard's Isaac, Gordon's Danni realizes that his father "had turned execution-er" and that "[t]hese people around him, these Arabs, they did not feel like the enemy. They felt like himself."[17] It was not God testing Abraham, but Abraham God.

"Abraham I cannot understand, in a certain sense there is noth-ing I can learn from him but astonishment," observed Kierkegaard.[18] He contended that "either Abraham was every minute a murderer, or we are confronted by a paradox which is higher than all mediation."[19] In the story of Abraham the temptation is the ethical itself. A superior telos makes Abraham's silence incomprehensible yet possessed of a religious paradox that forces upon him a kind of action that is marked-ly different from that of ordinary murder; unethical, purposeless action with invocation of a superior telos likewise makes certain kinds of mil-itary activity deeply disturbing morally and intellectually. Soldiers and rebels are both ordered by their superiors to commit atrocities. Perpetrators and victims at the same time, their situation is one of trag-ic responsibility and ironic innocence. They are ordered into action by their superiors with the assurance that "God is on our side."

The nuclear version of such paradox—the readiness to kill inno-cent civilians when demanded by a higher purpose—was underscored by President Truman the day after the civilian populations of Hiroshima and Nagasaki had been scorched to death en masse: "We thank God that it [the atomic bomb] has come to us instead of our enemies: and we pray that He may guide us to use it in His ways and for His purposes." The ethics of targeting noncombatant populations for a higher military purpose has been the driving force behind the Cold War's arms' race. The destruction of a city in order to send a message to the rulers of an enemy power has become the possibility of obliterating the human race if that be "His purpose." Abraham's aberration could not be made more final.

II

Innocence is the quintessential condition of terrorist victimology.
                                    —R. A. Friedlander, *Terrorism and the Law*

Terrorist warfare plays with the shocking incongruence that the perfect victim is chosen randomly and is therefore innocent. The killing
of an enemy soldier is conventional war; planting a bomb in London's
Oxford Street or at the federal building in Oklahoma City is "terrorism." As such a cornerstone of terrorism culture, "innocence" requires
close scrutiny.

The issue of innocent victimology is recognized, yet remains insuf-
ficiently understood, within terrorism discourse. Schmid notes,

> In our samples many authors either stress or at least refer to the inno-
> cence of the victims of terrorism (e.g., Arendt, Bassiouni, Bouthoul,
> Bite, Crenshaw, Fromkin, Friedlander, Green, Gross, Lador-Lederer,
> Leiser, Jenkins, Monday, Post, Sobel, Waldmann, Wilkinson).
> Innocence of what? Not a single author has, to our knowledge, made
> an attempt to develop criteria for establishing this innocence.[20]

He argues that even if innocent people are killed by the explosion of a
bomb in a marketplace, "it cannot be said that they were killed because
of their innocence" but rather "despite their innocence."[21] And he
goes on to ask: "If innocence is irrelevant or at any rate not a condition for becoming a victim, what better substitute can there be?"[22]

Yet the alleged innocence of the victim is clearly not a trivial issue.
At first glance, within the daily rhetorics of terrorism it is the aspect
that is most shocking. We must recognize that, in the same manner
that Abraham's absurd story hides the paradox of religious transcendence, so does terrorist "innocence" conceal an intriguing incongruity
that opens a window upon the entire behavior.

The killing of innocent victims is, obviously, far from restricted to
"terrorism." At the core of liberal belief are the distinctions between
state and society, government and individual, soldier and civilian. Yet
more civilians than soldiers were in fact victimized by the wars of the
second half of the twentieth century. During World War I only around
11 percent of the casualties were civilian, whereas by World War II the
proportion had risen to 53 percent. In the wars of the 1960s, 1970s,
and 1980s it was 52, 68, and 76 percent respectively.[23] In the current
conflicts the estimate is 90 percent.[24] While the practice is not condoned by the Geneva Convention, the destruction of an enemy's cities
by aerial bombing (in which civilian deaths are inflicted deliberately)
has become accepted practice in this century's warfare. The similarity
between the terrorist's car bomb and a bomb dropped from a plane
is too obvious to be ignored.[25] Yet the former commands front-page
attention while the 35,000 victims of the Dresden bombing, for exam-

ple, recede from memory. And what about nuclear warfare? As noted by Wheeler, "One can ask if the distinction of military from civilian is not an anachronism in the nuclear age."[26] Chance even played a part in the selection of Nagasaki for nuclear destruction on August 9, 1945: the target was to have been the city of Kokura, but that morning it was hidden under heavy clouds.

Nevertheless, despite Orwell's plausible question, "Why is it worse to kill civilians than soldiers?,"[27] we do not consider the distinction civilian/combatant irrelevant. Indeed, its frequency notwithstanding, the killing of civilians constitutes a war crime, one for which at least the vanquished may be tried by the victors. Terrorist tactics, too, target innocent bystanders. Thus, the killing of civilians, whether by armies or terrorists, violates the warfare condition that the target should be a combatant. It is precisely the innocence of civilian victims that makes certain acts of war particularly odious.

How is it that successful conventional warfare requires its Gernikas, Dresdens, and Hiroshimas? The indiscriminate killing of civilians has quite different connotations than the destroying of military targets, for it is clearly designed to demoralize the enemy. An exchange of fire among military units takes place within the strategic space of equals and is "limited" by the technology and conventions of warfare. The killing of unarmed people belongs to a different domain; it implies total warfare, in which any pretence of limiting the fight to its military goals is abandoned in favor of attacking the entire enemy community. Thus, there is the qualitative leap in which not only are the combatants to be destroyed but also those associated with them, as if they were guilty by "contagion" through their ties of kinship, culture, and co-citizenship.

Warfare may infer the threat and the reality of a full-fledged attack on the enemy population. This is, however, in conventional warfare the last resort rather than the norm (nuclear warfare is less discriminating). "Terrorism," as ideally portrayed, is nothing but that last inhumane resort to all-out violence. Most so-called terrorist groups would vehemently deny that civilians are their primary targets, but it is also true that they routinely kidnap or kill innocent bystanders. So how can terrorists "justify" such inhumanity?

Ritual sacrifice is the one anthropological model that illuminates the sweeping assault on civilian populations, whether by conventional, nuclear, or terrorist warfare. In this ultimate situation the play with "chance" and the manipulation of "innocence" become *logically* interconnected necessities.

III

Terror is most effective when it is indiscriminate in appearance but highly discriminate in fact.

—T. P. Thornton, "Terror as a Weapon of Political Agitation"

A central part of terrorism discourse characterizes its violence as "random," "indiscriminate," "arbitrary," and "unpredictable." This capriciousness is again proof for Schmid that "innocence or a noncombatant status does not matter"[28] in becoming a terrorist target.

Yet we cannot say that terrorist violence is completely indiscriminate, for clearly some persons run higher risks of becoming victims than others; nor is terrorism as random as mugging. In fact, as noted by Thornton, in most cases victimization appears to be simultaneously both selective and indiscriminate, and its efficiency derives precisely from such confusion of target categories.

Indeed, there seems to be an anomaly in terrorism's selection of targets. On the one hand, there can be such apparent precision that the logic of the message is evident to everyone. The killing of a representative of the established order is a prime example in which the indexical sign (the attack) directs the attention of the audience (the public) to the object (the terrorist's cause) through the catalyst of spectacular publicity (the media). It is the clear purpose of such acts to remove the struggle from the frameworks of law, parliamentary process, or conventional military confrontation. Rather, there is the resort to obvious indexical signing[29] which seeks maximum symbolic impact by employing ritualistic (as opposed to instrumental) political violence. By attacking a representative, the political activist calls into question the legitimacy of the institutionalized status quo, while at the same time sending the message to all of its representatives that "you could be next." Clearly, the efficacy of such an implicit threat is enhanced by the prominence of the victim. Thus, while the private in the army or the cop on his beat may serve the terrorist's purpose at some minimal level, the most indexical message of all derives from the demonstrated ability to strike at the general or prime minister. In this respect, the target of the terrorist attack may be stripped of all ambiguity.

At the same time, however, the selection of terrorist victims may be said to be "random," "arbitrary," and "indiscriminate." It is easy to regard terrorist incidents as inherently irrational, the desperate acts of unbalanced persons. A different view, however, might see them as carefully contrived attempts by the activists to play with chance and innocence as a means of augmenting the shock value of their actions. To appreciate these points it is necessary to disaggregate chance and innocence into gradated, rather than monolithic, categories. In this fashion it becomes possible to understand the terrorist's perspective.

There is little randomness in the selection of the *class* of targets, as defined by national, religious, ethnic, political, or social class features. And, even within the class, the sacrificial victim must possess at least a modicum of symbolic value. Thus, to kidnap an American professor in Boston does not have the same significance as it would in Beirut. Pan Am 103 was selected by the Middle Eastern bombers, not an Air India flight. The government building, the bank or other financial institutions, and the company headquarters of large firms are frequent and obvious targets. Then, too, there is the department store at Christmas season, the subway system at rush hour, the tavern frequented by police officers; all of these are more likely targets than the public library, a church, or a small business. Shock value is a critical consideration.

However, it is equally true that within the class of targets there is considerable randomness. It is this very fact that inspires the terror that the terrorist requires. Thus, any American carrier and any other Pan Am flight would have served the bombers' purposes as well as the ill-fated flight 103. At this point, we are confronted with the paradox and tragedy of innocence.

These actions in which we now engage do not denote what those actions for which they stand *would denote.*

—G. Bateson, *Steps to an Ecology of Mind*

We are primarily interested in the semantics and rhetorics of innocence—in particular with the staging and self-serving use of the word "innocence," as well as its antonym "guilt." A simple comparison will suffice. During the 1980s, on several occasions an aircraft carrying hundreds of passengers was deliberately downed. Consider three instances: in 1983 a South Korean airliner, KAL's flight 007 was shot down off the southwestern coast of Sakhalin Island with 269 people on board; on July 3, 1988, it was Iran Air Flight 655 in the Persian Gulf, on its regular flight from Bandar Abbas to Dubai, with 290 people on board; on December 21, 1988, Pan Am flight 103 was destroyed over Lockerbie, Scotland, on its regular flight from London to New York, with the loss of 259 lives. The first two were attacked by the former USSR and U.S. military forces, respectively; it is still unclear who downed the third aircraft.

No book on terrorism is likely to include KAL 007 and Iran Air 655 tragedies as "terrorist" attacks; Pan Am 103 has become the very paradigm of terrorist atrocity. The U.S. and the former USSR have an easy explanation for their actions: "error." Consequently there was no guilt, no penalty, no reparation to the families' victims, no breach of international law on the part of the perpetrators. The civilian passengers were noncombatants, and it is presumed that they were all "innocent"; yet the two superpowers did not intentionally go after innocent people—they simply "erred"—and it would be inappropriate to say that they massacred innocent people. So those who fired on the luckless Korean and Iranian aircrafts are also "innocent" themselves. The assumption of "We did not mean it" may be invoked to absolve any military atrocity, for there is a kind of play behind the deadly seriousness of warfare, a sort of "We don't really want to kill you; should it happen, it is just accidental, never intentional murder; it is not our purpose to terrorize innocent civilians." The "terrorists," however, are depicted in opposite fashion: they went after innocent passengers, randomly, anonymously, and purposefully. They acted out of complete unconcern for humanity and with the intention of terrorizing the American public.

Thus, any warring faction will advocate an innocent perspective for itself predicated upon the enemy's culpability. This results in glaring instances of a double standard regarding what constitutes "terrorism," as when the literature considers the Beirut attack on U.S. Marines a major terrorist event but not the massacre of 1,800–3,500 noncombatants, mostly women and children, killed in the Sabra-Shatilla conflicts by the Lebanese Phalangists under the supervision of the Israeli army. The construction of "innocence" regarding politically motivated violence may diverge diametrically within the same society as well. In societies containing significant minorities supportive of underground armed violence against the established order, the same event that appears to most as inhumanely brutal may be exculpated by some as quite absolvable. This has to do with the underlying interpretation of causation in starkly different contexts. Consider a typical example: an armed organization places a hidden bomb set to go off within the hour in a supermarket filled with shoppers and then alerts the police. The authorities, through skepticism, ineptness, or conscious decision, withhold the information and a massacre ensues.

Who are the guilty? One can scarcely absolve the bombers, for had they not placed the device nothing would have happened. Can we absolve the authorities? The act of placing the bomb might be perceived, by the supporters of the violent group, as innocuous when compared with the failure to alert the population. It was not the activists' "intention," they would argue, to massacre innocent civilians—this was the result of the police's inaction. This has been ETA's justification after its most deadly actions in train stations and supermarkets; it was also Menachem Begin's argument while maintaining his "innocence" after the group he led, the Irgun, bombed the King David Hotel in Jerusalem in 1946, killing or injuring more than 200 people.[30] Within a context pervaded by chance, therefore, the premising of good and bad intentions is capable of absolving anything at a subjective level.

Yet the most typical "terrorist act" is one in which the activists unabashedly plant bombs in public places in order to kill innocent bystanders and thereby create terror. Violence that is "meant as punishment" is, by its very nature, "not terroristic."[31] If the terrorists' victims deserved punishment, or even death, actions against them would not be terroristic, but rather acts of justice. If skyjackers act in simple retaliation for a wrong previously done to them, such behavior—despite its cruelty—is too comprehensible to arouse the bewilderment that "terrorism" requires. The skyjackers know, of course, that the passengers of the seized or destroyed airplane are not personally guilty and therefore deserving of individual punishment.

Remember Kierkegaard: the sacrificial innocence of Isaac is the paradigm of the absurd extremes that faith may require. Similarly, the very innocence of the victims becomes the paramount message that the activists wish to exploit to their advantage. The tactic of killing innocent bystanders or seizing passengers implies this kind of paradoxical statement: "We know that you consider our victims to be innocent and that you are outraged by this act; we too consider them innocent. Yet we consider ourselves to be innocent since we are forced by circumstances to take into our hands their innocent lives." Such implicit statements make "terrorism" most baffling and incomprehensible.

"Innocence" and "guilt" are compounded by playing with the confusion of categories—one member of a given party (group, nation, religion) stands for the entire class, is the sacrificial lamb. Terrorism is "war by proxy" or "surrogate warfare," we are told. The killing of a few ATF federal agents in Oklahoma City was intended as a blow against the entire organization. This is also how historically the stereotype of "the scapegoat" has operated.[32] The following is an instance of such categorical confusion. In one of ETA's actions seven civil guards were assassinated; and the central government responded by sending 7,000 civil guards to the Basque region. The asymmetrical disproportion (killing one requires replacement of a thousand) is an obvious statement regarding the economy and symbolic nature of terrorist killing. If one casualty can be made to stand for an entire class, then we are not in a context of antagonistic warfare—where strict literalness derives from body count—nor in a conventional war in which technological and strategic superiority prevail. This is warfare in which the physical-terrain/symbolic-territory relationship is obviously confused. It is reminiscent of the inability of so-called primary-process or unconscious thinking to discriminate between "some" and "all"—that is, both the ETA militants and the police perceive "one" killing to be literally the equivalent of "many."

Such difficulties in distinguishing one from many—member from class—have been analyzed by Bateson regarding play activity. It conforms to his glossing of the message, "This is play," as meaning that certain actions do not denote what the actions for which they stand denote. A bite stands for aggression, but a playful bite does not denote aggression. Threat behavior is likewise well known for such difference between what actions denote versus what actually happens, and by now we are accustomed to the argument that a great part of what appears to be combat among animals is simply bluff. Other behaviors, such as risk taking, can also be seen to have their roots in a combination of threat and play. Social dramas, such as the Moro affair, may also turn into a "morality play."[33] We have already considered the properties of ritual, in which discrimination between the action and that which it denotes is not always clearly drawn. "Terrorism" belongs fully to this category of phenomena. It makes a world of difference in understanding terrorism whether we situate it, as is usually done by the literature and in the media, in a context of deadly literalness and instrumental warfare, as opposed to one of deceptive play (threat, histrionics, risk taking, and the like). Then, too, there are the notorious difficulties in drawing the distinction between physical terrain and symbolic territory in contexts pervaded with religious or patriotic sacrament, as is the case with most of terrorism.

It is the combination of being deadly serious (but at the same time engaged in mere provocation, boastful threat, or a trickster's make-believe), of purposefully perpetrating real acts of violence (but with lots of bluff and deception), of deliberately manipulating audiences and the media (while also engaged in life-or-death risk taking) that turns "terrorism" into such a field of semantic confusion. The ease with which both terrorist and counterterrorist can manipulate the categories of innocence (for one's own benefit) and guilt (for the other) gives an indication of the extent to which violence introduces its perpetrators into a playlike frame; that is, the regular meanings of human action disintegrate only to be replaced by arbitrarily symbolic acts, fictional representations of Terror become as factual as actual events, and there is no longer the possibility of achieving consensus regarding what is "real" and what is an "as if" type of violence.

V

The movement of playing has no goal which brings it to an end; rather it renews itself in constant repetition.

—H-G. Gadamer, *Truth and Method*

The life-or-death situation of the underground paramilitary activist, tested with concrete "actions" turned into ordeals by fire, amounts to the fateful experience of a repeated ritual of initiation. This way of life radically molds the personality of the armed militant, and gets engraved in every reaction of the body. The initiated activist, ready for killing and dying, is a *moriturus*.

Yet this situation of ultimate consequence results not only in fear and martyrdom; total acceptance of the *amor fati* can also be experienced as *deep play*, a game turned into a source of exhilaration that all but replaces fear. For the militant activist thus ready, real hardship consists not in the challenge of combat but rather in not being able to carry out "actions." It is action that provides release and long sought gratification, the ultimate accomplishment. In the midst of supreme risk, the play experience, as expressed in song, laughter, camaraderie, and sheer enjoyment, might be so intense as to make the activist feel entirely fearless.[34]

The ritual components become so immediate that the question emerges as to whether the combat, despite its brutal reality, should be considered genuine or spurious, real or pretense. Such questioning, however, makes no sense to the militant player for whom being and playing are one and the same. All is "play," yet nothing is more real and true. Gadamer writes that play encompasses a serious dimension that is "even sacred."[35] The risks may be self-imposed but are nonetheless truly alarming. The difference between the literal and the metaphoric, the real and the feigned, the instrumental and the expressive, evaporates in ritual action. The "war" of a few pistol-toting teenagers against the massive military might of a modern state is surely fictional, an insolent joke at best, yet sufficient affront to provoke an entire army.

Viewed from the perspective of the activists themselves, their willingness to incur personal martyrdom for the cause is an initiatory rite that confers on them warrior status. Rather than being anointed soldiers in the ranks of an army, the activists might be likened more to knights-errant in pursuit of their holy grails. From their perspective, the struggle is epic precisely because it transpires between two ludicrously uneven forces. For the activists to engage their enemy in set, serious battle would clearly be suicidal, hence the recourse to stealth, surprise, suddenness, the selection of targets for their symbolic value. In short, each action becomes more an incident than an encounter, an irritation more than an engagement, and hence suffused with certain qualities of playfulness. Indeed, it is part of the efficacy of the strategy that it seeks to frustrate the enemy by ridiculing its inability to bring its vaunted forces to bear. Authority is humorless and never more vulnerable than when it can be "played" with, particularly with apparent impunity. Thus, despite its deadly dimensions, the rebels' struggle with the authorities is contemplated by their sympathizers as a kind of athletic contest, a source of entertainment. Each new action is greeted with a sense of "Can you believe what they have done now?" It is in this regard that a successful terrorist action may be likened to "scoring a goal" and the reactions of the enraged authorities to that of the bull charging the matador's cape.

For the activist, then, the several ritual and even playful properties of his actions and very existence are far from trivial. Indeed, they are critical to the sustenance of the morale of both the organization and its individual members. For, given the obvious disparity between the forces at play, it is difficult for the activists to perceive a timetable for victory or even its final certainty. Thus, that which sustains momentum and morale is the quest itself rather than its outcome, at least on a daily basis. In short, since each activist is aware that the outcome is quite in doubt, and that even if the quest is finally successful that its attainment will likely transpire at some distant time outside his/her own personal frame of reference, for the individual the game may become more important than the prize.

Consequently, to one deeply immersed in the ritual play, it matters whether there is purposive conclusion at hand. The player is aware, of course, that the cause has serious goals but, in its constant repetition, "the movement of playing has no goal which brings it to an end."[36] Action itself becomes self-sustaining and effortless, purposiveness is not essential to it, the player succumbs to the spell of the game.

The *reductio ad absurdum* creates in the spectators a sense of ironic absurdity that was beautifully captured by Conrad when the secret agent was exhorted by an *agent provocateur* to blow up the first meridian at the Greenwich Observatory! In one of the best exegeses on symbolic violence ever written, we are told (in 1907) that in the secular world an attack upon royalty or religion would be pointless. Rather, "The sacrosanct fetish of to-day is science." The *agent provocateur* then notes:

> Madness alone is truly terrifying, inasmuch as you cannot placate it either by threats, persuasion or bribes. Moreover, I am a civilized man. I would never dream of directing you to organize a mere butchery, even if I expected the best results from it. But I wouldn't expect from a butchery the result I want. Murder is always with us. It is almost an institution. The demonstration must be against learning—science. But not every science will do. The attack must have all the shocking senselessness of gratuitous blasphemy. Since bombs are your means of expression, it would be really telling if one could throw a bomb into pure mathematics. But that is impossible…. What do you think of having a go at astronomy?…
>
> There could be nothing better. Such an outrage combines the greatest possible regard for humanity with the most alarming display of ferocious imbecility. I defy the ingenuity of journalists to persuade their public that any given member of the proletariat can have a personal grievance against astronomy. Starvation itself could hardly be dragged in there—eh? And there are other advantages. The whole civilized world has heard of Greenwich.[37]

Even though it may appear as delirium to strangers, the play of the underground rebel or terrorist is clearly fateful. To become such a character implies entering the realm of death and revival, personal ordeals, and distant journeys. The catch phrase, sanctioned almost as a religious principle by their sympathizers, is likely to be: "They wagered their own lives"; writers on war invoke the same perspective when they discuss war for its own sake.[38] We are once again faced with the closure of self-transcendence. As the making of a soldier requires the initiation of military conscription and training, that of the underground militant derives from self-imposed eschewal of law, society, personal comfort, and a "normal" life. Although not couched in the strict conformity to the highly formalized, hierarchical structure of a regular army, the activist's initiation and life style are no less arduous than the soldier's service. If the soldier's training combines preparations for battle with actual defensive operations such as mounting guard, the activist's character is tested by carrying out actions while enduring extreme threats and vexations. He or she is also a *moriturus* who must live daily with the soldier's dilemma of killing or being killed. Such readiness to die and kill under superior orders, accepted as a condition of life, characterizes the very condition of the activist warrior.

All of this applies not only to the members of the IRA or PLO, but also to Tim McVeigh of the Oklahoma City explosion—and his ilk. When questioned about his role, the ex-army veteran McVeigh reportedly followed the instructions for POWs in a manual published by the Michigan Militia—responding only with his name, rank, and date of birth. He became not only a "patriot," but also a "prisoner of war." McVeigh had actually been in the U.S. army, where he rose to the rank of sergeant and served in Operation Desert Storm, in which he won several medals. According to a roommate, "Tim was the perfect soldier." One of his former commanders described him as "a very normal, good American serving his country."[39] The descent of "the hero" of Desert Storm to "the terrorist" of Oklahoma City is hard to fathom for his ex-comrades, yet the two roles might not be that far apart in McVeigh's warrior soul. If someone was required to turn the dream of antigovernment violence into reality, the *moriturus* of Desert Storm could serve as the *moriturus* of Oklahoma City. Within the booming paramilitary culture of post-Vietnam "warrior dreams"[40] and post-Waco apocalyptic conspiracies, he found a community to nourish and share his fears, a culture that might ascribe the martyr's "heroism" and "innocence" to his actions.

VI

The essential characteristic of non-harmonic tones, however, is said to be that they appear by chance.

—A. Schoenberg, *Theory of Harmony*

The play with purpose and intention is notoriously self-deceptive; any atrocity, whether in the service of "terrorism" or of "counterterrorism," can be easily justified in that context. A field of action is generated by which "our" goal makes sense and excludes "theirs." The connection between act and purpose is internal to this field, a subjective link that outsiders may fail to recognize, thus generating perplexingly opposite interpretations of the same process.

We might compare again the downing of the Iranian airplane in the Persian Gulf by the *Vincennes* and the subsequent destruction of Pan Am flight 103 over Lockerbie. The former was, from the American perspective, an unplanned "accident" having nothing to do with purpose or intention, a view that could hardly be shared by the Iranians; on the other hand, to Americans the Lockerbie incident was a deliberate massacre by "terrorists." If, however, the perpetrators of Lockerbie were Iranians, as many experts have assumed on the basis of the available evidence, then from their perspective the Lockerbie action was retaliation for the loss of the Iranian airplane. Such linkage makes no sense to the families of the Lockerbie victims, who see it as a totally unwarranted act of arbitrary atrocity. It is by appending purposes and switching intentions that the same events might be construed in starkly contradictory terms. This is the kind of teleological play typical of both religion and militarism.

The play with transcendent chance and innocence in the end assumes frightening relevance. If chance "decides" that certain passengers become hostages in a skyjacking to further the political agenda of their captors, such "external" purpose transcends the lives of the victims *and* the perpetrators. Indeed, this capacity to instill such public fear, by designing an action so that each citizen can imagine himself/herself in the victim's stead, is an important measure of the efficacy of "terrorism," as well as of the relative success or failure of a particular act of violence.

The logic of randomness and the play with chance is not defined solely from the perspective of the victim. As we have noted, the activists, too, are largely incapable of affecting the external process, since they are acting on behalf of a cause with its wider organization and in a manner that quite deliberately reduces the set of alternatives by introducing noncorrective elements (such as ultimatums) into the process. They have their orders, which do not empower them to negotiate of their own volition or on their own behalf. In this regard their personal safety is as irrelevant as that of the victims; they are bound by an ethic of personal martyrdom. Thus the fate of the activists, once an action is initiated, is equally "decided" by an external purpose over which they exercise no personal control. It is this perception, again however dimly understood, that lends an additional frightening and sinister dimension to the terrorist action.

We might illustrate the foregoing points by considering the kid-napping of the Basque industrialist, Berazadi, by four ETA activists. Mere teenagers, they took their hostage to their village and held him in the loft of an abandoned barn that belonged to the family of one of the kidnappers. The incident dragged on for several weeks as ETA sought concessions from the Spanish authorities and a ransom from the victim's family. At least publicly, both refused to negotiate. Meanwhile the youths and their hostage became fast friends. He became their cook; they debated politics, played cards, and made plans to have a reunion dinner together in France once their common ordeal was over.

One day the mother of the boy whose family owned the hideout entered the barn and heard noises in the loft. Her son told her what was going on and the captors then informed ETA of the new develop-ment. In light of the protracted and unsuccessful "negotiations," and the growing likelihood that the authorities might rescue the hostage and possibly capture the perpetrators, ETA's inner council met and considered Berazadi's fate. Twice there was a tie in the voting; then one abstained, and by the margin of a single vote it was decided that he must be killed in the interest of ETA's credibility.

The order went out and was carried out by the young men, who were only too aware of their victim's personal innocence. Indeed, there was the added irony that Berazadi, while a moderate, was himself a Basque nationalist. Yet—and this underscores the terrible inhuman-ity inherent in playing with the logic of innocence—the activists too proclaimed their personal innocence in the tragedy!

How so? The military rationale can readily find answers: they were acting out a logic of chance in which random events decided the course of the action (unplanned developments such as being discov-ered and the irony that, unbeknownst to ETA, Berazadi's family was on its way to France with the ransom money the morning he was killed, played a decisive role in the shocking outcome of the affair). They did not purposefully seek to kill Berazadi; they, too, were the vic-tims of chance, the military rationale would argue. Most of all, the entire process was governed by a hierarchical logic in which the final decision rested entirely with the organization, while demanding from its subordinates a disposition of unquestioning obedience and sacri-ficial action.[41] Thus the youths did not kill Berazadi; chance and exter-nal purposes did. It is precisely by virtue of the ritual nature of the act, in which the link between means and ends is neither intrinsic nor immanent but rather refers to a transcendent order, that these stories become so strange and terrifying. Such are the terrors of military innocence.

"What is the purpose of such killing?" we ask in bewilderment. There is in fact "an inevitable tendency to reserve the label [terrorism] not so much for the methods as for the purposes."[42] When asked about such purposes and functions of terrorism, there is agreement that the principal one is "to terrorize."[43] Others, when distinguishing between victim and the target group, note "the purpose is not primarily to terrorize, but to communicate."[44] Instead of asserting redundantly that the main business of terrorism is to terrorize or to communicate, we should examine the *nature* of its purpose. To the extent that "terrorism" is guided by a logic of chance and randomness, it is essentially nonpredictive and hence, strictly speaking, "purposeless." This lack of obvious purpose is uniquely terrifying to contemplate. At first blush, it is what makes the bombings at the World Trade Center and Oklahoma City so bewildering.

In point of fact, terroristic actions are often limited to threats rather than actual violence; it is common practice to plant a bomb with a timing device (thereby ensuring credibility) and then advising the authorities before it goes off. Indeed, terrorist activity often begins with a cycle of threats and actual bombings against targets that have been carefully selected in order to avoid casualties (e.g., the night bombing of a public monument). Since the purpose is to publicize a cause by creating the fear in each citizen that s/he *might* become the innocent victim of seemingly indiscriminate acts, actual casualties are unnecessary, at least until such time that the public and the media become inured to a particular level of political violence. At that point there is, indeed, likely to be a deadly escalation in the frequency and kind of terrorist attacks in an effort to regain the shock value that ensures attention.

The efficacy of "terrorism" therefore turns not so much upon fear struck through sheer numbers of casualties, since one victim is as sufficient as ten or a hundred. Action must be frequent enough to retain credibility yet infrequent enough so as not to abuse the limelight. It is in this light that the militants' resort to infrequent concrete action, intermingled with threat, and bluff, becomes more understandable as a design to raise the level of public apprehension and awareness. Anticipation is always more delicious or frightening, as the case may be, than is the actual experiencing of pleasure or pain. In the terrorism framework it is this very anticipation which translates into the tension inspired by imagined terror, the most terrifying of its possible guises.

It would be wrong to contend that every "terrorist act" is so carefully calculated and so expertly executed as to maximize symbolic impact while minimizing casualties. Terrorist bombs have had the unintended consequences of killing the activists themselves. Things go wrong—coincidence places unintended victims at the wrong place at the wrong time; police officers stumble upon an action in progress, leading to an unplanned shoot-out. Then, too, the typical "terrorist" is likely to be a young male, with all the exuberance and brashness of youth, resulting in a potent mix of bravado and zeal. Of course, there is also the veteran activist, steeled in combat and possibly inured to death, for whom killing may have become "a way of life." Consequently, it is sometimes impossible for even the paramilitary organization to control fully the actions of all its operatives. Still and all, the seemingly rash and random (i.e., logically purposeless) nature of particular acts and activists, however devastating their effects, should not be confused with intentional purpose(lessness) as we seek to understand the phenomenon called "terrorism."

Another limitation upon the arbitrariness of activists is their need to preserve legitimacy in the eyes of their own supporters. For a rebel movement to be significant it must represent more than a cause to be held dear by a few dozen or a few hundred activists themselves. Rather, at the very least its goals, if not necessarily its means, must strike a sympathetic chord within a significant minority of the affected population. This places certain limitations upon the terrorist organization's range of flexibility. It must, at all costs, avoid alienating its own constituency.

In this regard underground militant organizations are quite capable of committing "historic error." A prime example was the bombing by ETA of a supermarket in Barcelona. While ETA—which does not have a policy of planting bombs to produce civilian casualties[45]—claims that it informed the authorities prior to the explosion and nothing was done; the blast killed 22 persons. This prompted mass demonstrations in Catalonia (where shortly before 40,000 voters supported the HB political party closely aligned with ETA). Several prominent Basque activists disaffiliated with the organization and denounced the deaths as indefensible murders. In short, the incident was a total internal and public-relations disaster for ETA, a fact largely acknowledged by the organization itself.

Ultimately, the "terrorist" seeks to shock the public by playing with nonimmanent purpose and easily renders, as if by contagion, single acts of sparse violence into alarming symbolic statements of all-out challenge to the established order. But the actual reality of such a threat resides in the perception and interpretation of the audience. To the extent that it terrifies the public, terrorism achieves its goal; to the extent it provokes awareness of the symbolic nature of the provocation, it loses its grip on the collective imagination. Only then can we redirect our attention from the imaginary terror of alien invisible forces to the real terror of "ordinary" militarism in the contemporary world.

Militant activism is adamant in stating, "This is war." Yet, at the same time, the playful elements of such an obviously symbolic behavior cannot avoid raising the question, "Is this war?" The positive or negative answer to the question appears to depend on the reaction it provokes. If an entire army is mobilized to respond to the hesitant challenge posed by terrorist provocation, then obviously this is *real* war and the ritual threat has achieved its goal. If obliterating one police officer requires a thousandfold substitution, then the single heinous act is tantamount to a massive elimination. The art of the *trompe l'oeil* school of painting consists in imitating nature so perfectly that the viewer is invited to be fooled while perceiving the skillful deception itself. The art of terrorism is based upon concealment of the deceptive psychological realism of Terror; the traumatized viewer must be incapable of suspecting any manipulation of the semantics in the act.

In short, we are confronted with a system so different that its violent stridency sounds completely chaotic when experienced with the conventional chords of accepted functional harmony. As Schoenberg observed in his new theory of harmony, the essential characteristic of nonharmonic tones is that they seem to appear "by chance." Such action is "arbitrary" from the viewpoint of the subject; yet what is noise in terms of ordinary language turns out to be meaningful music in the "nonharmonic" system of atonality or ritual behavior.

Purposefulness, as defined here, is quite independent of causality, initial or final.... Since we consider purposefulness a concept necessary for the understanding of certain modes of behavior we suggest that a teleological study is useful if it avoids problems of causality and concerns itself merely with an investigation of purpose.

—A. Rosenblueth, N. Wiener, and J. Bigelow,
"Behavior, Purpose and Teleology"

In order to understand terrorist "arbitrariness" and the "innocence" of its victims, the key issue to be considered is that the action takes place, ideal-typically, within a logical space dominated by *chance* election. It is not that the victim is chosen "on the condition" that s/he be innocent (in which case the guilty would be excluded), but by a logic of chance which removes the action to a different realm of possibility and meaning.

Confronted with chance, the distinction between innocence and guilt simply disappears—one is not personally responsible for one's fate. Chance makes all outcomes equally innocent; such innocence is not the result of personal subjectivity, it is implied by the very logic of fortuitous chance.

It is indispensable to realize that chance causation and the innocence of the victim logically imply one another; when innocent bystanders suffer the seemingly unplanned consequences of random terrorist actions, it is "by accident." Yet these are the very ingredients essential to the creation of a context of ritual sacrifice. To ensure the innocence of the sacrificial victim, many societies have instituted the practice of drawing lots. Chance election guarantees general awareness that the victim is personally innocent.[46]

To kill a person for an offense is an act of justice; to kill in order to placate an angry god is ritual sacrifice. "Terrorism," like ritual sacrifice, requires that its offering be pure, that is, the victim (which condenses the purpose and meaning of the action) has to be ideally innocent, thereby invoking a logic of chance through random selection.

Randomness is accompanied, however, by a limited set of alternatives, and playing with chance approximates magical kinds of causation rather than instrumental ones. This means that the billiard-ball model of cause and effect has to be dismissed in favor of ritual or "negative" types of causation. In the contrast between ritual logic based on chance and instrumental logic based on technical means-ends linkages, the very notions of feedback, form, and process are essentially different. Failure to appreciate this distinction converts the concept of "terrorism" into the anomalous aberration that is so prevalent in the depictions of it by both the popular and scientific literatures.

Systems theory and cybernetics provide the means for avoiding the billiard-ball model of positive causation. Cybernetically, what matter are the alternative possibilities, those that could have occurred but did not because there were restraints—explanation in this mode is a kind of *reductio ad absurdum*. Asked about why they do what they do, the militant activists reply, "There is no other way, no other solution." It is thus particularly promising to focus upon purpose rather than cause. Terrorist madness, as much as Abraham's absurdity, derives from the manipulations and deceptions of teleology. The inner logic of "terrorism," in its ideal performance, should be studied as a deliberate play with purpose and as a deceptive confusion of various teleological levels.

In fact, the victim/target differentiation is regarded in the literature as a major *fundamenta divisionis* of terrorism. That is, we must distinguish between the victim who is the "target of violence" but not the prime "target of terror," a wider specific group which is the "target of demands" and the general public that is the "target of attention." The structure of the terrorist event implies thus a triangular relationship between perpetrator, victim, and target. Schmid illustrates the point with the attempted murder of U.S. President Ronald Reagan (victim) by John W. Hinkley Jr. (perpetrator) to impress the actress Jodie Foster (target).[47] Schmid notes, "This differentiation should be one of the most important elements in any definition of terrorism."[48] This characterization of terrorism has been gaining support ever since Walter and Thornton first suggested it in 1964. Yet what is so "terroristic" about such a triadic structure, particularly when Schmid himself is well aware that it is germane to any type of warfare as well as to standard (i.e., nonterroristic) kidnapping and assassination? It is even present in nonviolent struggles such as a strike over better wages.

According to the discourse we are examining, what distinguishes "terrorism" is its recourse to a transcendent logic of chance and an ethic of personal martyrdom. In this regard it does not constitute a rational-technical behavior of immanent purpose, such as is the case with conventional warfare, standard political violence, and industrial strife. Such "transcendence" derives initially from the purely logical terms of higher purpose. If "chance" has disposed that certain passengers be in a particular skyjacking and that they be held hostage for the obtainment of political objectives, such external purpose transcends the lives of the victims and renders them powerless to influence their own fate. If the hostages could influence the behavior of the skyjackers, by negotiating with them, for instance, the system would have immanent feedback and purpose, and the nature of the triadic relationship would change radically. Such *external* purpose and the innocence and impotence of the victim regarding his or her own fate are logically implicated.

A related transcendence that distinguishes "the terrorist" from the soldier, the hit man, or the simply deranged or disgruntled perpetrator of a violent act, is his total and open-ended devotion to *a cause.* Thus, a soldier is a salaried temporary employee whose personal agenda may, but more frequently does not, include a willingness to die. A contract killer is a professional whose services are for hire. He is most certainly not predisposed to personal martyrdom, though a sense of professional pride or "ethics" may seal his lips if apprehended by the authorities. A deranged or disgruntled person may throw personal caution to the winds, and even lose his/her life in near suicidal fashion in a burst of violence.

On the basis of this connection between terrorism and a cause, the attempted assassination of President Reagan would qualify not as a terrorist act but as the violent outburst of a deranged individual, such as when a sociopathic racist guns down school children or a disgruntled employee fired from his job shoots his former employer. In this latter event we might see a headline "Former Employee Terrorizes Workplace," but we would never read "Terrorist Attacks Former Workplace." There is a world of difference between the verb "terrorize" and the noun "terrorist." The former is applied in generic fashion and is often a euphemism for "sudden" or "random" violence, whereas the latter is much more specific. The difference is respected in practice by the media, if not always perceived in the abstract. In making the distinction there is at least implicit recognition that "terrorism" is purposive behavior, even when its purposes are but dimly perceived, if at all.

In short, it is pointless to maintain that terrorist groups have no purposes of their own. To the contrary, as if to respond to such accusations, terrorists usually accompany their most publicized actions with quite explicit statements about their goals. Indeed, it is the purpose of the former to call attention to the latter.

Dealing with the simultaneously purposeful and purposeless dimensions of the terrorist act places us squarely within the realm of symbolic violence. Thornton was the first to characterize terrorism as a "symbolic act." However, he added that this does not imply that the victim is killed "only symbolically and not in fact; rather, it means that the terroristic act is intended and perceived as a symbol."[49] The symbolic concept permitted Thornton to distinguish terrorism from sabotage and assassination, which, as a general rule, are "nonsymbolic." This approach has been further developed by Crenshaw, for whom

> sabotage and assassination are means of terrorism only if they are facets of a broader strategy. When such acts of violence accomplish in

themselves the total objective of the assassin or the saboteur, their political significance is limited.[50]

Assassination can thus be seen as murder that achieves its ends through the act itself, whereas terrorist murders have an ulterior purpose. By this standard definition, Oklahoma City is not "terrorism."

In the same manner that a gaming device can be designed to produce random outcomes and Russian roulette surrenders even personal life to the play with chance, so can political or military action make use of purposelessness as a weapon against convention. "Terrorism," in its extreme form, can be portrayed exclusively as a military strategy premised on deliberate purposelessness. The weapon in the hands of a regular soldier has the clear purpose of firing upon a well-determined enemy target; the same weapon in the hands of "a terrorist" can be said to be "purposeless" in the sense that it does not have a definite target. From this perspective, if the IRA or ETA strike against British or Spanish military targets, it is guerrilla warfare between two belligerents within clearly defined military methods and goals; when they engage in indiscriminate bombings of public places in London or Madrid, it is sheer "terrorism"—the targets are chosen randomly in a deliberate attempt to shock the population. Since their enemy's military targets are so much more powerful in number and capacity, the only tactical advantage remaining to small militant groups seems to consist in changing the very rules of the game: they cannot inflict military defeat, but they can impose a new system in which targets will be selected by chance. Such purposelessness with respect to its victims, while purposeful to the interests of the organization, is the reason why terrorism discourse is so difficult to understand.

The study of purpose, as indicated by the opening epigraph of this section, is a crucial field of inquiry in behavioral sciences. A primary distinction is that purposeful behavior can be subdivided into its teleological ("feedback") and nonteleological ("nonfeedback") aspects. In its restricted negative sense, the term feedback is used "to signify that the behavior of an object is controlled by the margin of error at which the object stands at a given time with reference to a relatively specific goal."[51] If feedback is required for purposeful behavior, "by non-feed-back behavior is meant that in which there are no signals from the goal which modify the activity of the object *in the course of the behavior*."[52]

To be effective, many types of military and nonmilitary violence incorporate a dimension of nonfeedback or deliberate purposelessness. That is, the actual victim cannot affect the outcome during the course of the action. The daily murder by a "stray bullet" in New York is perhaps the most telling instance of purposeless nonmilitary violence—what goes "astray" has no target yet kills. The most blatant example of military purposelessness is nuclear arms,[53] in general, a degree of "purposeless" killing of innocent victims is intrinsic to all types of conventional warfare. Yet it is "terrorism" that, according to its discourse, epitomizes the killings of innocent victims chosen randomly. Terrorist "anomaly" imputes "normalcy" to state violence.

Ironically, the same period in history in which nations have created military weapons systems capable of destroying humanity itself, a holocaust that could be triggered by a technological error, is also the one that creates the figure of the loathsome Terrorist intent on nothing but random killing. The absurdity of the believer Abraham—ready to kill yet blameless—like the absurdity of warrior McVeighs—who massacre innocents yet turn into POWs—is the nemesis of business-as-usual militarism's play with purpose and innocence in the defense of national boundaries and democratic values.

6

TERROR, TABOO, AND THE WILD MAN

"Taboo," that familiar yet most exotic of terms in both everyday speech and academic jargon, regards the unspeakable. "The unspeakable act of terrorism" is the quintessential taboo in contemporary political discourse. As with any tabooed subject, its mere invocation would appear to foreclose the need for any further discussion. If there is any such thing as consensus in this world, shouldn't we all be able to agree that terrorism is a heinous crime—end of the story? Even for the anthropologist, accustomed to examining other peoples' taboos "objectively," the one on terrorism within our own social time and social space might seem such a logical appeal to universal human values as to preclude any need for further investigation.

Indeed, the very attempt to "know" how the terrorist thinks or lives can be deemed an abomination. Such a viewpoint is found not only in newspaper editorials but in the works of prominent terrorism writers such as Conor Cruise O'Brien. When *The Guardian* argued that the IRA's political motivations needed to be recognized, and appealed, socratically, to "know thine enemy," O'Brien noted in *The Observer*, "When we are summoned to make an effort to understand them…it is a way of deflecting indignation and preparing surrender—'know thine enemy' may be a first stage in giving in to him…. It is an invitation in fact to acquiesce in legitimating terror."[1] We know of no other field in which the call for tabooing knowledge in the interest of moral indignation can be issued by a leading figure.

In this chapter we will equate "terrorism" and "taboo," not only in order to bring to the fore the antinomies of norm and anomaly, lawfulness and lawlessness, normalcy and pathology, pattern and chaos, the civilized and the barbaric—in short, the dynamics of form and formlessness—but also to reveal the extent to which transgression and terror are, in the final analysis, cultural constructions amenable to demythification. We call particular attention to the absurdity of attributing enormous power to "terrorists" who have been mythified and then tabooed.

The politics of blacklisting archetypal "enemies" of the liberal state by ascribing the label "terrorist" to those singled out by the State Department is key to the efficacy of terrorism discourse. So we must examine how the figure of the loathed villain is constructed. This is semantic territory rich in cultural tradition.

In this regard we might say that "terrorism" is the latest embodiment of an old theme—civilization locked in deadly struggle with wildness. Terrorist literature is filled with the horror of savagery. If the creation of the science of anthropology has been perceived as a manifestation of the modernist fascination with the primitive, the even more recent birth of terrorism studies is, far from any anthropological romance, a new scholarly attempt to penetrate the dark mysteries of "savage political evil." Hence, it is instructive to see how anthropology has dealt with all sorts of savagery—from incest to killing, from headhunting to cannibalism. For the purposes of this essay it is particularly enlightening to examine the ways in which wildness has been continuously invoked in the name of order, and how savage instincts have been manufactured from the fears of the colonizers' imagination. The mimetic result between the savagery attributed to the Native Americans and the one perpetrated on them by the European colonists is all too well known; in Taussig's words, "the colonizer reifies his myths about the savage, becomes subject to their power, and in so doing seeks salvation from the civilization that torments him as much as the savage on whom he has projected his anti-self."[2]

̣
I

*Ritual pollution...arises from the interplay of form and surrounding form-
lessness. Pollution dangers strike when form has been attacked.*
                                        —M. Douglas, *Purity and Danger*

Abjection is above all ambiguity.
                                        —J. Kristeva, *Powers of Horror*

According to terrorism discourse, abrogation of form is quintessential
to all aspects of terroristic warfare. Explicit structure, whether social,
logical, legal, or moral, is systematically violated and replaced with the
polluting formless powers of terrifying chaos and near magical action.
Such transgression of form characterizes everything intrinsic to whatever is labeled "terrorism" (its logic of chance and innocence, its disregard for any fixed rule, the bluff of ritual threat, the condensation of
action, the contagiousness of taboo, even the very self of the defiled
terrorist) and transforms it into a paramount candidate for the
vagaries of the collective imagination.

According to the anthropological literature, performances governed by metaphysical ideas and powers, such as positive luck and
mana or negative sorcery and taboo, are dependent on the interplay
between form and formlessness. These powers and dangers may not
pertain to the formal social structure but are still decisive in the social
and conceptual organization of the community that is governed by it.
That interplay characterizes ritual pollution. If polluting dirt is essentially disorder—that which must not be included if a pattern is to be
maintained—"terrorism," too, implies systemic disorder and, like dirt,
is itself a residual category. Disorder, however, symbolizes both danger
and power—the more disorderly and dangerous a behavior, the more
power it exerts against the ordered system. Terrorism discourse makes
good use of the premise that "ritual recognizes the potency of disorder."[3] Dirt, lawlessness, the lack of boundaries are all formless, yet have
the power to create new social forms.

Difficulties with control are typical of the terrorism phenomenon.
As befits contagious plagues, it is not easily "contained." Inexorably, it
tends to be "international." Consider a typical opening statement of a
book on terrorism:

> Mostly indiscriminate and often state supported, terrorism has
> emerged over the years as perhaps the most complex amd least pre-
> dictable threat to the security of the United States, its allies, and other

nations as well. No longer a weapon used only by marginal, isolated groups, terrorism relies on networks of communication that transcend international boundaries linking these groups with one another.[4]

At the same time, while the public may perceive "the terrorists" as utterly undisciplined and unpredictable, many of them claim to be "soldiers." Underground activism does not lack its own forms of hierarchy and formal structure but, when compared with the institutionalized formality and regularity of a conventional soldier's lifestyle, these tend to be latent and informal. The formlessness of an ethnic insurgency, for example, frequently begins with its being the cause of a "stateless nation," one without national institutions or recognition under international law. The hierarchical structure may be so rudimentary in an underground group that it appears to be absent altogether. Formal pledges of loyalty to the flag or the country are unnecessary; military stripes, etiquette, forms of address, and other ceremonial formulae can be omitted. The territorial entity for which the insurgent group fights is likely to be defined more by a legendary past and cultural symbolism than by recognized present boundaries. The activists' mode of fighting cannot replicate the technical-mechanical methods of a quantitatively vastly superior army. Rather, they must rely upon ritualized means of stratagem, bluff, play, and other inconstant forms of momentous action.

By extending this ethnographic allegory, we might add that formlessness affects, ultimately, the very persona of "the terrorist" who, like the witch, shaman, or trickster in traditional cultures, has to assume fundamental ambiguity at the margins of society; this is what explains his capacity to encompass the seemingly contradictory functions of hero and criminal, guardian angel and demon, martyr and murderer.

II

To us it [taboo] means, on the one hand, "sacred," "consecrated," and on the other, "uncanny," "dangerous," "forbidden," "unclean."

—S. Freud, *Totem and Taboo*

As Freud's description in the epigraph underscores, there is an odd proximity between the notions of the "sacred" and the "tabooed." The common perception, turned by now into a cliché, that "one man's terrorist is another man's freedom fighter," reflects similar ambivalence about persons who are simultaneously dangerous and consecrated. It is both paradox and puzzlement that the very same subjects are loathsome, murderous terrorists for a large segment of the population yet patriotic, Christ-like heroes for others. This antinomian quality makes "terrorism" into an incomprehensible phenomenon unless we recognize in such ambivalence the essential proximity between the sacred and the defiled.

Freud reminded us that we can speak of the unconscious only by analogies, and that most of what we can say about that "dark inaccessible part of our personality; what little we know of it…is of a negative character and can be described only as a contrast to the ego."[5] Nothing captures those negative aspects as emblematically as a taboo.

Taboos are rooted in the fundamental need to control dangerous behavior. Steiner concluded that the two social functions of taboo are: (1) the classification and identification of transgressions, and (2) the institutional situating of danger, both by the segregation of it and by protecting society from it.[6] "Terrorism," currently portrayed as the most intractable politico-military danger in many national and international scenarios, fulfills these two functions to a tee. The "problem" has become extraordinarily acute given contemporary awareness of the threat of human annihilation in the nuclear age. Even with the end of the Cold War, terrorism remains the unyielding danger, the genie out of the bottle that no system or canon can control. With the terrorist menace, then, we are at the very heart of the political darkness of danger and taboo.

What "terrorism" brings to the fore is the relevance of anomaly for social science. Far from being an oddity, we are regularly confronted with social anomaly throughout history, as illustrated egregiously by millennial cults, the ritual killing of kings, the burning of alleged witches in sixteenth-century Europe, infamous massacres such as the one on St. Bartholomew's Day in France in 1572, macabre exhumations of corpses in revolutionary Spain during the 1930s, the Kenyan Mau-Mau movement, the North American Ghost Dance, the Iranian Revolution, and so many other events. "A paradoxical relation and a dialectic tension thus exists between taxonomy and anomaly," wrote Lincoln.[7] Taxonomic structures are potentially threatened by marginal anomalies that, by their very existence, reveal the shortcomings, contradictions, and arbitrariness of such structures. Hence, anomaly and danger are closely related. Deliberate sacrilege, violation of taboos, displays of obscenity are common in revolutionary or millenarian upheavals. This liminal stage of "no rules" evokes the existence of underlying ritual processes before "new rules" are formulated;

ritual recognizes the potency of disorder. If the relationship between taxonomy and anomaly is both paradoxical and dialectical, so is the connection between "terrorism" and the social group that practices it.

Nothing is inherently anomalous; it is within the framework of a given taxonomic system that some things become so. Yet, as Lincoln points out, two contrasting formulations can be granted to the same countertaxonomy: "(1) an anomaly is any entity that defies the rules of an operative taxonomy or (2) an anomaly is an entity, the existence of which an operative taxonomy is incapable of acknowledging."[8] Just as social deviance produces outlaws when the legitimacy of the system is affirmed and rebels when the system is judged illegitimate, so does the same underground military activism yield freedom fighters and terrorists, depending on the legitimacy granted to the cause. Lévi-Strauss's observation about totemism is applicable here: "It is not because they are totemic that such systems must be regarded as irregular; it is because they are irregular that they can only be totemic."[9] As irregular systems become "totemic" and cultural anomalies are isolated by the prohibitions of "taboo," so are antinomian personalities and uncompromising forms of struggle ostracized as "terrorist." The discourse on terrorism is about such aberrant anomaly.

Men with one eye, and others with dog's noses, who ate men, and that when they took a man, they cut off his head and drank his blood and castrated him.
                    —C. Columbus, *The Voyages of Christopher Columbus*

The great historical encounters with native savages forced western man to face his own alarming vagueness concerning the definition of "humanity." Suddenly everything was assaulted by anomaly. Thus John of Holywood described the natives of America in 1498 as "blue in colour and with square heads."[10] History tells us that Columbus found the Caribbeans to be human beings and not monsters when he first met them, but soon rumors were spread that dog-headed cannibals (the term "cannibal" derives from Columbus's name for Carib) inhabited the as-yet unvisited islands, which then provided a moral justification for the extermination of the locals in order to found European plantations worked by African slaves.[11]

But the greatest confusion of the civilized Europeans was over the nature of their own humanity as reflected in their attitudes and beliefs toward the barbarians of the New World. Upon the discovery of

America, the proponents of classifying the natives as "natural slaves" adduced cannibalism and incest and invoked Aristotle to make their case.[12] Yet the long debates were not primarily about behavior or attributes, but regarded the *essential qualities* of the brutalized natives' humanity. In short, did they possess a *human* soul?

For Greek and Roman thinkers, humanity was differentiated by largely benign physical and cultural factors, whereas for Hebrew and Christian thinkers such differences became far more essentialist and imbued with moral and metaphysical overtones. The Judeo-Christian qualitative and hierarchical distinctions between animal and human souls was far beyond the horizontal/relational one in Greek thought between city dwellers and the barbarians out in the wilderness, i.e., beyond social bounds. The hierarchical view was that, as human/animal distinctions were qualitatively different states of being (immortality being a major consequence of the difference), so also were the we/normal versus they/native differences within humanity. Animal souls were nothing but pure desire; rational man had the right to domesticate or hunt the beasts. A similar fate awaited people with animal souls.[13]

Wild men during the Middle Ages, much as the "barbarians" during the classical Greek period, were contrasted with civilized people on the basis of *law*. For Aristotle, humanity was the capacity to behave as "a political animal" within the confines of the city (although urban women, slaves, and merchants were denied such privilege); those outside its borders had no possibility of full humanity because they were beyond the law. In premodern thought, the myth of the Wild Man, with its various archetypal forms and variations, held irrepressible fascination for western civilization. With "wildness" we got the closely related notions of "savagery," "madness," "heresy," "barbarism." As a testament to its enduring power, the second part of the twentieth century has added a new type to this old myth, a "monster" that furthers arbitrary evil—namely, "the terrorist."

The "terrorist" perpetrates a frontal assault on any type of norm, whether tactical, political, or moral. It is antinomy in its most naked form. Terrorism discourse is the attempt to taxonomize anomaly, narrativize nonsensical logic, categorize chaos itself. Such attempts are futile, but the failures of the students and reporters of "terrorism" are far from inconsequential. The single enemy, identified as international in scope and situated in a nuclear era, falls beyond the ordinary realm of humanity. This translates immediately into the premise that we cannot afford to be too humane when confronting terroristic inhumanity, that perhaps we should not be overly concerned with law while combatting evil itself; that we, too, perhaps must practice a little terrorism, but of the right kind, in order to contain the malignancy. Confronted by the unmitigated evil of "terrorism," shouldn't we accordingly be prepared to break, or at least bend, any rule ourselves in order to behead the repellent monster?

Terrorists are "the new barbarians." Lawless youths or extemporary warriors may embrace the "terrorist" myths of boundless power. Yet we too should not forget the ancient western tradition of fearing imaginary monsters that are always located outside of one's own community and its moral spheres. If for centuries the alienated and repressed part of humanity kept reappearing in the Occidental collective imagination in the dreadful forms of the Wild Man, currently the Terrorist appears to be the epitome of such savagery for the western psyche. He is, we are told by the daily news, a Palestinian, a Muslim, an Iranian, an Irishman, a Basque, a Colombian. We may call this, with Hayden White, a "*re*mythification" of the Wild Man, for it works in the same way that myth worked in ancient cultures:

> That is, as a projection of repressed desires and anxieties, as an example of a mode of thought in which the distinction between the physical and the mental worlds has been dissolved and in which fictions (such as wildness, barbarism, savagery) are treated, not as *conceptual instruments* for designating an area of inquiry or for constructing a catalogue of human possibilities, or as *symbols* representing a relationship between two areas of experience, but as *signs* designating the existence of things or entities whose attributes bear just those qualities that the imagination, for whatever reasons, insists they must bear.[14]

If the myth of the Wild Man sustained the perception of dog-headed cannibals when Europeans met American natives, such canine imagery is far from extinct when dealing with terrorist subjects. President Reagan, for example, set up his order for an attack on Qaddafi's life in 1986 by first calling him a "mad dog."[15] "Why the Dogs Had to Die" was the front page news in Britain's *The Sun*, referring to the unarmed IRA men killed at Gibraltar by the British police in March of 1988. The literal crudity of such animal analogies in the literature on terrorism may be appreciated from examples such as the following:

> Although, as has been pointed out, the way to defeat the terrorist is to keep him out, like a poisonous snake, it can be argued that even

poisonous snakes have their place in the balance of nature. Moreover, the terrorist is more intelligent and resourceful than a snake and has political and intellectual as well as merely instinctive motives.[16]

Similarly, the Likud leader Benjamin Netanyahu invokes "the realization that wild beasts prowl our airways and waterways...fleeing to countries which respect, indeed worship, the law of the jungle."[17] The natural reaction called for by such depictions of loathsome beasts is one of the merciless hunt. This is an instance taken from an editorial of a Madrid newspaper:

> The activists of ETA, who are not men, who are beasts. To what degree do beasts deserve human rights?... Beasts are enclosed behind the heaviest bars that there are in the village; first they are hunted by all kinds of tricks. And if in the venture someone is killed, bad luck, or good luck.... No human rights come into play when a tiger must be hunted. The tiger is searched after, is hounded, is captured, and if necessary is killed.[18]

The very definition of the "monstrous" natives' essence as subhuman justified the European colonizer's extermination, ownership, or subdual of them. Similar ironic predications between colonizer and colonized countries are far from extinct at the end of the twentieth century. In 1986, for instance, under U.S. pressure after its own raids on Libya, the twelve countries that make up the European Community produced at the Tokyo summit a blacklist of nations in which almost all their indigent neighboring countries of Africa and the Middle East were identified as terrorist.[19] When we watch historically holier-than-thou countries such as England, Germany, Spain, France, Italy, Holland...stigmatizing their Third World neighbors Libya, Syria, Iran, Iraq, Tunisia, Jordan, Algeria, Sudan, North Yemen, South Yemen...as "terrorist" nations, globally and categorically, then we are reminded once again of Columbus's impudently ironic use of native inhumanity as justification for European barbarism. Since defending her borders from African starvation and Middle East violence has become one of the major obsessions of the new Europe, it is quite useful for it to define the excluded as terrifying savages. Yet the ploy does not quite work, since at some level we find ourselves confused as to the content of our humanity as reflected in our own attitudes and actions regarding destitute and "barbarous" peoples.

IV

The common links between my two stories are, as you can see, the themes of terroristic massacre, cannibalism by imaginary dog-headed monsters, a political opportunism that makes your opponents virtuous or monstrous as a matter of convenience without any regard for empirical facts of the case, and the principle that if the lack of shared moral values is so complete that the "other" comes to be categorised as a wild animal, then every imaginable form of terroristic atrocity is not only attributed to the other side but becomes permissible for oneself. Indeed, counter terrorism becomes, in a bizarre sense, a religiously sanctioned moral duty.

— E. Leach, *Custom, Law, and Terrorist Violence*

Consider the public discussion in Great Britain as to whether terrorist suspects can be lawfully shot to death in cold blood. In 1982 the Ulster police killed six unarmed Irish youths;[20] the government ordered an internal investigation to determine whether the police had a secret shoot-to-kill policy regarding terrorist suspects. The police officer in charge of the British investigation, John Stalker, was relieved of his post and then expelled from the corps when, as revealed later in his book of memoirs,[21] he was on the verge of uncovering definitive proof that there was such a policy. The same issue reappeared in March of 1988 in Gibraltar when British security agents wounded and then coldly finished off three Irish youths who not only were unarmed but, according to a witness, had surrendered with their hands in the air.[22] British television, resisting considerable British Government pressure, broadcast reports of the event, forcing the matter into the courts. On trial was a policy implicitly condoned by Thatcher's government and supported by a large majority of the British population, who believed that any measure is justified when employed against "terrorists." The court ruled that the killings were "lawful." As the leader of the Social Democratic and Labour Party, John Hume MP, put it: "It is quite clear that a section of the RUC and the British Army have now been authorized to shoot to kill anyone about whom they are suspicious."[23]

In Germany, likewise, on June 27, 1993, a suspected leader of the Red Army Faction (charged not with committing terrorist acts but simply of belonging to a terrorist organization) was arrested and executed by the antiterrorist commandos known as GSG-9 as he lay bound helpless in police custody; the testimony of twenty-two witnesses forced the resignation of Interior Minister Rudolf Seiters.[24] In July 1993, Peru's President Alberto Fujimori, in a meeting of Latin American leaders in Brazil, bragged openly that had he ever met the Maoist guerrilla leader Abimael Guzmán face to face while armed, "I would have sent him to hell."[25] Similarly, Spain's Socialist Party and government under Felipe González organized a state-financed, anti-ETA group named GAL ("Anti-Terrorist Liberation Group"). These death squads under official Spanish protection have claimed responsibility for killing twenty-seven Basque political refugees in Southern France between 1983 and 1987.[26] Such is the power of the terrorist bogeyman to turn even heads of state into vigilantes.

These examples pose an obvious dilemma. The terrorists themselves shoot to kill without warning, so what is wrong with answering in kind? The difference, of course, has to do with the formal legitimacy and behavior of a legally constituted government versus the "formless" illegitimacy of terrorists. What is portrayed as ordinary terrorist behavior is most extraordinary as government response to it. Arbitrary terroristic killings make no claim of legality; indeed, they are extralegal statements questioning the legitimacy of the constituted legal order. When the constitutional forces of that order resort to similar tactics, there is the need to justify them in the name of "lawful killing."

Indeed, in the counterterrorism campaign, due process is apt to become the first victim. It did not come as a surprise, therefore, that in the early 1990s several judicial decisions were overturned in Great Britain when people sentenced to life imprisonment as terrorists were found innocent after serving many years in prison. The best-known cases were those of the Birmingham Six and the Guildford Four. In the latter case, made famous by the movie *In the Name of the Father*, after the convicted had already served fourteen years in prison the original verdicts were dismissed when it was proven that the state had intentionally fabricated evidence and withheld crucial information from the defense.[27] In another extraordinary legal case, in 1992 the U.S. Supreme Court decided that anybody suspected of terrorism residing in a foreign country could be forcibly abducted by American agents and brought to the United States to stand trial irrespective of the legal niceties and inconveniences of mere matters such as extradition treaties. The United Nations condemns as contrary to international law such international abduction of even the most notorious of criminals.

Counterterrorism's shoot-to-kill policy, its abrogation of due process, its frequent resort to torture "point to a central truth—that there are few areas of state activity in which the temptation to abandon important ethical norms is so strong and so pervasive." Adam Roberts further tells us that all too often the legitimate efforts to combat terrorist movements and actions end up as "the use of terrorism against terrorism."[28] Prominent counterterrorism specialists, such as Brian Jenkins, in fact seem to advocate coopting terroristic strategy as part of "indirect forms of warfare."[29] And thus we are all urged to become terrorists. At this juncture, we fall fully into the trap envisioned by Conrad expressed through the words of "The Professor," the bombmaker, who notes:

> To break up the superstition and worship of legality should be our aim. Nothing would please me more than to see Inspector Heat and his likes take to shooting us down in broad daylight with the approval of the public. Half our battle would be won then; the disintegration of the old morality would have set in its very temple.[30]

In the final analysis we are confronted with the "epistemic murk" by which narratives of terrorist savagery become indispensable for maintaining terrorism discourse and policy. This reminds us of the "diseased imagination" of European colonizers in Colombia early in this century who, in the words of the judge Rómulo Paredes, "saw everywhere attacks by Indians, conspiracies, uprisings, treachery, etc.; and in order to save themselves from these fancied perils…they killed, and killed without compassion."[31] Just as the same culture of terror dominated both whites and natives, terrorist narratives scare not only their victims but their promoters as well. In a startling inversion, the attribution of wildness to the colonized or unknown other, objectified as magical essence, returns to haunt the consciousness of the conqueror.[32]

In U.S. law-enforcement history, the Ruby Ridge case encapsulates this logic to perfection. Attributing wild savagery to the holed-up Weaver family, the FBI changed its rules of engagement to a shoot-on-sight policy so that "the agents 'could and should' use lethal force even *before* the FBI announced its presence and called for the Weavers' surrender."[33] The tragic results of such demonization and the cover-up of the unconstitutional use of force would haunt the FBI long after the Oklahoma City explosion.

V

Talk of the devil and he'll appear.

—Erasmus, *Adagiorum Collectanea*

The bombing of the federal building in Oklahoma City meant the resurrection of the Weaver case and more particularly of Waco.

Oklahoma City transpired on the second anniversary of the Waco raid, which had resulted in the death of eighty-six Branch Davidians, twenty-four of whom were children. FBI and media reports alike stressed the linkage of Waco and Oklahoma City in the thinking of the tens of thousands of armed militiamen—who, in several states, practice weekend paramilitary maneuvers while dressed in camouflage uniforms. The main culprit charged with the bombing, Timothy McVeigh, had made a pilgrimage to Waco and was reportedly enraged over the conduct of law-enforcement agents there. Oklahoma City has been widely perceived as revenge for the Waco disaster. So it seems appropriate that we gain a minimal understanding of the referential baseline for the latest wave of terrorism discourse in the United States.

Numerous journalists and writers were very critical of the government's intervention in Waco. From the initial raid on February 28, 1993, to the final holocaust on April 19, the media reported a litany of gross blunders and a demonstrable pattern of deception on the part of law-enforcement agencies. The Justice Department's own analysis on the killing of the four federal agents and eighty-six Davidians made it clear that "from beginning to end there were fundamental errors in the way the Government approached the case."[34] The Treasury Department's report likewise "chronicled how law enforcement officials at a Treasury agency had made fatal mistakes in planning and executing the February raid and had then lied about them."[35]

In the United States does a "cultist" have religious or civil rights of any sort, including the right to be left alone? The right of religious association and the right to bear arms are both constitutional; but aren't they just excesses once we are dealing with "cults," those secretive and potentially criminal organizations? This seems to be the conclusion if we consider that, ironically, after the Oklahoma City tragedy, Larry Potts was promoted to deputy director of the FBI. Mr. Potts was a senior FBI official who helped plan the Waco assault and who was also the primary supervisor of the mismanaged standoff in Ruby Ridge, Idaho, with Randall Weaver, the survivalist who believed in an imminent biblical Apocalypse.

This textbook case of the reality-making power of discourse all began when the ATF paid $5,000 to an informer to buy two illegally sawed-off shotguns from Weaver who, caught in a weapon's violation, was then asked to spy on neo-Nazi groups in exchange for not being prosecuted. An extreme Christian fundamentalist whose religious views had led him to reject modern society, Weaver refused. He secluded his family in their cabin at Ruby Ridge for eighteen months. After

Weaver failed to appear in court, the well-publicized standoff ensued. The initial encounter began when Weaver's dog detected the marshals, and the shoot-out ended in the deaths of one of the marshals and Weaver's fourteen-year-old son. The next day Mrs. Weaver was killed by an FBI sharpshooter while standing in the doorway of her cabin holding her ten-month-old baby. Weaver was later acquitted of murder in the marshal's death by an Idaho jury.

The real scandal, the embarrassment that led to a cover-up, had to do with the new rules of engagement approved by the FBI. Reminiscent of antiterrorism's shoot-to-kill policy, Potts was censured for Ruby Ridge because "the FBI crisis team was given a 'shoot on sight' rule for dealing with weapon-carrying separatists in place of the ordinary rule of firing only when life was in danger."[36] The new rules said in effect the agents "could and should" use lethal force. The Justice Department found that in doing so the FBI violated its own rules and procedures. If we want to understand how the selling of two sawed-off shotguns might result in three deaths, millions of dollars expended, and prominent careers destroyed, we need only examine the power of discourse to generate its own reality—beginning with the initial entrapment of Weaver. Zealots of the right to bear arms have turned the Weaver fiasco, along with Waco, into *causes célèbres* that made it possible to conceive of the Oklahoma City tragedy.

Enter now Oklahoma City and antiterrorism. Larry Potts was put in charge of the Oklahoma investigation and promoted to the second highest position at the FBI. The FBI Director and the Attorney General apparently considered that his fatal mistakes in the Weaver and Waco affairs were but minor blunders. President Clinton likewise, after the Oklahoma City explosion, lashed out at any criticism of the federal raid on Waco, calling the Branch Davidians murderers, thus "simplifying complex events into a morality tale."[37] Despite the militiamen's fantasy wars in the woods, paranoia is not yet a crime in the United States, and the government's response was both arrogant and extralegal. Later Mr. Potts was demoted and then suspended; along with four other top-ranking FBI officials, he became the subject of a criminal investigation for possible obstruction of justice. This is one more instance in which the transgressors of established legal order and their violence-prone opposition are in league. We are obviously in the realm of terrorism discourse whereby, with overly facile demonization of the enemy, both sides tend to downplay or ignore due process. We are reminded again of the "animal soul" of the Wild Man, a citizen with no political attributes or legal rights because he is essentially inhuman.

It is worth focusing on the main reason adduced by both President Clinton and Attorney General Janet Reno for the decision to approve the final assault plan on Waco—child abuse. Both claimed that there was "mounting evidence of the children being continually abused." Yet, of all people, it was FBI Director William Sessions who himself stated that there were no grounds for the charge.

His career under attack and desperately in need of an FBI triumph, Sessions had argued forcefully for Reno to approve the final gas assault on Waco. On April 12, 14, 15, and 16 she refused, asking, "Why now?" Sessions, with his two deputies, Floyd Clarke and Larry Potts, persisted. After they produced the requested "documentation," Reno reversed herself and sanctioned the raid. Peter Boyer has chronicled the sequence of events whereby Reno was apparently misled by the FBI, but it also seems she did not read the prepared statement carefully. Reno acted in the belief that Koresh was engaging in ongoing child abuse when, in fact, Sessions' report contended he was incapable of such action after having been wounded in the initial shootout. Dr. Bruce Perry, the head psychiatrist of the crisis team that took charge of the twenty-one children released from the compound during the standoff, and who did not find them to be victims of sexual abuse, was perplexed by Reno's insistence that the gas assault was needed to save the children. Yet someone must have convinced her. In Perry's words, "The FBI maximized things they knew would ring a bell with her."[38] It is still an unanswered question who told her there was ongoing child abuse, but several writers have pointed to a likely source.

Nothing can demonize anyone more insidiously than the sensational charge of child abuse. Such allegations against Koresh were first made in 1991 by Marc Breault, a defector who plotted to take over the Davidians' Australian chapter. He contacted the noncustodial father of the young teenager Kiri Jewell, living in Waco with her mother, and convinced him to file for custody. Mr. Jewell and his new wife maintained visiting rights and had spent the holidays with Kiri at their home practically every year since the divorce ten years earlier. It was during the last of these visits that David Jewell arranged for Kiri's deprogramming, which "was later discovered to be a very well orchestated and planned action...executed with precision by Cult Awareness Network (CAN) experts."[39] After nearly four months of deprogramming, Kiri was taken to a judge and the court allowed her to stay with her father and stepmother. She then provided on national television the "testimony" of child abuse sought by the CAN deprogrammers. Among those skeptical of her story was her own mother. Later during

the Waco hearings of July 1995, Kiri became the star witness of
Democrats seeking to justify the ATF's assault on the Davidian compound on the basis of Koresh's depravity.

In response to the charges brought by Breault and David Jewell,
the Texas Department of Protective and Regulatory Services conducted a nine-week-long investigation. It found that there was no evidence
to substantiate child abuse. Other reports spoke of Koresh as routinely having sex with children, severely beating infants, fathering "lots of
babies," and so on. In an interview on National Public Radio, Joyce
Sparks, the caseworker supervisor of the Protective Services' investigation of the Branch Davidians, averred there was no evidence that any
minor had been sexually abused, there were no cases of pregnant
minors, and the children were characterized as well-adjusted. During
the Waco hearings, in July of 1995, Ms. Sparks confirmed that she had
been allowed to question the children, but had had limited access; Kiri
Jewell had been unwilling to testify against Koresh. No new charges or
evidence emerged after that investigation. Asked about the ATF
assault, her reply was that the result was most predictable, that it was
simply "the fulfillment of their prophecies." Nevertheless, the stigma of
such public accusations is hard to remove. The media's portrayal of
the "Wacko from Waco" made most people see Koresh as mentally ill,
another basic strategy for demonizing borderline persons.

Koresh was admittedly an unsavory figure. Yet the unconventional living arrangements of religious sects are scarcely a rarity (from the
celibacy of many Christian orders to the "complex marriage" of the
Oneida Community and the "celestial marriage" of Mormon
polygamy). However, while the public has great tolerance for bizarre
recreational sexual practices and promiscuity of the prominent, religiously motivated and unconventional sexual arrangements are highly suspect.

Similarly, the self-imposed "messiah" label likely leads to dire consequences for its claimant (from the crucifixion of Jesus Christ to the
lynching of Joseph Smith, messiahs have not fared very well), but there
is no law against it.[40] According to Hofstadter, a distinctive characteristic of the paranoid style in interpreting social and historical events is
that "decisive events are not taken as part of the stream of history, but
as the consequences of someone's will."[41] It is the charismatic individual with special techniques of control, demonic powers, and dark
secrets, who is held personally responsible for the particular widespread evil. According to the CAN experts, the Branch Davidians were
"hostages," "brainwashed," and held "captive" by Koresh's "mind con-

trol." Sociology and psychology may reject the theory of "mind control" to the point that the victim loses his/her capacity for voluntary action (the argument is not admissible as "expert testimony" in trials since the federal court decision of *U.S. v. Fishaman*).[42]

It was no accident that Janet Reno decided to ignore the reports of the Department of Child Prevention. For there was another influential source for interpretation of Waco's "cultists"—the Cult Awareness Network. CAN has been engaged in an unceasing war on satanism. In his book *In Pursuit of Satan*, Robert Hicks repeatedly features CAN as a major player in the denunciation of satanic rituals. Such "experts" on satanic cults believe that there is an international underground of satanists responsible for over 50,000 human sacrifices annually.[43] The abuse of children is in itself a form of worship for satanists. CAN distributed, for example, Catherine Gould's checklist of satanic behavioral symptoms in teens; Gould is the most frequently cited researcher promoting the stories of satanic abuse in day-care centers. The former president of CAN, the Reverend Michael Rokos, at one point provided his own checklist of signs of teenage satanism and warned: "*Any* teenager who has not been educated about satanic cult methods and tactics flirts with the occult without realizing it."[44]

Several writers have documented the pivotal influence of CAN upon the government's decision making concerning Waco. Alexander Cockburn wrote in the *Los Angeles Times*: "The role in Waco of the Cult Awareness Network, whose members are respectfully cited in the press as 'experts,' may well have been crucial."[45] After the initial deadly raid, it was learned that CAN deprogrammer Rick Ross had advised the ATF prior to the assault. Mr. Ross—an ex-con with an extensive record of psychiatric problems, with no professional training in counseling, arrested in January 1991 following a failed deprogramming—stated, in self-promotional interviews with CBS and NBC, that he had warned the ATF against the caches of arms inside the compound and that he had been in touch with the FBI "over the long haul."[46] He described the Davidians as "a very dangerous group" in an interview with the *Waco Tribune-Herald*, and, in the words of Dr. James Lewis of the Association of World Academics for Religious Education, "whatever Ross may have communicated to the ATF, it is certain it promoted the worst stereotypes of alternative religions…. [S]cholars have time and again rejected this stereotype as simply unfounded."[47]

We get a sense of Ross's disinterested approach to the ills of brainwashed cultists when we learn that he makes his living by "deprogramming" them—at $35,000 to $50,000 a pop![48] David Block, a former Branch Davidian deprogrammed by Rick Ross and Priscilla Coates, was interviewed by the ATF, and his information contributed to the decision to storm the compound. Nor is Priscilla Coates herself immune. In 1984 she and another CAN deprogrammer, Galen Kelley (convicted in May 1993 of violently kidnapping a woman for the purpose of deprogramming), were involved in a notorious case when they "so alarmed the authorities with fantasized allegations of child abuse by members of a religious commune in Island Pond in Vermont that the movement was illegally raided and its children removed into custody.... A judge ruled that the raid had been 'grossly unlawful' and ordered the children released."[49] Waco was obviously a huge target of opportunity for CAN.

In the aftermath of the initial disastrous raid, CAN experts flooded the media, offering their advice on how to deal with the almost subhuman, brainwashed Davidians. For example, CAN's president, Patricia Ryan, told the *Houston Chronicle* that Koresh should be arrested by whatever means necessary, "including lethal force." Contrast this with the view of former prosecutors who had previously dealt with the Davidians. Vic Feazell, for instance, former district attorney for the county, explained to the Associated Press how he had arrested Koresh in 1987 without bloodshed: "If they'd called and talked to them, the Davidians would've given them what they wanted. We had to arrest them to prosecute them.... [W]e treated them like human beings, instead of storming the place. They were extremely polite people."[50] Even within the FBI forces at Waco there were apparently two factions distinctly at odds—the negotiators, who tried to build confidence and brought about the release of twenty-one children and several adults; and the Hostage Rescue Team, whose harassing tactics undermined the negotiations.

Tragically, the ATF, the FBI, and the Attorney General chose to ignore the advice of local law authorities and health officials who had dealt directly with the Davidians. Instead they listened to CAN deprogrammers who were exploiting the tense situation to promote their own agenda. Even after the firestorm had killed over eighty people and the FBI director had denied allegations of continuing child abuse, Priscilla Coates maintained, in an interview with the *Washington Post*, "I know how these groups work and children are always abused."[51] Similarly, Patricia Ryan and Herbert Rosedale, president of the American Family Foundation, issued a joint statement in which, without providing any evidence, they insisted on "the risk cults pose to the health, and sometimes even the lives, of children."[52] CAN experts were later eager to deprogram the survivors of Waco to ensure that their testimony confirmed CAN's own prejudgment that mass suicide occurred in Waco.

Why did Attorney General Janet Reno favor the advice of dubious CAN "experts" over that of health officials, a former district attorney, and credible specialists? Once again we must consider the persistence of long-standing mythical constructs, such as the archetypal image of the Wild Man, and even satanism, whose murderous rituals Reno had prosecuted forcefully in the past. We have become accustomed to accusations of child abuse in child custody and care cases, which is almost *de rigueur* in the criticism of "cults." But it should be noted that Janet Reno "had, in a sense, risen to her position partly on the child abuse issue."[53] She knew what was best for the children. Herself the abused daughter of a loving but extremely difficult and alcoholic mother, as a state attorney she became "a rescuer" of abused children. As a Miami federal prosecutor she argued several cases of satanic and ritual child abuse. One of Reno's unsuccessful, but highly newsworthy, prosecutions was the trial of a fourteen-year-old boy, Bobby Fijnje, who worked as a babysitter at a church. With the help of specialists, the children "disclosed" tales of Bobby killing and eating babies, flying witches, and more, mostly during the day-time services at a Presbyterian church. After having spent a year and eight months in jail, the boy was found to be innocent and was freed. The ritual-child-abuse issue swept the country during the late 1980s, largely as a result of media hype promoted by the "experts" of CAN and supported by fundamentalist Christians. After a number of hoaxes were uncovered, the whole scheme was later exposed by authors such as Robert Hicks.[54] Yet Waco provided Reno the Rescuer with one more opportunity to save children.

Andrew Milne provides evidence to suggest that, through Congressman William Hughes of New Jersey, Janet Reno was fed CAN's "tactics and hysteria" concerning alternative religions.[55] The initial House Judiciary Committee hearings disclosed the connection, although the Attorney General denied that she herself had spoken to CAN "experts" during the standoff. On March 30 (at the height of the siege), Patricia Ryan, Herbert Rosedale, and psychologist Margaret Singer of the American Family Foundation contributed statements on "cults" to a congressional committee. It should be noted that the American Psychological Association rejected Singer's research as lacking scientific merit, and that Ryan and Rosedale cited the writings of Louis West, a discredited psychiatrist known for his promotion of mind-altering drugs and his proposals to use ethnic and racial minorities as experimental subjects.

Why should the government grant credibility to what is mostly scientifically discredited? Humble objective facts are but pale details when confronted with myth. Both the far-right, anti-government conspiracies and the official credibility granted to "experts" share similar themes deeply embedded in apocalyptic culture. Above all, we view the susceptibility of public officials to such stories of satanic ritual not "as evidence of therapeutical and prosecutorial mischief," but rather "as evidence of the reality-making force of discursive practices generally."[56] Had we not been exposed for so many years to the "reality-making force" of terrorism discourse and the tales of its "experts," we might be skeptical of the claims by various writers that CAN's advice, however indirectly, was in fact significant in Janet Reno's disastrous handling of Waco. Terrorism experts, who defined the standoff as a "barricade/hostage situation," were also consulted. We are therefore not surprised that, regarding Koresh, the conspiratorial views of CAN were more influential than the findings of the Department of Health and Human Services. It is typical that federal agencies would pay close attention to the likes of Rick Ross who, though short on evidence, gain tremendous credibility by simply voicing the possibility of worst-case scenarios that echo the deep-seated beliefs concerning mythical Wild Men and satanic plots.

Like ideas held about witchcraft during the Middle Ages, such premises, whether believed by an antisatanism crusader or by the Attorney General of the United States, are so deeply embedded among millions of American believers as to be impervious to any superficial act of exorcism. David Koresh reminded us that we are living through the Last Days before the Apocalypse. Religious scholars in contact with him believed that the Branch Davidian group saw itself as playing out the events of the "fifth seal" as found in chapter six of the Book of Revelations. Such small Christian apocalyptic groups need to enact their End Time stories. Yet in America there are also an estimated 10–15 million born-again Christians with their own futurist schemes of premillennial "dispensationalism," plus another 10–15 million charismatic Christians with similar beliefs. Dispensationalism, in Susan Harding's definition, "is the way most Bible-believing Christians in America read current history and the daily news."[57] Therefore, while not exactly mainstream, the apocalyptic vision of the end of the world is held by a significant number of Americans.

It is not only the David Koreshes but also American presidents who share such beliefs. Ronald Reagan, for one, believed the dispensationalist scheme. His interior secretary, James Watt, declared The End was near. President George Bush, during the Gulf War crisis, frequently consulted dispensationalist preacher Billy Graham and did so before he ordered the bombing of Baghdad. Was the Gulf War God's historical destiny for the president and the Christians who supported it? Harding questions the politics of those apocalyptic readings; she analyzes how to read dispensationalism as "discourse that constitutes reality."[58] If modern historians were to expel God from history, dispensationalists would return to the battle between God and Satan as the true pattern of history. Janet Reno, favoring the apocalyptic version of antisatanist CAN experts, was, after all, simply in concert with the millions of American premillennialists.

In the Waco tragedy, a compound with forty children inside was assaulted with a fusillade of bullets. Electricity and other utilities essential to the maintenance of health standards were cut off—all in the name of eliminating "child abuse." The area was bombarded with spotlights, loud music, and bizarre sounds (such as that of rabbits being slaughtered)—all for the children's sake. Their safety also required employing tanks as battering rams and the use of CS gas ("banned for battlefield use by 100 nations."[59]) Finally, twenty-four children were immolated in a fire that should have been foreseen as the likely outcome of the final assault. Indeed, "there is little doubt the FBI planners anticipated that the compound could go up in flames. They alerted a hospital burn unit in Dallas on the day of the attack."[60] In any case, a two-month investigation by the *Los Angeles Times* staff writer Glenn Bunting, involving more than seventy-five interviews and an examination of confidential documents, showed that "the government's role in—and explanation of—the deadly fire is murkier and more open to criticism that its categorical assertions suggest."[61] Nevertheless, "Through some fantastically contorted mental exertions, the federal government, the media, and the Americans in general have blamed Koresh and the other Branch Davidian adults for the suffering of these children."[62] This is what Leach had in mind when he charged that, by turning your opponents into monstrous wild animals, "every imaginable form of terroristic atrocity is not only attributed to the other side but becomes permissible for oneself."[63] Thus, Janet Reno, a well-meaning child advocate, ended up sending in tanks and CS gas to save children. In the process, unwittingly yet ominously, the government created a foundational event that became a rallying cry for tens of thousands of future militiamen and which so far has prompted one catastrophic explosion.

Yet the inquisitorial logic of redemption through bonfire—burn bodies to save souls—provided in Waco a statement too clear to be missed by those prone to fear of government conspiracies. The immolation of Koresh's cult in front of TV cameras was a potent and public anticultist ritual of purification in the name of law and morality. The morality play of Koresh's demise was so compelling that the FBI allowed the press within one-and-a-half miles of the compound, while keeping the fire fighters miles away. Once the blaze started, the authorities waited at least ten minutes before calling them in. When the fire trucks finally did arrive, they were held at the checkpoint under FBI control for another sixteen minutes. It was more important to consummate the purification of the villain. Then the tale required a redeeming heroine, and the Washington establishment proceeded to make one out of Janet Reno. She assumed ultimate responsibility for the catastrophe, repeating the mantra "The buck stops here," to the applause of Democrats and Republicans alike.

Not everyone was, of course, edified by Washington's morality play. If Koresh's love for guns was so threatening as to prompt a government massacre with impunity, many felt they, too, were under threat. Many decided to better organize themselves into militias, and have done so in thirty-three states. But it is for Waco pilgrims such as McVeigh that mere talk about government conspiracy and readiness for action are insufficient. The "hero" must act out what others only voice. Somebody must reenact the decisive battle, bring about the inferno of the final judgment. Someone must become "the chosen one" to speak real truth through action. The phony driver's license in McVeigh's possession at the time of his arrest was dated April 19—the date of the Waco tragedy. As we learn more about him, it would seem that his message can only be: "Oklahoma City *is* Waco!"

For the militants, outraged by the Ruby Ridge and the Waco affairs, what rhetorics could epitomize government wickedness? There was, of course, one frightening discourse that specialized in demonizing enemies to the point that they were beyond all law and "innocence"—terrorism. When McVeigh went target shooting while in the army, at least once he practiced against "a target of a terrorist holding a hostage."[64] It is the ultimate irony that nobody would seem to better understand McVeigh's rage than the so-called "constitutional activists" who have turned Waco into a tourist attraction and pilgrimage site. Thus, in its perverse way, and as an indelible gift of the terrorism discourse regarding distant madmen so assiduously promoted by the government over the last two decades, McVeigh's pithy message intended by the Oklahoma City explosion appears to be: "Government *is* terrorism!"

VI

The question of terrorism is political in a still more precise sense, in that the issue of the state and its legitimacy is, or should be, quite central to the discussion of terrorism at both the empirical and moral levels.

  —A. Arblaster, "Terrorism: Myths, Meaning and Morals"

The tension between legality and illegality is intrinsic to the notions of state, law, and criminality that regulate modern societies. "Terrorism" provides a crucial test of an established state's willingness and capacity to abide by its own rules. Although we postulate that law should be free from arbitrary decisions and value judgements, the very notions of "law" and "crime" can be problematic, as anthropologists learned long ago.[65] The issue of what constitutes a political crime, for example, is disputed by various specialists,[66] though most authors do recognize a basic distinction between common and political crimes—the latter motivated by the desire to change extant laws and policies. One does not need to visit a primitive society to discover that legitimacy and criminality do not always depend on the facts of the case, but rather that "legitimacy is evaluative."[67] The histories of nearly all the major nation-states provide striking illustration that the legitimate actions of the ruler readily become redefined as the criminal acts of the ex-ruler.

Functionalist anthropologists make a sharp distinction between the *is* and the *ought* of customs and practices. Such discrepancies between praxis and norm should make it clear that frequently "the moral status of any particular item of practical behavior will depend upon how it is interpreted."[68] One should therefore not be surprised that there is also considerable difficulty and discrepancy when determining what is terroristic. As Bonanate put it, "deciding whether an action is terrorist…is more the result of a verdict than the establishing of a fact."[69] Even the terrorism experts analyzing the Basque case recognized that "under the dictatorship the resort to violence appeared justified and those who engaged in it were looked upon as heroes."[70] The experts assumed that the change from dictatorship to democracy changed the moral status of a course of behavior, even when they were aware that the likelihood of a new military intervention, given the Spanish army's long tradition for coups, could not be discounted.[71] The hard-line Basque view that Madrid—not a particular dictator or political system—is the enemy was simply left out of account.

Preposterous as it sounds to democrats, supporters of terrorist methods are most suspicious of the assumption that democracy is an incorruptible, ultimate political value. Many agree with Rabbi Meir Kahane that democracy is "an alien, Gentile idea."[72] But the liberal press, too, can be accused of unconcern for democracy when it comes to combatting terrorism, as was the case when Fujimori suspended Peru's constitution and dissolved its congress in April of 1992. The U.S. media's acceptance of Fujimori's dictatorship was rebuked by the Peruvian writer Gustavo Gorriti, arrested himself after the *autogolpe*: "I'm afraid this belies a certain hypocrisy on the part of many of the liberal press, a sense that democracy is good for us but not for them."[73] The press couldn't care less that Fujimori all but abrogated due process and that Peru's new antiterrorist law "defines collaboration so broadly that it could include almost anyone, and it means twenty years in jail."[74]

As argued by Taylor,[75] the study of comparative politics may be vitiated by our faith in the universal value of a North Atlantic-type polity and the failure to recognize the cultural and conjunctural specificity of our basic political notions such as "negotiation," "legitimacy," or "freedom." Written or codified legislation is essential to our statist societies, yet we should remember that in the broader context of global human history it is rather unusual. Most societies have been, and still are, ruled by oral procedures and tradition. Convention, custom, and law belong on the same continuum. Writers such as Vico—whose main interest is in the history of law and who describes the framework of mythology (oral and written) in which a society develops its political culture—stress that we cannot ignore the historical role of poetic and mythic impulses in shaping the moral imagination of a people.

The obvious point is that the perception of what constitutes law and its moral legitimation may vary substantially from society to society and from one situation to the next. A universal concept of "terrorism" glaringly fails to address such contextual realities. The depiction of Menachem Begin and Yitzhak Shamir as ruthless, outlawed freedom fighters, "terrorists" against British rule, and as the prime ministers of Israel provide but one example. The same can be said of the political premise that the state is the unquestioned source of legality and guarantor of legitimacy.[76] Writers who argue that, above all, terrorists are intent upon attacking the liberal state overlook the fact that the fundamental goal of some "terrorist" organizations is precisely the creation of such a state.

Ehud Sprinzak analyzes the telling case of Israel concerning the problems that may arise between the State and the rule of law. Some religious ultraorthodox groups consider the State of Israel an apostasy, whereas others, such as Gush Emunim, glorify the State but display systematic disrespect of the rule of law.[77] Their extralegalism has gone so far that several distinguished members of the movement have advocated premeditated killings of Arabs. The most notorious of these was Rabbi Meir Kahane, whose "real program included an entire overhaul of the Israeli legal system, the expulsion of the Arabs, the removal of the Muslim shrines on Temple Mount, the establishment of Jewish anti-terror squads."[78] His followers of the Jewish Defense League absorbed his message of anti-Arab terror and committed in New York various acts of terrorism, which led the FBI consistently to categorize the JDL as a terrorist organization.[79] Yet it is not these extremist groups but the pervasiveness of vigilantism in Israel that really bothers Sprinzak. What characterizes the vigilante mentality is the conviction that the government has failed to enforce the law; therefore, taking it into one's hand in the name of self-defense is consonant with any concept of law. A 1983 account found that 27 percent of all West Bank male and 5 percent of all female settlers had engaged in anti-Arab vigilante activity, and that 65 percent of the entire community of settlers agreed with vigilantism.[80]

Then, too, there is the cynicism engendered by the evident double standard of the western democracies when dealing with foreign policy as distinct from domestic affairs. Constituted as territorially defined states, there is the underlying premise that each should pursue its "national interest" vis-à-vis the others which, carried to its logical conclusion, results in a permanent state of international tension and mutual antagonism.[81] Peace results not so much from international consensus and good will among nations as from a balance of power, one might even say a balance of terror. Hence, the appeal to universal human values and respect for individual human rights implicit in the democratic ideals that informs domestic political debate is largely conspicuous by its absence in the arena of international relations as each country pursues its national interests and guarantees its national defense. Indeed, such "realism" informs and permeates the political thought of such influential liberal democratic political theorists as Hans Morgenthau and Henry Kissinger.

In short, whether dealing with either domestic or foreign policy, the exercise of condoning or condemning particular agendas, organizations, and behaviors is at least as much rhetorical and political as it is philosophical. Even some Spanish military officials disagree with the view that a guerrilla fighter should be juridically unprotected and treated as a "vulgar criminal."[82] Conversely, it is rather common practice among governments to carry out secret conversations and even open negotiations with their adversaries while publicly stigmatizing them as terrorist murderers with whom compromise is unthinkable.[83] "Murder is murder irrespective of the circumstances"[84] is the kind of edifying pronouncement that might be accepted unquestioningly by any citizen, were it not for the daily fact that world politics is better described by Voltaire's pronouncement that killing is murder unless you do it to the sound of trumpets. As we learn from the "lawful" killings of three unarmed IRA activists, there are vast differences among murders.

The arrogation of the right to kill by a (typically) small group with no formal legitimation is what makes "terrorism" such a frightening phenomenon. Yet anthropologists are familiar with other contexts in which the right to commit legitimate murder is contested. One such instructive contrast is that between the nature of Swazi kingship prior to colonialism and its status during the colonial period of Boer and British domination. The essential difference concerns the formidable system of self-defense enjoyed by the Swazi kings in precolonial times, namely, "the right to kill" those suspected of sorcery against the throne.[85] Ironically, the right of summary execution became a major weakness vis-à-vis the new colonial enemies, who themselves made royal executions a prominent ploy in their campaign to undermine independent Swazi rule. That is, Europeans justified their execution of Swazi kings by charging that the barbarous monarchs themselves executed their enemies. This is but one minor example in colonial history whereby depriving a group of the right to kill is seen by the colonizers as a major civilizing step, whereas for the colonized it marks essential subordination. As a Swazi royal councilor put it to the Europeans, "We do not see that unless you allow us to rule in our own way there is any independence at all. Our way of ruling is to kill each other, and what shall be the rule if we are not allowed to kill?"[86]

Guerrilla and terrorist organizations use much the same logic of "not according to the state the monopoly of violence." It is not difficult for them, at least in their own view, to legitimize their actions by underscoring historical atrocities and the present injustices in world

affairs. The paradoxes between "us" and "them" regarding the barbaric right to kill—if they can, then why can't we; if we should be held
to a higher morality, then why not they—are too obvious for a Swazi or
"a terrorist" to ignore.

The critical point about the semantics of terrorism in relation to
law should be obvious by now: by charging the other with terrorist lawlessness, it allows oneself to dispense with the rule of law. This was the
case with the U.S. military raids on Libya by the Reagan administration on behalf of Germany and Italy,[87] an act that was censured by a
General Assembly resolution at the UN. A related matter consists in
launching an attack on another state as anticipatory self-defense.
Examples are the bombing by Israel of Iraq's nuclear reactor at Osirik
in 1981 or the sabotage of Libya's Rabta chemical factory in March of
1990. Under normal circumstances there is no right for such preemptive strikes against other states, but the harder one hits Saddam
Hussein or Mu'ammar Qaddafi the harder one hits terrorism itself, so
who can deny its direct contribution to international order and legality? Demonizing the enemy on the one hand while claiming exemp-
tion from legal accountability for oneself on the other[88]—in recent
decades nothing has done so much as terrorism discourse to rekindle
their age-old mutual dependence. A perfect example is the response
of Amos Oz to Begin's statement that destroying Arafat's headquarters in Beirut made him feel as if he had sent the Israeli defense forces
to Berlin to eliminate Hitler in his bunker: "Hitler is already dead, my
dear Prime Minister…. Again and again, Mr. Begin, you reveal to the
public eye a strange urge to resuscitate Hitler in order to kill him every
day anew in the guise of terrorists."[89]

The *Achille Lauro* affair, inflamed by the heinous crime of killing a
paraplegic simply because he was a Jew, is a paradigmatic example of
deteriorating international relations over terrorism. Its complex legal
implications have been studied by Antonio Cassese.[90] He has concentrated on U.S. embarrassment after having intercepted an Egyptian
airliner "in a way that was totally unjustified under international law"
and on the allegorical rationale given by the Americans that it was
done because the terrorists were "a kind of modern incarnation of the
pirates of former times."[91] Egypt was humiliated to the point that
Mubarak spoke of being "stabbed in the back" and denounced it as an
"act of piracy…without precedent in any international code or law";[92]
the Italian Prime Minister Craxi sent a note of protest over the
American violation of Italy's territorial sovereignty. With the exception of Israel, the reaction of other states was negative. Cassese's con-

clusion is unambiguous: "The United States preferred violence to law, leaving behind an unfortunate legacy that has polluted international law and aggravated political and diplomatic relations between states."[93] In short, the incident highlights the weaknesses of international legal regulation of state response to terrorism, since a superpower can always twist the laws to fit its political interests.

Lawlessness is what made the barbarians less than human for Aristotle. In our liberal democracies, too, the tension between civilization and barbarism turns upon issues of legality. We cannot ignore, therefore, that under the guise of fighting terrorism the United States has rejected agreements such as the 1977 Geneva Protocol I, which "provides one clear set of internationally-agreed criteria by which one can assess, and criticize, acts of terrorism."[94] Reagan's view that the Protocol would give recognition and protection to terrorist groups was strongly countered.[95] Some critical legal scholars have no qualms in describing the U.S. counterterrorist policy as "itself both terroristic and illegal."[96]

In the case of post-Franco Spain's remarkable transition from dictatorship to democracy, the Constitution of 1978 was touted as the birth of a new legal system. But, as Vercher observes, there were "two qualifying factors" to be taken into consideration: first, the Constitution failed to abrogate all previous laws; second, the civil service, judiciary, and police remain significantly staffed by the old guard.[97] Regarding the new Constitution's rules for detention and trial, "There have been substantial amendments...in terrorist cases."[98] In fact, on December 4, 1978, or two days before the Constitutional Referendum, "the first antiterrorist Law in democratic Spain appeared...[which] was very much like the antiterrorist decrees and laws that had been inherited from the Franco years."[99] The justification for such laws was that "it is extremely difficult to obtain evidence," the reason being that "witnesses are almost impossible to find," and therefore "the police have to resort to any available means in order to conduct the investigation. In those circumstances the law facilitates not only the use of prolonged detention [up to ten days] but also the rendering incommunicado of the detainee."[100]

Vercher documents notorious cases of victims tortured to death in democratic Spain, for "judicial control of prolonged detention in terrorist cases is far from effective."[101] Once again, only savage "terrorism" can justify the preservation of the old regime's most dubious practices such as torture and evasion of the law.

The dangers of a policy based on simplistic premises of good versus evil, while shunning international legality, turned into a paradigm of folly in the Iran-Contra fiasco. First there was the disproportional prioritizing of terrorism as the major foreign policy issue to the detriment of other international problems; thus the United States and the UN did nothing to stop the Iraqi invasion of Iran or the Israeli invasion of Lebanon. Then there was the public labeling of entire countries as terrorist, imposing upon them a pariah status—a taboo, however, that came to haunt its originator when business with the untouchable enemy was in order. A tragic instance of the consequences of international lawlessness under the guise of counterterrorism was the kidnapping and killing of four Iranians—three diplomats and a journalist—after their car bearing diplomatic plates and accompanied by a police escort was stopped by the Israeli-backed Christian militia in Lebanon in 1982. The local governments and the United States ignored the fate of the Iranians, and the incident marked the genesis of the dramatic hostage phenomenon in Lebanon that led to the kidnapping of approximately 130 foreigners from 18 nations. It was subsequently acknowledged that officials in Washington and international diplomats recognized "that the Iranian abduction established a new context for political violence against the various forces in Lebanon that was later to be widely reenacted."[102] It was the sum of all these elements in orbit around the Evil of terrorism—a combination of taboo and folly—that led to the Iran-Contra debacle.

Similarly, in retaliation for Saddam Hussein's "state terrorism" and violation of Kuwait's internationally recognized border, the Bush Administration shielded Kurdish nationalists with a no-flight zone enforced from Turkey. Subsequently, the Clinton administration gave its blessings to the Turks when their army, equally unconcerned with the sanctity of international borders, invaded Northern Iraq in search of "several thousand terrorists" among the Kurds.[103] Once again, our former heroic fighters became our current loathsome terrorists; yesterday's zeal for international law absolves today's disregard of it. All that is needed to justify the shift is the rhetoric of terrorism discourse.

Myopia and self-deception are the almost certain outcomes of the politics of terrorism labeling. There is a long list of politicians and public officials—from Presidents Carter to Reagan to Bush, from Giscard d'Estaing to Chirac, from Oliver North to William Casey—who were consumed by the terrorist monster created by their own propaganda. Such politics of labeling deceives nobody more than its proponents, as when the United States regarded the PLO to be a terrorist organization, whereas all Arab states recognized it as the representative of the Palestinians. Overly simplifying our understanding of the Middle East by calling Arabs either terrorists or terrorism sympathizers readily translates into flagrant policy errors.

True to the pattern that today's archterrorist was yesterday's close friend—whether Qaddafi, Noriega, or Saddam Hussein—most recently the United States transformed Sheik Omar Abdul Rahman into the latest embodiment of "terrorism." After months in which the press trumpeted that the sheik had a record of violent incitement to terrorism in Egypt, and that he entered the country illegally despite being on a list of terrorist suspects, we were finally told that his real role, and that of his followers suspected in the bombing of the World Trade Center, was that of partner in Reagan's anti-Communist crusade in Afghanistan.

The suspicion that the sheik and his men were being protected by the CIA prior to the explosion was shared by many. Not surprisingly, Attorney General Janet Reno was initially opposed to the sheik's arrest; a week before she acquiesced, she had stated publicly that there was no substance to the charges against the sheik. In fact, while the established ideology and legality will harshly prohibit any contact with the tabooed subjects, it is official policy, condoned by the State Department, that the CIA can make bargains with terrorists, for "there are occasions where it is appropriate, perhaps even necessary, to deal with them."[104] As the infamous Aldrich Ames put it, "War is war. If you use your access to these foreign police and military services to recruit, you're not recruiting those guys to stop the war. You're recruiting those guys to help the war."[105] Therefore, ever true to the logic of taboo, terrorism culture must incur the polluting intimacy of men like Noriega, Saddam Hussein, and Sheik Omar Abdul Rahman who alternatively became our most trusted allies as well as our most frightening monsters. It is the State Department, depending on the political expediency of the moment, that endorses one stereotype or the other.

VII

If someone comes to kill you, rise and kill him first.

—The *Talmud*

To illustrate the dynamics by which tabooing people and adopting crusading attitudes feed into one another, anthropologist Edmund Leach resorts to history and mentions the case of Pope Gregory IX. He harangued Christianity into undertaking a crusade by depicting the

Mongols as dog-headed people who ate dead human bodies, leaving the bones to the vultures.

One characteristic of the work of terrorism experts is the very *pro-hibition* upon personal discourse with their subjects. Authors writing about terrorism must abide by this taboo. It is telling that one can claim expertise regarding "terrorists" without ever having seen or talked to one. This complete lack of contact with the subjects under study is not only usual but is even touted as the inevitable and desirable condition in the field of counterterrorism. One can, of course, know a lot about people one has never met, but it is odd to predicate expertise upon such systematic avoidance. That such an oddity can transpire is conditioned by the fact that the investigators themselves abide by the general rule: terrorists are by their very nature "untouchables," highly dangerous, polluting persons with whom contact is to be avoided at all costs. This rule obeys the perception that, whatever else they might be, terrorists are wholly unlike ordinary people.

There is further reason for the experts' avoidance of the subjects they are studying, which has to do with the aftermath of their investigations and the policy they recommend. Namely, that the fight against "terrorists" demands that they be "contained" and "isolated." According to the expert report on Basque terrorism, for instance, viewing even one terrorist on television is highly pernicious and should therefore be prohibited by the authorities. Such personal television appearances must be avoided because they "facilitate a personal and direct rapprochement with the masses...for people can see as well as hear the person being interviewed."[106] Beware of seeing a terrorist's face on television; beware of hearing his voice on a radio! Scientific expertise is thus adduced for championing specific instructions for stigmatizing members of the society when, in fact, in the Basque political context, any citizen is likely to have known, and possibly lionized, an alleged "terrorist." For many families the death or existence of a member in prison or exile is an intimate and ongoing tragedy. Nevertheless, it is the stated strategy to first conceal the fact that for thousands of people membership in a violent nationalist organization has amounted to a baptism by fire akin to an initiation ritual and then, by surrounding them with an aura of estrangement and aberration, literally to taboo them.

The same expert recommendations offered to the Basques were in fact implemented in Britain when, in October 1988, Thatcher's government prohibited the broadcast by radio and television of interviews with "terrorists" and politicians that support them. The terrorism experts in possession of such burning antiterrorist zeal might do well to consider the extent to which they are simply prepossessed by religious illusion, for, as Leach noted, "indeed, counter terrorism becomes, in a bizarre sense, a religiously sanctioned duty."[107] This spirit of religious self-righteousness, which would be regarded as an aberration when informing other social concerns, appears to writers on terrorism to be not only legitimate but also morally requisite. A writer may feel so personally besieged by the subjects he is studying that he concludes a paper in an international conference on terrorism with the words from the Talmud: "If someone comes to kill you, rise and kill him first."[108]

Questioning the anomalous and amoral depiction of the terrorist, contemplating his very ambivalent nature, recognizing that one's knowledge of such unruly action must by necessity be problematic, seeking to place it in broader social and political context—all threaten to undermine the terrorism expert's basic conceptual and moral taxonomies; indeed, the very object of discourse threatens to evaporate. There is hardly any doubt that a bomb will go off somewhere killing casual bystanders, that neighboring groups will engage in fratricidal warfare, that people will be kidnapped and murdered, that all sorts of senseless violence will be perpetrated for unclear reasons and for incomprehensible causes. Yet once we are persuaded to doubt their unity as a categorical phenomenon, the entire edifice of the "terrorist other" crumbles.

Faced with the apparently unbridgeable discontinuity of terrorist behavior, one is reminded of Leibnitz's doctrine of continuity, according to which the anomaly of a "monstrous" or inherently "irrational" man reflected a lack of knowledge or an inadequate notion of human nature.[109] And so did Freud continuously undermine the distinction between the pathological and the normal in the interest of a common humanity. As to the possibility of anthropological knowledge, Lévi-Strauss's remark about "the (conscious and unconscious) subjective comprehension that we would adopt if, men after all, ourselves would live the fact as a native instead of observing it as an ethnographer"[110] signals the necessity of considering the native's point of view. All of this is *forbidden* to the terrorism expert. There must be no common ground between terrorist Unreason and political Reason. There can be no ambiguity, no problem, no possibility of alternative plots for the same events. Realist discourse is masked as moral imperative. Ironic and skeptical perspectives must be ruled out.

Every perspective is best defined by the limits it places upon the viewer; each intellectual discipline is primarily constituted by the taboos it imposes upon its practitioners. What are the restrictions imposed by terrorism discourse on its framers? Personally, politically, and morally, terrorism is the utterly untouchable. If contact with, empathy for, or understanding of the terrorist is contaminating and proscribed, the taboo itself empowers the terrorist identity with near-magical efficacy, and thereby constitutes the very problem it seeks to resolve.

Discourse implies the give and take between alternative or contrasting perspectives. Indeed, from the viewpoint of the tabooed actors, the very notion of such intercourse would appear highly ironic, since terrorism discourse demands interdiction of an I/you dialogue with the subjects responsible for generating the phenomenon. By definition, terrorism is an anomaly that must be met with the prohibition and horror of taboo, and we ourselves can never be terrorists. The last thing a terrorism expert can suggest is that there be a congruence of views with the terrorist. It simply falls outside the taxonomy of our political definitions that whatever dirty work is carried out by our own government—whether arming insurgents against democratically elected governments or assassinating foreign heads of state—should be classed as terrorism. The terrorist is simply the anomalous "other." Those rare yet powerful exceptions, such as Robin Morgan[111] talking in the first person of her past as a terrorist, only confirm the rule, for a "confessed" terrorist is no longer one.

The discourse of the terrorism expert is buttressed by the scientistic idea that true knowledge must afford the objectivity that allows one to talk about society in terms of universal criteria. Such knowledge dealing with the very behavior of people whose faces one has never seen and whose voices one has never heard, obtained by reading the works of writers who likewise have never seen or heard them, is so removed from the terrorist's personal decision-making and motivations that whatever factual information one indirectly obtains about the actors pales before the imaginative "If I were a horse" type of fictional reconstruction of the impenetrable terror.

Most humanist disciplines subscribe to the opposite Durkheimian position that cognition is socially determined, which does not imply that all thought reflects established structures but rather that any given society presents contradictions in its thinking and discourse. That the writer should speak from "within" the community is authorially taboo in the sinister field of terrorism. Yet when, rarely, writers such as Ehud Sprinzak[112] or Gustavo Gorriti Ellenbogen[113] speak to

us, critically and passionately, about their own countries' slide into terrorist violence, their voices carry a different conviction. Their
antipode—and mentor of most counterterrorism specialists—is the
armchair anthropologist who, having written many volumes on the savages, when asked whether he had ever seen one, replied, "God forbid!"

Discourse derives from the Latin *discurrere*, suggesting a movement
"back and forth" between received conceptions of reality and the actual events that defy explanation by them, or between alternative ways of
encoding what counts as true and real. In the strident give and take
between the violent actor and the various kinds of communal identifications and consternated audiences affected by him, each side reacts
to the other in ultimate concern. The actor supplies anomaly; the
audience responds with denial through taboo.

A discourse is not only about the topic of discussion but also about
the premises of the discourse itself. *Meta*terrorism is required in order
to understand how the discourse on terrorism creates its object—the
logical interdependence, paradoxical yet dialectical, between anomaly and taxonomy. Reflexivity, however, is taboo as well. Such avoidance
is quintessential to the constitution of terrorism studies as an academic discipline. It is a discourse grounded in the very prohibition of
discourse. The Terrorist is simply the latest embodiment of the
Barbarian we must avoid at all costs.

VIII

*We may therefore well call those people barbarians in respect to the rules of
reason, but not in respect to ourselves, who surpass them in every kind of
barbarity.*

—M. Montaigne, *The Essays*

People of all cultures have struggled to delimit the precarious borders of what it is to be human. Far from being a fixed category,
"humanity" is a shifty concept whose metaphoric hierarchical movement places people somewhere between Gods and Monsters.
Terrorism discourse makes frequent use of such dissolution of
human/bestial categories.[114]

In the long tradition of the myth of the Wild Man, what makes
the Terrorist such a grand candidate for the workings of the collective
imagination? Formless ambiguity, for one thing. What qualifies some
acts of political violence, but not others, as terroristic is their successful abrogation of: logical form (the play with chance); predictable

tactics (the illusion that the targets are chosen randomly); military structure (improvisation of a loosely structured, underground organization); conventional military strategy (the resort to bluff rather than actual force; action, when taken, for action's sake); morality (the innocence of the victims); normative constraints (the willingness to murder in the pursuit of a self-proclaimed just cause); and a normal persona (the simultaneous and irreconcilable interpretations of the activist as hero and criminal).

Imagination is also characterized by such inconstancy of form,[115] and terrorism can be made to feed into it directly. In the anthropological literature, shamans, witches, prophets, saints, and the like are credited with the typical immunity from ordinary constraint that characterizes myth; such collective representations are witness to, as Needham put it, "an intrinsic vagrancy of the imagination and a constant impulsion to evade external limitations."[116] It is therefore not surprising to hear anthropologists confess to ironies such as "we learnt the most profound lesson about consciousness in rural South Africa from a madman,"[117] and even concede, with a certain conceit, that, "looking into dragons, not domesticating or abominating them, nor drowning them in vats of theory, is what anthropology has been all about."[118] Contemporary terrorists appear to be qualified candidates to be included in this class of mercurial dragonesque personages.

"Terrorism" is an enormously efficacious stimulant of the collective imagination, since it clearly garners and holds media attention all out of proportion to the course of actual events. The fate of a few hostages can rivet public attention for months and even years, or long after the world has wearied of the predicament of whole battalions of troops mired in dirty little wars. We have argued that it is terrorism's play with radical formlessness that empowers it as the modern world's enchanted discourse. Other frequently cited examples of collective enchantment that have generated extraordinary historical stereotypes still haunting us are the Jewish conspiracy, the witch craze, or the Red Scare. Each, like "terrorism," resulted in a chimerical construction so steeped in imaginary fear and terror as to blur the distinction between fiction and reality.

Collective representations are intimately related to the intellectual and moral space of a particular period.[119] When we examine the intellectual context of the recent discovery of terrorism as a salient factor in world politics, we cannot help but notice its simultaneous birth with the real taboo of our times—nuclear energy. Terrorism discourse and nuclear deterrence are symbiotically related. Once there is nuclear capability, the possibility of its falling into the hands of a madman, or even of a chance nuclear cataclysm, becomes unbearably real—true "terrorism" has now been created. In the military imagination of our times, then, there is a clear interdependence between the "formless" powers of terrorism and nuclear terror. Such formlessness is also manifest in the "colorless, odorless" lethal gas of biological warfare. If we can talk of the formless powers of taboo and the abrogation of form as quintessential to the strategy of the terrorist, such depiction is not alien to the ways in which we think about atomic disintegration and biological poisoning. Our imagining of modern technological terrors is informed by the prospect of "boundless" physical energy produced by "breaking" the atom and "unchaining" an endless reaction of "uncontrollable" radiation. Then, too, there is the "unleashing" of the "amorphous" cloud of toxic gas. This is the basic matrix of how we assume nature to work once nuclear and biological technologies are released; it fashions our military imagination grown familiar with depictions of the potential horrors with which we live as late twentieth-century denizens of Planet Earth.

Our western governments are interested in nuclear weapons and biological warfare solely for the purposes of deterrence, or so we are encouraged to believe; but what would the terrorists do with them? With terrorism being typically depicted as the denial of all concern for humanity, we can easily imagine that a Gadaffi or a Saddam Hussein would use the Bomb against us. It is in this regard that we can understand Secretary of State Alexander Haig's statement that "terrorism" was the Reagan administration's major international problem. Were someone to question whether it is justified for us to have the bomb but not so for other countries, the tacit reply is that we know our intentions to be good and therefore we, unlike others, should be trusted. In other words, Hiroshima's *intention* was not terrorism, but the intentions of terrorist states would surely be to instill terror. Despite the apparent irony, such posturing readily makes sense once the perception of terrorism is situated in the apocalyptic soil of a nuclearized imagination.

Yet how has the end of the Cold War and the dwindling of the nuclear threat affected the representation of "terrorism"? It is no accident that those charged with the Oklahoma City explosion were nourished by the newly invigorated culture of rampant worldwide conspiracies following the demise of the East/West armaments race. Ironically, it was President Bush's declaration of a New World Order, imposed by America as its only superpower that prompted such paranoic reactions in the United States. If the Reagan administration used "to confuse terrorism with communism"[120] and Moscow was, according to Sterling, the source and soul of a worldwide terrorist conspiracy, it was not surprising that the Oklahoma bombing was blamed on Japan by the head of the Michigan militia and on the U.S. government itself by others. The Soviet Union is no longer the terrorist enemy, and only days after his solemn participation in the Oklahoma City funeral, President Clinton was sitting next to President Yeltsin in Moscow. The visit had been preceded by reports of massacres by the Russian army in Chechnya. Clinton listened in silence as his host equated Chechnya and Oklahoma City as domestic conflicts rather than warfare.

Without apparent threats from the accustomed external Cold War enemy, it was inevitable that terrorism would finally come "home" where the "heart" is. First, it was the World Trade Center bombing in New York City, ostensibly perpetuated by anti-Communist heroes of the Afghan war left without a mission after the collapse of the Soviet Union, infiltrated by shadowy informers, with purported fanciful conspiracies to blow up every tunnel and every bridge in sight, and thereby feeding the public's negative stereotyping of anything "Muslim."

Then there was Oklahoma City's "terror in the heartland" perpetrated by a former hero of the Gulf War—the emblematic war of Bush's New World Order. Thus, distant, world-menacing "terrorism," so much abominated and promoted by successive U.S. administrations, comes to America itself, ironically the weapon of (of all people!) Reagan's and Bush's ex-warriors. The very triumphant concept of a New World Order, for which they had fought so valiantly, had itself become their worst conspiratorial nightmare. It was not in vain that the Gulf War had aroused millennial dreams among many born-again Christians and provoked a boom in apocalyptic literature. Premillennialist believers wondered: "Is this Armageddon? Is Saddam Hussein the Antichrist? Is his rebuilding of Babylon a fulfillment of Bible prophecy?"[121] God supported America in the war, but Satan was not idle. Jerry Falwell preached a sermon in February 1993, called "America Declares War against God," in which he depicted the state of America under Bill Clinton in cataclysmic terms. If Iranians chanted in their demonstrations that America was "The Great Satan," premillennial dispensationalism and the Department of State had their own cast of satanic figures to be kept in check under the New World Order—the "terrorists." The new order, predicated on confirming and countering the evils of terrorists, was so intimately associated with "them" (the mercenaries of the Afghanistans and Nicaraguas, the

Saddam Husseins, the CIA's Sheik Omars, the ex-army veteran McVeighs) that they become the monster slayers converted into monsters. The alternative was to invent, and then to market, a whole new cast of characters. In the present climate, it is the role (and contribution) of the "terrorist" at home (and the "rogue state" at a distance) to grant legitimacy to apocalyptic fears that drive and justify military and police budgets.

It is not our purpose to ascribe innocence or guilt to either Sheik Omar or McVeigh, determinations that (as of this writing) have yet to be made. Rather, it is our point that *they* stand accused, and there is no small measure of irony regardless of the outcome of their trials. If guilty, then we have the agents of our own antiterrorist campaign turned against their masters. If innocent, then we are the victims of our own terrorist rhetoric, which has regularly demonized Arabs and now includes domestic right-wing extremists (just as in the 1960s, it was left-wingers like the SDS who served as the terrorist bogeyman).

IX

It is the dissolution of these grounds...that permits us to distinguish between wildness as a myth and as a fiction, as an ontological state and as a historical stage of human development, as a moral condition and as an analytical category of cultural anthropology, and, finally, to recognize in the notion of the Wild Man an instrument of cultural projection that is as anomalous in conception as it is vicious in application.

—Hayden White, *Tropics of Discourse*

"Terrorism" ultimately becomes emblematic of the times in which we live. Collective representations of terror can be seen as the photographic negatives depicting the potential chaos of our political culture. Yet by looking at our terrorized images we may learn not only about the barbarian within but also about the transformative powers of our imaginations. Metaphors and allegories rescue the mind from the language of literal meanings and conceptual reifications. Barbarism in the end derives from the failure of the mind to be dialogic and to make of itself a fable. Militarism is particularly close to literalness and has a relevant place in the contemporary experience of a tragic sense of history. The goal of dissolving the culture of terror takes us back to a reappraisal of the tasks of ritual and of the imagination as ways of creating distance from our own modes of acting and knowing.

By turning terror into a projective fantasy of bizarre plots and utter anomaly dreamed up by others wholly unlike us, the real terrors in our daily lives are concealed and granted normalcy. Daniel Patrick Moynihan has argued that criminal violence in the United States has been defined downward;[122] that is, the crime rate has become both so lunatic and so trivialized that what in the Chicago of the 1930s was so shockingly outrageous as to become legendary is nowadays but an ordinary event during any weekend in any American city. The *Journal of the American Medical Association*, in its June 14, 1995, issue, stated that firearms kill 40,000 and harm another 240,000 each year in the United States; the direct and indirect costs surpass $14 billion annually. In 1991, firearm-related deaths were the leading or second-leading cause of injury or death in fifteen states. Firearm homicide among males aged fifteen to nineteen more than tripled in the ten years between 1984 and 1993. Nonfatal assaults occur one hundred times as frequently as those that result in death. If the trend continues, "then between 1993 and 2000 we can expect something like 350,000 firearms deaths in the United States, predominantly among children, teenagers, and young adults."[123] A recent poll by Louis Harris[124] found that 9 percent of sixth-to-twelfth grade students had fired a shot at someone at some time, and eleven percent had been shot at in the past year. Yet none of this is really so abnormal as to pose a threat to national security or provoke any major debate; rather it is grist for the routine journalistic op-ed mill. This is now part of life in America.

Yet there are crimes and there are crimes. In a typical year, such as 1992, worldwide two Americans might be killed and one injured by terrorism.[125] Still, "terrorism" continued at the top of the list of national security problems. Billions were spent annually in preventing it. And yet, as the World Trade Center explosion proved, it wasn't enough. Just as steps were taken in 1990 to protect all airports from the menace, other measures have been made to secure nuclear power plants and other sensitive buildings from terrorist sabotage. Yet guarding nuclear plants alone will not be enough and never will be enough, for "terrorism" is by now perceived as an ineradicable plague. It is the embodiment of anomaly itself. Unlike other rates, such as motor vehicle deaths or the number of institutionalized mental patients, which are very much subject to a "normalizing/abnormalizing" dynamic,[126] terrorism is the ultimate taboo that cannot be measured in statistical terms alone. How else can we explain that the three people killed by the Unabomber over a span of seventeen years can create a national crisis, whereas the tens of thousands of firearm-related deaths in America annually have become a part of "normal" life?

Ordinarily we do not think of murderers as polluted sinners, but it is when we are shocked by some particularly horrible crime that we are reminded that "some crimes *are* also sins. And it is precisely *these* crimes...which lie at the core of our ideas about criminality."[127] The crimes of Nazism and Stalinism fall into this category, and in current political discourse terrorism has emerged as the prototype of such sinful criminality against which the public reacts with the horror of taboo.

Moynihan sees "a dynamic" in the (conservative) upward and the (liberal) downward redefining of what constitutes normalcy. Yet we sense another element at play: since there is always the possibility of manipulating the boundary between the normal and the abnormal, and since society must maintain checks and balances between the two camps, we can always draw the line in such a manner that we can define downward the normalcy of *our* own crimes indefinitely, as long as we define upward the abnormalcy of *their* crimes. For example, there is seemingly nothing "abnormal," certainly nothing "terrorist," about the availability of drugs in American cities and the drug-related homicides. Yet Colombian peasants who grow coca leaves and the traffickers in them are engaged in "narco-terrorism." We are urged to wage a war against them, for it is they who are to blame for our ills. In her book on "narco-terrorism," Rachel Ehrenfeld makes this position explicit: "The real enemy in this war on drugs is not the American people; it is those states [Colombia, Peru, Bolivia] and organizations who combine drugs with terror in a still largely clandestine war against Western societies, above all, the American one."[128] What must, then, be done? Identify the clandestine "root causes"[129] and wage war against them.

In brief, despite the occasional admission that "violence is as American as cherry pie," it is easier to think of our crimes as "normal" as long as we have terrorism to characterize the truly abnormal. Places like Ireland and Palestine are plagued with terror; others, such as Japan, Germany, or France may occasionally turned into a breeding ground of terrorist groups. A favorite rhetorical strategy in terrorism reporting in the American press is to present some awful event in a foreign land and then ask: Could it happen here? The question assumes that so far the United States is free from the unthinkable that transpires elsewhere. For the American citizen, who fears visiting such places as Northern Ireland and Israel, there is little thought given to our homicide rate that is ten times that of Germany, France, or Greece, and seventeen times that of Ireland or Japan![130] In 1992, there were

13,220 homocides in the United States committed with handguns; in Australia there were 13; in the United Kingdom, 33; in Japan, 60.[131]

It is therefore not surprising that the very week the *New York Times* reported that 11 percent of American second graders were shot at during the previous year, the *New Yorker*'s cover page depicted a cartoon captioned "Castles in the Sand" in which a boy with an Arab turban jumps from the surf upon a twin tower while the children who built it are terrified. Gunplay by school children produce normal crime; bombs among suspect Muslims produces anomalous crime. In other words, it is far more important for New Yorkers to keep the blind sheik in jail than to deal with violence in their schools. "Terrorism" is the ultimate bogeyman, the perfect taboo with which to identify and to contain what is presumed to be supreme danger, while glossing over the real terrors of urban life. While obsessed with "terrorism," for example, the media and the public can forget surreal revelations that millions of unknowing Americans have been systematically exposed to radiation experiments, recommended by scientists, during the Cold War. Terrorism also offers the illusion of practical solution; it is a relatively simple and straightforward proposition to incarcerate the sheik, whereas no one really has the answer for urban violence. If terrorism is action, by jailing suspected terrorists we are at least *doing something*—the niceties and legalities of our actions notwithstanding. Once the sheik is in jail we all sleep a bit better in our beds, as when a serial killer is removed from the streets. The reality that the detention of a Son of Sam has no demonstrable value in deterring future serial killings is too unbearable a thought to inform that evening's reverie!

Either in stretching the limits of our normalcy or raising the levels of their anomaly, what becomes apparent is a fetishistic relationship toward violence and its tools. (By *fetish* we mean magical belief, extravagant devotion, and pathological erotic displacement onto an object.) As Marx examined the "fetishism of gold" (the one that confuses the thing for its meaning as a "means" of exchange, the "form" for its "content"),[132] White sees fetishistic components in the monstrous forms of native Wild Men who are at the same time the ultimate objects of desire,[133] whether in the figure of the Proletariat as brute yet as eschatological class, or the extolling of the European as the highest form of humanity on the bases of the fetishes of race and social class.

Fascination with violence (on television and in real life) is what is most notorious about popular culture in the United States. Through it we have access to the Wild Man within (the Wild West, Rambo, the Terminator, Dirty Harry), qualitatively different from the Terrorist

(Monster) without. We experience our violent selves by unleashing vicariously our wrath upon hypothetical evil others; with their savage violence, it is they who are our foils and deserving of our civilized retribution. Recently, Taussig's narration of a "culture of terror" in the midst of colonialism reminded us once again that our notions of civilized self and the barbaric other are still awaiting demythification and reenchantment.

There is an intellectual attitude that distances itself from such attempts at reconstituting a discourse that, in the final analysis, remythifies the figure of the all-too-dangerous Wild Man or the all-too-powerful Terrorist in order to imitate his aberrant anomalies. This can be illustrated by the ironic mode in which Montaigne uses the concept of savagery to question the myths whereby his own society understood civilization, without implying that he was asking his readers to unleash their own cannibalistic instincts. "Terrorism," too, can be invoked as a fictional construct to gain critical distance from our own political discourse. If what best typifies terrorism is the blatant transgression of form, this is also perhaps what best captures the spirit of the present times; we live in a postmodern world in which conceptual fixities are dislodged and are undergoing a crisis of representation, and in which military conventions have been superseded by the new realities of nuclear deterrence and low-intensity warfare. The contemporary fascination with horror as a salient source of mass aesthetic stimulation[134] and with terrorism as the political emblem of our times reflects the same reality. By deliberately playing with the extremes of terrorist "savagery" versus "civilized" militarism and nuclearism, we get closer to the complexities of the world we live in. Instead of further adding to the remythification of the Wild Man as a terrorist, a skeptical view suggests that we can learn much from fictionalizing the myths of terrorism and thereby exorcise the terrors of our own Cold War imaginations.

7

FACES OF TERROR
AND LAUGHTER

This chapter presents the view from hell. We ask the victims of terror to show their faces. As ethnographers we must witness them. Yet we are aware that bearing witness can itself be illusory, that lying may be inherent to any confession, and that implicitly apologetic discourses can mask self-righteousness. We can hardly claim to be true witnesses; we live far removed from the horror of the victims' everyday lives. Nor can we pretend that the interpretations we impose on their narratives are the correct ones. Still, despite the silence that overwhelms any inquiry into human torture and killing, and despite the danger that we might appear to be creating excuses for what is in itself inexcusable, we choose not to hide the pain of the victims—whether of terrorists or counterterrorists. By refusing to stigmatize the activists and their communities, we know that we must be ready to accept the accusation that we are tainted by personal proximity and sympathy.

Experiences of victimization and torture are emblematic in that they move us, as Taussig puts it, "through that space of death where reality is up for grabs. And here we but begin to see the magnitude of the task, which calls neither for demystification nor remystification but for a quite different poetics of destruction and revelation."[1] The cases that we will examine have the power to go beyond the rhetorical subversion of a mythical discourse. They reflect embodied terror and are engaged not in moral indignation from the sidelines but in working through the madness of personal experience in the quest for new means of social and political healing. They radically question categorical distinctions between "us" and "them," the saved and the damned.

Confronted with the phantoms of terrorist discourse's postmodern "hyperreality" and its atmosphere of contagion and taboo, our counterdiscourse consists, ironically, of a return to the premodern risks of what Levinas has called "the very straightforwardness of the face to face." For us such face-to-face contact with terrorism is initially an ethnographic encounter, but it also transcends both the intimacy of fieldwork and the ethics of mere dialogue. The paramount expression of terrorism discourse is official ideology; its primary mode consists in demonizing and imposing on the violent actor a *cordon sanitaire*, infringement of which amounts to the transgression of a taboo and commitment of a crime. The mere suggestion that we take into account discourse-as-dialogue and discourse-as-subjectivity[2] is, in itself, a direct assault on much of the extant terrorism discourse. We do not limit our purview to the sanitized "subject" proposed by terrorism experts but rather, as ethnographers are wont to do, we speak freely to the actual subjects caught up in the political violence. In keeping with the recent theoretical prominence ascribed to the human body in social analysis—the locus of manifold material and symbolic practices,[3]—we witness the bodies of the victims of violence as the privileged site of political agency and subjectivation.

I

And it is then, in this moment when no longer fleeing we accept to look the victim and the murderer in the eye—like Myshkin looks at Rogozhin—that we remember we are human, that this is a misfortune, but it is a trying joy. Human equally: humanity passes through you and me, and through Macbeth and the king and the beggar, and we understand ourselves and each other.

    —H. Cixous, "The Place of Crime, The Place of Forgiveness"

Her father had been killed an hour earlier. Cristina Cuesta, a twenty-year-old journalism student, was answering the matter-of-fact questions of a court clerk:

"*When did you know that something had happened?*"
"At five past three P.M."
"*How did you hear about it?*"
"My neighbor called me."
"*What did she tell you?*"
"Run down the stairs because something has happened to your father."
"*Did you see your father there?*"
"No, he had been taken to the hospital."
"*Who took you to the hospital?*"
"The municipal police."
"*How many times was he shot?*"
"….!!"

Cristina could not answer "two." She happened to be at home in San Sebastian that Friday afternoon at five past three, March 26, 1982, when the telephone rang. She had come from Bilbao to celebrate her birthday with the family. A female voice told her to run downstairs because something had happened to her father. Without saying a word to her mother and her younger sister, she rushed to the scene. She saw the people, the blood—a friend embraced her and said he had been taken to the hospital. The municipal police drove the two of them there. The hospital was no more than a mile away but it seemed much further. She concentrated all of her energy upon refusing to believe that her father could be dead. At the hospital, they wouldn't let her see him. She insisted and people around her began to shout that she was the daughter, that she was an adult, and that she had a right. She was allowed to enter the morgue. She threw herself upon her dead father's body, while shouting "*¡Hijos de puta!*" ("Whore's sons!") over and over. The authorities had to separate her forcibly from the corpse in order to take her to the justice court to give evidence. It was there that the clerk asked her about how many bullets had pierced her father's heart and, in her horror, she could not utter the word "two." A psychiatrist gave her some tranquilizers, so she can scarcely remember more details from that fateful day.

Twelve years later Cristina still cannot talk about these events with her mother and her younger sister; they cannot cope yet with what happened. They heard the news on national TV at about 3:30. The fourteen-year-old girl also ran downstairs looking for her father, but someone intercepted her and took her back home. Cristina's mother refused to believe her husband was dead. That night the two sisters went to sleep locked in a tearful embrace.

Cristina's father was the local director of the National Telephone System in San Sebastian. It was taken for granted that state agents would eavesdrop in its search for information regarding ETA. The director had to turn a blind eye to such police intervention; for ETA this was tantamount to being a collaborator in state espionage and deserving of death. To his wife and daughters he had likened his situation to one "as if the police stop you at a roadblock and demand to see your papers; you swallow it and shut up." The orders came from on high and had nothing to do with him. He simply knew what was transpiring. He had even petitioned the Ministry of Interior to prohibit such police abuse of the telephone system, maintaining that no telephone worker should have to be a collaborator. Born in the adjacent region of the Rioja, he had married a Basque woman and felt himself to be Basque.

After her father's murder, Cristina had to assume responsibility for her younger, traumatized sister and her mother, who became mentally ill. At first this responsibility kept Cristina strong and determined, but after a year she collapsed. In the meantime she found herself changing almost without realizing it. If she read a political slogan spray-painted on a wall it would nauseate her. She found antigovernment political demonstrations to be infuriating. News of the death of some activists made her happy. Each new detention was now a triumph. She came to approve of torture—the more the better. But it all began to disturb her. She could no longer recognize herself in such reactions. They were not her.

This is but one example of the trauma and tragedy experienced by the families of ETA's victims. By June of 1993 ETA had killed 749 people, of whom 453 were members of state security forces and 296 were civilians (25 children).[4] There are no statistics regarding the wounded, but their numbers are much greater. Each victim implies the victimization of an entire family. Of the victims interviewed for one study in the province of Gipuzkoa,[5] 23 percent of civilian casualties had been caused "by error," 65.4 percent of those interviewed still suffered psychological trauma, and 73 percent of them cited negative "social consequences." In 65.4 percent of the cases their economic circumstances had worsened. Nothing better captures in cold numbers the vastness of ETA's real violence than these hundreds of victimized families.

Social workers who attend to such survivors underscore the victims' overwhelming desire to meet *face-to-face* with the killer of their loved one. They are aware that staring into one another's eyes would be the most revelatory moment. What do victims feel toward the aggressors? "Hatred and rage" (34 percent of the cases), "impotence" (34 percent), "sadness" (26 percent), "nothing" (3 percent). Does the word "pardon" mean anything to them? Of the victims, 57 percent don't know or can't answer, 23 percent say yes, 19 percent say no. There are towns in which ETA perpetrators and family members of their victims can come across each other on the street. (Many of the victims claim to be able to identify their assailant.) Thus far there have not been cases of revenge, although the possibility is there.

Victims, then, by a large majority of 73 percent, say they would like to have a chance to talk to their aggressors. They long for that face-to-face interaction in which naked humanity would communicate. When asked what they would ask of their aggressors, over half replied "just being begged forgiveness." A face-to-face apology might radically change that impenetrable burden of pain and perplexity. The faces of terrorized victims might get transformed if simply they had a chance to cry out to the mute yet ever-present face of the killer, "Why did you do it?" Enduring such an encounter would entail a recognition of each other's humanity.

Cristina Cuesta's story is exceptional in that it eventually incorporates reconciliation and personal courage. Shocked by her own dark transformation that made her rejoice in the murder of others, she became uncomfortable with herself. She began a period of reflection and of active search for a way out of her state of mind. Then one day she realized that those murdered by Spain's state terrorism were as much victims of violence as herself. The case of the mother of Mikel Zabalza, arrested and found dead while in police custody in 1985, was particularly crucial in Cristina's change of heart. She could identify with the mother's pronouncements of her feelings of rage and impotence. She discovered that the common pain that bound all the victims of the violence was far more intense than that which separated them ideologically. Cristina had been ascribed and relegated to one of the two sides of the confrontation without her choice. The protagonists of history might want nothing to do with her, she realized, but at the very least she could try to bridge the gap between the victims of both sides by accepting the other's pain as one's own.

Cristina found an apt opportunity to issue her bold and potent message. During an international conference on violence and the media, when the audience was given a chance to intervene, she rose to her feet. In plain words she said that she was a victim of terrorism, that she hadn't chosen her trench in the war, that she had hated enough, and that she wanted to issue a call to Mikel Zabalza's mother and to a family member of one of GAL's victims to join forces in a search for reconciliation. If the victims of violence from the opposing parties were able to work for peace together, she added, institutions and political parties should follow suit. Zabalza's mother replied positively to Cristina's call. There was no going back, and in 1986 Cristina created an association for peace in the Basque Country to which she has devoted herself ever since.

This is the type of truth that is not merely "the interrogator's violence reaudited and redoubled as truth."[6] It is the truth that may emerge in the eyes of the victims and the actors' audiences forced to witness the drama. It happens when the victimized community has the courage to overcome the initial reaction of hatred and to take center stage. The community can no longer remain a mere victim; it must either turn away in horror or become an accomplice. By awakening to the unfolding, real-life tragedy, the community becomes capable of breaking the repetitive, violent plot and of seeing through the seduction and complacency of uncritical self-righteousness.

This action is similar to aesthetic distancing in the search for truth, as when Gadamer writes about "art as the raising up of this [untransformed] reality into its truth."[7] It requires, however, that the players—both aggressors and victims—not be deprived of their communities and that they be recognized as genuine subjects profoundly transformed by their experience. In this fashion, the violent actor is stripped of disguise, of pretending to be somebody else, and is scorched to the core of his/her being by the *amor fati* that have overtaken his/her life. This is not the truth of the inquisitor or the interrogator, nor is it any sort of representational truth or absolute veracity waiting to be discovered by the fortunate. It is rather the common sense of experience and of multiperspectivity forced upon the community through its new-found awareness of its own contingency.

This adoption of the victim's perspective as one way of avoiding the delusions of a single representation is reminiscent of Blake's powerful allegory in the "Marriage of Heaven and Hell." Through corrosive satire of moralistic orthodoxy, he forces the vain "angel" to see the hellish vision of his own heavenly condition. The problem with the Swedenborgian angel is that he has never spoken to devils; had he visited hell, Blake contends, the angel would have grown wiser by hearing both sides of the story. This allegory of angels and devils and their mutual transformation is a tale about man's ambivalent impulses. Freedom from restriction is ultimately obtained by harnessing the power of multiple perspectives. This is also the higher irony of thinkers such as Vico, for whom falsehood can be viewed as a necessary stage in the attainment of truth.

Terrorism discourse is vitiated by the lack of a multiple perspective. The Blakean vision announces that "Without Contraries is no progression"; the angelic view that only sees the good lacks multiple perspective and is of no value for an understanding of the drama and "progression" of humanity, which can only result from a marriage of contrary perspectives. In psychoanalytic vocabulary, this is the marriage of consciousness and unconsciousness, thought and energy; in the religious realm, of metaphor and sacrament. Moralizing contraries, and then privileging one interpretation to the exclusion of the other, is the source of the priest's uncompromising single code.

It is tempting to be conclusive and to say that any text can have only one literal meaning and one moral sense and must ultimately be right or wrong. But matters are not so simple, either in biblical interpretation or in these morality plays of terror producing innocence and experience. Cristina Cuesta's transformation bears witness to these moral complexities.

II

Then they told me that they would do me a favor, and the one who had tortured me the most forced me to look at his face. I hated it.

                                           —E. Martínez

Eyes world-blind,
eyes in the fissure of dying,
eyes eyes

                                  —P. Celan, "Snow-bed"

Head down and eyes closed!—are the very first orders the torturer issues to his victim. Tortured people are systematically blindfolded or hooded in Spain. Victims relate long days of torture without ever having seen a face. Occasionally when, after endless torment, the torturers have to admit to their victim that s/he is innocent, the order might be given to raise one's eyes. Being forced to see the torturer's face can be a most frightening experience for the victim. The straightforwardness of the facial confrontation condenses the revelatory potential for both intimacy (solidarity) as well as distance (terror) in human interaction.

For the militant who has surrendered his life to a cause, the prospect of systematic torture might be even more frightening than death itself. Torture is the ordeal by fire and the usual fate reserved by governments for underground activists. The message that torture engraves upon one's humiliated body is an unforgiving and unforgettable inscription, an everlasting initiation to an unfrequented human space and condition. The terrors of innocence and of experience climax there. The broken body both secures and reflects an indelible verity.

"The beginning was a kind of ritual." That's how Joxe Domingo Aizpurua begins his story; he is a slim, tall, vulnerable-looking, handsome man in his early forties, a philosophy student, his voice somewhat cracked, both fright and determination visible in his eyes. It is the evening of August 12, 1994; upon our request, he is about to relate his experiences beginning June 2, when, having completed a prison term in France as an alleged ETA operative, he was handed over to the Spanish police at the Basque frontier.

> Unexpectedly they put a bandage over my eyes in absolute silence. Suddenly one grabbed me by one arm and another by the other. Twelve, or maybe fifteen, men stood around me in a circle. They made me walk about forty or fifty steps. Suddenly the silence was broken, and one of them spoke in my ear softly: "Whore's son, we are going to kill you, we are going to assassinate you, we are going to tear you apart, just like Arregi" [who perished by torture while in the custody of the Spanish police]. And then the other repeated the threat softly in my other ear. And those around, standing in the circle, shouted loudly and together like a chorus: "We are going to kill you!" while at the same time marking march steps. This was the initiation ritual, that's how I have defined it. It lasted about two minutes. I can remember perfectly how those voices, one in one ear, the other in the other, while the rest shouted and marched, how those words penetrated the depths of my brain. After the two minutes, silence.

This is ritualization in the plain sense of formalized performance. It is prior to the ritualized "duel for truth" that Foucault observed in torture. Formalization serves as a mechanism to induce a state of terror in the blindfolded victim while controlling the actions of the torturers.

> Then the torture began. They put a plastic bag over my head, always with the blindfold over my eyes, and I would feel the suffocation. My hands were tied. The twelve or fifteen men continued around me in

a circle. Two of them always held me up. One touched me gently. He was taking my pulse so as to give the order "Take it off!" when I was about to faint. And they would take it off. I don't know how long I endured the asphyxia. And then they would tell me: "Well, you have three seconds to talk. One, two, three!" Again they would put the bag on me. Again the asphyxia. Always the one who controlled my pulse gave the order. And again and again, it seemed like an infinity, beyond reckoning. When that was over, it was time for the electric shocks. They applied the electrodes all over my body. They would always apply the electrodes over my clothes. [Pointing to his body] Here, here, here. When facing them, they would put the electrodes right on my penis. When from behind they would put them on my testicles. On my nipples, my lips, all over the body. After the shocks they would give me a glass of water, and when I would take it they turned on the electricity. The spilling of the water multiplied the discharge effect. Then came the blows from all the men still in their circle. I always remained blindfolded. They would push me from one side to the other. Blows all over my body. When they would hit me on my face and chest, they would do so with their hands open so as not to leave marks. They hit me over the head with something like a telephone book, which makes your brain feel swollen. And then came the round of punches as I was passed from one to another, and then another. And after that again the hood and the suffocation. Then more electric shocks and blows. I lost consciousness an infinity of times. They would hold me up, they would make me stand. This was all accompanied by insults. I have estimated that I was tortured like this in San Sebastián for eleven hours (because I was handed over to the Spanish police by the French at 9 P.M. and it was daylight when they took me to Madrid). They introduced me in a police van that had individual compartments. They turned up the volume of the music to the limit. I made the entire trip in a foetal position, trembling. I could not stand up, I was shaking. In Madrid, after they made me wait in the van for an hour or two in very high heat, they dragged me from the van amid kicks and blows and put me in a dark cell. There I lost entirely any sense of time, of day or night, of anything at all.

The man telling the story has detailed narration at his disposal. His voice is neutral, his gestures matter-of-fact, his eyes express no particular emotion as he speaks. The listener has heard about torture and has a vague idea that it is likely to exist somewhere. Told in the first

person in one's living room, its sheer brutality presents, at least initially, problems of discomfort and readjustment. One asks questions
in order to mark time and be able to decide if the shocking narration
is possible. Yes, yes, one hears occasionally about Amnesty
International's yearly report that torture is routine in a very long list
of countries; in fact, one struggles to remember, wasn't it alleged that
most European countries practice it? But the tortured face is annoyed
by such requests for additional information; the story overtakes its
teller and allows for no interruptions. Yes, yes, let us assume this is
true. But then it is not an historical account about Hitler's Germany
or Stalin's Russia. This face in one's living room is a neighbor reporting something that happened to him a few weeks earlier, something
that seems out of the ordinary yet is also routine, all in a European
democracy in 1994. Again, one is embarrassed by one's own naivete,
as if there should be some contradiction between democracy and torture, or torture should be at most some "premodern," accidental, and
momentary feature of modern politics. There are no signs of hatred,
no anger, no request for pity in the face of the man telling the story.
Not a hint of pride or claim to personal worth for what happened to
him. He is simply replying to a request to tell his story.

Rather than for reasons of state, torture, as Scarry has noted, has
much more to do with "the display of the fiction of power."[8] The example we have just related can be taken as a case in point. When, after
having completed his four-year prison sentence in France, this man
was handed over to the Spanish police, there was no extradiction petition for him pending nor was there any indictment against him in the
Spanish courts. His lawyers even contested the legality of his delivery
to the Spanish authorities (other prisoners in the same situation
appealed and were granted residence in other parts of France). After
several days of torture, in which ordinarily the victim admits to any
charge, and after two weeks of being held incommunicado, the case
against him proved so unsubstantial that he was released on proba-
tion. He was, in fact, told by the torturers that his case had to do mostly with "propaganda." A week later there were to be elections to the
European Parliament and the Spanish Minister of Interior was, during those days of torture, in Paris talking with his French counterpart
about issues of international counterterrorism. Governments needed
to show to their outraged constituents some "successes" of international collaboration in the war against terrorism. The handing over of
a militant could be partly explained in terms of its propaganda effect.
Aizpurua's case conforms to Rajali's view that "they [the tortured] are

of no use except as parts of a system of media representations."[9]

Joxe Domingo Aizpurua's travails were followed by the arrest and the widespread torture of another sixty-two people in June of 1994, of whom only six were subsequently kept in custody. The inflicted tortures mirrored the horror of terrorist savagery the police feared and fictionalized. The incalculable consequence of such use of repression is that the authorities thereby "validate the sociological assumptions that animate terrorist ideologies and practice."[10]

These examples illustrate that it is not for extreme reasons of state that torture is administered. During the 1980s it was estimated that 85 percent of the tortured people in the Basque Country were subsequently released without charges. In 1985, for example, 1,181 detentions related to terrorism resulted in only 69 prison sentences.[11] Similarly, according to one source, in Northern Ireland in 1973, one-fifth of all houses were subjected to police and army raids; the indictment rate of those arrested in a 1980 raid was 11 percent; and of the 75 percent of those who were charged, indictment was predicated mainly on confession.[12] The experience of prison and torture being central to the political culture of terror, it is commonplace that "through arrest and interrogation the state imposes a kind of information taxation on society."[13] Reports on torture, as in the case of Argentina, mention that "prisoners were routinely terrorized with torture before and during interrogation, before execution, or before regaining freedom. In other cases people were tortured and released without ever being interrogated."[14] As students of torture point out, it "does not produce any better intelligence results than ordinary police work."[15] In the case of Spain, Vercher notes, "the evidence so obtained has usually been of poor quality."[16] Torture becomes an end in itself. As Peters noted, "It is not primarily the victim's information, but the victim, that torture seeks to win—or reduce to powerlessness."[17] If anything, we could say with Sartre that its goal is to create a different "race," the species of the nonhuman.

The fate of the woman Enkarni Martínez, mother of two children, tortured in the summer of 1994, illustrates such banal arbitrariness.

> I was arrested at 4 or 5 in the morning, but out of revenge. They came for my husband but since he was not at home they arrested me instead. As I entered their car the threats began. "Here we are in charge; lower your head, close your eyes, and if you say or do anything we'll hit you." I lost track of where we were going. One of them said loudly: "What this whore fox needs is a prick in the asshole that'll come out of her mouth." This greatly impressed me….

The initial ritual was the following: they put me against the wall, they ordered me not to ever open my eyes and not to lean on the wall. All was silence, and suddenly I heard the steps of someone. Bang! He gave me a slap that sent me reeling against the opposite wall. And then all of them started punching me, and giving me electric shocks, and so on. They would fondle me a lot with their hands. I had my period and while in the bathroom they were staring at me. But much worse than the electric shocks were the threats against my son. That was the hardest. They pretended they had him there.... During the interrogation someone might come from behind me saying that he was going to rape me, while others pretended to scold him: "Come on, we are eight people here watching you." And the insults: "whore fox," "filthy one," "sow." They put a hood made of cloth over my head, and over it a plastic bag. What I feared most was losing consciousness and then being told I had admitted to things I had not done.... I was tortured from June 5 to June 8, 1994. When they set me free I went to the doctor to be examined. As soon as they read the results of the tests they were alarmed and ordered my immediate hospitalization. If muscles normally have 160 enzymes, I had over 24,000. If not for the test, they told me, I could have lost my kidney. I denounced it all in front of Judge Garzón. I told him: "Do you want me to show you the marks?" He replied: "No, no, no."

If one looks at the newspapers of the day in need of reassurance about the reality of these events, they are indeed recorded. In Enkarni's case, obscene photos of her body injuries are included. The June 11 issue of the pro-ETA newspaper Egin had a front-page color photograph of the wound that could have cost Enkarni her kidney, and another displaying some of the thirty-three bruises on her body.

The interdictions imposed on the faces of tortured people are uniquely revelatory of the power relations. The victim must lower his/her face at all times; the eyes must be closed or blindfolded. The tortured must never see the face of the torturer. A primary reason for this, of course, is to avoid the possibility of future identifications in the event that the torturer is denounced and brought to justice. Yet such asymmetries of vision reveal far more than simple caution. The following instance in Enkarni's story shows the powerful implications of a face-to-face encounter:

When it was over they told me that they were very sorry, that they begged my pardon. Since everybody claims to be innocent how else could they learn the truth? They wanted to know what was I thinking about them at that moment. I told them that I hated them. Then they said that they would do me a favor, and the one that had tortured me the most forced me to look at his face. I hated it. He knew that I would be set free, and I think that the point of showing me his face was that I would be left with the fear that I might see him again when I was out on the street.

This is the communication "from darkness to darkness." As Celan's poem noted: "You opened your eyes—I saw my darkness live."[18]

Ultimately, truth that emerges from such interaction derives perhaps from having imposed what Foucault calls a "theater of hell," that is, a two-way "torture of the truth" between the torturer and the victim,[19] its impossible goal being, as Sartre put it, "to force from *one* tongue...the secret of *everything*."[20] Linked together in agonistic duel, the torturer strives to connect events to their authors, whereas the victim seeks truth in the silence of self-perseverance. As Feldman puts it, "Interrogation is a ceremony of verification, not only of crime but of agency. It revolves around techniques of encapsulation and transubstantiation that render power tangible, immediate, and circumscribed."[21] The faceless torturer may "reward" his victim with the sight of his face once the experiment is over.

An extreme instance of seeking truth by manipulating facial interaction is evident in the next narration. Patxi Lizaso was publicly charged by the province's civil governor of belonging to an ETA cell responsible for killing three people, but after days of torture he was released with no charges against him.

> When they saw that I would not admit the actions they imputed to me, they brought in two guys. One of them was from Usurbil [Patxi's home town]; he had been arrested about five hours earlier. They let me see his face when they unhooded him for a moment, but they would not let him see me. It was a kind of confrontation, although they would not let me speak. They put the hood on him and made him testify in front of me, although he didn't know I was there. And then they brought in the other one, whose face they did not let me see, and he made the same accusations against me. They both said that I was the one who had provided them the arms, that I was the head of the cell. What my neighbor had to say was all prearranged. And they would ask him: "And in such and such action, what was Patxi Lizaso's role?" And he would respond with whatever had been prearranged. And then the other one, whose face they did not show me and who could very well have been one of them, repeated the same things.

After that confrontation they took me to another room. An old "dog" [police officer] of about fifty-five years old took off my hood, he made me lift my head, and after looking at me (his was the only face I had seen since my arrest), he told me: "Are you convinced that they are heaping on you all the blame?" "Yeah, but everything is made up by you." He wanted to climb up the walls when I told him that.

In another interrogation they brought the same man from Usurbil again to testify against me. They put the same questions to him and he began to say the same things. I was absolutely forbidden to speak but I couldn't stand it any more and I said to myself: "They can't beat me any more than they already have." So I spoke to him: "X [his personal name], why aren't you telling the truth?" That was terrible. I was hit so hard that I was knocked to the floor more than once and left there unable to stand up. They gave me electric shocks.

Besides their presence in torture chambers, facial coverings have a sinister pedigree in terrorism iconography. The activist's actions with the IRA, for example, are labeled "hooding activities."[22] If there is an emblematic stereotype of guerrillas or terrorists in action, it is of the masked men/women holding submachine guns.[23] It is not their weapons but rather their masked facelessness that is the perfect icon for their expatriation from society. Withdrawal of face is denial of social interaction and personal responsibility. If the very act of concealing the face is charged with symbolism, the persona typified by a faceless mask is beyond the human sphere. Victims kidnapped by an armed organization, as well as suspects arrested by the police, will remain for days and weeks without ever seeing the faces of their custodians. Withdrawal of a human face that will take direct responsibility for a victim's fate is ultimate terror.

Systematicness is a point stressed by students of torture; it is not fortuitous or the result of one individual's pathological sadism, but is rather a well-planned and hierarchically sanctioned policy turned into a basic repressive instrument by the state. The political establishment proudly trumpets and appropriates as its own victories the "great successes" of such police interrogations. Nor is torture an anomalous aberration from the values of western civilization; on the contrary, as any student of colonialism is well aware, such rites of terror have a deep civilizing history.

It is estimated by Basque sources that during the Spanish democratic period alone (that is, since 1978), over 14,000 Basques have been arrested for political reasons,[24] and that about 85 percent of those arrested are subjected to torture and maltreatment of all kinds.[25] If we take into account that this repression has taken place almost exclusively among the so-called patriotic left, which votes for the pro-ETA Herri Batasuna Party and which accounts for about 250,000 Basques, approximately one out of twenty in their ranks has suffered the harrowing effects of arrest and potential torture during the democratic period. While estimates vary, by one count during ETA's 35-year history, 5 people have died under torture, 10 have died while in jail, 67 people have been killed as a result of the so-called dirty war at the hands of state-sponsored mercenaries, and 119 have perished as a result of police actions. The wounded number many more. An estimated 2,000 persons have been forced into political exile. There is a permanent prison population of about 500 activists, of whom 84 declared they were tortured during 1993 while being transported from one jail to another.[26]

On March 23, 1995, it was reported that the bodies of two Basque guerrillas who had disappeared twelve years earlier had been found.[27] It was revealed that following their kidnapping in France, both had been tortured at a Ministry of Interior building in San Sebastián where they remained for weeks before being taken to Alicante and murdered. There they remained, lying in a morgue.[28]

These discoveries followed the revelations of two former police officers convicted in 1991 for murder while organizing and operating the hit squads known as GAL, linked to the Socialist Government of Prime Minister Felipe González. The men implicated superior officers, and several former police and Interior Ministry officials were jailed as a result. The chain of accusations reached its zenith in the summer of 1995 when a former Basque socialist leader, Ricardo García Damborenea, confessed that he had been one of the organizers of the anti-ETA state terrorist group GAL. He added that he had personally informed González about GAL's operations and obtained his approval, a charge denied by the Spanish leader. Judge Baltasar Garzón charged González in the Spanish Supreme Court with being a founder and leader of GAL. The Supreme Court declined to investigate him for lack of evidence.

Europe is no exception to the fact that two-thirds of the world's countries regularly practice human rights abuses. European governments try hard to mask the evidence of their systematic torture. Amnesty International's 1993 report recorded torture and ill treatment of prisoners in twenty-seven European countries and claims that torture was apparently responsible for the deaths of more than forty persons in about ten European countries during the year. Indeed, there is a European Committee for Prevention of Torture, of which Spain is member. In the case of Joxe Domingo Aizpurua, the Committee was called in and three of its experts interviewed the tortured man. But reports are ruled by discretion, and governments can impede their publication, so the findings were not made public. This is all democracy at work. At the time the Spanish government ordered its own investigation that, once the furor was over, was soon canceled with declarations that there were no "proofs" of torture.

III

We victims and victimizers, we're part of the same humanity, colleagues in the same endeavor to prove the existence of ideologies, feelings, heroic deeds, religions, obsessions.

—J. Timerman, *Prisoner without a Name,*
Cell without a Number

The most disturbing incongruity is that the torturer is all too human. Even more surreal than the victim's torment is the sudden visit to the torturer of his wife, mantilla in hand, on her way to mass; or when he picks up the phone to speak lovingly to his children. Eva Forest describes one such phone call.[29] She had been awakened from unconsciousness by water poured on her and the torturer had handed her a cup of coffee. She was against the wall, all wet and shivering with cold, an iron grip holding her arm each time she staggered, waiting to see "a very important man." Suddenly the door opened and she was pushed inside. And there he was, solemn and immense, exquisitely dressed, the man on the other side of the large table in a comfortable office with soft armchairs, politely telling her to come closer, to have a seat, while offering her a cigarette. The torturer sat on the armchair next to her. While everybody waited respectfully, the very important man rang home to let his mother know that he had "a visit" and would be late for dinner. She was threatened, hit, guns were aimed at her—while the important man's role in the game was to plead for calm from his impassive distance. He delayed his filial responsibilities toward his mother in order to assume a paternal role towards the victim.

Yet Forest adamantly refuses to ratify the torturer's benevolence. She wrote a piece after reading in *El País International* a rather extensive obituary regarding the life of José Sainz—she had later found that to be the name of "the very important man"—during Spain's transition period to democracy. According to the newspaper, his death posed an irreparable loss to society. His obituary was side by side, equal in length and significance, to that of the great Catalan poet J.V. Foix. Forest obstinately clung to her memory and resisted sanitizing history to erase the differences between the two men.[30]

The torturer is so human that he may even beg his victim's pardon, as we saw in the case of Enkarni Martinez. What follows is Patxi Lizaso's concluding "reconciliation" with his torturers:

> Later on, when they took me to testify in front of the lawyer in charge [state-appointed rather than designated by the accused], they put me in a corner. They told me I could lift my head, but that I was not to look at them. And they asked my forgiveness. They said that I was right, that they had been mistaken, that I was clean, that I had been very honest in not giving the names of innocents, that they disliked having innocent persons. This left me worse off than before. I felt completely impotent. I didn't say a word, I couldn't utter a single one. They told me I was right and clean, and added: "Now when you go to the lawyer in charge to testify we advise you not to declare anything [i.e., about torture]. And tomorrow, after you are processed, you will be out on the street." Those were their words.

Torture, too, pertains to that class of events afflicted by a radical failure of witnessing[31]—the startling fact that an event eliminates its own witness. Hence, denouncing one's torture publicly, after having been savagely exposed to it, is itself most difficult for the terrified victim. After all, there are no independent witnesses. In Spain, arrested persons can be held by the police without access to their lawyer for up to five days (until 1987 arrested people could be held incommunicado for ten days). The judge may attribute signs such as redness on the legs to an allergic reaction to one's stockings, or a swollen head to an insect's sting; and there is always recourse to the possibility that one's injuries are self-inflicted (particularly if fatal). There were 448 denunciations for torture in the Spanish state during 1993, yet no one knows what percentage of the victims fail to come forward because of the risks of going public.

The exorbitance of torture is such that forgetting it becomes almost a necessity; its obscenity makes denial seem almost more reasonable than accepting it as fact. Thus talk about "torture" is almost taboo in the media, except as a footnote that refers to a report by some human rights organization. Studiously avoiding the word torture, there are standard expressions such as someone being "subjected to heavy-handed tactics."[32] On September 24 and 26, 1993, for example, Gurutze Yanci and Xabier Galparsoro died while they were in police custody and under interrogation in the Basque Country. If one accepts matter-of-factly the attestations presented in this chapter, it is not unthinkable that something may have gone wrong during the macabre ritual of "custody and interrogation." The three newspapers we have consulted—the *New York Times, El País Internacional, Deia*—were able to report the Yanei and Galparsoro deaths without once mentioning the word "torture" even as a possibility or a suspicion. The invisibility of the unwitnessed, tormented body in the torture chamber finds its replica in the invisibility of the unwritten word "torture" in the report. The thirty-one-year-old Gurutze Yanci died of heart failure twenty-six hours after she was arrested in the same police station in which Aizpurua had been tortured (described above); those who were arrested along with her, her husband included, could hear Yanci's screams during the night; they themselves were subject to agonies similar to those of Aizpurua. The "causes" adduced by the media for Yanci's death were that she smoked or that she was overweight. Xabier Galparsoro's death was explained as a suicide when he threw himself from the police headquarter's window. In Feldman's words, "The performance of torture does not apply power; rather it manufactures it from the 'raw' ingredient of the captive's body. The surface of the body is the stage where the state is made to appear as an effective material force."[33] The state ensures its reproduction by the right to dispose of the bodies of its subjects with impunity.

In the United States, newspapers such as the *New York Times* abet the practice by giving front-page news coverage to "confessions" provided by government officials who have extracted them through torture; indeed, it is not the torture that makes the news, since it is known that the practice is "pretty common for the Egyptians."[34] The real issue concerning torture is, of course, its widespread practice by governments, many of them cohorts of the United States,[35] including democracies such as Spain,[36] France,[37] Great Britain,[38] and Israel.[39]

The possibility that the United States might resort to systematic torture is somewhat remote. Yet we suspect that, if anything, "counterterrorism" has the greatest potential for legitimating such behavior. In legal terms, the standard prelude to authoritarian regimes condoning torture is the suspension of *habeas corpus*, that "great historic remedy to injustice" that in the United States permits federal courts to "set aside the convictions of state prisoners because they were tortured into confessing or convicted by other unconstitutional means."[40] Should we, therefore, be surprised that the counterterrorism bill passed by Congress after the Oklahoma City explosion provided stringent restrictions on *habeas corpus* that, according to experts, "may effectively eliminate it."[41] President Clinton went along with attaching the *habeas corpus* provision to the counterterrorism bill—"the worst cave-in" according to an editorial in the *New York Times*[42]—apparently in the belief that the political mileage obtained from seeming tough on terrorism is more important than preserving the Great Writ, as it is called.

After the Oklahoma City explosion, at least one voice openly advocated that the United States use torture in cases of suspected terrorists. On May 14, 1995, National Public Radio interviewed a criminal law specialist from Israel who advocated it on the basis of his own country's systematic use of the practice on Palestinian detainees.[43] He acknowledged that there might be some initial resistance, just as there was in placing metal detectors in airports, but that the public would get used to it. Asked why Israel keeps secret its resort to torture, he replied that, aside from potential embarrassment there is the advantage that secrecy makes the practice more effective. To the objection that a few days earlier, as a consequence of "moderate shaking," a detained Palestinian had died at the hands of the police, the interviewee posed this final question: "Wouldn't you have put a plastic bag over McVeigh's head for half an hour if you thought that would have prevented the Oklahoma City explosion?"

Chapter 6 addressed the question of whether there is anything that can justify the use of torture in a democracy. There is no other more compelling argument than the need for "counterterrorism" to blur the issue of the intrinsic inhumanity of torture. The mainstream terrorism literature at times even defends its practice when employed against terrorists.[44] Here, the conclusion by Leach that "counter terrorism becomes, in a bizarre sense, a religiously sanctioned moral duty,"[45] attains its zenith.

If Aristotle denied a human soul to slaves, thereby permitting philosophers to defend the right of the Athenians to maltreat them, it scarcely comes as a surprise that many would advocate that "under certain circumstances" states have such a right. It takes the idealism and the clarity of thinking of a Wayne Booth to argue that physical torture is *always* wrong. The utilitarian calculations of the consequentialist argument (according to which the well-being of 500 versus that of an individual translates into a personal worth of the accused of one-five-hundredth) has been the common argument to defend torture by all its practitioners, from Nazis to Communists. We are reminded: "Do not send to ask whom the torturer is torturing: he is torturing thee."[46]

I recall that in the middle of a "round" of punches [in the torture chamber] someone opened the door and said: Do you remember that there is boxing on TV tonight? And all of them left immediately leaving me to rest until the next day, and I began to laugh, and became frightened that I was going mad.
—E. Forest, *Testimonios de Lucha y Resistencia*

Carnival-like laughter in the midst of torture, the experience of systematic agony suddenly turned into a kind of illumination, the pain of ultimate disintegration mixed with the lucidity of madness…these conditions, too, are engraved in the faces of terror and underscore the view of the body as a political institution.

Eva Forest, arrested and tortured under the dictatorship for her association with the ETA activists who killed Carrero Blanco (General Franco's hand-picked successor), and author of several books on torture, underscores in a conversation the particular density of experience that transpires at the limits of human endurance:

> Any outer limit situation breaks your patterns…. [Y]ou can either remain frozen by it or you can overcome it and enrich yourself….
> [I]t is such a source of richness that it is impossible to communicate…there is also the deep feeling that no one will believe you.

One of the qualities hard to convey is the sensation of surreal strangeness that may lead to laughter. It is the victim's irresistible wish for a tape recorder while the military man is mouthing atrocities that shatters the mood. Or it is the sudden imaginative revelation, as when Forest, daughter of a painter, understood Picasso's *Guernica* in a different light:

> I liked it before, but it was in one of those moments of torture that I gained real comprehension of Picasso's *Guernica* and the great pleasure of feeling identified with it. It was an incredible aesthetic moment when I said to myself: "Of course, this is it; reality has been smashed, split apart, broken into pieces and now it is as if they would seek to rejoin again and they no longer fit together."

The victim begins to perceive the world differently:

Many [tortured people] have told me: "how can I tell my parents that I was lying on the floor and suddenly one of them came and played a cassette tape. While I was listening to *flamenco* I could see the feet of the man who was kicking me and I was saying to myself: 'wow, how shiny those shoes are!' And I can remember that black shoe." And this is nothing. You also have the grotesque; for example, those [policemen] who came in drunk, and so on. That is also part of torture.

Forest perceives the torturers' merriment—"Can't you hear them roaring with laughter?"[47] Laughter becomes an inevitable expression of the new world revealed by the Dantesque experience.

Everybody has their experiences, and, it being so hard to communicate about torture, you can deceive yourself into thinking you have understood it. I have found many tortured people who told me they had to hold their private parts so as not to wet themselves from laughter. That's when you understand surrealism, the oneiric world, and it is all real.

The case of the twelve women who were tortured and then released while their husbands were kept in jail comes to mind. One night there was no room for all of them in the *guardia civil*'s police station. Two boys from ETA were also there. And since there was no room for them, one was kept at the end of the corridor and the other was tied to a radiator. The man in charge of the station came and said: "that one [the boy in the corridor] has to stand at attention and every quarter of an hour say, 'I am so and so, an assassin from ETA.'" At first the women were horrified; all of this was happening in a corridor, you could hear everything and besides the boy was wounded. He would come every quarter of an hour and say, "I am so and so, an assassin from ETA." If initially the people were scared, by the time the night was over, at dawn, everybody was roaring with laughter, included the guy who had to present himself: "I am an assassin from ETA, ha, ha, ha." Even the man in charge of the station was laughing. Everybody was laughing their heads off. Something like this happens during the vigils for the dead as well.

Objectively torture is horrible, but I would not say whether the experience of it is positive or negative. It can be fatal for some, liberating for others…. There comes a point in which you realize that all the schemes you had internalized collapse and you no longer know where the boundaries are: what is madness, what is normal, which are the valid criteria for beauty or ugliness, what is morality. It is like being in jail and coming to realize that there is not such a big difference between being inside and outside. You don't need physical torture for this; psychic torture can be even worse.

And Forest describes the case of the blindfolded woman lying nude on a table whom the torturers told they had advanced technology to sterilize her through some type of ray. They placed on her womb what was most likely an electric light bulb, but for her that was far more terrible than all the other usual physical tortures. Another victim was particularly broken after being tortured by a woman, which is unusual.

Forest insists on the indelible mark that turns into a seal of secrecy: "Tortured people will describe to you in vivid detail their painful experiences, but they will never tell you the most important thing; such outer limits situations are almost impossible to communicate, even to those who were tortured like yourself, your brothers in communion so to speak." Forest had studied and denounced torture under Franco's regime for some time before she was subject to the experience herself and realized that "I knew nothing about torture." That most unspeakable experience had to do with laughter in the torture chamber.

V̄

But how can that be?

—Women from Itziar

Yet it is the community of faces witnessing the horrors of violence that we regard as the most instructive. This was our case when, as anthropologists, we undertook fieldwork. We came face-to-face not with the abstractions of "Terrorism" but with the agonizing perplexity in the faces of ordinary people suddenly turned into victims of the violence of one side or the other, startled by having to witness murder in their neighborhood, frightened by the implicit complicity with the violence.

This is how Zulaika began his work on Basque political violence:

This ethnography began on a summer day in 1975…when several Itziar women, who had just witnessed the killing of a villager, assailed me with wide-open eyes and the question, "But how can that be?" It was not properly a question but the expression of an unanswerable puzzlement, as when spectators are compelled to witness an epic drama in which men become gods and beasts and are capable of heroic deeds and tragic errors.[48]

The man killed that morning inside a bus filled with rural house-wives on a trip to market was Carlos, the driver and alleged police informer of the village. When the village suffered political polarization he was singled out as the potential informer; false rumors about him became undisputed social facts. Later he assumed the scapegoat role by openly associating himself with the Spanish police. After shouting at him, "You are a dog!" his assailants shot him to death in front of his brother, sister, and the horrified women. The blood of Carlos, spilled on the public road, remained visible for days. That morning remains indelible in the memory of the ethnographer: "Their eyes were spearing me, pleading for an answer. I remained mute. 'But how can that be?' It was not a question. It was the inexpressible."[49] Thus, paradox and silence became inevitable argumentative components of the anthropologist's dramatic plot.

The political antagonist of Carlos was Martin. When Carlos became the suspected villain, Martin was the patriotic hero. Both had been nursed by Carlos's mother after Martin's had died. Profoundly aware of their common sustenance, in their early adulthood they were the closest of friends while engaged in various social activities to revitalize the village. When political polarization became an unavoidable fact, their opposed family allegiances led them to pursue divergent courses. Each felt betrayed by the other. Years after Carlos's death and a few months before his own from leukemia, Martin talked to the anthropologist about his milk brother Carlos with exceptional compassion. He knew that man only too well, he kept repeating, much better than the Spanish policemen Carlos befriended or the ETA militants who executed him. According to Martin, despite his alleged role as informer, Carlos did not deserve the infamy of such a death. His observation was underscored with an intense look.

At the conclusion of the fieldwork, the anthropologist was asked by the villagers to give them a lecture expounding his "findings." He welcomed that exceptional opportunity, but in the process the ironies of the role of ethnographer were to become disturbingly embarrassing. He had no answer of any sort to the deeply perplexing political questions of his neighbors. Nor had he any new factual information that was of true concern to his audience.

All he had was a parable drawn from recent local history: a priest who became secularized and then attempted, inadequately, to explain to his ex-parishioners the essence of this "sacramental change of status." He was as helpless as the ex-priest, the anthropologist insisted, as were they, since they could hardly explain what they knew about the violence. There were no objective grounds on which to compare the life of the same man when he was a priest and when he was not, no ultimate rule to judge the movement back and forth from sacrament to metaphor, from ritual to theater. The audience, who knew and admired the ex-priest, understood at once. The historical analogy between the local ex-priest and the local ex-"terrorist" seemed to capture the essence of the violence for all of them—personally and collectively.

The ethnographer's framing of their experience prompted a vital dialogue between the competing political and moral identities within the village. Local experience, as exemplary parable, turned into a powerful source of communal solidarity and tolerance. The very history of the village provided the ethical and political tension required for the necessary distancing. There were unmistakable voices in that history that spoke of a deeply experienced conversion to Catholic sacramentalism, of a sincere belief in socialist utopia, of an ardently felt promised land of nationalist freedom, as well as of a disillusioned skepticism regarding modernity. Nor could they ignore the ambiguities and repugnant contradictions that arise from a situation of at times violent political engagement. Prominent among such contradictions was generalized and simultaneous allegiance to the Catholic Church, whose morality is one of unambiguous abhorrence of killing, and the support for ETA's course of action, in which such killing is indispensable. Still, nobody claimed a position of moral superiority from which to condemn as inhuman, and thereby to criminalize, the histories of lifelong neighbors.

That "priests and murderers" were willing to listen to the voicing of altogether different perspectives was the ultimate irony. Representative ex-militants, who had risked their own lives and sacrificed those of others, were most vocal in critiquing military solutions and highlighting their chaotic results! People who had not undergone the initiatory ordeal of being arrested and accused of terrorism wondered how those consecrated as heroes could now oppose bloody heroism. The truly subversive displacement concerning the "heroism of terror" was transpiring in that communal meeting far more poignantly than in any textual interpretation entertained by the writer. It was the disbelief of the former heroes that was stunning. The seeming plenitude of meaning was declared "passé" and "meaningless" by the very subjects who had constituted us into a community of violence. The consequence of that twist was unsurpassable irony. But it was irony constructed and then decoded by the community itself. The writing task, therefore, consisted in listening to dissenting voices in order to sketch the outlines of contrasting representations of the violence. The ethical distance between the "is" and the "ought" was as abysmal as could be, but it was not dogmatically imposed by any political or authorial force; rather it was an ineluctable part of the intimate self of each member as product of the community's dynamics. Individual behaviors could at times step outside the village's shared frames of reference, but there was a primary sense in which the "ethical" was delimited from within the community. The villagers' standards of the good and the just were replete with uncertainty and unending debate, yet whatever was most reasonable for them had to take into account the community and its history.

The fieldworker's requested exposition provided, therefore, an occasion for openly debating such ultimate political-*cum*-religious constructions. The nature of the violent action itself, as well as the political antagonism generated by it, depended on communal definition and a plurality of views needed to be taken into account and negotiated. This was a radical dialogue with the contrarian perspective that could even deprive oneself and one's adversary of the right to life; there was no point in turning the debate into an abstraction such as "terrorism" when the pronouns "I" and "you" were on the table, at times backed by two decades of family history in a fight that, when antifascist, was unequivocally courageous, but when antidemocratic became dubiously so. The facts could be described and legitimated in various ways; they were dealing with interpretations that were their own life histories. If there was no correct interpretation, even among the community's actors, how could a cultural interpreter presume to impose one?

That communication between a notion of politics as sacrament—uncompromising, life-giving and life-taking, unconscious communion with the community's values—and a notion of politics as metaphor—conscious of the mythology of their own origins, the relativity of all heroism, the art of the possible—undermined both a martyred sense of life as well as a view of society so enlightened by universal values as to be repelled by local beliefs and sentiments. That such debate did occur vindicated the ethnographer's task. It permitted the community itself to effect a sort of ethnographic distancing from its own modes of believing and acting. The more starkly that one view of authenticity was presented, the more it was contested. They themselves were fighting for their own "hearts and minds" in a debate that configured their "politics of morality."[50]

An anthropologist might say that they were confronted in their daily lives with the Frazerian question, foundational to anthropology, of murder experienced as ritual necessity. Such complicity between murder and ritual, far from being an ethnographic curiosity, is rather commonplace. Social science has long recognized that "the deviant characteristics of the hero and of the criminal are essentially the same."[51] This sense of perplexity, the awareness that there is no readily attainable "objective characterization" of the facts at hand, is crucial if one is to become sensitive to the discursive strategies that constitute contrasting modes of consciousness in history and ethnography. The writer who aims at mediating between them is driven progressively "toward the ironic recognition that any given linguistic protocol will obscure as much as it reveals about the reality it seeks to capture in an order of words."[52] Terrorism discourse finds it much easier to dismiss the deviant actor and his community as "criminal," and to place the whole subject under a taboo, thereby avoiding the intrinsically problematical task of having to deal with essential ambiguity.

We are haunted by these faces of terror. We believe that the occurrence of this kind of communal encounter promises a transformation. Contrast this with the way, after Oklahoma City, Timothy McVeigh and Terry Nichols were distanced from the militia groups and the survivalist culture that nurtured them. The spin placed on them concluded that they were simply two isolated "kooks" acting on their own. As *Time* magazine put it, "No wide-ranging conspiracy. No criminal masterminds. Not even any hardened zealots dedicating their life to the disciplined terrorist pursuit of an ideological cause. Just two drifters and misfits with a rented truck and a homemade bomb."[53] Their action was wholly aberrant, the irrational result of two perturbed individuals. The accounts emphasize their truncated biographies and broken family histories. Yet nothing reported about them thus far—the divorce of their parents, their status as army veterans, their love of guns—makes them so different from ordinary Americans. It is, of course, far more disturbing to regard them as typical citizens acting out, albeit in a violent fashion, the values and goals shared by a large survivalist culture. In fact, as noted earlier, millions of Americans interpret the historical changes taking place worldwide in apocalyptic terms. It is easy to say that Oklahoma City had nothing to do with America's gun culture, with Weaver and Waco, with the militia movement, with survivalist propaganda, with the military training of the accused. We do not claim that any of these factors "caused" Oklahoma City; but depriving an action of its context, thereby making it meaningless and bizarre, and depriving actors of their ordinary community by turning them into kooks with whom no one shares anything, is not a formula for ultimate understanding—regardless of the beneficial cathartic effects that it may have upon a citizenry and its polity as an exercise in self-exoneration.

Self-exoneration is a far cry from the attitude of Itziar villagers in the town meeting described above. Rather than shrinking from and effacing their violent actors, the neighbors proposed confronting and contemplating them. When violent ex-militants and their community gathered, there were no definitive arguments of any sort, but there was a majestic factor—the presence of faces that had assumed responsibility for acting out or supporting political violence. This was not the media(ted) exchange between anchor and televiewer. There were no decontextualized kooks for whom the community was unaccountable. The villagers preferred the view that murderers are *made*, not born. So there were the unmediated faces of young killers, of ex-prisoners welcomed as heroes, of mothers with dead sons, of family members of the imprisoned or tortured, of political antagonists who would never reconcile themselves ideologically no matter how hard they tried. Yet there was a promise of reconciliation in faces that were for once unburdened of false representations, of rumors, of perspectives imposed by outsiders, and imbued instead with the immediacy of one another's compelling presence. The villagers *addressed* each other.

Whatever else the "terrorist" was, he or she was not a faceless man or woman in that meeting. Their voices might be muted, their hearing deafened, their gaze intense with the burden of their action, yet they were not people wholly unlike the rest of us. It was possible to carry out an I-Thou conversation with them. The "problem" with terrorism was not principally one of intellectual elaboration, but simply how to react, what to say to significant others, what to think of the ideas and actions that led to the violent disruption of the social order in the first place. Contemplating, literally and figuratively, the faces of the effaced activist and his or her intimates becomes a condition for understanding the inferno of action. Such confrontation rescues us from obfuscating allegory and representation.

VI

The very straightforwardness of the face to face, without the intermediary of any image, in one's nudity, that is, in one's destitution and hunger.

—E. Levinas, *Totality and Infinity*

"Am I my brother's keeper?" When Cain's desolate question regarding his absent, murdered sibling attains existential urgency, the exorbitance of the perplexity—"But how can that be?" "I do not know; am I my brother's keeper?"—admits no easy rational answer. It is easier to undo faulty categories and point out their rhetorical emplotments than to recreate, intellectually and politically, a new process that will respect both radical difference and systemic integration. If searching for the laws of universal reason cannot provide a conclusive solution to the dilemmas, neither can one capitulate to a final "interpretation" of murder. Violence is mute. "'Crime? What crime?' he suddenly shouted.... 'I understand my crime less than ever!'" Raskolnikov's words regarding the abysmal incomprehensibility of human murder also regard the community that must shelter and endure such inhumanity. "We are all responsible for everyone else—but I am more responsible than all the others,"[54] the words of Alyosha Karamazov, in their Levinasian "asymmetry," weigh upon us as well.

We are commanded to a "living dialogue" with the Other, not only by theologians such as Buber, but also by the demanding dialogism of social thinkers like Bakhtin and ontological philosophers of Levinas's caliber. Theorists as iconoclastically diverse as MacIntyre and Rorty appeal in the end to notions such as "community" and "solidarity." An anthropologically informed approach may also conclude, with Edmund Leach, "The point of my sermon is simply this. However incomprehensible the acts of terrorists may seem to be, our judges, our policemen, and our politicians must never be allowed to forget that terrorism is an activity by fellow human beings and *not* of dog-headed cannibals."[55] The narratives considered here remind us of the Dantean movement from despair to grace through descent into evil and the world of the dead.

But dialogue with a terrorist? Should we uphold ethical principles such as the Levinasian *absolute* alterity of the Other, or should we commit ourselves to a radical ethnographic encounter in which "looking into dragons, not domesticating or abominating them"[56] should be our primary concern? For those of us nurtured at best in the affirmative amoralism of Nietzsche or in the value-free science of Weber, such uncompromising intersubjectivity is unknown territory.

While ethics, either deferred or discredited, are notoriously absent in social scientific analysis generally, within terrorism studies they are mostly invoked as an exercise in moral indignation. Yet there is little attempt to focus upon the ethics of ignoring our own implication with the violent actors. This essay is an invitation to such confrontation. It presents a view of "the terrorist" that will not exempt the viewer (either through romantic faith or inquisitorial zeal) as well as a call to relate to the unknown feared Other without dehumanizing ourselves. It is only by combining these two concerns that we will avoid the dangers of creating a fictionalized and tabooed subject, an enchanted world impervious to comprehension.

We have insisted on the intellectual therapy of a multiple perspective, the Blakean vision of the marriage of Heaven and Hell, in which the chaotic and the destructive have an autonomy of their own. But this is far from implying adoption of a relative point of view concerning the evils of terror. Still, terrorism forces upon us a paradox and an alternative. Simply put, the paradox is that a symmetrical response to the blind forces and values of terror with the same weapons of reactive terrorism and indifference amounts to the victory of the terrorist agenda. The alternative is the ethical asymmetry of an expansive vision.

We must advocate justice, but this does not rescue authority and morality from their internal paradoxes. This is nowhere more apparent than in the recourse to violence. As Walter Benjamin wrote, "Among all the forms of violence permitted by both natural law and positive law there is not one that is free of the gravely problematic nature...of all legal violence," and yet, at the same time, "every conceivable solution to human problems...remains impossible if violence is totally excluded in principle."[57] Yet, Levinas reminds us, politics and ethics are different domains, interrelated but frequently contradictory as well, each with its own justification. Individuals are at times exhorted to uphold an ethical standard that transcends political or military purposes; this is epitomized by face-to-face interaction, the interpersonal contact that commands "Thou shalt not commit murder." This primordial expression should be understood not just in pacifist terms but rather as the contemplation and comprehension of, as well as empathy with, the alterity of the Other, which surpasses all control or annihilation.

The relationship between politics and ethics in the present world is decided, at times emblematically, in the recreation and manipulation of "terrorism." The accusation of terrorism, like that of witchcraft and demonic possession in former times, allows us to efface the person and thereby deprive the individual of humanity. In this fashion we ourselves are no longer bound by the commandment against murder; we become immune to having to respond, "I am my brother's keeper." Cain is wrong only if we assume responsibility for others.

We are accustomed to the idea that the final judgment of any moral principle must be in relation to truth or knowledge. Yet it is precisely the very absence of knowledge that is so prominent in the perplexing "But how can that be?" For the women of the village, responsibility toward their slain neighbor took precedence over any knowledge concerning the victim's political culpability or, indeed, whether there was any political cause that could justify such killing. This ethical priority of sociability over knowledge cries out for the convergence of ethics and epistemology. Cain was condemned by the very indifference expressed in his question regarding Abel; their moral agony saved the village women from Cain's fate even though they were forced to witness the murder of a neighbor for whose life they felt responsible. We perceive our role as writers to be one of witnessing rather than judging. Primo Levi, himself a victim of the Nazis in Auschwitz and committed to remembering the Holocaust, wrote that "he preferred the role of witness to that of judge"[58] when contemplating his captors. We agree with Aretxaga who, after having studied how ten IRA members reached the decision to die in a hunger strike in 1981, concluded: "It is not for me to decide whether the hunger strikers were right or wrong or if what they achieved was worse than what they were trying to overcome."[59]

The autonomy of knowledge (representation, epistemology) is dashed by such prior responsibility to the destituted Other. The presence of the real face, its commanding proximity, proves to be more compelling than any fiction, allegory, ritual, or narrative. Knowledge scorns such immediacy, which it knows time and again to be mediated. But the goal of knowledge is only more knowledge; its only transcendence is intentionality; reason is its most compelling argument. Yet the kind of puzzlement that might force the question "But how can that be?" demands movement beyond reason. It calls for the power to contest knowledge in the name of the Other's absolute alterity, as is best expressed in the revelatory power of the human face.

This is why, after writing on the cultures of violence and terror, we are still either powerless or unwilling to dismiss Martin Buber's thought that one individual has nothing to say about another. The Other cannot be thematized. The enlightened sixteenth century inquisitor Salazar spoke *to* the alleged witches, not to know them in order to accuse them of a crime, but rather to exorcise them from official discourses and at times even to convince them of their own tragic self-deception. He refused to subordinate their alterity to the witchcraft discourse concocted by the Church. Such resistance was grounded in an ethics that was skeptical of the Church's official morality and that became the death knell of witchcraft epistemology. In that face-to-face encounter between the witch and the inquisitor, the consciousness of both was radically transformed to a point of no return.

Our ethical stance, then, is best captured by the exorbitant and asymmetrical responsibility toward the Other (always provoking the unsettling "Am I my brother's keeper?"), which is best captured in Levinas' face-to-face encounter. Such an ethic cannot be based on any theoretical justification, but rather entails sustaining, despite the fact that s/he is a potential murderer, a radical acceptance of the other's humanity without mediation of a concept, discourse, or taboo. This critique of an ameliorating term that neutralizes the shock of a direct encounter with the Other is aimed at revealing such excess of alterity; it does not entail unproblematic return to immediacy, nor does it assume that such alterity is exhausted by its immersion in one's cultural context. Such "asymmetry," as Derrida observes, implies a radicalness that "can make us tremble" and that goes far beyond the "formal" and "private" I-Thou relationship. Whether we turn the encounter into scholarship, inquisition, literature, aesthetics, or expertise, in the final analysis we are all struggling with truth while describing the Other.

VII

Every man testifies to the crimes of all others.

—A. Camus, *The Fall*

Your son is gone. Your son is gone. Where is the fucking symbolism?

—N. Gordon, *Sacrifice of Isaac*

Terrorism attests to the relevance of the role of the witness—both as a promise of redemption and as a failure—in the contemporary history of crime. A face-to-face confrontation with the killers and victims can radically affect the witness. Such a transformation was partially achieved in the town meeting that concluded the anthropologist's fieldwork. Witnessing another's views and destitution taught a seemingly unique lesson in history and ethics. In one sense there was a promise of resolution in the very act of letting an entire community bear witness. "By provoking such dialogue between irreconcilable worldviews," the anthropologist wrote confidently, "I felt I was sharing with my Itziar neighbors and friends anthropology's subversive character;" that is, ethnography became "a distancing device by pointing out the 'otherness' of what people experience, the ethnographer included, within the boundaries of their cultural constructions" and, in so doing, the anthropologist was "inviting his culture to understand and ultimately question the role of the native."[60]

Yet were such intimations of a testimonial breakthrough signs of real transformation, or were they merely the delusions of a writer seeking redemption? The community of neighbors wanted to feel implicated in one another's lives, to assume mutual responsibility, and thereby to find salvation in the very act of bearing witness to each other's actions. Accepting the risks while commanding the presence of each other's face was a revelatory event, in itself an act of transformation. That testimony to an unwanted history of violence and victimization seemed to provide a new awareness of the community's cultural meltdown; it could be regarded as a belated attempt at a collective confession and request for forgiveness.

However, another village meeting quickly dispelled such illusions about understanding and forgiving. The occasion was to consider the intention of a television producer to film a documentary of the violence in Itziar—based on the published ethnography.[61] Confronted with the prospect of recounting their recent history of division and murder to the unrelenting eye of the camera—that final witness in defining terrorism and its victims—the anthropologist and the community failed miserably in their testimonial task. Old accusations of mutual victimization were brought to life. Former antagonistic scenarios became overpowering and ultimately the villagers refused to collaborate in a common narration of their political story. The community's earlier self-confessional spirit dissipated in failure. There were wounds that simply could not be healed. For the camera, i.e., the external world, there was no community capable of witnessing.

Such failure only underscores the problematic nature of the role of the witness. It reminds us that "confession fails to close off a discourse,"[62] and that no excuse can undo violence. Felman understands that active silence—"as the absolute refusal of any trivializing or legitimating discourse (of apology, of narrative, or of psychologizing explanation of recent history)"—can turn into "the most radical and irrevocable assumption of historical responsibility."[63] Pleas of "innocence"—a linchpin trope in terrorism rhetorics—are no less problematic when they lead to complacency regarding the truthfulness of one's testimony or the self-righteous integrity of one's moral position. Our own appropriation of Levinas's moral high ground in the previous section can also be seen in part as a morality play, an exercise in apologetic discourse—an act of confession demanding from the reader absolution from the inescapable impossibility of resolving the dilemmas posed by terrorism.

Levinas himself was asked whether Israel was innocent or responsible for the massacre at Sabra and Shatilla. He replied in terms "of the responsibility of those 'who have done nothing,' of an original responsibility of man for the other person.... This is the responsibility of those we call innocent!"[64] Levinas went on to say that, "Unfortunately for ethics, politics has its own justification" and "the Zionist idea...has an ethical justification."[65] Even Levinas's work, from which we have learned the most about ethics and politics, is incapable of immunizing us from "the temptation of innocence."[66] Any Israeli soldier repulsed by having to be present at the massacre, yet under orders not to witness it, could have rebutted Levinas with the blunt words of an angry Luke Benami who, in Gordon's novel, reacts thus to being reminded of the Holocaust as justification of Sabra and Shatilla:

> "To excuse a police state because of the Final Solution is bullshit; the precise opposite should be happening. Instead the army bulldozes the Arab's house in Jericho, they blame it on Auschwitz, then they build a nuclear reactor in South Africa, and excuse that one with Majdanek."
>
> A silence. Then Luke, more calmly: "Look. I don't say there's not a proper reaction to the Holocaust; there is. There is, and it should inform every fucking minute of our lives. Every minute. But it's not self-righteousness—not even righteousness at all. Not anymore.... I just don't believe that the Holocaust was ever about 'them and us,' you know? It was always about *us*, all of *us*, and if there was ever any doubt about that, then the Israeli occupation's made it crystal fucking clear."[67]

We agree with the arguments for the unique historical horror of the Holocaust and reject the efforts to minimize or trivialize it. Still, we believe that the true ethical breakthrough must come from writers like Gordon who refuse to give in to the temptations of innocence and speak about the guilt of "all of *us*." For them there is no qualitative difference in the humanity of any victimized person. And if even the terrible Holocaust should not divide humanity into "them" and "us," how can we allow terrorism to do so? If there is anything that is obvious in the recent history of governments fighting terrorism—Spain, Great Britain, Germany, Israel, Peru—it is that they themselves have engaged in actions that, according to their own definitions, fall clearly under the rubric of "terrorism."

"Innocence" is what Abraham claimed for himself when, in an ultimate act of idolatry, he was ready to sacrifice Isaac, for "he could not comprehend that it was a sin to be willing to offer to God the best thing he possessed."[68] Abraham would want us to believe that it was all for a higher Purpose. Yet Isaac, the innocent son, did witness what happened. The Kierkegaardian story of Abraham's murderous action would remain unforgettable for both as an irresolvable paradox. The father's act of faith forced the son to lose his.

Abraham's story is incomprehensible for Kierkegaard—a paradox without resolution. Equally so for Levinas are the contemporary conflicts between ethics and politics—as in the case of Sabra and Shatilla. De Man referred to this predicament—being compelled to choose while the occasion itself destroys the bases of any choice—as the impossibility of reading.[69] It is this impossibility of knowing how to read their own immediate historical circumstances that is so common in situations of violence—the startling fact that people, like the villagers of Itziar, are drawn to political and moral perspectives that are fundamentally opposed and then have no means of reconciling them. "*I do not know,* am I my brother's keeper?" The consequences of such awareness are devastating and can easily lead to realizations such as, "In my country we are all born guilty," or "This is Europe. Everyone's guilty."[70] Camus concluded that, "We cannot assert the innocence of anyone, whereas we can state with certainty the guilt of all."[71]

Confronted with the question, "What does it mean to *inhabit history* as crime, as the space of the annihilation of the Other?" then "innocence can only mean lack of awareness of one's participation in the crime," for "there is no longer any place of innocence from where to testify."[72] Far from an unquestioning belief in the untainted innocence of one's testimony, for Camus we are all accomplices in the atrocities of contemporary history, characterized by the alarming fact that the roles of judge, victim, executioner, bystander, and witness have suffered continuous permutations.[73] Terrorism discourse remains (indeed requires us to be) oblivious to this predicament in order to— consonant with its claim to absolute truth—establish categorical differences between the saved and the damned, soldiers and terrorists, "them" and "us." We prefer to confront the radical difficulty of reading this century's criminal history, of which "terrorism" is but one instance. We learn the most from writers who are painfully conscious of their failings while representing others, and who are aware that various kinds of ideological constraint are built inescapably into the very language of discourse.

Kierkegaard's Abraham wanted to believe that nobody had seen the pyre, the ropes binding his son, the fateful knife brandished. Erasing any witness is a major concern of any murderer. Hitler sought to perfect murder by erasing an entire people without leaving any witnesses. Students of the Holocaust underscore this paradigmatic "crisis of witnessing"—the occurrence of "an event without a witness."[74] They conceptualize witnessing as "a *critical* activity"[75] in every sense of the word. The relationship between witnessing and truth could not be more germane.

An anomaly that sums up our arguments concerning the taboo of terrorism could be made in terms of the strict prohibition upon witnessing. The official line in matters of terrorism is that, excepting surveillance, any type of witnessing is forbidden. It begins with a categorical prevention of any interaction with terrorists. The faces and voices of terrorists are banned from being shown and heard in the media of most countries dealing with the problem. Ethnography of terrorism is, to be sure, also anathema. We were not surprised to be told by a committee of terrorism experts[76] that our work should be an appendage to that of the police. Sustaining a posture of political or intellectual witnessing is most suspect. The moral paradoxes we have encountered concerning the phenomenon are, in this regard, related to such a "crisis of witnessing."

Another aspect of the crisis is that, while neutral witnesses are unwanted, the work of shadowy informers is actively promoted and their testimony given full credit. Thus people suspected of terrorism can be charged without proof, as has happened to scores of people in Northern Ireland. Or the FBI engages in the questionable practice of paying $1 million to an informer such as Emad Salem, the main witness in the bomb conspiracy trial against Sheik Omar Abdul Rahman and ten others. Salem "began his testimony by admitting that he had lied to just about everybody he ever met." The *New York Times* questioned "whether the abundance of details he has provided outweighs his glaring flaws as a witness." He is "always ready with another believe-it-or-not exploit." Mr. Salem's testimony sounded "like sheer fantasy."[77]

We fail to see the moral value of tabooing true witnesses and promoting shadowy informers. We prefer the stance of the Itziar villagers for two reasons: first, the testimonial meeting was an act of taking responsibility for the community's crimes; second, and just as important, by detabooing the role of the witness it was also possible to go beyond any illusion of communal redemption through exemplary testimony. It is the repressed or criminalized witness who ends up confusing testimony with ultimate truth, and who is thereby unable to escape a secret loyalty toward the violent actor. It is after being allowed to bear free testimony that one can problematize the claims of innocence for both the agent and the witness.

It was while working in the field as ethnographers that we were exposed to the equivocal yet critical nexus between witnessing and truth in matters of terrorism. It is in a world of secrecy, masks, and hidden agendas that violence prospers—that is, in situations in which witnessing is not allowed to impact on the lives of the violent actors. If we learned anything from the successful town meeting, it was the crucial role that face-to-face encounters could have in revising collective representations and promoting tolerance. It is the kidnapper and the torturer who abhor the witness. Counterterrorism's policy of defacing the activist and reducing his/her narratives to sheer criminality only replicates the violence's original logic of secrecy and dehumanization. Both the terrorist and the counterterrorist join forces in eradicating the witness. Both are engaged in systematically ignoring the human condition of the other.

A requisite for achieving this mutual nonintelligibility is adherence to a discourse of strict literalness in which any ambiguity can be singled out as an abomination. Abraham ended up accepting the ritual substitution of a ram for his beloved son. But no such symbolic equivalence can be tolerated by a discourse bent on demonizing the enemy with metaphors of unredeemable bestiality. In such contexts of univocal truth and survival strategy, the gift of symbolism—ritually substituting an offering for actual murder, dismantling one's mythology to save the life of the son—is most unwelcome.

Taboo and the sacred are two aspects of the same coin, as Freud insisted. The stronger the imposition of a taboo by the counterterrorist, the greater the sacredness obtained by the realm of violence. Detabooing terrorism implies liberating its victims. It is the decanonization of terrorism—the unveiling of masks, the transgression of silence, "the liberation of the testimony through its desacralization"[78]—that counterterrorism cannot bear.[79]

Epilogue as Prologue
THE APOTHEOSIS OF
TERRORISM FORETOLD

History, I read recently, does not light the way forward but, like the stern lamp on a ship, illuminates its wake. Perhaps what offends the Western nations most about their victory over Communism is that in cutting a path to the future, they have unleashed the sleeping demons of their accusing past.
— John le Carré, "The Shame of the West"

As we write these last lines, Carlos the Jackal sits in a French jail await-ing trial, seemingly ignominiously traduced by the Sudanese hosts grown weary of harboring a debauched, middle-aged, international fugitive. Abimael Guzmán, the leader of Peru's "Shining Path"—the most notorious "terrorist" group in South America—languishes in prison. Sheik Omar Abdul Rahman is also incarcerated, in New York State, more an embarrassment than an exemplar for a U.S. foreign policy now more obsessed with a Middle East Peace Accord than with Arab-bashing. The hapless Saddam Hussein and Muammar Gadaffi, yesterday's bogeymen and today's international pariahs, maintain the lowest of profiles, while Yassir Arafat and Shimon Peres stand shoul-der to shoulder (albeit perched precariously) against Hamas and Zionist zealots. The ANC is now the ruling party in South Africa. The Brigata Rossa and Baader Meinhof are but recent memories in a west-ern Europe increasingly preoccupied more by the revival of fascism and a racist backlash against its political and economic refugees than by class warfare. Sinn Fein has been negotiating with Great Britain and Ireland on behalf of an IRA that agreed to a cease-fire. ETA is increasingly isolated within both Spanish and Basque societies. In short, our generation's cast of terrorist activists and movements seems all but moribund. A blinkered optimist with little sense of history might even be prepared to pronounce "terrorism" itself dead.

Yet there is suddenly a new promised land for terrorism—the United States. Its major networks now dispatch their reporters to London to determine how civilized Europe adjusted to mindless terrorism. They send back the sobering warning that Americans better get used to it. William Pierce, author of *The Turner Diaries* and spiritual father of the militia movement sweeping the country, agrees. After the Oklahoma City explosion, he predicted in a radio address that resentment among "normal Americans" of politicians, Jews, minorities, and female executives would lead to more terrorism "on a scale that the world has never seen before."[1]

Our terrorism discourse closes its circle, its apotheosis expressed in the sealing off of Pennsylvania Avenue by a president besieged in his White House. Two world wars, a Cold War with its terrorist networks masterminded from Moscow, and the domestic divisions of the Vietnam era all failed to merit such a quarantine. Seemingly, the New World Order equates to a new Era of Terror. What a triumph for Timothy McVeigh—to accomplish what all the horrors of the twentieth century could not! And what vindication for the army of public officials, experts, journalists, and academics who orchestrate terrorism discourse. As for the rest of us, we are left to inhabit a world configured by the *True Lies* of our terrorized imaginations.

The most recent actor in the "new" terrorism discourse is McVeigh—"the American terrorist." There is, however, a sense that in considering the Oklahoma City bombing to be a terrorist act we are stretching the categorical bounds of conventional wisdom regarding "terrorism." Hitherto, for terrorism experts, the term referred to the political violence of disaffected groups; as yet, it remains to be seen whether McVeigh acted for an organization in the name of its cause. Curiously, Oklahoma City (like the World Trade Center bombing) remained unclaimed, scarcely the *modus operandi* of the "old" terrorism. If McVeigh's action turns out to be the personal political statement of an army veteran who was denied the honor of becoming a Green Beret, we may actually be dealing with an act more akin to the random shootings by the demented, dismissed employee (a not uncommon occurrence in American life) than with the actions of an IRA, PLO, or ETA. Indeed, by reducing a common form of American violence to "terrorism," the future of terrorism discourse should be guaranteed.

Yet we oppose the practice of transforming the Oliver Norths into heroes and the McVeighs into tabooed kooks. Seeking to understand them in their own terms is the only viable alternative to the proliferation of metal detectors and the further closure of avenues—whether Pennsylvania or simply those of communication. McVeigh adopted the pseudonym taken from the avenger T. Tuttle as his alias on his mail drop and along the gun show trail. If we fail to understand what made him do so, we indeed face the prospect of one day living in some kind of futuristic "Brazil"—a world in which bombings are commonplace and civil liberties minimal as society musters most of its resources for the counterterrorism campaign of a ruthless, dehumanized bureaucracy. The future can be discerned in the counterterrorism bill prompted by the Oklahoma City bombing which provides for 1,000 additional counterterrorism agents, fewer impediments on the arbitrary deportation of foreigners, a broadened authority to wiretap, and tighter restrictions upon the legal appeal process of prisoners under sentence of death.[2]

Thus, lest any citizen of the New World Order be so foolhardy as to relax, counterterrorism experts assure the public that Terrorism is alive and well. Could we even imagine a world without it? Indeed, so we are told, it has become much worse. The capture of Carlos, for example, gave *The Economist* more pause for thought than cause for celebration. While noting that the state-sponsored terrorism that formerly gave employment to Carlos and his kind might be waning, nevertheless, "Terrorism has not gone away." In fact,

> the terrorism of autonomous groups is harder to deal with. They have no protector to be leaned on, no vital interests other than their own cause—or lives—to be threatened. Some have goals so utopian that no compromise exists that could entice them to cease fire.[3]

If we are to assess the truly dangerous situation of the world out there, all we have to do is combine this autonomy of the various potential terrorist groups with the quintessential terror of the nuclear age:

> What is worse is that the technology available to terrorists is becoming more sophisticated. Twice within days German police have seized samples of Russian plutonium. True, building a nuclear bomb demands more than a bit of plutonium and a spanner. Yet the problems are not insuperable for a serious group. Even if they were, radioactive material could be packed around a conventional device to threaten a city center. And nuclear-armed terrorists could be more

dangerous than a nuclear-armed state. Sane or crazy, a state's leaders must always fear a counter-attack upon their own cities. How
could one threaten some Sikh dreamer's "Khalistan," let alone the
wildest-eyed bearers of an ideal called Islam?[4]

As for the Russian plutonium, the *New York Times* reported the
words of a high-ranking German official: "This could turn into the
most serious security threat since the end of the cold war, and it is getting steadily worse."[5] There followed suggestions that the smugglers
were possibly negotiating with Iraq or Iran. The worst fears concerning
nuclear terrorism, long anticipated by the experts, were seemingly
becoming true. The problem was that the operation had been "a plot
concocted by the German secret agencies" themselves, with the con-
sent of German politicians.[6] Why the deception of what came to be
known as "plutoniumgate"? The collapse of the Soviet Union had left
thousands of German spies with no enemy to fight. What better to do
than create some antiterrorism hysteria so as to preserve their jobs?
As the spokesman of the Social Democratic party in the European
Parliament put it, "Those who are fighting this market are those who
created it."[7] Leaders of the opposition argued that the operation was
orchestrated to help Chancellor Helmut Kohl win reelection.[8]

It is, in fact, not difficult to fabricate such reality, since it only
requires a slight distortion of the existing thriving international arms'
bazaar, a "furtive and frantic market" in which American companies
buy Russian arms and nuclear technology in a "feeding frenzy."[9] This
should not concern us, presumably. The only real danger is the possibility of the crazy terrorists acquiring any of the coveted merchandise.
It is legitimate business as usual for *our* markets, it is an apocalyptic
taboo for *them.*[10] Nor does there seem to be anything wrong with
democratic armies stockpiling obscene arsenals of mustard gas and
other agents of chemical and biological warfare for the next virtuous
war, except for the danger that terrorists may get hold of them. And
so, with the grey certainties of the Cold War no longer obtaining, it
seems that probing the New World Order is becoming a lot like the
earlier exploration of the New World, during which the fearful yet fascinated imaginations of the explorers created their own phantas-
magoric bestiaries. Once again we are exhorted to contemplate dog-
headed cannibals, only now they are armed with nuclear weapons and
poison gas.

The sham of plutoniumgate is an all too obvious case of the culture itself imposing the reality. Far more insidious are the instances in

which the reality-making force of the discourse is concealed under layers of mythical stereotypes, fundamentalist premises, or morality tales.
Consider, for example, critical cases such as the "disposal problem"
posed by CIA-trained and financed by anti-Communist crusaders who
apparently recycled their jihad in Afghanistan into the World Trade
Center explosion. Revolutionary freedom fighters when attacking
Soviet communism for the sake of Islam, they are depicted as loathsome terrorists when fighting capitalism for the same cause. If Sheik
Omar's followers fought side by side with the Green Berets in
Afghanistan,[11] a prospective Green Beret repudiated by the Army,
Timothy McVeigh, had the opportunity to fulfill his warrior dreams as
a civilian in Oklahoma City. Educated in the Reagan-Bush period of
massive military intervention against "terrorist" targets, the alternatives for a war hero like McVeigh seemingly oscillated between becoming a defending Rambo or an avenging Rebel. In this sense the counterterrorist and the terrorist are not so different.

Remember Oliver North, the hero of the Reagan administration's
Iran-Contra fiasco, the counterterrorist who promoted counterinsur-
gencies of his own while making secret deals with alleged terrorists?
Should we be surprised to learn that McVeigh viewed North as a role
model and actually campaigned for him?[12] To suggest an ideological
link between the "patriotism" of the two men was far too disturbing
for the public. Instead of seeing Oklahoma City as "motivated by a
brand of politics not as detached from the mainstream as we'd like to
think,"[13] the media and the public were quick to attribute it initially
to Muslim fundamentalists. When this proved wrong, it was easier and
more palatable to conclude that the bombing was the senseless action
of a pair of "lunatics." Blaming the Oklahoma City tragedy on a couple of "kooks," thereby ignoring the cultural connection between the
militia movement and its potential for violence, is a way of denying any
relationship between the counterterrorist/terrorist, Rambo/ Rebel
alternatives. Since we are considering the power of discourse to generate its own reality, remember also that Oklahoma City was meant to
commemorate Waco, itself an egregious example of self-fulfilling
prophecy on the part of both the Davidians and the ATF police.

What about Pan Am flight 103? Was it also the result of terrorism
rhetorics? The tragic incident over Lockerbie epitomizes, for the
American public, the ultimate proof of terrorism's extreme danger.
What is altogether missing is a public appreciation of the extent to
which terrorism discourse itself might have contributed decisively to
the tragedy. Pan Am flight 103 was preceded by the downing, "by mis-

take," of an Iranian passanger airliner by the American warship *Vincennes*. Most experts and family members of the Pan Am victims remained skeptical with the official version that blamed two Libyan officers; the clues pointing to Iran were simply too obvious to ignore. In any case, what made the crew of the *Vincennes* commit so grave a mistake as to sacrifice with impunity the lives of 290 airline passengers? Isn't this the reality-making force of a discourse that allows itself to act as it assumes the enemy will? In doing so it provokes as well the self-fulfilling reaction from the enemy that proves that it was the feared monster after all. Nevertheless, the incident that has turned into the paradigm of terrorism for the American public has been viewed by some terrorism experts as a type of "blood feud." It is by forgetting the symmetry between the Iranian airliner and Pan Am flight 103, and by erasing the assumptions and justifications surrounding the *Vincennes'* "error," that terrorism discourse conceals its own self-generating logic.

As we have seen, the use and abuse of the Unabomber by the authorities provide a classic example of the categorical and definitional vagaries of terrorism discourse. Glittery "terrorist" when it suits the forces of counterterrorism and unglamorous "serial killer" when it doesn't, the Unabomber, more than any other example, exposes the game. But the threat posed by the Unabomber acquired credibility due partly to the explosion of Pan Am flight 103. According to some reports, because of the lack of appropriate scanning technology "passengers are travelling virtually unprotected."[14] Yet this begs a question. If bombing an airliner is so simple and the world is so populated with lethal masterminds (including the agents of anti-American "terrorist" governments), why haven't there been a dozen or more Pan Am 103s? That would seem to be the real question that the promoters of terrorism discourse—from the Transportation Secretary to the FBI to the experts and the media—should answer for the frightened public.

We were once astonished that the politicians and the media could confidently include under the same "terrorist" rubric such disaparate characters as Sheik Omar, Mr. McVeigh, the Unabomber, and the Chechen Dudayev. From now on our real surprise will be if the counterterrorism crusade does not increasingly regale the American public with a new "war" game and all sorts of "successes" against terrorism. We assume that the reality-making power of terrorism discourse is by now almost unstoppable. All that is necessary to produce the loathsome thing are some CIA-trained "rebels" turned against their mentors (as with Sheik Omar and his followers) or a military "error" (as in the shooting down of the Iranian passenger flight that preceded Pan

Am 103) or a disgruntled, Ramboesque army veteran (such as Timothy McVeigh) or some uncontrolled arm smuggler in the thriving post-Cold War arms bazaar (as in plutoniumgate). This emerging terrorism "reality" appears to be already a blooming, self-fulfilling prophecy in the United States. The prognosis is bullish for the counterterrorism industry, whether made manifest in security, academia, or journalistic circles.

If, until now, modern terrorism discourse has been to a large extent a function of the Cold War confrontation and nuclear predicament, many of its premises are currently in flux. The full detail of the emerging political agenda remains unclear, but certain trends are obvious.

First, it is clear that the repeated use and abuse of terrorism discourse has enshrined the term—with all its vagueness and vagaries—into late-twentieth-century global consciousness. As an instance, it has been codified as "sin" by the Catholic Church, which in its recently released catechism stated:

> RESPECT FOR BODILY INTEGRITY
>
> 2297 *Kidnapping* and *hostage taking* bring on a reign of terror; by means of threats they subject their victims to intolerable pressures. They are morally wrong. *Terrorism* which threatens, wounds, and kills indiscriminately is gravely against justice and charity.[15]

Unfortunately, the Catholic theologians fail to specify which one of the hundreds of definitions of terrorism we should accept.

Second, as the sole superpower, the United States now has a new-found love affair with the United Nations that is nothing short of startling. Suddenly, Washington issues solemn pronouncements in support of "international law" and threatens to punish its violators, when for the past two decades in the eyes of the rest of the world, it has scarcely been a paragon of international virtue—consider Grenada, Panama, Libya, the Iran-Contra affair.

One can only speculate that the *Pax Americana* will have to invent its enemies. We are reminded incessantly that the post-Cold War world is a "most dangerous place" and that "New World Disorder" is becoming the more appropriate label. There are currently more than one hundred wars being fought around the globe. In a world no longer populated by convenient Communist foils and constrained by a super-power balance of nuclear terror, it seems likely that the clarion call to fear might actually require a greater range of "terrorist" adversaries than in the past.

Third, future terrorism discourse is likely to be nourished by the flawed democracies proliferating throughout much of the former Soviet empire and sphere of influence. The temptation to brand their opponents as terrorists in order to demonize them as the first step in legitimizing their eradication is proving to be quite tempting. The invasion of Chechnya was justified in part as a cleansing of a nest of "bandits and terrorists," while the outgunned Chechen leader, Dudayev, placed the Russians on notice by dispatching a team of hostage takers to the Russian heartland itself.

Fourth, the threat posed by Muslim fundamentalists who attack foreign residents and tourists in Algeria and Egypt, while unnerving governments throughout the Middle East, is akin to the kinds of political violence that we have considered in this text—violence that is high in symbolism and relatively low in casualties. The perpetrators have been labeled "terrorists" by their respective governments as a first step in a no-holds-barred campaign to obliterate adversaries. Indeed, for many governments this all too familiar ploy has seemingly not lost any of its demonstrable appeal—witness developments in Argentina and India.

In the wake of the bombing of the Jewish community center in Buenos Aires, President Menem "has created a security agency to oversee the military, the police and the intelligence-gathering services in emergencies, reviving memories of a time when an all-powerful military terrorized the country." According to the director for human rights at Argentina's Center for Legal and Social Studies, "This is but one more example of what has always happened in Argentina: facing a real and concrete necessity—in this case the fight against international terrorism—the military is used to render the common individual totally defenseless against the powers of the state."[16]

India legislated its Terrorist and Disruptive Activities Act (TADA) in 1985 to quell terrorism in the Punjab. By 1994, 65,000 persons had been detained under its provisions, including 19,000 in Gujarat, "where there is no terrorist activity." There even have been environmentalists arrested under TADA. According to one source, the act "enables the police to detain people temporarily without charge. Witnesses who give evidence of crimes need not be named. The act allows confessions made before senior police officers to be used in court, even if these are later retracted. Human rights activists believe this has opened the door...for confessions extracted by torture."[17]

Finally, terrorism discourse has not lost any of its allure for world leaders in political difficulty. Benjamin Netanyahu, leader of the Likud party is a good case in point. According to various reports, his chances for becoming prime minister depended largely on whether terrorist attacks occurred or not in Israel, and "Netanyahu's future is thus heavily dependent on terror."[18] This fits well with his entire career for he, "a sort of Israeli Rambo," has always seen himself as the leader of the antiterrorism cause. Even if "not perceived in Israel as having anything particularly interesting or authoritative to say about terror, or anything else," he has, nevertheless, "built a successful career in the U.S. as a regular and articulate participant in talk shows, much sought after because of his reputation as a leading expert in 'the war against terrorism.'"[19] One of his "students" was Ronald Reagan who, as claimed by Netanyahu himself, decided to attack Libya after he read in *Time* magazine excerpts from a conference that Netanyahu organized at the Jonathan Institute.

After the Oklahoma City bombing and the gas attack in Japan, "Terrorism is back—with a vengeance," Netanyahu wrote in the opening line of his new book, *Fighting Terrorism*. Late Prime Minister Rabin's words were not mere sarcasm: "Bibi Netanyahu is a Hamas collaborator."[20] It only attests to how strong the umbilical cord is between terrorists and counterterrorists.

In typical irony, the very day on which Yitzhak Rabin was assassinated Netanyahu had published an op-ed article in the *New York Times*, entitled "Act Now Against the Terror Network." It began: "The West had better wake up to the new terrorism. When even a small group like Islamic Holy War can threaten worldwide attacks..."[21] The article warned of the existence of at least 14 terrorist militant groups in Europe, "their active membership reaching tens of thousands," as well as "a number of terrorist groups" in America with widespread connections to Iran, Sudan, Egypt, Gaza, Tunisia, Pakistan and Indonesia. "This new terrorism poses unprecedented dangers," he went on, "especially because...a nuclear Iran could resort to indirect blackmail."[22] One thing that Netanyahu didn't alert the readers about was the possibility that, as the columnist Thomas Friedman put it, his own Prime Minister and political adversary Rabin might be murdered by a "gunman whose politics is virtually identical with that of Mr. Netanyahu's Likud Party and its allies in the Orthodox Jewish right."[23] In his op-ed article Netanyahu demanded a "systematic investigation of groups openly preaching terror," but had no qualms in allowing himself to be photographed in the company of West Bank settlers who "routinely described Rabin as an evil killer."[24]

President Clinton, too, has learned how to get political mileage out of terrorism. During his first two years in office, smarting from the criticism that he is unschooled in international affairs and a draft evader, the president alternatively sought to transcend his predecessors as both historic peacemaker and consummate world policeman. Consequently, in autumn of 1994 he traveled to Syria to meet with Assad, who the president proclaimed a "great statesman," and on St. Patrick's Day he invited Sinn Fein's Gerry Adams to the White House (to the utter chagrin of the British).

Conversely, Iran is, for the Clinton administration, *the* terrorist state, even though during Clinton's first two years in office the United States was Iran's largest trading partner and American exports to Iran had increased tenfold since 1989,[25] notwithstanding the charade of blocking oil exploration by American firms in that country. In his recent State of the Union address, touted as the most important political speech in the beleaguered president's career, Clinton confounded his own supporters with a lengthy declaration of war against international terrorists, which included a pledge to seize their American bank accounts. The next day administration officials conceded that they were unaware of such assets. One confused terrorism expert, who had served Clinton, was at a loss to explain "what—other than the terrible bombings in Israel—brought the terrorism issue to such prominence in the State of the Union speech."[26] However, as the *New York Times* noted, "Secretary of State Warren Christopher has made the fight against terrorism a linchpin of American foreign policy, and has searched for creative ways—however farfetched—to make it happen."[27]

In view of such highly choreographed sermons by their presidents, it is not surprising that the American public is terrified of terrorism. Even before Oklahoma City, Clinton had proposed a new Omnibus Counterterrorism Act. In an article entitled "Back to McCarthy," Anthony Lewis criticized the bill because it "imposes guilt by association" with groups defined as terrorist by the government. Lewis observes that, under the new law, the thousands of American who gave money to support Mandela's ANC "would now be punishable by 10 years in prison." This would take us back to the McCarthy era when "officials often insisted that they denied a fair process to the accused because the national security was at stake—but in time, case after case was shown to have been built on lies. And judges, far from being vigilant, usually deferred to the executive's supposed expertise."[28]

The new antiterrorism powers sought by the FBI after the Oklahoma City explosion were sternly criticized by both the left and the right. In William Safire's words, they amounted to "proposing a bureaucratic subversion of our civil liberties."[29] Wary of "the paranoid streak in American politics," the press issued warnings of "False Choices on Terrorism."[30] Even Louis Freeh, the Director of the FBI, told the Senate that his agency did not need the relaxation of investigative guidelines proposed by the White House. "Desperately in Need of Winning Streak," the *New York Times* entitled a front-page piece, and went on to report Clinton delivering "rousing red-meat speeches on Mideast terrorism (to Jewish groups)" to rally voter support.[31] In short, another U.S. administration had learned that counterterrorism is politically expedient as a substitute for thornier and riskier public policy—both foreign and domestic. The Waco and Ruby Ridge Hearings during the summer of 1995 helped to defeat the broad new counterterrorism legislation that earlier in the year had passed in the Senate by the lopsided vote of 91 to 8. However, in the latest political waltz, it was revived and made into law.

The latest terrorism dynamic in the United States has a particularly ominous component: the mutually reinforcing roles of official discourse and right-wing violent activism. This is conducive to a process that is reminiscent of the strategies proposed by the guerrilla manuals of the 1960s under the slogan "action/reaction/ action." The primary goal of insurgent action was deemed to be to provoke more government repression (assumed necessary to raise the consciousness of the people) resulting, in turn, in more popular action. Nothing is more relevant than reelection in American politics, and if terrorism can help to bolster a beleaguered president's standing in the polls by raising the specter of national security (as Clinton most clearly did after Oklahoma City), then barricading Pennsylvania Avenue, getting tough with terrorism (even at the expense of *habeas corpus*), and turning counterterrorism into the "linchpin" of foreign policy is all good for the reelection campaign.

In the meantime the time-honored politics of imprisoning yesterday's friend and turning him into today's archterrorist continues under the Clinton Administration. In the tradition of Noriega, Sheik Omar and others, the latest case involves Haiti's Emmanuel Constant, the leader of the hit squad FRAPH, who, beginning in mid-1993 while working for the CIA, launched a campaign of terror with arms shipped from the United States. This continued even after the knowledge "of the myriad murders, arsons, rapes and tortures then being attributed—often openly—to Constant's men in FRAPH. The United States, though, kept on paying Constant, and the weapons flow increased."[32] Constant declared: "People say the C.I.A. was opposed to Clinton, but

I don't think so. Clinton knew everything concerning me."[33] Various reports from Aristide advisers and U.S. envoy Lawrence Pezzullo confirm that the Administration did indeed use the threat of FRAPH to pressure Aristide in Washington.[34] The expert Brian Jenkins didn't need to invoke the future when he wrote that "national governments will recognize...and begin to employ"[35] terrorism as a new form of warfare. As we have insisted throughout this book, one of the royal advantages of controlling terrorism discourse is that our most trusted allies can, by the stroke of a pen, be redefined as frightening monsters, while we ourselves, acting as their judges, remain innocent and even enhance our moral legitimacy.

In this book we have argued that the American quest for "terrorism" has had a lot to do with a Beckettian theater of the absurd as well as with the political manipulations of collective fantasies of nuclearism and savagery. It doesn't take an uncommon sagacity to perceive that the journalistic and academic fashionings of the "thing" itself are flawed and self-deceptive. But, even if we have concentrated on showing the discursive basis of the culture of terrorism, there is a point in which the thing itself (whether the created category is "race" or "ethnicity" or "taboo"), no matter how reified or distorted or banal, becomes a structural reality and a historical force. It appears that "terrorism" is fast becoming a dominant medium through which American society and domestic politics need to be interpreted. We may laugh at an American public overwhelmingly obssessed with terrorism during the 1980s—a time when little terrorism actually transpired. Yet the rhetorical forces and foreign policy interests that promoted it in the first place are not becoming a thing of the past. Terrorism is now becoming a functional reality of American politics, an autonomous prime mover of enormous consequence affecting national policy and legislation. This is no longer mere phantasmagoria but rather an irreducible dimension of a political ideology that profoundly affects the material reality of American society. Terrorism has been "naturalized" into a constant risk that is omnipresent out there, a sort of chaotic principle always ready to strike and create havoc, and against which society must now marshall all its resources in an unending struggle. Now that it has become a prime *raison d'état*, its perpetuation seems guaranteed.

It is against such a prospect that we have engaged ourselves in scrutinizing terrorism discourse in order to challenge both the inquisition and its witches. As the world moves forward into uncharted political waters, it is well to deprive both sides unchallenged access to, and control of, terrorism discourse, since ultimately it is we, the public, who are the real targets (and victims) of the manipulation. If we take away their witches from the self-styled, emblematic protectors of the moral order, elected or otherwise, then they must justify their activities in other terms. Stripped of their scapegoats, the architects of the New World Order and its flawed democracies will have to explicate and defend their agendas in terms of political rather than terroristic discourse. Similarly, by dissolving the category and unmasking the rhetorics of terrorism, the "terrorists," denied their roles within a plausible script would cease to be actors capable of a credible apocalyptic performance. Terrorism discourse must be disenchanted if it is to lose its efficacy for all concerned.

Notes

PREFACE

1. As an instance, the A section of May 16, 1995, includes a typical array of terrorism stories: one about the Japanese group Aum Shinrikyo, one about Iran's "outlaw state spreading global terror," one about the Oklahoma City explosion, one about Clinton's push for passing anti-terrorism legislation, one about the FBI's files on protest groups and its lack of authority to infiltrate them unless they have "a firm connection with terrorism," an editorial that begins with a reference to "Muslim terrorists," a letter about the Oklahoma City suspect McVeigh, an op-ed article about "how to foil bomb makers" of the Oklahoma City type by exercising "the imagination of disaster," another op-ed about Iran's "terrorist state," and finally a story about a New York congressman who laments that in order to get media attention "I'm going to become a terrorist, too."
2. *The Washington Post*, May 21, 1995, p. A1.
3. See Douglass and Zulaika, "On the Interpretation of Terrorist Violence," and Zulaika, *Basque Violence*.
4. Taussig, *Shamanism, Colonialism, and the Wild Man*, p. xiii.

1: WAITING FOR TERROR

1. Hofstadter, "The Paranoid Style in American Politics," p. 37.
2. Davis, *Fiction in the Archives*, p. 3.
3. For the extensive literature on terrorism and the media, see particularly the very relevant work of Schlesinger, Murdock, and Elliot, *Televising "Terrorism"*; Schmid and de Graaf, *Violence as Communication*; Schlesinger, *Media, State, and Nation*; and Paletz and Schmid, *Terrorism and the Media*.
4. Palmerton, "The Rhetoric of Terrorism," p. 107.
5. In Barthes, *The Rustle of Language*, p. 147. Such "reality effect" consists in operationalizing Barthes's "referential illusion": "The truth of this illusion is this: eliminated from the realist speech-act as a signified of denotation, the 'real' returns to it as a signified of connotation; for just when these details are reputed to *denote* the real directly, all that they do—without saying so—is *signify* it." p. 147
6. Quoted in Palmerton, "The Rhetoric of Terrorism," p. 106.
7. As reported by Hinckley in "American Opinion Toward Terrorism," six surveys in 1987–88 showed 68–80 percent of the public considered terrorism an "extreme" or "very" serious threat.
8. Freedman, et al., *Terrorism and International Order*, p. 45.
9. *New York Times*, April 27, 1986, p. 23.
10. Hinckley, "American Opinion toward Terrorism," p. 388.
11. As for Americans killed overseas in terrorist attacks, different numbers are given by different authors. A standard estimate is given by Bennet that, "During the 1980s, terrorists killed 571 Americans around the world" (p. 22). Two attacks—the 1983 suicide bomb against the Marine barracks in Beirut and the destruction

of Pan Am flight 103 over Lockerbie—are responsible for most of these casualties. The Beirut explosion, produced after Lebanon had been invaded by Israel and American troops had come to her aid, was responsible for the killing of 241 American soldiers. The destruction of Pan Am flight103 took the lives of 189 Americans; this was, however, a very special case of "terrorism." It has received extensive treatment in the literature and we shall consider it in greater detail. Apart from these two major incidents, at the peak of the terrorism scare there would seem to have been an annual average of fourteen American deaths attributable to terrorism worldwide.

12. Worldwide, thirty-four Americans were killed during those four years.
13. Bennet, "Mission Impossible."
14. On why people emphasize certain risks while ignoring others, see Douglas and Wildavsky, *Risk and Culture.*
15. Barthes, *The Rustle of Language,* p. 148.
16. Nacos, Fan, and Young, "Terrorism and the Print Media," p. 108.
17. Schmid, "Terrorism and the Media," p. 556.
18. Quoted in Farnen, "Terrorism and the Mass Media," p. 112.
19. Sluka, *Hearts and Minds, Water and Fish,* p. 288.
20. *New York Times Magazine,* April 21, 1991.
21. Ibid., p. 31.
22. Eser, "Repairing Our War-torn Industry," p. 40.
23. Nor at this juncture do they bear the burden of proof, since obviously millions *believe* in terrorism, and faith is not easily shaken by facts. Stated differently, faith tends to arrange facts selectively, accepting uncritically the evidence supporting belief and dismissing that which challenges it. It is testimony to the success of the counterterrorism campaign that docile public acceptance of the reality of its nemesis is so pervasive.
24. Herman and O'Sullivan, *The "Terror" Industry,* pp. 57–59, 128.
25. Martin and Walcott, *Best Laid Plans,* p. 201.
26. Herman and O'Sullivan, *The "Terror" Industry,* p. 126.
27. See chapter 2 of Coates, *Armed and Dangerous.*
28. *New York Times,* August 21, 1995, p. A1.
29. See, for instance, White, *Metahistory;* Davis, *Fiction in the Archives.*
30. White, *Tropics of Discourse,* p. 154. Similarly, the Freud of *Totem and Taboo,* pp. 159–160, insisted on the role of "fantasy" and underlined the preeminence of "psychical realities" to the detriment of "factual" ones in the genesis of neurosis.
31. Rothstein, "When Fiction is Fact," p. 375.
32. As an instance of such reactions, the noted terrorism experts Robert and Tamara Kupperman wrote in an op-ed article in the *New York Times* (November 16, 1991): "compelling evidence still suggests that Iran commissioned the bombing and with Syria's help paid Ahmed Jibril's terrorist organization…to carry it out…. For now, political considerations have taken precedence." p. 19.
33. Weinberg and Eubank, "Political Terrorism and Political Development," p. 32.
34. Livingston, *The Terrorism Spectacle.*
35. Ibid., chapter 2.
36. Ibid., pp. 30–31.
37. Quoted in Herman and O'Sullivan, *The "Terror" Industry,* pp. xii–xiii.
38. The words of former ambassador and university president Lincoln Gordon; in Martin and Walcott, *Best Laid Plans,* p. 53.

39. Ibid., p. 54.

40. We can agree with Livingston that it is not particularly startling that a State Department publication may emphasize the terrorism of its enemies while ignoring the violence perpetrated by America's proxy armies. However, "What *was* surprising…was the degree to which a world class newspaper like the *New York Times* was capable of doing the same thing. Even more surprising still was the degree to which *Times* was capable of ignoring its own stories" (*The Terrorism Spectacle*, p. 48).

41. Alexander and Picard, *In the Camera's Eye*, p. 14.

42. The fact is that dozens of American terrorist groups populated the United States not long ago. By one authoritative calculation, in the 1960s there were 35 terrorist groups and 476 known terrorists in the United States (see Handler, "Socioeconomic Profile"). It is not coincidental that this was also a period when America was preoccupied with the countercultural movement. Terrorism is always about fear and power; the violent actions of another that challenge one's own precepts or self-image are always prime candidates for the terrorist label.

    As to present-day acts of terror, it is well known that many bombings and threats do occur in the United States for political and moral reasons. According to the FBI, in 1992 alone there were 2,493 bombings in the United States (*New York Times*, December 22, 1994, p. A13). This is basically a semantic issue since, for instance, during the Reagan and Bush years' pro-life administrations, the hundreds of bombings and death threats directed against abortion clinics were, according to the FBI, nonterrorist and hence were not reported in the media as terrorism (see Wilson and Lynxwiler, "Abortion Clinic Violence as Terrorism"). Under a pro-choice Clinton administration, the terrorism label is regularly leveled at violent opponents of abortion. What makes one person's bombing terror and another's not? Again, the answer is obviously the politics of labeling.

    Ironically, the portrayed impossibility of American terrorism is accompanied by reports of the presence of foreign terrorist groups on U.S. soil. How convenient for the agencies of counterterrorism that, while there are no longer American terrorists, every major international terrorist organization has a surrogate or branch operation in the United States. See, for instance, Mullins, XX. *Terrorist Organizations in the United States.*

43. Sick, *All Fall Down.*

44. Martin and Walcott, *Best Laid Plans.*

45. Sick, *All Fall Down*, p. 42.

46. Ibid., p. 171.

47. Herman and O'Sullivan, *The "Terror" Industry*, p. 171. For Sterling's treatment of the Basque case, see chapter 2 of this book.

48. Martin and Walcott, *Best Laid Plans*, p. 50.

49. Ibid., p. 48.

50. Ibid., p. 56.

51. *New York Times*, April 27, 1986, p. E23.

52. Livingston, *The Terrorism Spectacle*, p. 173.

53. Ibid., p. 136.

54. White, *Tropics of Discourse*, chapter 5.

55. See Chomsky and Herman, *The Political Economy of Human Rights*; and Herman, *The Real Terror Network.*

56. See Geifman, *Thou Shalt Kill*, for a history of "terrorist" activity that claimed more than 17,000 victims.

57. Hardman, "Terrorism," p. 579.

58. The present work is scarcely the place to develop an adequate treatment of the labyrinthian issues and arguments engendered by the Israel conundrum. Indeed it might be argued that no such treatment is even possible given the vastness of the published debate, the myriad number of viewpoints, and the degree to which they are polarized. For present purposes, suffice it to say that the conundrum has provided us with the archetypal terrorist figure—the PLO activist—and the archetypal examples of state terrorism—Syria, Iraq, Iran, Libya. The fact that the negative stereotypy regards the Arab side of the ledger is, itself, testimony to the success of Israel's proponents to control the terms of the debate. The counterexamples that emphasize the bombs, assassinations, and kidnappings of the Stern gang in the 1940s, or the willingness of Israel's armed forces and the Mossad to conduct strikes well beyond the confines of Israel, are largely underplayed or even defended as "preemptive" in the western press. Thus, books like Bowyer Bell's *Terror Out of Zion*, run the risk of garnering for their authors the accusation of being anti-Semites, while Chomsky is labeled "traitor" by some for penning *The Fateful Triangle: The United States, Israel and the Palestinians*, as is the French historian Rodinson for books like *Israel and the Arabs* and *Israel: A Colonial-Settler State?* For an overview of the difficulties that Israeli scholars themselves encounter when they become critical of the Zionist movement, see Uri Ram, "The Colonization Perspective in Israeli Sociology." As for the U.S. side of the ledger, we are told by William F. Buckley, Jr. that "Israel, as my sociologist friend Jack Cuddihy, a profound student of Jewish-Christian relations observes, is 'the issue that makes strong men tremble.' Everyone in journalism knows that you criticize Israel at your own risk" (in *In Search of Anti-Semitism*, p. 96).

This timidity is not limited to journalists alone. For example, Horowitz penned *Ethnic Groups in Conflict*, the most ambitious synthesis to date regarding the subject. Yet the work studiously avoids the issue of Israel/Palestine, arguably *the* most serious ethnic conflict in the contemporary world—one that has on occasion threatened the planet with escalation toward a nuclear holocaust!

It is difficult to prove our contention that there is a tilt toward Israel in U.S. foreign policy, one that is contested by scholars such as Glazer who, in his article "Anti-Zionism—A Global Phenomenon," argues the opposite by counting the anti-Israel books on display in bookstore windows of Cambridge, Massachusetts, in the aftermath of the invasion of Lebanon. However, there does remain one inescapable bit of evidence: namely that, despite a recent history of certain disagreements between Israeli and U.S. authorities, Israel receives enormous amounts of U.S. foreign aid. By 1975 the Middle East had surpassed Asia as the world region receiving the most American foreign aid, and by 1982 it accounted for more than 50 percent of the total (Guess, *The Politics of United States Foreign Aid*, p. 223). By 1985, 19 percent of the Israeli budget derived from U.S. foreign aid; the country accounted for 33 percent of American aid to the Middle East as well as 50 percent of all American military assistance (Guess, p. 224). In 1990 Israel, with a population of about 4.5 million inhabitants, received almost $3 billion in U.S. assistance, or three times the amount given to the entire African continent and half again as much as the U.S. provided to all of Latin America. Egypt, as a continuing reward for signing the Camp David accord with Israel, received about $2.4 billion. The next largest recipient was Pakistan, which received almost $591 million (American Foreign Policy Council, *Modernizing Foreign Assistance*, pp. 135–139).

59. In Isaacson and Kelly, "We Distorted our Minds," p. 32.
60. Moynihan, "Do We Still Need the CIA?" pY15.
61. Wilkinson, "Trends in International Terrorism and the American Response," p. 45.
62. See Douglass and Zulaika, "On the Interpretation of Terrorist Violence."
63. Barthes, *The Rustle of Language*, p. 148.
64. Taussig, *Shamanism, Colonialism, and the Wild Man*, p. 121.
65. There is a list of 1,600 easily obtainable publications and manuals on bomb building. See the *New York Times*, December 22, 1994, p. A13.
66. *New York Times*, February 8, 1995, p. A1.
67. Friedman, "The CIA's *Jihad*," p. 38.
68. Ibid., pp. 36–47.
69. Melton, "Epilogue: A Fiery Ending," pp. 257–58.
70. See Lewis, "Showdown at the Waco Corral," p. 92.
71. Allen, "Reader-Oriented Criticism and Television," p. 75.
72. Fish, *Is There a Text in This Class?* p. 335.
73. Neill, "Fear, Fiction, and Make Believe," p. 51

2: WRITING TERRORISM

1. Numbers produced through a search of the OCLC WorldCat Database.
2. See particularly Derrida, *Of Grammatology*, and *Writing and Difference*.
3. See for example Hicks, "Cult Label Made Waco Violence Inevitable"; Oliver, "Killed by Semantics"; and Goldberg, "FBI Uses 'Cults' as Bait." See our critique of the label "cult" in chapter 4.
4. *New York Times*, April 26, 1995 p. A12.
5. Douglass and Zulaika, "On the Interpretation of Terrorist Violence."
6. See Zulaika, *Basque Violence*.
7. See Martin and Walcott, *Best Laid Plans*, p. 362. The base is called "Strike U" and was created by the Navy in response to its dismal performance in Lebanon in December of 1983. Beginning in the fall of 1987, Navy pilots encountered a new missile—the American-made Hawk—on their training ranges. Why? The Iranians were able to use the spare parts that the Reagan administration sold them to activate Hawk missile batteries. Each training session on Hawk missile defense costs about $1 million.
8. Gramsci, *The Modern Prince and Other Writings*, p. 22.
9. Hordago, *Documentos*, I:104.
10. Tololyan, "Cultural Narrative and the Motivation of the Terrorist," p. 218.
11. Ibid., p. 219.
12. Ibid., p. 222.
13. Hordago, *Documentos*, I:412.
14. Ibid., II:506.
15. Ibid., I:133.
16. See Zulaika, *Basque Violence*, for a description of the Itziar events.
17. Douglass, *Death in Murelaga*.
18. As one of the anthropologists who worked in Spain during the Franco years, I (Douglass) now share in the accusation leveled by Spanish new-guard anthropology that we were silent regarding the real issues of the day while we went about

producing benign descriptions of culturally exotic, backwater places. The charge is accurate up to a point, although it invites the obvious retort that the political climate itself determined the parameters of our inquiry. There was a far more telling issue, however, which was the ethical one. I felt as constrained not to write about Basque nationalism in Murelaga as about the contraband system in the frontier village of Echalar. Twenty years ago had I presented my detailed knowledge regarding either, many lives would have been jeopardized.

19. *El Diario Vasco*, May 20, 1969.
20. Evans-Pritchard, "The Divine Kingship of the Shilluk of the Nilotic Sudan," p. 77.
21. See Crelinsten, "Images of Terrorism," p. 173.
22. Sterling, *The Terror Network*, p. 11.
23. Ibid., p. 171.
24. See Gambetta, "In the Beginning Was the Word," p. 64.
25. Trevanian, *Shibumi*, p. 290.
26. See Cooper, "Terrorism and Perspectivist Philosophy," p. 11.
27. See Zulaika, "Terror, Totem, and Taboo."
28. Rose, et al., *Report of the International Commission on Violence in the Basque Country*, #9.1.21.
29. Ibid., #9.1.14.
30. Nordstrom and Martin, "The Culture of Conflict," p. 4.
31. Wilkinson, "Some Observations on the Relationships between Terrorism and Freedom," p. 47.
32. Pollack and Hunter, "Dictatorship, Democracy and Terrorism in Spain," p. 144, n.45.
33. Ibid.
34. Schlesinger, *Media, State and Nation*, pp. 74, 86.
35. Sterling, *The Terror Network*, pp. 12–13.
36. Ibid., p. 4.
37. Ibid., p. 7.
38. Sterling writes that Spanish Basques barely exceed 1.5 million in population, whereas in actuality there are 2.7 million. She says they are equaled if not outnumbered by immigrant workers; migrants constitute less than 40 percent of the population. She says Basque is spoken perhaps by one in twenty; it is spoken by one in four.
39. She spells *sopa de marisco* as *zupa de marrascos*.
40. "Iñaki"'s real name was not José Ignacio Bustamante Otaduy, as stated by Sterling, but José Ignacio Pérez Beotegi. Hundreds of Basque emigrants living in London knew Iñaki personally, and his real name was no secret to anyone after he became prominent in a hunger strike protesting the Burgos trial, staged in Trafalgar Square in December 1970. He was one of a handful of ETA operatives working during the early 1970s, and his name was constantly in the newspapers. The fact that Sterling's superinformed sources committed such a basic error underscores their unreliability.
41. See Zulaika, *Basque Violence*, chapter 3.
42. Sterling, *The Terror Network*, p. 4.
43. Ibid., p. 7.
44. Quoted in Hofstadter, "The Paranoid Style in American Politics," p. 11.
45. Ibid., p. 14.
46. Post, "Worlds in Collision, Worlds in Collusion," p. 241.

47. Ibid., p. 247.

48. Clark, "Patterns in the Lives of ETA Members."

49. In the abstract of the paper, Clark states: "The study finds ETA members to be not the alienated and pathologically distressed individuals who join other insurgent organizations, but rather they are psychologically healthy persons for the most part, strongly supported by their families and their ethnic community" (Clark, p. 423). Post's selective use of Clark's findings as to the 8 and 40 percent figures can be detected from simply quoting the next sentence Clark writes regarding the same table: "More than 80 percent of all *etarras* [ETA members] have at least one Basque parent, as compared with slightly less than 60 percent of the province's overall population." This bluntly negates Post's conclusions. Aside from Post's obvious distortion of his sources, there is a major problem with Clark's data in that what are tabulated are the *surnames* of both parents of arrested ETA members; it is simply common sense that many culturally Basque persons have non-Basque surnames and vice versa, and that this cannot be equated, as does Post, with "Basque ethnicity," much less with "Basque parentage." Post's conclusion that ETA activists are marginal people with dubious Basque credentials is a fabrication that contradicts virtually everything written on Basque violence.

50. See for instance Post's 1987 paper in which the theory of alienation once again invokes the Basques: "Only 8 percent of families are of mixed Spanish-Basque heritage, and the children of these families are scorned and rejected. Yet fully 40 percent of the members of ETA…come from such mixed-parent families" (p. 432).

51. See, for instance, Long, *The Anatomy of Terrorism*, p. 22. In typical fashion, in order to argue that Basque terrorism is of an "ethnic" kind, he describes the Basques with the most outdated stereotypes of "self-contained, and self-sufficient race of herders and fishermen" (p. 49).

52. Bremer, "Terrorism: Myths and Reality."

53. Quoted in R. Friedman, "One Man's *Jihad*," p. 656.

54. Quoted ibid.

55. Emerson, "Exchange: Journalist's *Jihad*," p. 186.

56. Wievorka, *The Making of Terrorism*, p. 178

57. Ibid., p. 196.

58. Ibid., p. 201.

59. Ibid., p. 213.

60. Ibid., p. 211.

61. Ibid., p. 147.

62. Ibid., p. 296.

63. Ibid., p. 297.

64. Derrida, "Signature event context," p. 181.

65. A forthright account of the intellectual and personal difficulties a fieldworker encounters in situations of political violence is presented by Sluka, *Hearts and Minds, Water and Fish.*

66. After the publication of *The Secret Agent,* Conrad endured severe criticism for having broached the tabooed subject of terrorism. In a preface to a later edition (1920), Conrad stated that in telling the tale "I have not intended to commit a gratuitous outrage on the feelings of mankind" (1993, p. 7). At the same time he underscored the dilemma that the serious novelist shares with the ethnographer—the need to empathize with one's subjects in order to be true to their tale. In Conrad's words:

I have no doubt...that there had been moments during the writing of the book when I was an extreme revolutionist, I won't say more convinced than they but certainly cherishing a more concentrated purpose than any of them.... I don't say this to boast. I was simply attending to my business. In the matter of all of my books...I have attended to it with complete surrender. I could not have done otherwise. It would have bored me too much to make-believe. (Ibid.).

67. In 1970, sixteen ETA members were brought before a military tribunal in Burgos. From the outset the notorious "Burgos Trial," as it came to be known, was more concerned with making an example of the defendants than with rules of evidence. The attempt to conduct the proceedings in secret failed, and in open court all of the defendants repudiated their confessions and declared that they had been exacted under torture. The prosecution demanded death for six of them and lengthy prison sentences for the remainder.

The Burgos trial quickly became a *cause célèbre*. Several European countries withdrew their ambassadors for consultation, and there were demonstrations before the Spanish embassy in a number of European capitals. In the Basque Country, public manifestations in support of the Burgos 16 were common and, at times, violent. Public figures from around the world urged Franco to be moderate.

In the final analysis, Franco did compromise up to a point. Caught between world opinion and the demands of his hardliners that no quarter be given—and further squeezed by an ETA kidnapping of the honorary West German consul in San Sebastián (whose release was then predicated upon leniency for the Burgos 16)—the Spanish authorities found the defendants guilty and handed out harsh sentences, but the death ones were then commuted by Franco to prison terms.

68. Shedd, *Silence in Bilbao.*
69. Douglass and da Silva, "Basque Nationalism."
70. See Juaristi, "Héroes y traidores."
71. Aranzadi, "Sangre simbólica e impostura antropológica." See Zulaika's reply, "El antropólogo como impostor."
72. See Zulaika, "The Anthropologist as Terrorist."
73. Foucault quoted in Miller, *The Passion of Michel Foucault*, p. 228.

3: TROPICS OF TERROR

1. Feldman, *Formations of Violence*, p. 14.
2. Wagner-Pacifici, *The Moro Morality Play*, p. 273.
3. See Pepper, *World Hypothesis.*
4. Jenkins, *Terrorism and Beyond*, p. 9.
5. Ibid., p. 11.
6. Crenshaw, "The Causes of Terrorism."
7. Bateson, "Cybernetic Explanation," in *Steps to an Ecology of Mind*, pp. 375–86.
8. As an example of what we mean by analyzing "negatively" a violent sequence, see Zulaika, *Basque Violence*, chapter 13.
9. See Leach, "Ritualization in Man in Relation to Conceptual and Social Development."
10. Evans-Pritchard, *Social Anthropology*, p. 38.
11. Weber, *The Methodology of the Social Sciences*, p. 78.
12. Geertz, *The Interpretation of Cultures*, p. 316. For further critiques of causal argu-

ments, see Needham, *Structure and Sentiment.*

13. In fact, conspiratorial theories about taxes being the root of all evil and of an America about to be devoured by the New World Order presided over by the United Nations and controlled by Jewish international bankers (see Smolowe, "Enemies of the State") are not that original. They have been around since the passage of the income tax amendment to the Constitution in 1913 and reached their apogee during Roosevelt's New Deal. For decades, writers have been charging that the United Nations was "the principal instrument of a gigantic conspiracy to control the foreign and domestic policies of the United States" (quoted in Hofstadter, "The Paranoid Style in American Politics," p. 25, n. 9).

14. Hofstadter, "The Paranoid Style in American Politics," p. 32.

15. *New York Times*, editorial article "The Trial of Omar Abdel Rahman," Oct. 3, 1995, p. A14; emphasis added.

16. Ibid.

17. Kermode, "Secrets and Narrative Sequence," p. 84.

18. Ibid., p. 87.

19. Sterling, *The Terror Network*, p. 30.

20. Ibid., p. 45.

21. Hill, "The Political Dilemmas for Western Governments," p. 85.

22. Aron, *Peace and War*, p. 170.

23. Evans-Pritchard, *Theories of Primitive Religion*, p. 44.

24. Lévi-Strauss, *Totemism*, p. 71.

25. Fernandez, *Persuasions and Performances.*

26. Bateson, "Some Components of Socialization for Trance," p. 147.

27. Sapir, "The Emergence of the Concept of Personality in a Study of Cultures," p. 412.

28. White, "The Value of Narrativity in the Representation of Reality," p. 27.

29. For a discussion of political agency—particularly regarding the body—as the result of situated practices, see Feldman, *Formations of Violence.*

30. To see how this modeling on an all-or-nothing game can be realized, see Zulaika, *Basque Violence*, chapter 13. In American football, the desperate forward pass of a team facing a seemingly insurmountable situation in terms of necessary yardage or elapsing time is referred to as "the bomb."

31. See Bateson, *Mind and Nature*, pp. 195–96, for a comparison between scatter-gunning with a shotgun versus aiming with a rifle.

32. See Zulaika, *Basque Violence*, and Douglass and Zulaika, "On the Interpretation of Terrorist Violence."

33. Benveniste quoted in Gennette, "Boundaries of Narrative," p. 9.

34. Ibid., p. 8. Italics in original.

35. Jenkins, "International Terrorism."

36. See, among others, the works of Jenkins, Crenshaw, Merari, and Wilkinson.

37. Van Creveld, *Transformation of War*, p. 30.

38. See the definitions of these labels in Huxley, *A Discussion of Ritualization of Behavior.*

39. Aron, *Peace and War*, p. 67.

40. Fox, "The Inherent Rules of Violence."

41. See Wilkinson, *Terrorism and the Liberal State*, p. 181; Jenkins, "International Terrorism", p. 30, foresees a similar scenario.

42. See Arques and Miralles, *Amedo.*

43. See references to the Stalker Affair in chapter 6.

44. Arbastler, "Terrorism," p. 419.

45. See the report on the conclusions of the Fifth Course of the International School of Disarmament and Research on Conflicts by Leurdijk, "Summary of Proceedings."

46. Merari, *Kingfisher Game*, p. 136.

47. This is suggested, for instance, by the title of Netanyahu's book, *Terrorism: How the West Can Win*.

48. Goody, "Religion and Ritual," p. 159.

49. Moore and Myerhoff, *Secular Ritual*, p. 17.

50. Rappaport, *Ecology, Meaning, and Religion*, p. 174.

51. Huxley, *A Discussion of Ritualization of Behavior*, p. 258.

52. See Morris, "The Rigidification of Behavior," p. 329.

53. Erikson, "Ontogeny of Ritualization in Man," p. 339. Italics in original.

54. See Paine, *Politically Speaking*.

55. V. Turner, "Social Dramas and Stories about Them," pp. 161, 163.

56. See Van Gennep, *The Rites of Passage*.

57. Lincoln, *Religion, Rebellion, Revolution*, p. 280.

58. Fox, "The Violent Imagination," p. 24.

59. Hardman, "Terrorism," p. 576.

60. Schmid, *Political Terrorism*, p. 101.

61. Wheeler, "Terrorism and Military Theory," pp. 24–25.

62. Redfield, *Nature and Culture in the Iliad*, p. 128.

63. White, *Metahistory*, p. 31. Italics in original.

64. Girard, *Violence and the Sacred*, p. 110.

65. Fernandez, "Symbolic Consensus in a Fang Reformative Cult."

66. Geertz, *The Interpretation of Cultures*, p. 167.

67. In its extreme form, conventionally noncommunicative behavior may be used to communicate; silence and opposition to any mediating mechanism may become ends in themselves. As with that of the psychotic, "This type of communication has its own rules: it is highly formalized; it is limited in temporal sequence; it is resistant to change; it is cryptic" (Laing, "Ritualization and Abnormal Behavior," p. 334). Such behavioral abnormalities may be viewed as "metarituals," in which "deritualization of normal human rituals" occurs; through their increased rigidity, they become "an aberration of an aberration" (Ibid., p. 335).

4: CATEGORIES AND ALLEGORIES

1. Quoted in Miller, *The Passion of Michel Foucault*, p. 150.

2. Words attributed to the Unabomber in *Newsweek*, July 10, 1995, p. 45.

3. Quoted in *Newsweek*, July 10, 1995, p. 45.

4. *Newsweek*, July 10, 1995, p. 40.

5. *Los Angeles Times*, June 29, 1995, A30.

6. Ibid.

7. *New York Times*, Nov. 6, 1995, p. A16.

8. Ibid.

9. Ibid.

10. Ibid., p. A1.

11. Ibid.

12. Ibid., p. A16.
13. *Newsweek*, July 10, 1995, p. 42.
14. *New York Times*, Nov. 6, 1995, p. A16.
15. McLennan, "The Worship of Animals and Plants."
16. Rivers, *The History of Melanesian Society*.
17. Boas, "The Origin of Totemism."
18. Lévi-Strauss, *Totemism*, pp. 17–18.
19. Ibid., p. 45.
20. Trevor-Roper, *The European Witch-Craze*, p. 177.
21. Crick, *Explorations in Language and Meaning*, p. 112.
22. Bell, "Trends on Terror," pp. 481–82.
23. Schmid, *Political Terrorism*, p. 12.
24. Schmid, Jongman, et al., *Political Terrorism*.
25. See Sederberg, "Defining Terrorism."
26. "Terrorism is a method of combat in which random or symbolic victims serve as an instrumental *target of violence*. These instrumental victims share group or class characteristics which form the basis for their selection for victimization. Through previous use of violence or the credible threat of violence other members of that group or class are put in a *state of chronic fear (terror)*. This group or class, whose members' sense of security is purposively undermined, is the *target of terror*. The victimization of the target of violence is considered extranormal by most observers from the witnessing audience on the basis of its atrocity; the time (e.g., peacetime) or place (not a battlefield) of victimization or the disregard for rules of combat accepted in conventional warfare. The norm violation creates an attentive audience beyond the target of terror; sectors of this audience might in turn form the main object of manipulation. The purpose of this indirect method of combat is either to immobilize the target of terror in order to produce disorientation and/or compliance, or to mobilize secondary *targets of demands* (e.g., a government) or *targets of attention* (e.g., public opinion) to changes of attitude or behavior favoring the short or long-term interests of the users of this method of combat" (Schmid, *Politcal Terrorism*, p. 111. Italics in original).
27. Hitchens, "Wanton Acts of Usage."
28. Livingstone and Arnold, *Fighting Back*.
29. Hitchens, "Wanton Acts of Usage," pp. 67–68.
30. Margalit, "The Terror Master,".p. 19.
31. See for example Slater and Stohl, "Introduction."
32. Schmid, *Political Terrorism*, p. 8.
33. Beidelman, "Towards More Open Theoretical Interpretations," p. 351.
34. See, for example, Winzeler, "Shaman, Priest and Spirit Medium."
35. Beidelman, "Towards More Open Theoretical Interpretations," p. 351.
36. Gurr, "Empirical Research on Political Terrorism."
37. Wilkinson, *Terrorism and the Liberal State*, p. xiii.
38. Weber, *The Methodology of the Social Sciences*, p. 85. Italics in original.
39. Wilkinson, "Trends in International Terrorism and the American Response."
40. Bell, *Transnational Terror*.
41. As examples, see Wilkinson, "Trends in International Terrorism and the American Response"; and Bell, "Trends on Terror."
42. Hardman, "Terrorism."
43. See Merari and Friedland, "Social Psychological Aspects of Political Terrorism."

44. Crick, *Explorations in Language and Meaning*, p. 116.
45. Gambetta, "In the Beginning Was the Word," p. 66. Italics in original.
46. Quoted in Gambetta, "In the Beginning Was the Word," p. 68.
47. Urban, *A Discourse-Centered Approach to Culture*, p. 10.
48. Hicks, "Cult Label Made Waco Violence Inevitable," p. 00. In James Lewis, *From the Ashes*, p. 63.
49. Ibid.
50. Oliver, "Killed by Semantics," p. 72.
51. Ibid.
52. Melton, "Epilogue: A Fiery Ending," p. 260.
53. Barkun, "Reflections after Waco," p. 43.
54. See Bromley, "The Mythology of Cults."
55. Weber, *Economy and Society*, Vol. 1, p. 13. Italics in original.
56. Rose, et al., *Report of the International Commission on Violence in The Basque Country*, #9.1.1.
57. Weber, *Economy and Society*, Vol. 1, p. 395.
58. See Comaroff, "Of Totemism and Ethnicity."
59. Fox, "The Violent Imagination."
60. Wagner-Pacifici, *The Moro Morality Play*.
61. Comaroff, "Of Totemism and Ethnicity," p. 303.
62. Ibid., p. 304.
63. Bateson, "Some Components of Socialization for Trance," p. 147. Italics in original.
64. Rudé, *Robespierre*, p. 76.
65. See, for example, Lincoln, *Religion, Rebellion, Revolution*.
66. See, among many others, Thornton, "Terror as a Weapon of Political Agitation"; Laqueur, *Terrorism;* Rapoport, "Fear and Trembling"; Rapoport and Alexander, *The Morality of Terrorism*.
67. Rapoport, "Fear and Trembling," p. 659.
68. Ibid., p. 662.
69. Ibid.
70. Ibid., p. 663.
71. Trevor-Roper, *The European Witch-Craze*, p. 109.
72. Taussig, *Shamanism, Colonialism, and the Wild Man*, p. 121.
73. Behler, *Irony and the Discourse of Modernity*, p. 103.
74. Clifford, "On Ethnographic Allegory," p. 99.
75. For a comprehensive bibliography on religion and violence, see Candland, *The Spirit of Violence*.
76. See, for instance, Geertz, *The Interpretation of Cultures*, p. 40.
77. Jorgensen, "Religious Solutions and Native American Struggles."
78. See Robertson, "The Development and Implications of the Classical Sociological Perspective on Religion and Revolution."
79. Kroeber, *Anthropology Today*.
80. Rapoport, "Fear and Trembling," pp. 674, 675.
81. Weber, *The Methodology of the Social Sciences*, p. 110.
82. Ibid., p. 110. Italics in original.
83. Ibid.
84. Ibid., p. 111.
85. Freud, *Totem and Taboo*.
86. Lowie, *Primitive Religion*.

87. Radin, *Primitive Religion.*
88. Malinowski, *Crime and Custom in Savage Society.*
89. See Needham, *Structure and Sentiment.*
90. See, for instance, Crenshaw, "The Causes of Terrorism"; Ferracuti, "Psychiatric Aspects of Italian Left Wing and Right Wing Terrorism"; Rubinstein, *Alchemists of Revolution.*
91. Post, "Notes on a Psychodynamic Theory of Terrorist Behavior," p. 241.
92. Jenkins, *Terrorism and Beyond*, p. 54.
93. These arguments were divulged in the International Scientific Conference on Terrorism held in Berlin in December of 1978.
94. Deleuze quoted in Miller, *The Passion of Michel Foucault*, p. 152.
95. Wittgenstein, "Remarks on Frazer's 'Golden Bough'," p. 29.
96. Ibid., p. 234.
97. Vico, *The New Science of Giambattista Vico*, p. 210.
98. Ibid., p. 405.
99. Ibid.
100. Fernandez, *Persuasions and Performances.*
101. Black, *Models and Metaphors*, p. 229. Italics in original.
102. Weber, *The Methodology of the Social Sciences*, p. 88. Italics in original.
103. Geertz, *The Interpretation of Cultures*, p. 93.
104. Wilkinson, *Terrorism and the Liberal State*, p. x.
105. Conrad chose a similar approach:

    "The Secret Agent" is a perfectly genuine piece of work. Even the purely artistic purpose, that of applying an ironic method to a subject to that kind, was formulated with deliberation and in the earnest belief that ironic treatment alone would enable me to say all I felt I would have to say in scorn as well as in pity. It is one of the minor satisfactions of my writing life that having taken this resolve I did manage, it seems to me, to carry it right through to the end. (*The Secret Agent*, 1993, p. 6)

5: FATEFUL PURPOSE, FEARFUL INNOCENCE

1. Blake, *Complete Works*, p. 221.
2. Kierkegaard, *Fear and Trembling*, p. 26.
3. Ibid., p. 27.
4. Ibid., p. 28.
5. Ibid.
6. Ibid., p. 29.
7. Burke, *A Rhetoric of Motives*, p. 244.
8. Kierkegaard, *Fear and Trembling*, p. 67.
9. Ibid.
10. Quoted in Sprinzak, "Violence and Catastrophe in the Theology of Rabbi Meir Kahane," p. 62.
11. See Ben-Yehuda, "Conflict Resolution in an Underground Group."
12. Kierkegaard, *Fear and Trembling*, p. 29.
13. Gordon, *Sacrifice of Isaac*, p. 55.
14. Ibid., p. 267.
15. Ibid., p. 192.
16. Ibid.

17. Ibid., p. 268.
18. Kierkegaard, *Fear and Trembling*, p. 48.
19. Ibid., pp. 76–77.
20. Schmid, *Political Terrorism*, p. 79.
21. Ibid.
22. Ibid., p. 80.
23. Kaldor and Anderson, *Mad Dogs*, p. 67.
24. See Nordstrom and Martin, "The Culture of Conflict," p. 14.
25. Mallin, "Terrorism as a Military Weapon," p. 397.
26. Wheeler, "Terrorism and Military Theory," p. 23.
27. Orwell, "Killing Civilians," p. 102.
28. Schmid, *Political Terrorism*, p. 85.
29. We are using these sign categories in Peircean terms; see Peirce, *Philosophical Writings*.
30. See Taylor and Ryan, "Fanaticism, Political Suicide and Terrorism," p. 94. See also Begin, *The Revolt*.
31. Schmid, *Political Terrorism*, p. 93.
32. See Girard, *Violence and the Sacred*.
33. This has been argued by Wagner-Pacifici, *The Moro Morality Play*.
34. See Zulaika, *Basque Violence*, p. 185.
35. Gadamer, *Truth and Method*, p. 102.
36. Ibid., p. 103.
37. Conrad, *The Secret Agent*, pp. 36–37.
38. See Van Creveld, *Transformation of War*, p. 22.
39. Gleick, "Something Big Is Going to Happen," p. 52.
40. Gibson, *Warrior Dreams*.
41. See T. Turner, "Transformation, Hierarchy and Transcendence," on the hierarchical logic of ritual.
42. Freedman, "Terrorism and Strategy," p. 56.
43. Schmid, *Political Terrorism*, pp. 96–97.
44. Ibid., p. 87.
45. See Clark, *The Basque Insurgents*, on this point.
46. See Girard, *Violence and the Sacred*, p. 312.
47. Schmid, *Political Terrorism*, p. 95.
48. Ibid., p. 96.
49. Thornton, "Terror as a Weapon of Political Agitation," p. 77.
50. Crenshaw, *Revolutionary Terrorism*, p. 20.
51. Rosenblueth, Wiener, and Bigelow, "Behavior, Purpose and Teleology," p. 19.
52. Ibid. Italics in original.
53. War, as a systemic arrangement whereby one group seeks armed victory over another, has become altogether "purposeless" in the nuclear era. In the words of Robert McNamara, former U.S. Secretary of Defense, "nuclear weapons serve no military purpose whatsoever. They are totally useless—except only to deter one's opponent from using them" (*New York Times*, September 10, 1983, p. A27). The purpose is no longer to win the war but to avoid it. As with terrorism and ritual, with nuclear armaments, too, we are in the domain of partly nonintrinsic causality between means and ends; here, too, premises of chance, bluff, and belief introduce nonfunctional elements that are decisive throughout the entire course of the behavior.

6: TERROR, TABOO, AND THE WILD MAN

1. Quoted in Schlesinger, Murdock, and Elliot, *Televising "Terrorism,"* pp. 20–21.
2. Taussig, *Shamanism, Colonialism, and the Wild Man*, p. 211.
3. Douglas, *Purity and Danger*, p. 94.
4. Serfaty, "Foreword," p. vii.
5. Freud, *New Introductory Lectures on Psychoanalysis*, p. 73.
6. Steiner, *Taboo*.
7. Lincoln, *Discourse and the Construction of Society*, p. 166.
8. Ibid., 165.
9. Lévi-Strauss, *Totemism*, p. 53.
10. Quoted in Hanke, *Aristotle and the American Indians*, p. 4.
11. See Robe, "Wild Man and Spain's Brave New World."
12. See Hanke, *Aristotle and the American Indians*.
13. Yet Christian doctrine is also one of redemption through grace. All creatures come from and return to God; there is a graded hierarchy of being that presupposes a common essence, each creature being governed by the attributes specific to its species. Aquinas, unlike Averroes, held that the human soul is immortal; Aquinas also held that the souls of animals, however, are not immortal.

    Philosophy waited until Hume to rid "substance" from psychological concepts such as Self, soul, or subject. Such ambiguity concerning spiritual essence was partly responsible for the popularity of another adjunctive thesis, namely, the degeneracy and the monstrosity that derives from mixing different types of species. Whatever the state of physical degeneracy, the soul was potentially salvageable, in the Christian scheme. In Saint Augustine's view, even the most monstrous people reported by ancient travelers were still people who should not be denied essential humanity. The possibility of a man with the soul of an animal, so that it could not be saved even by God's grace, was the subject of a peculiarly medieval theological debate.
14. White, *Tropics of Discourse*, p. 154. Italics in original.
15. For an example of ETA activists calling their victim "dog" before executing him, see Zulaika, *Basque Violence*, p. 74.
16. Clutterbuck, *Living with Terrorism*, p. 123.
17. Netanyahu, *Terrorism: How the West Can Win*, p. 202.
18. *Diario 16*, March 23, 1981.
19. Lodge, *The Threat of Terrorism*, pp. 248–49.
20. The suspicion of the existence of an unofficial "shoot-to-kill" policy began in 1977, when undercover units of the British Army killed ten people during one year, of whom three were innocent civilians. The other seven, connected with the IRA, were shot in disputed circumstances. Between November 1982 and the end of 1983, security forces killed fourteen civilians, most of them unarmed. See Smyth, "Stretching the Boundaries."
21. See Stalker, *Stalker: Ireland, "Shoot to Kill" and the "Affair."*
22. *El País*, Sept. 6, 1988.
23. Quoted in Schelesinger, Murdock, and Elliott, *Televising "Terrorism"*, p. 27.
24. See the *New York Times*, July 11 and August 13, 1993.
25. *New York Times*, August 6, 1993, p. A5.
26. See Miralles and Arques, *Amedo: El Estado contra ETA*, for an extensive, in-depth journalistic account of the entire affair.

27. See Nelson, "Terrorist Challenge to the Rule of Law," p. 234.
28. Roberts, "Ethics, Terrorism and Counter Terrorism," p. 62.
29. "Indirect forms of warfare include clandestine and covert military operations carried out by other than the regular armed forces of a nation, providing asylum and support for guerrillas in an adjacent country, providing support—and sometimes operational direction—to terrorist groups opposing a rival or enemy regime, and governmental use of terrorist tactics, such as assassinating foreign foes or troublesome exiles" (Jenkins, "New Modes of Conflict," p. v).
30. Conrad, *The Secret Agent*, p. 70.
31. Quoted in Taussig, *Shamanism, Colonialism, and the Wild Man*, p. 121.
32. Ibid., 213.
33. *Newsweek*, August 28, 1995, p. 26.
34. *New York Times*, October 2, 1993, pp. A1–A8.
35. *New York Times*, October 9, 1993, p. A11.
36. Editorial of the *New York Times*, "Censure and Promotion at the FBI" May 9, 1995, p. A26.
37. Postrel, "Post-Mortem on the Waco Disaster," p. 24.
38. Quoted in Boyer, "Children of Waco," p. 42.
39. Robertson, "Suffer the Little Children," p. 177.
40. See Kelley, "Open Season on Messiahs?" p. 218.
41. Hofstadter, "The Paranoid Style in American Politics," p. 32.
42. See Kelley, "Open Session on Messiahs?" p. 219; and Robbins and Anthony, "'Cults,' 'Mind Control,' and the State," p. 130.
43. Hicks, *In Pursuit of Satan*, p. 56.
44. Quoted in ibid., p. 276.
45. Quoted in Milne, "The Cult Awareness Network," p. 137.
46. Quoted in ibid., p. 138.
47. Quoted in ibid.
48. See Lewis, "Introduction: Responses to the Branch Davidian Tragedy," p. xiv.
49. Milne, "The Cult Awareness Network," p. 140.
50. Quoted in ibid., p. 138.
51. Quoted in ibid., p. 139.
52. Quoted in ibid.
53. Lilliston, "Who Committed Child Abuse at Waco?" p. 170.
54. Hicks, *In Pursuit of Satan*.
55. Milne, "The Cult Awareness Network," p. 142.
56. Harding, "Knowing Satan," pp. 1–2.
57. Harding, "Imagining the Last Days," p. 16.
58. Ibid., p. 21.
59. *Newsweek*, July 31, 1995, p. 28.
60. *Los Angeles Times*, July 16, 1995, p. A14.
61. Bunting, "Embers of Doubt Remain about Cause of Waco Blaze," p. A1.
62. Lilliston, "Who Committed Child Abuse at Waco?" p. 173.
63. Leach, *Custom, Law, and Terrorist Violence*, p. 36.
64. *New York Times*, December 31, 1995, p. Y12.
65. See Malinowski, *Crime and Custom in Savage Society*, and Radcliffe-Brown, "Public and Private Delicts in Primitive Law."
66. See Schmid, *Political Terrorism*, pp. 25–32.
67. Lipset, *Political Man*, p. 64.

68. Leach, *Custom, Law, and Terrorist Violence*, p. 12.

69. Bonanate, "Some Unanticipated Consequences of Terrorism," p. 197.

70. Rose, et al., *Report of the International Commission on Violence in the Basque Country*, #2.6.

71. See for instance Janke's remarks in "Basque Separatism," p. 163. In fact, new revelations in 1991 showed that the very year (1985) in which the experts were writing the report, the Spanish military had a carefully orchestrated plan to stage a coup.

72. Sprinzak, *The Ascendancy of Israel's Radical Right*, p. 227.

73. Kerr, "Fujimori's Plot," p. 18.

74. Ibid.

75. Taylor, "Interpretation and the Sciences of Man."

76. According to Weber, "The case which is by far the most complicated and most interesting [is] the problem of the logical structure of the *concept of the state*" (*The Methodology of the Social Sciences*, p. 99; italics in original). The literature on terrorism is oblivious to this basic issue. The conclusion that the state represents the "ultimate" political value and that all social actions should be evaluated in terms of their relation to its interests is scorned by him as "an inadmissible deduction of a value-judgment from a statement of fact," for "there are certain things which the state cannot do. This is the case even in the sphere of military activity, which might be regarded as its most proper domain" (Ibid., p. 46). He granted the state an auxiliary status for the realization of other values from which it derives its own value.

77. Sprinzak, *The Ascendancy of Israel's Radical Right*, pp. 117–121.

78. Ibid., p. 233.

79. Ibid., p. 235.

80. Ibid., pp. 91–92.

81. Jáuregui Bereciartu, *The Decline of the Nation State*.

82. Díez Alegría, *Ejército y Sociedad*, p. 148.

83. See, for example, Clark, *Negotiating with ETA*.

84. Rose, et al., *Report of the International Commission on Violence in the Basque Country*, #8.36.

85. Lincoln, *Discourse and the Construction of Society*, pp. 61–66.

86. Ibid., p. 62.

87. In the case of Libya, and despite the well-known ties of Qaddafi to terrorist groups, the literature is unanimous that none of these countries ever produced any evidence to back up the charges of Libyan involvement in the events leading to those raids.

88. For further elaboration of this interrelationship in recent American policy, see Falk, *Revolutionaries and Functionaries*.

89. Quoted in Margalit, "The Uses of the Holocaust," p. 10.

90. Cassese, *Terror, Politics, and the Law*.

91. Ibid., pp. 67, 127.

92. Ibid., pp. 78, 129.

93. Ibid., p. 80.

94. Roberts, "Ethics, Terrorism and Counter Terrorism," p. 65.

95. See Gasser, "An Appeal for Ratification by the United States," pp. 912–25.

96. Falk, *Revolutionaries and Functionaries*, p. 147.

97. Vercher, *Terrorism in Europe*, p. 228.

98. Ibid., p. 229.

99. Ibid., p. 390.

100. Ibid., p. 230.

101. Ibid., p. 233.

102. Jenkins and Wright, "Why Hostage Taking is so Popular with Terrorists," p. 145.

103. *New York Times*, March 29, 1995, p. A4.

104. The Justice Department spokesman Carl Stern quoted by Tim Weiner in "CIA Re-examines Hiring of Ex-Terrorist as Agent" *The New York Times*, August 21, 1995, p. A2.

105. Quoted in Corn, "A Talk with Aldrich Ames," p. 240.

106. Rose, et al., *Report of the International Commission on Violence in the Basque Country*, #8.18.

107. Leach, *Custom, Law, and Terrorist Violence*, p. 36.

108. Horchem, "Pre-empting Terror," p. 312.

109. White, *Topics of Discourse*, p. 137.

110. Lévi-Strauss, "Introduction a l'oeuvre de Marcel Mauss," p. xxvii.

111. Morgan, *The Demon Lover*.

112. Sprinzak, *The Ascendancy of Israel's Radical Right*.

113. Gorriti Ellenbogen, *Sendero*.

114. See Zulaika, "Further Encounters with the Wild Man."

115. The concept of "the imagination" can be reformulated to account for the processes with which the individual puts together knowledge, perceptions, and emotions (Friedrich, *The Language Parallax*, p. 18). It is both analytic and highly synthetic in its creative use of language and other symbolic systems. It includes emotions, aesthetic apprehension, and mythic forms of imagining, as well as cognition and practical reason. Of particular interest for the arguments of this section is that maximum freedom from formal constraints, either in language or imagery, is granted by the imagination, which has therefore a significantly chaotic element emerging from the sense of individual self.

116. Needham, *Primordial Characters*, p. 64.

117. Comaroff and Comaroff, "The Madman and the Migrant," p. 191.

118. Geertz, "Anti anti-relativism," p. 275.

119. A "collective representation" is, in the Durkheimian sense, an imaginary construct or concept shared by many people, with a reality of its own that is external to any individual conscience and sufficiently similar to allow effective communication and social action among those holding it. Collective representations are also collective affections. They serve as the basis for classifying the world. The real task of the social scientist, Durkheim and Mauss contended in *Primitive Classifications*, is that of studying such collective representations that reveal the deeper layers of social cohesion.

120. Martin and Walcott, *Best Laid Plans*, p. 56.

121. See Harding, "Imagining the Last Days," pp. 39–40.

122. Moynihan, "Defining Deviancy Down."

123. Charles Marwick, "A Public Health Approach to Making Guns Safer," *JAMA*, June 14, 1995, 273 (22): 1743.

124. *New York Times*, July 20, 1993, p. A6.

125. See the freely distributed *Patterns of Global Terrorism 1992*, published by the Department of State.

126. During the 1960s the "carnage" of over 50,000 motor vehicle deaths a year in the

United States was considered unacceptable, whereas now that annual rate is pretty much regarded as "normal." In 1955 there were 93,314 mental patients in New York State, whereas in 1992 there were 11,363—a result of "redefining" rather than "curing" mental illness. In this fashion, most pressing issues of modern life—mental illness, family welfare, gays in the military—can be defined and redefined upward or downward on the priority scale, the consequences of such redefinitions being critical for social policy. Such dynamics underscore the extent to which notions of what constitutes normalcy and anomaly are not embedded in the very nature of things; rather it is a matter of definition and public perception.

127. Leach, *Custom, Law, and Terrorist Violence*, p. 32. Italics in original.
128. Ehrenfeld, *Narco-Terrorism*, p. 185.
129. Ibid., p. 184.
130. Thomas, "Our 'Subculture of Violence'," p. 37.
131. *JAMA*, June 14, 1995, 273 (22): 1743.
132. Marx, "The Fetishism of Commodities and the Secret thereof."
133. White, *Tropics of Discourse*.
134. See Carrol, "The Nature of Horror."

7: FACES OF TERROR AND LAUGHTER

1. Taussig, *Shamanism, Colonialism, and the Wild Man*, p. 9.
2. For the distinctions between "discourse as language," "discourse as ideology," and "discourse as subjectivity," see Easthope, *Poetry as Discourse*.
3. A fundamental reference for the relationship between systems of punishment and the political economy of the body is Foucault's seminal *Discipline and Punish*. Feldman's *Formations of Violence* provides an ethnographically sustained and philosophically based argument regarding "the instrumental staging and commodification of the body by political violence" (p. 8).
4. Data taken from Pulgar Gutiérrez, *Las víctimas del terrorismo de ETA*.
5. Cuesta, *Víctimas civiles del terrorismo residentes en Guipúzcoa*, p. 39.
6. Feldman, *Formations of Violence*, p. 136.
7. Gadamer, *Truth and Method*, p. 113.
8. Scarry, *The Body in Pain*, p. 56.
9. Rajali, *Torture and Modernity*, p. 163.
10. Feldman, *Formations of Violence*, p. 86.
11. See Pollack and Hunter, "Dictatorship, Democracy and Terrorism in Spain," p. 133.
12. These are Hillyard's and Walsh's estimates quoted in Feldman, *Formations of Violence*, pp. 88 and 113, respectively.
13. Ibid., p. 86.
14. Suárez-Orozco, "A Grammar of Terror," p. 239.
15. Rajali, *Torture and Modernity*, p. 175.
16. Vercher, *Terrorism in Europe*, p. 247.
17. Peters, *Torture*, p. 164.
18. Celan, "From Darkness to Darkness," p. 79.
19. Foucault, *Discipline and Punish*, p. 40.
20. Sartre, "Preface," p. 23.
21. Feldman, *Formations of Violence*, p. 115.
22. Sluka, *Hearts and Minds, Water and Fish*, p. 283.

23. For an interesting historical overview on the use of masks for the purpose of inducing terror, see Caro Baroja, *Terror y Terrorismo*.
24. Moraza and Basterra, *La columna infame*, p. 205. Similarly, it is estimated that more than 10,000 persons were arrested in the Basque Country during the years 1968–75; for the numbers of yearly detainees, see Castells Arteche 1982, p. 104.
25. See Jacques, "Spain: Systematic Torture in a Democratic State," p. 60.
26. TAT, *1993 Informe anual.*
27. See the *New York Times*, March 23, 1995, p. A8.
28. See *El País. Edicion Internacional*, August 7, 1995, p. 11.
29. Forest, *Diez Años de Tortura y Democracia*, pp. 259–62.
30. She wrote this piece from the University of California, Irvine, where her husband Alfonso Sastre, a prominent Spanish playwright, was teaching at the time. Later in 1992, Sastre was denied a visa to teach as a distinguished professor at Irvine because he and Forest had joined the ranks of 200 European intellectuals signing a letter protesting the Gulf War.
31. On the "crisis of witnessing," see the seminal essays by Felman and Laub, *Testimony: Crises of Witnessing in Literature, Psychoanalysis, and History.*
32. *New York Times*, August 16, 1995, p. A6.
33. Feldman, *Formations of Violence*, p. 115.
34. A federal official quoted in the *New York Times*, March 27, 1993, p. 7A.
35. According to Herman and O'Sullivan, *The "Terror" Industry*, p. 18, 74 percent of an estimated 35 countries using torture on a regular administrative basis were clients of the United States.
36. For many years, both during Franco's dictatorship and afterward, Amnesty International's yearly report has routinely accused Spain of systematic use of torture.
37. See Crenshaw, *Revolutionary Terrorism.*
38. For a list of documented cases of systematic torture in Great Britain, see, for instance, Schlesinger, Murdock, and Elliot, *Televising "Terrorism,"* p. 23.
39. For data about systematic torture in Israel, see Herman and O'Sullivan, *The "Terror" Industry*, p. 32.
40. Lewis, "Mr. Clinton's Betrayal," p. A17.
41. Ibid.
42. *New York Times*, June 9, 1995, p. A14.
43. On August 16, 1995, once again the Israeli government extended the authority of the secret services to use torture on Palestinian suspects, specifically the authority to violently shake the detainees, a technique previously banned by the Israeli Attorney General. The decision followed an appeal to the government from Amnesty International that charged that "Palestinian detainees in Israel have been systematically subjected to methods of torture including hooding, shaking, beating, sleep deprivation while standing or sitting in painful positions and prolongued confinement in closet-sized cells" (*New York Times*, August 17, 1995, p. A6).
44. See Gerstein, "Do the Terrorists Have Rights?"
45. Leach, *Custom, Law, and Terrorist Violence*, p. 36.
46. Booth, "Individualism and the Mystery of the Social Self," p. 97.
47. Forest, "Bajo los efectos de un viaje," p. 37.
48. Zulaika, *Basque Violence*, p. xxviii.
49. Ibid., p. 75.

50. For similar moral debates in the Irish case, see Sluka, *Hearts and Minds, Water and Fish*; and Burton, *The Politics of Legitimacy.*

51. Leach, *Custom, Law, and Terrorist Violence*, p. 27.

52. White, *Tropics of Discourse*, p. 130.

53. *Time*, August 21, 1995, p. 22.

54. Quoted repeatedly in Levinas's work.

55. Leach, *Custom, Law, and Terrorist Violence*, p. 36.

56. Geertz, "Anti anti-relativism," p. 275.

57. Benjamin, "Critique of Violence," p. 293.

58. Levi, "Afterward," p. 388.

59. Aretxaga, "Striking with Hunger," p. 246.

60. Zulaika, *Basque Violence*, p. 350.

61. For a description of the incident, see the final section of chapter 2.

62. De Man, *Allegories of Reading*, p. 282.

63. Felman and Laub, *Testimony*, p. 152.

64. Levinas and Finkielkraut interviewed by Shlomo Malka on Radio Communauté, Semptember 28, 1982. In Levinas, *The Levinas Reader*, p. 290.

65. Ibid., p. 292.

66. An expression used by Alain Finkieldraut in the same radio interview. In Levinas, *The Levinas Reader*, p. 291.

67. Gordon, *Sacrifice of Isaac*, pp. 193–94.

68. Kierkegaard, *Fear and Trembling*, p. 28.

69. De Man, *Allegories of Reading*, p. 245.

70. Gordon, *Sacrifice of Isaac*, pp. 30, 184.

71. Camus, *The Fall*, p. 110.

72. Felman. In Felman and Laub, *Testimony*, pp. 189, 196.

73. Ibid., p. 198.

74. See Felman and Laub, *Testimony*, p. xvii.

75. Felman and Laub, *Testimony*, p. 206.

76. See chapter 2 of this volume.

77. *New York Times*, March 19, 1995, p. A9.

78. Felman. In Felman and Laub, *Testimony*, p. 219.

79. This very writing—concerned with detabooing the witnesses of the violence— remains for some readers highly suspect and threatening. Time and again we have noted that our text can be perceived as a breach of the taboo proscribing terrorists. It is emblematic, for example, that the editorial board of a major university press rejected the dialogic approach advocated herein. "Talk to a McVeigh?" In a most unusual move, board members voted down publication of this book after our manuscript had passed satisfactorily a four-year process of review and revision. Ironically, it was while we were in Atlanta's Carter Center, while trying to broker peace talks to find a solution to the question of Basque violence, that we received a fax that members of that editorial board were disturbed by our argument. Meeting in the emotional climate less than a week after the Oklahoma City explosion, they concluded that our text was inadmissible because of a hidden "political agenda." They were simply abiding by the taboos of official terrorism discourse, much as the learned theologians and lawyers of the Inquisition respected the medieval Church's doctrine concerning witchcraft. "Talk to a McVeigh?" they marveled, while adding, "That's a *non sequitur!*" But no less perplexing is Arafat shaking hands with Rabin in Washington or Gerry Adams visiting the White

House. Were Kurt Vonnegut Jr. writing the script, he would surely add, "And so it goes."

EPILOGUE AS PROLOGUE

1. Quoted in Rich, "The Rambo Culture," p. A19.
2. Editorial, "A Hasty Response to Terrorism" *New York Times*, June 9, 1995.
3. *The Economist*, August 20, 1994, p. 13.
4. Ibid.
5. *New York Times*, August 12, 1994 p. A1.
6. See *El País. Edition Internacional*, May 15, 1995, p. 3.
7. Words by Martin Schulz, the *New York Times*, May 18, 1995, A4.
8. *New York Times*, April 21, 1995, p. A8.
9. *New York Times*, Dec. 24, 1994, p. A7.
10. See Perlez, "Tracing a Nuclear Risk," p. A3.
11. See R. Friedman, "The CIA's *Jihad*," *New York*, March 27, 1995, pp. 41–43.
12. Lapham, "Seen But Not Heard."
13. E. J. Dionne, in the *Washington Post*. Quoted in Lapham, "Seen But Not Heard," p. 32.
14. *USA Today*, June 30, 1995, p. 5B.
15. *Catechism of the Catholic Church*, p. 553.
16. *New York Times*, September 11, 1994, p. A8.
17. *The Economist*, August 27, 1994, p. 32.
18. Margalit, "The Terror Master," p. 17.
19. Ibid., pp. 17–18.
20. Quoted in ibid., p. 19.
21. *New York Times*, Nov. 4, 1995, p. A14.
22. Ibid.
23. "How About You?" *New York Times*, Nov. 8, 1995, p. A17.
24. *Washington Post National Weekly Edition*, Nov. 13-19, 1995, p. 7.
25. See Friedman, "Wednesday News Quiz."
26. Sciolino, "Bankrupting Terror," p. A5.
27. Ibid., p. A5.
28. Lewis, "Back to McCarthy," p. A15.
29. *New York Times*, May 8, 1995, p. A13.
30. Editorial, *New York Times*, April 30, 1995, p. E14.
31. *New York Times*, May 7, 1995, p. A1.
32. Allan Nairn, "Haiti Under the Gun: How U.S. Intelligence Has Been Exercising Crowd Control." *The Nation*, Jan. 8/15, 1996, p. 14.
33. Quoted in ibid.
34. Ibid.
35. Jenkins, "International Terrorism," p. 30.

Bibliography

Alexander, Yonah, and Robert Picard. 1991. *In the Camera's Eye: News Coverage of Terrorist Events*. Washington, DC: Brassey's.

American Foreign Policy Council. 1992. *Modernizing Foreign Assistance. Resource Management as an Instrument of Foreign Policy*. Westport: Praeger.

Aranzadi, Juan. 1994. "Sangre simbólica e impostura antropológica." *Antropología* 6 : 65–96.

Arblaster, Anthony. 1977. "Terrorism: Myths, Meaning and Morals." *Political Studies* 25 (3): 413–24.

Aretxaga, Begoña. 1993. "Striking with Hunger: Cultural Meanings of Political Violence in Northern Ireland." In K. Warren, ed., *The Violence Within*. Boulder, CO: Westview Press, pp. 219–253.

Aron, Raymond. 1966. *Peace and War*. London: Weidenfeld and Nicolson.

Arques, Ricardo, and Melchor Miralles. 1989. *Amedo: El Estado contra ETA*. Barcelona: Plaza y Janés.

Barkun, Michael. 1993. "Reflections after Waco: Millennialists and the State." *Christian Century*, June 2–9. Reprinted in James Lewis, ed., *From the Ashes: Making Sense of Waco*. London: Rowman & Littlefield, pp. 41–49.

Barthes, Roland. 1968. *The Rustle of Language*. New York: Hill and Wang.

Bateson, Gregory. 1951. "Conventions of Communication: Where Validity Depends upon Belief." In J. Ruesch and G. Bateson, eds., *Communication: The Social Matrix of Psychiatry*. New York: W.W. Norton, pp. 212–227.

———. 1973. *Steps to an Ecology of Mind*. New York: Ballantine.

———. 1975. "Some Components of Socialization for Trance." *Ethos* 3 (2): 143–56.

———. 1979 *Mind and Nature*. New York: E.P. Dutton.

Beckett, Samuel. 1970. *Waiting for Godot*. New York: Grove.

Begin, Menachem. 1951. *The Revolt*. New York: Nash.

Behler, Ernst. 1990. *Irony and the Discourse of Modernity*. Seattle: University of Washington Press.

Beidelman, Thomas. 1970. "Towards More Open Theoretical Interpretations." In Mary Douglas, ed., *Witchcraft Confessions and Accusations*. London: Tavistock.

Bell, J. Bowyer. 1975. *Transnational Terror*. Washington: American Enterprise Institute for Public Policy Research.

———. 1977. "Trends on Terror: The Analysis of Political Violence." *World Politics* 29 (3): 476–88.

———. 1977. *Terror Out of Zion: Irgun Zuai Leumi, LEHI, and the Palestinian Underground, 1929–1949*. New York: St. Martin's.

Benjamin, Walter. 1978. "Critique of Violence." In *Reflections: Essays, Aphorisms, Autobiographical Writings*. New York: Harcourt Brace Jovanovich.

Bennet, James. 1990. "Mission Improbable: Why—10 Years after Desert One—the U.S. Still Isn't Ready to Fight the War Against Terrorism." *Washington Monthly*, June 1990: 22–23.

Ben-Yehuda, Nachman. 1989. "Conflict Resolution in an Underground Group: The Shamir-Giladi Clash." *Terrorism* 12 (3): 199–212.

———. 1995. "Behind Bomb Fugitive's Arrest, Quick Action on Informer's Tip." *New York Times*, February 10, p. A1.

Black, Max. 1962. *Models and Metaphors: Studies in Language and Philosophy*. Ithaca NY: Cornell University Press.

Blake, William. 1969. *Complete Works*. Edited by G. Keynes. London: Oxford University Press.

Boas, Franz. 1916. "The Origin of Totemism." *American Anthropologist* 18: 319–26.

Bodley, John. 1992. "Anthropology and the Politics of Genocide." In C. Nordstrom and J. Martin eds., *The Paths to Dominion, Resistance, and Terror*. Berkeley: University of California Press, pp. 37–51.

Bonanate, Luigi. 1979. "Some Unanticipated Consequences of Terrorism." *Journal of Peace Research* 16 (3): 196–211.

Booth, Waine. 1993. "Individualism and the Mystery of the Social Self; or, Does Amnesty Have a Leg to Stand On?" In B. Johnson, ed., *Freedom and Interpretation: The Oxford Amnesty Lectures 1992*. New York: Basic Books, pp. 69–101.

Boyer, Peter. 1995. "Children of Waco." *New Yorker*, May 15, pp. 38–45.

Bremer, Paul. 1988. "Terrorism: Myths and Reality." *Current Policy*, No. 1047, pp. 1–3.

Bromley, David. 1993. "The Mythology of Cults." *Style Weekly*, May 11, pp. 14–18.

Buckley, Jr., William F. 1992. *In Search of Anti-Semitism*. New York: Continuum.

Bunting, Glenn. 1995. "Embers of Doubt Remain about Cause of Waco Blaze." *Los Angeles Times*, July 16, pp. A1, A13–A14.

Burke, Kenneth. 1950. *A Rhetoric of Motives*. New York: Prentice-Hall.

Burton, Frank. 1978. *The Politics of Legitimacy: Struggles in a Belfast Community*. London: Routledge and Kegan.

Camus, Albert. 1956. *The Fall*. New York: Knopf.

Candland, Christopher. 1992. *The Spirit of Violence: An Interdisciplinary Bibliography of Religion and Violence*. New York: Occasional Papers of the Harry Frank Guggenheim Foundation.

Caro Baroja, Julio. 1989. *Terror y Terrorismo*. Barcelona: Plaza and Janes/Cambio 16.

Carré, John le. 1994. "The Shame of the West." *New York Times*, December 14, p. A19.

Carrol, Noel. 1987. "The Nature of Horror." *The Journal of Aesthetics and Art Criticism* 46 : 51–59.

Cassese, Antonio. 1989. *Terror, Politics, and the Law: The Achille Lauro Affair*. Princeton, NJ: Princeton University Press.

Castells Arteche, Miguel. 1982. *Radiografía de un modelo represivo*. San Sebastián: Ediciones Vascas.

———. *Catechism of the Catholic Church*. Liguori: Libreria Editrice Vaticana.

Celan, Paul. 1988. *Poems of Paul Celan*. Translated with an introduction by Michael Hamburger. New York: Persea Books.

Chomsky, Noam. 1983. *The Fateful Triangle: The United States, Israel and the Palestinians*. Boston: South End Press.

———. 1988. *The Culture of Terrorism*. Boston: South End Press.

Chomsky, Noam and Edward Herman. 1979. *The Political Economy of Human Rights*. 2 vols. Nottingham, UK: Spokesman.

Cixous, Hélène. 1994. "The Place of Crime. The Place of Forgiveness." In S. Seller, ed., *The Hélène Cixous Reader*. New York: Routledge, pp. 150–56.

Clark, Robert. 1983. "Patterns in the Lives of ETA Members." *Terrorism: An International Journal* 6 (3): 423–54.

———. 1990. *Negotiating with ETA: Obstacles to Peace in the Basque Country, 1975–1988.* Reno: University of Nevada Press.

Clifford, James. 1986. "On Ethnographic Allegory." In J. Clifford and G. E. Marcus, eds., *Writing Culture: The Poetics and Politics of Ethnography.* Berkeley: University of California Press.

Clutterbuck, Richard. 1975. *Living with Terrorism.* London: Faber and Faber.

Coates, James. 1987. *Armed and Dangerous: The Rise of the Survivalist Right.* New York: Hill and Wang.

Columbus, Christopher. 1892. *The Voyages of Christopher Columbus: The Story of the Discovery of America.* New York: Press of the Society.

Comaroff, John L. 1987. "Of Totemism and Ethnicity: Consciousness, Practice and the Signs of Inequality." *Ethnos* 52: 301–323.

Comaroff, John L., and Jean Comaroff. 1987. "The Madman and the Migrant: Work and Labor in the Historical Consciousness of a South African People." *American Ethnologist* 14: 191–209.

Corn, David. 1995. "A Talk With Aldrich Ames." *The Nation*, September 11, p. 240

Conrad, Joseph. 1993. *The Secret Agent.* Hertfordshire, UK: Wordsworth Classics.

Cooper, Thomas. 1991. "Terrorism and Perspectivist Philosophy: Understanding Adversarial News Coverage." In Y. Alexander and R. Picard, eds., *In the Camera's Eye.* Washington, DC: Brassey's, pp. 10–29.

Crelinsten, Ronald. 1989. "Images of Terrorism in the Media: 1966–1985." *Terrorism* 12: 167–98.

Crenshaw, Martha. 1978. *Revolutionary Terrorism. The FLN in Algeria, 1954–1962.* Stanford, CA: Hoover Institution.

———. 1981. "The Causes of Terrorism." *Comparative Politics* 13 (4): 379–99.

Crick, Malcolm. 1976. *Explorations in Language and Meaning: Towards a Semantic Anthropology.* New York: Wiley.

Cuesta, Cristina. 1994. *Víctimas civiles del terrorismo residentes en Guipúzcoa: Situación personal y respuesta social e institucional.* Master's thesis. Universidad del País Vasco.

Davis, Natalie. 1987. *Fiction in the Archives: Pardon Tales and their Tellers in Sixteenth-Century France.* Stanford, CA: Stanford University Press.

De Man, Paul. 1979. *Allegories of Reading: Figural Language in Rousseau, Nietzsche, Rilke, and Proust.* New Haven: Yale University Press.

Department of State Publications. 1993. *Patterns of Global Terrorism 1992.* Publication no.10054.

Derrida, Jacques. 1976. *Of Grammatology.* Trans. Gayatri Chakravorty Spivak. Baltimore, MD: Johns Hopkins University Press.

———. 1977. "Signature event context." *Glyph* 1: 172–97.

———. 1978. *Writing and Difference.* Chicago: University of Chicago Press.

———. 1988. "Like the Sound of the Sea Deep Within the Shell: Paul de Man's War." *Critical Inquiry* 14: 590–652.

Díez-Alegría, Manuel. 1972. *Ejército y Sociedad.* Madrid: Alianza Editorial.

Dostoevsky, Fyodor. 1948. *Brothers Karamazov.* New York: Grosset and Dunlap.

———. 1975. *Crime and Punishment.* Trans. Jessie Coulson. New York: Norton.

Douglas, Mary. 1966. *Purity and Danger.* London: Routledge and Kegan Paul.

Douglas, Mary, and Wildavsky, Aaron. 1982. *Risk and Culture: An Essay on the Selection of Technological and Environmental Dangers.* Berkeley: University of California Press.

Douglass, William. 1969. *Death in Murelaga.* Seattle: University of Washington Press.

Douglass, William and da Silva, Milton. 1971. "Basque Nationalism." In Oriol Pi-Sunyer, ed., *The Limits of Integration: Ethnicity and Nation in Modern Europe.* Research Reports, no. 9, Department of Anthropology. Amherst: University of Massachussets.

Douglass, William, and Joseba Zulaika. 1990. "On the Interpretation of Terrorist Violence: ETA and the Basque Political Process." *Comparative Studies in Society and History* 32: 238–57.

Durkheim, Emile. 1938. *The Rules of Sociological Method.* New York: Free Press.

Durkheim, Emile, and Marcel Mauss. 1963. *Primitive Classification.* Chicago: Chicago University Press.

Easthope, Antony. 1983. *Poetry as Discourse.* New York: Routledge.

The Economist.

Ehrenfeld, Rachel. 1990. *Narco-Terrorism.* New York: Basic Books.

El País.

Emerson, Steven. 1991. "The Capture of a Terrorist: The Hunter and Her Witness." *New York Times Magazine,* April 21, p. 31.

———. 1995. "Exchange: Journalist's *Jihad.*" *The Nation,* August 28/ September 4, p. 186.

Erasmus, Desiderius. 1500. *Adagiorum Collectanea.* Parhisiis: J. Philipp.

———. 1970. *The Praise of Folly.* New Haven, CT: Yale University Press.

Erikson, Erik. 1966. "Ontogeny of Ritualization in Man." In J.S. Huxley, ed., *A Discussion of Ritualization of Behavior in Animals and Man.* Series B. Vol 251. London: Royal Society, pp. 337–349.

Eser, G.O. 1991. "Repairing Our War-torn Industry." *Airline Executive International,* April 1991: 40.

Evans-Pritchard, Edward. 1951. *Social Anthropology.* London: Cohen and West.

———. 1962. "The Divine Kingship of the Shilluk of the Nilotic Sudan." In E. Evans-Pritchard, *Essays in Social Anthropology,* pp. 66–128. New York: Free Press, pp. 66–128.

———. 1965. *Theories of Primitive Religion.* Oxford: Clarendon.

Falk, Richard. 1988. *Revolutionaries and Functionaries.* New York: E.P. Dutton.

Farnen, Russell. 1990. "Terrorism and the Mass Media: A Systemic Analysis of a Symbiotic Process." *Terrorism* 13: 99–143.

Feldman, Allen. 1991. *Formations of Violence: The Narrative of the Body and Political Terror in Northern Ireland.* Chicago: University of Chicago Press.

Felman, Shoshana, and Dori Laub. 1992. *Testimony: Crises of Witnessing in Literature, Psychoanalysis, and History.* New York: Routledge.

Fernandez, James. 1965. "Symbolic Consensus in a Fang Reformative Cult." *American Anthropologist* 67: 902–929.

———. 1986. *Persuasions and Performances: The Play of Tropes in Culture.* Bloomington: Indiana University Press.

Ferracuti, Franco. 1983. "Psychiatric Aspects of Italian Left Wing and Right Wing Terrorism." Paper presented at the Seventh World Congress of Psychiatry, Vienna, Austria, July 1983.

Fish, Stanley. 1980. *Is There a Text in This Class?* Cambridge: Harvard University Press.

Forest, Eva. 1977. *Testimonios de Lucha y Resistencia.* Hendaye: Mugalde.

———. 1987. *Diez Años de Tortura y Democracia.* Hondarribia: Gestoras pro Amnistía de Euskadi.

———. 1993. "Bajo los efectos de un viaje." In *Dispersión.* Ondarribia: Gestoras pro Amnistía, pp. 9–54.

Foucault, Michel. 1977. *Discipline and Punish: The Birth of the Prison.* New York: Pantheon.

Fox, Robin. 1977. "The Inherent Rules of Violence." In P. Collett, ed., *Social Rules and*

Social Behavior. Oxford: Basil Blackwell, pp. 132–149.

———. 1982. "The Violent Imagination." In P. Marsh and A. Campbell, eds., *Agression and Violence.* Oxford: Basil Blackwell, pp. 6–26.

Frazer, James. 1963. *The Golden Bough: A Study in Magic and Religion.* New York: Macmillan.

Freedman, Lawrence. 1986. "Terrorism and Strategy." In Freedman, et al., eds., *Terrorism and International Order.* The Royal Institute of International Affairs. London: Routledge and Kegan Paul, pp. 56–76.

Freedman, Lawrence, Hill, Christopher, Roberts, Adam, Vincent, R. J., Wilkinson, Paul and Windsor, Philip. 1986. *Terrorism and International Order.* Chatham House Special Paper. London: Routledge and Kegan Paul.

Freud, Sigmund. 1950. *Totem and Taboo.* New York: W. W. Norton.

———. 1964. *New Introductory Lectures on Psychoanalysis.* Vol. 22 of *The Standard Edition of the Complete Psychological Works of Sigmund Freud.* Trans. by J. Strachey. London: Hogarth.

Friedman, Robert. 1995. "The CIA's *Jihad.*" *New York,* March 27, pp. 36–47.

———. 1995. "One Man's *Jihad.*" *The Nation,* May 15, p. 656.

Friedman, Thomas. 1995. "Wednesday News Quiz." The *New York Times,* March 31, p. A17.

———. 1995. "How About You?" *New York Times,* Nov. 8, p. A17.

Friedlander, Robert. 1980. *Terrorism and the Law: What Price Safety?* Gaithersburg, MD: IACP.

Friedrich, Paul. 1979. *Language, Context, and the Imagination: Essays by Paul Friedrich.* Stanford, CA: Stanford University Press.

———. 1986. *The Language Parallax: Linguistic Relativism and Poetic Indeterminacy.* Austin: University of Texas Press.

Frye, Northrop. 1957. *Anatomy of Criticism; four essays.* Princeton: Princeton University Press.

Gadamer, Hans George. 1989. *Truth and Method.* 2d, rev. ed. New York: Crossroad.

Gambetta, Diego. 1991. "In the Beginning Was the Word…. The Symbols of the Mafia." *Archives of European Sociology* 32: 53–77.

Gasser, Hans-Peter. 1987. "An Appeal for Ratification by the United States." *American Journal of International Law* 81 (4): 912–25.

Gatzaga Taldea. 1985. "Bost esperto ez dira bost esperto (bakarrik)." *Argia* 1078, suplemento, pp. i–viii.

Geertz, Clifford. 1973. *The Interpretation of Cultures.* New York: Basic Books.

———. 1984. "Anti anti-relativism." *American Anthropologist* 86: 263–78.

Geifman, Anna. 1993. *Thou Shalt Kill: Revolutionary Terrorism in Russia, 1894–1917.* Princeton, NJ: Princeton University Press.

Genette, Gerard. 1976. "Boundaries of Narrative." *New Literary History* 7: 1–13.

Gerstein, Robert. 1982. "Do the Terrorists Have Rights?" In D.C. Rapoport and Y. Alexander, eds., *The Morality of Terrorism: Religious and Secular Justifications.* New York: Pergamon.

Gibson, James William. 1994. *Warrior Dreams: Paramilitary Culture in Post-Vietnam America.* New York: Hill and Wang.

Girard, Rene. 1977. *Violence and the Sacred.* Baltimore, MD: Johns Hopkins University Press.

Glazer, Nathan. 1986. "Anti-Zionism—A Global Phenomenon." In Michael Curtis, ed., *Antisemitism in The Contemporary World* Boulder, CO: Westview Press, 155–63.

Gleick, Elizabeth. 1995. "Something Big Is Going to Happen." *Time,* May 8, 1995, pp. 50–53.

Goethe, Johann. 1932. *Faust: A Tragedy in Two Parts.* Trans. by B. Taylor. London: Oxford University Press.

Goldberg, Phyllis. 1993. "FBI Uses 'Cults' as Bait." *The National Alliance* (May 6), 14, no. 17.

Goody, Jack. 1961. "Religion and Ritual: The Definitional Problem." *British Journal of Sociology* 12: 142–64.

Gordon, Neil. 1995. *Sacrifice of Issac.* New York: Random House.

Gorriti Ellenbogen, Gustavo. 1990. *Sendero: historia de la guerra milenaria en el Perú.* Lima: Apoyo.

Gramsci, Antonio. 1957. *The Modern Prince and Other Writings.* New York: International Publishers.

Guess, George M. 1987. *The Politics of United States Foreign Aid.* New York: St. Martin's.

Gurr, Ted Robert. 1980. "On the Outcomes of Violent Conflict." In Ted Gurr, ed., *Handbook of Political Conflict: Theory and Research.* New York: Free Press.

———. 1988. "Empirical Research on Political Terrorism: The State of the Art and How It Might Be Improved." In R.O. Slater and M. Stohl, eds., *Current Perspectives on International Terrorism.* New York: Macmillan.

Hacker, Frederick. 1976. *Crusaders, Criminals, Crazies: Terror and Terrorism in Our Time.* New York: Norton.

Handler, Jerome. 1990. "Socioeconomic Profile of an American Terrorist: 1960 and 1970s." *Terrorism* 13: 195–213.

Hanke, Lewis. 1959. *Aristotle and the American Indians: A Study in Race Prejudice.* New York: Random House.

Harding, Susan. 1994. "Imagining the Last Days: The Politics of Apocalyptic Language." *The Bulletin of the American Academy of Arts and Sciences,* 48 (3): 14–44.

———. n.d. "Knowing Satan: Born-Again Technologies of the Demonic."

Hardman, Jacob. 1959. "Terrorism." In E.R. Seligman, ed., *Encyclopedia of the Social Sciences.* New York: Macmillan, vol. 14: 575–79.

Henningsen, Gustav. 1980. *The Witches' Advocate: Basque Witchcraft and the Spanish Inquisition (1609–1614).* Reno: University of Nevada Press.

Herman, Edward. 1982. *The Real Terror Network: Terrorism in Fact and Propaganda.* Boston: South End Press.

Herman, Edward, and Gerry O'Sullivan. 1989. *The "Terror" Industry: The Experts and Institutions that Shape Our View of Terror.* New York: Pantheon.

Hicks, Robert. 1990. *In Pursuit of Satan: The Police and the Occult.* New York: Prometheus.

———. 1993. "Cult Label Made Waco Violence Inevitable." *Pacific News Service,* March 12. Reprinted in James Lewis, ed., *From the Ashes: Making Sense of Waco.* London: Rowman and Littlefield, pp. 63–65.

Hill, Christopher. 1986. "The Political Dilemmas for Western Governments." In L. Freedman, et al., eds., *Terrorism and International Order.* The Royal Institute of International Affairs. London: Routledge and Kegan Paul, pp. 77–100.

Hinckley, Ronald. 1989. "American Opinion toward Terrorism: The Reagan Years." *Terrorism* 12: 387–99.

Hitchens, Christopher. 1986. "Wanton Acts of Usage. Terrorism: A Cliché in Search of Meaning." *Harper's* 273: 66–70.

Hofstadter, Richard. 1966. "The Paranoid Style in American Politics." In Richard Hofstadter, *The Paranoid Style in American Politics and Other Essays.* New York: Alfred A. Knopf, pp. 3–40.

Horchem, Hans. 1981. "Pre-empting Terror." In B. Netanyahu, ed., *International Terrorism:*

Challenge and Response. New Brunswick, NJ: Transaction Books, pp. 307–312.

Hordago. 1979. *Documentos*. 18 vols. San Sebastián, Spain: Lur.

Horowitz, Donald. 1985. *Ethnic Groups in Conflict*. Berkeley: University of California Press.

Humphries, Patrick, and Bauldie, John. 1991. *Absolutely Dylan*. New York: Viking Studio Books.

Huxley, Julian. 1966. *A Discussion of Ritualization of Behavior in Animals and Man*. Organized by Sir Julian Huxley. Series B, vol. 251. London: Royal Institute.

Isaacson, Alter, and James Kelly. 1993. "We Distorted our own Minds." *Time* (July 5), vol. 142, no. 1, pp. 32–33.

Jacques, Hylah. 1985. "Spain: Systematic Torture in a Democratic State." *Monthly Review* 37: 57–62.

Janke, Peter. 1986. "Basque Separatism: ETA's Threat to Basque Democracy." In W. Gutleridge, ed., *The New Terrorism*. The Institute for the Study of Conflict. London: Mansell, pp. 135–166.

Jáuregui Bereciartu, Gurutz. 1994. *The Decline of the Nation-State*. Reno: University of Nevada Press.

Jenkins, Brian. 1975. "International Terrorism: A New Model of Conflict." In D. Carlton and C. Schaerf, eds., *International Terrorism and World Security*. London: Croom Helm, pp. 13–49.

———. 1982. *Terrorism and Beyond: An International Conference on Terrorism and Low-Level Conflict*. Santa Monica, CA: Rand.

———. 1983. "New Modes of Conflict." Publication Series R-3009-DNA. Santa Monica, CA: Rand.

———. 1988. "Future Trends in International Terrorism." In R. Slater and M. Stohl, eds., *Current Perspectives on International Terrorism*. New York: St. Martin's, pp. 246–266.

Jenkins, Brian, and R. Wright. 1991. "Why Hostage Taking is so Popular with Terrorists." In B. Shechterman and M. Slann, eds., *Violence and Terrorism 91/92*. Guilford, CT: Dushkin Publishing Group, pp. 145–47.

Jorgensen, Joseph. 1985. "Religious Solutions and Native American Struggles: Ghost Dance, Sun Dance and Beyond." In B. Lincoln, ed., *Religion, Rebellion, Revolution*. New York: St. Martin's, pp. 97–128.

Journal of the American Medical Association.

Juaristi, Jon. 1990. "Héroes y traidores: el terrorismo y las falacias antropológicas." *El País*, May 20.

Kaldor, Mary and Paul Anderson, eds. 1986. *Mad Dogs: The U.S. Raids on Libya*. London: Pluto.

Kelley, Dean. 1994. "Open Session on Messiahs?" In James Lewis, ed., *From the Ashes: Making Sense of Waco*. London: Rowman and Littlefield, pp. 217–20.

Kermode, Frank. 1980. "Secrets and Narrative Sequence." *Critical Inquiry* 7: 83–101.

Kerr, Stanley. 1992. "Fujimori's Plot: An Interview with Gustavo Gorriti." *New York Times Review of Books*, June 25, p. 18.

Kierkegaard, Soren. 1968. *Fear and Trembling*. Trans. by W. Lowrie. Princeton, NJ: Princeton University Press.

Kristeva, Julia. 1982. *Powers of Horror: An Essay on Abjection*. New York: Columbia University Press.

Kroeber. Alfred. 1953. *Anthropology Today*. Chicago: University of Chicago Press.

Kuperman, Robert and Kuperman, Tamara. 1991. "Pan Am 103: Facts vs. Politics." *New York Times*, Nov. 16, p. 19.

Laing, Ronald. 1966. "Ritualization and Abnormal Behavior." In J.S. Huxley, ed., *A Discussion of Ritualization of Behavior in Animals and Man.* Series B, vol. 251. London: Royal Society, pp. 331–336.

Lapham, Lewis. 1995. "Seen But Not Heard: The Message of the Oklahoma Bombing." *Harper's,* July, pp. 29–36.

Laqueur, Walter. 1977. *Terrorism.* London: Weidenfeld and Nicolson.

Leach, Edmund. 1966. "Ritualization in Man in Relation to Conceptual and Social Development." In J.S. Huxley, ed., *A Discussion of Ritualization of Behavior in Animals and Man.* Series B, vol. 251. London: Royal Society, pp. 403–408.

———. 1977. *Custom, Law, and Terrorist Violence.* Edinburgh: Edinburgh University Press.

Leurdijk, Henk. 1975. "Summary of Proceedings: Our Violent Future." In D. Carlton and C. Shaerf, eds., *International Terrorism and World Security.* London: Croom Helm, pp. 1–12.

Leventhal, Paul, and Yonah Alexander. 1986. *Nuclear Terrorism: Defining the Threat.* Washington, DC: Pergamon.

———. 1987. *International Task Force on Prevention of Nuclear Terrorism.* Massachussetts: Lexington Books.

Levi, Primo. 1986. "Afterward: The Author's Answers to His Readers' Questions." In *Survival in Auschwitz and The Reawakening: Two Memoirs.* New York: Summit, pp. 375–397.

Levinas, Emmanuel. 1969. *Totality and Infinity.* Pittsburg, PA: Duquesne University Press.

———. 1989. *The Levinas Reader.* Edited by Seán Hand. Oxford: Basil Blackwell.

Lévi-Strauss, Claude. 1950. "Introduction a l'oeuvre de Marcel Mauss." In M. Mauss, *Sociologie and antropologie.* Paris: PUF, pp. 1-32.

———. 1963. *Totemism.* Boston: Beacon Press.

———. 1975. *Tristes Tropiques.* New York: Atheneum.

Lévy-Bruhl, L. 1923. *Primitive Mentality.* New York: Macmillan.

Lewis, Anthony. 1995. "Back to McCarthy." *New York Times,* Feb. 24, p. A15.

———. 1995. "Mr Clinton's Betrayal." *New York Times,* July 7, p. A17.

Lewis, James. 1994a. "Introduction: Responses to the Branch Davidian Tragedy." In James Lewis, ed., *From the Ashes: Making Sense of Waco.* London: Rowman and Littlefield, pp. xi-xvi.

———. 1994b. "Showdown at the Waco Corral: ATF Cowboys Shoot Themselves in the Foot." In James Lewis, ed., *From the Ashes: Making Sense of Waco.* London: Rowman and Littlefield, pp. 87–94.

———. 1994c. "Fanning the Flames of Suspicion: The Case against Mass Suicide at Waco." In James Lewis, ed., *From the Ashes: Making Sense of Waco.* London: Rowman and Littlefield, pp. 115–120.

Lilliston, Lawrence. 1994. "Who Committed Child Abuse at Waco?" In James Lewis, ed., *From the Ashes: Making Sense of Waco.* London: Rowman and Littlefield, pp. 169-73.

Lincoln, Bruce. 1985. *Religion, Rebellion, Revolution: An Interdisciplinary and Cross-Cultural Collection of Essays.* New York: St. Martin's.

———. 1989. *Discourse and the Construction of Society.* Oxford: Oxford University Press.

Lipset, Seymour. 1963. *Political Man: The Social Bases of Politics.* New York: Anchor.

Livingston, Steven. 1994. *The Terrorism Spectacle.* Boulder, CO: Westview Press.

Livingstone, Neil, and Terrel Arnold. 1986. *Fighting Back: Winning the War Against Terrorism.* Lexington, MA: Lexington Books.

Lodge, Juliet. 1988. *The Threat of Terrorism.* Boulder, CO: Westview Press.

Long, David. 1990. *The Anatomy of Terrorism.* New York: Free Press.

Lowie, Robert. 1925. *Primitive Religion.* New York: Liveright.

Macdonald, Andrew. 1980. *The Turner Diaries.* 2nd. ed. Hillsboro: National Vanguard Books.

Malinowski, Bronislaw. 1926. *Crime and Custom in Savage Society.* New York: Harcourt Brace.

Mallin, Jay. 1978. "Terrorism as a Military Weapon." In M.H. Livingston, L.B. Kress, and M.G. Wanek, eds., *International Terrorism in the Contemporary World.* Westport: Greenwood Press, pp. 389–401.

Marett, Robert. 1909. *The Threshold of Religion.* London: Methuen.

———. 1914. *The Threshold of Religion,* 2nd. ed. London: Methuen.

Margalit, Avishai. 1994. "The Uses of the Holocaust." *New York Review of Books,* 1, 4, pp. 7–10.

———. 1995. "The Terror Master." *New York Review of Books,* 42, 15, pp. 17–22.

Martin, David, and John Walcott. 1988. *Best Laid Plains: The Inside Story of America's War Against Terrorism.* New York: Harper and Row.

Marwick, Charles. 1995. "A Public Health Service Approach to Making Guns Safer." *JAMA,* June 14, 273(22): 1743–44.

Marx, Karl. 1967. "The Fetishism of Commodities and the Secret thereof." In K. Marx, *Capital,* vol 1. New York: International, pp. 81–95.

McLennan, John. 1869-70. "The Worship of Animals and Plants." *Fortnightly Review,* vols. 6 and 7.

Mead, Margaret. 1968. "Warfare Is Only an Invention—Not a Biological Necessity." In L. Bramson and G.W. Goethals, eds., *War: Studies from Psychology, Sociology, Anthropology.* New York: Basic Books, pp. 269–274.

Melton, J. Gordon. 1994. "Epilogue: A Fiery Ending." In James Lewis, ed., *From the Ashes: Making Sense of Waco.* London: Rowman and Littlefield, pp. 253–60.

Merari, Ariel. 1979. *Kingfisher Game: Summary of Procedure and Analysis.* Tel Aviv: Center for Strategic Studies and the Office of the Prime Minister's Adviser on Combatting Terrorism.

Merari, Ariel, and Nathan Friedland. 1985. "Social Psychological Aspects of Political Terrorism." In S. Oskamp, ed., *International Conflict and National Public Policy.* Vol. 6 of *Applied Social Psychology.* Beverly Hills, CA: Sage, pp. 185–205.

Miller, Jim. 1993. *The Passion of Michel Foucault.* New York: Simon and Schuster.

Milne, Andrew. 1994. "The Cult Awareness Network: Its Role in the Waco Tragedy." In James Lewis, ed., *From the Ashes: Making Sense of Waco.* London: Rowman and Littlefield, pp. 137–42.

Miralles, Melchor, and Ricardo Arques. 1989. *Amedo: El Estado contra ETA.* Barcelona: Plaza & Janes/Cambio 16.

Montaigne, Michel de. 1927. *The Essays of Montaigne.* London: Oxford University Press.

Moore, Sally, and Barbara Myerhoff. 1977. *Secular Ritual.* Assen/Amsterdam: Van Gorcum.

Moraza, Lurdes, and Mertxe Basterra. 1994. *La columna infame.* Tafalla Navarra: Txalaparta.

Morgan, Robin. 1989. *The Demon Lover: On the Sexuality of Terrorism.* New York: W. W. Norton.

Morris, David. 1966. "The Rigidification of Behavior." In J.S. Huxley, ed., *A Discussion of Ritualization of Behavior in Animals and Man.* series B, vol. 251. London: Royal Society, pp. 327–330.

Moynihan, Daniel. 1993. "Defining Deviancy Down." *The American Scholar,* 62: 17–30.

Moynihan, Patrick. 1991. "Do We Still Need the C.I.A.?" *New York Times*, May 19, p. A15.

Mullins, Wayman. 1988. *Terrorist Organizations in the United States: An Analysis of Issues, Organizations, Tactics and Responses*. Springfield: Charles Thomas.

Nacos, Brigitte, David Fan, and J.T. Young. 1989. "Terrorism and the Print Media: The 1985 TWA Hostage Crisis." *Terrorism* 12: 107–115.

Nairn, Allan. 1996. "Haiti Under the Gun: How U.S. Intelligence Has Been Exercising Crowd Control." *The Nation*, January 8/15, pp. 11–15.

Needham, Rodney. 1962. *Structure and Sentiment: A Test Case in Social Anthropology*. Chicago: Chicago University Press.

———. 1978. *Primordial Characters*. Charlottesville: University Press of Virginia.

Neill, Alexander. 1991. "Fear, Fiction, and Make-Believe." *The Journal of Aesthetics and Art Criticism* 49: 47–56.

Nelson, William. 1990. "Terrorist Challenge to the Rule of Law: The British Experience." *Terrorism* 13 (3): 227–36.

Netanyahu, Benjamin. 1995. *Fighting Terrorism: How Democracies Can Defeat Domestic and International Terrorists*. New York: Farrar, Straus and Giroux.

———. 1995. "Act Now Against Terrorism." *New York Times*, Nov. 4, p. A15.

———. 1986. "Terrorism: How the West Can Win." In Benjamin Netanyahu, ed., *Terrorism: How the West Can Win*. New York: Farrar, Straus & Giroux, pp. 196–226.

New York Times.

Newsweek.

Nordstrom, Carolyn, and Joann Martin. 1992. "The Culture of Conflict: Field Reality and Theory." In C. Nordstrom and J. Martin eds., *The Paths to Domination, Resistance, and Terror*. Berkeley: University of California Press, pp. 3–15.

Oliver, Moorman. 1994. "Killed by Semantics: Or Was It a Keystone Kaleidoscope Kaper?" In James Lewis, ed., *From the Ashes: Making Sense of Waco*. London: Rowman & Littlefield, pp. 71–86.

Orwell, George. 1990. "Killing Civilians." In S. Barnett and H. Bedan, eds., *Current Issues and Enduring Questions: Methods and Models of Argument*. 2d ed. Boston: St. Martin's, pp. 101–103.

Paine, Robert, ed. 1981. *Politically Speaking: Cross-Cultural Studies of Rhetoric*. Philadelphia: ISHI.

Paletz, David, and Alex Schmid. 1992. *Terrorism and the Media*. Newbury Park, CA: Sage.

Palmerton, Patricia. 1988. "The Rhetoric of Terrorism and the Media Response to the 'Crisis of Iran'." *Western Journal of Speech Communication* 52 (2): 105–121.

Peirce, Charles. 1955. *Philosophical Writings of Peirce*. Edited by J. Buchler. New York: Dover.

Pepper, Stephen. 1942. *World Hypothesis: A Study in Evidence*. Berkeley: University of California Press.

Perlez, Jane. 1995. "Tracing a Nuclear Risk: Stolen Enriched Uranium." *New York Times*, February 15, p. A3.

Peters, Edward. 1985. *Torture*. New York: Basic Blackwell.

Pollack, Benny, and Graham Hunter. 1988. "Dictatorship, Democracy and Terrorism in Spain." In Juliet Lodge, ed., *The Threat of Terrorism*. Boulder, CO: Westview Press, pp. 119–44.

Post, Jerrold. 1984. "Notes on a Psychodynamic Theory of Terrorist Behavior." *Terrorism* 7 (3): 241–56.

Post, Jerrold, and Raphael Ezekiel. 1988. "Worlds in Collision, Worlds in Collusion: The Uneasy Relationship Between the Counterterrorism Policy Community and the Academic Community." *Terrorism* 11 (6): 503–509.

Postrel, Virginia. 1995. "Post-Mortem on the Waco Disaster: Does the Federal Government Understand the Message It's Sending?" *Washington Post National Weekly Edition*, May 8-14, p. 24.

Pringle, Peter. 1986. "View from Washington." In M. Kaldor and P. Anderson, ed., *Mad Dogs: The U.S. Raids on Libya*. London: Pluto, pp. 54-64.

Pulgar Gutiérrez, Belen. 1993. *Las víctimas del terrorismo de ETA*. Master's thesis Universidad de León, Spain.

Radin, Paul. 1937. *Primitive Religion*. New York: Viking.

Rajali, Darius. 1994. *Torture and Modernity: Self, Society, and State in Modern Iran*. Boulder, CO: Westview Press.

Ram, Uri. 1993. "The Colonization Perspective in Israeli Sociology: Internal and External Comparisons." *Journal of Historical Sociology* 6 (3): 327-50.

Rapoport, David. 1984. "Fear and Trembling: Terrorism in Three Religious Traditions." *American Political Science Review* 78 (3): 658-77.

Rapoport, David, and Yonah Alexander, eds. 1982. *The Morality of Terrorism: Religious and Secular Justifications*. New York: Pergamon.

Rappaport, Roy. 1979. *Ecology, Meaning, and Religion*. Richmond: North Atlantic Books.

Redfield, James. 1975. *Nature and Culture in the Iliad: The Tragedy of Hector*. Chicago: University of Chicago Press.

Report of an Amnesty International Mission to Spain. 1975. London: Amnesty International Publications.

Rich, Frank. 1995. "The Rambo Culture." *New York Times*, May 11, p. A19.

Rivers, William. 1941. *The History of Melanesian Society*. 2 vols. Cambridge: Cambridge University Press.

Robbins, Thomas, and Dick Anthony. 1994. "'Cults,' 'Mind Control,' and the State." In James Lewis, ed., *From the Ashes: Making Sense of Waco*. London: Rowman and Littlefield, pp. 125-35.

Robe, Stanley. 1972. "Wild Man and Spain's Brave New World." In E. Dudley and M.E. Novak, eds., *The Wild Man Within: An Image in Western Thought from the Renaissance to Romanticism*. Pittsburgh, PA: University of Pittsburgh Press, pp. 39-54.

Roberts, Adam. 1989. "Ethics, Terrorism and Counter Terrorism." *Terrorism and Political Violence* 1 (1): 62.

Robertson, George. 1994. "Suffer the Little Children." In James Lewis, ed., *From the Ashes: Makind Sense of Waco*. London: Rowman and Littlefield, pp. 175-180.

Rose, C., F. Ferracuti, H. Horchem, P. Janke, and J.Leaute. 1986. *Report of the International Commission on Violence in the Basque Country*. Vitoria, Spain: Eusko Jaurlaritza.

Rosenblueth, Arturo, Norbert Wiener, and J. Bigelow. 1943. "Behavior, Purpose and Teleology." *Philosophy of Science* 10: 18-24.

Rothstein, Marian. 1986. "When Fiction is Fact: Perceptions in Sixteenth-Century France." *Studies in Philology* 83: 359-75.

Rubinstein, Richard. 1987. *Alchemists of Revolution: Terrorism in the Modern World*. New York: Tauris and Co..

Rudé, George. 1967. *Robespierre*. Englewood Cliffs, NJ: Prentice-Hall.

Sapir, Edward. 1934. "The Emergence of the Concept of Personality in a Study of Cultures." *Journal of Social Psychology* 5: 412.

Sartre, Jean Paul. 1958. "Preface." In H. Alleg, ed., *The Question*. Translated by John Calder. New York: George Braziller, pp. 1-12.

Scarry. Elaine. 1985. *The Body in Pain: The Making and Unmaking of the World*. New York: Oxford University Press.

Schlesinger, Philip. 1991. *Media, State, and Nation: Political Violence and Collective Identities.* London: Sage.

Schlesinger, Philip, George Murdock, and Philip Elliott. 1983. *Televising "Terrorism": Political Violence in Popular Culture.* London: Comedia Publishing.

Schmid, Alex. 1983. *Political Terrorism: A Research Guide to Concepts, Theories, Data Bases and Literature.* New Brunswick, NJ: Transaction Books.

———. 1989. "Terrorism and the Media: The Ethics of Publicity." *Terrorism and Political Violence* 1: 539–65.

Schmid, Alex, and Janny de Graaf. 1982. *Violence as Communication: Insurgent Terrorism and the Western News Media.* Beverly Hills, CA: Sage.

Schmid, Alex and Albert Jongman. 1988. *Political Terrorism: A New Guide to Actors, Authors, Concepts, Data Bases, Theories and Literature.* New Brunswick, NJ: Transaction Books.

Schoenberg, Arnold. 1978. *Theory of Harmony.* Berkeley: University of California Press.

Sciolino, Elaine. 1995. "Bankrupting Terror." *New York Times,* January 26, p. A5.

Sederberg, Peter. 1991. "Defining Terrorism." In P.C. Sederberg, ed., *Terrorism: Contending Themes in Contemporary Research.* New York: Garland.

Serfaty, Simon. 1990. "Foreword." In Barry Rubin, ed., *The Politics of Counterterrorism: The Ordeal of Democratic States,* Washington, DC: Johns Hopkins Foreign Policy Institute, pp. vii–ix.

Shedd, Margaret. 1974. *Silence in Bilbao.* New York: Doubleday.

Sick, Gary. 1985. *All Fall Down: America's Tragic Encounter with Iran.* New York: Random House.

Slater, Philip. 1970. *The Pursuit of Loneliness, American Culture at the Breaking Point.* Boston: Beacon Press.

Slater, Robert, and Michael Stohl. 1988. "Introduction." In R. Slater and M. Stohl, eds., *Current Perspectives on International Terrorism.* New York: Macmillan, pp. 1–11.

Sleeman, John L. 1933. *Thugs; or a Million Murders.* London: S. Low and Marston.

Sluka, Jeffrey. 1989. *Hearts and Minds, Water and Fish: Support for the IRA and INLA in a Northern Irish Ghetto.* Greenwich, UK: Jai Press.

Smolowe, Jill. 1995. "Enemies of the State." *Time,* May 8, pp. 58–69.

Smyth, Jim. 1988. "Stretching the Boundaries: The Control of Dissent in Northern Ireland." *Terrorism* 11: 289–308.

Spencer, Herbert. 1882. *The Principles of Sociology.* New York: Appleton and Co.

Sprinzak, Ehud. 1991a. *The Ascendancy of Israel's Radical Right.* New York: Oxford University Press.

———. 1991b. "Violence and Catastrophe in the Theology of Rabbi Meir Kahane: The Ideologization of Mimetic Desire." *Terrorism and Political Violence* 3 (3): 48–70.

Stalker, James. 1988. *Stalker: Ireland, "Shoot to Kill" and the "Affair."* Harmondsworth, UK: Penguin.

Steiner, Franz. 1967. *Taboo.* Harmondsworth, UK: Penguin.

Sterling, Claire. 1981. *The Terror Network: The Secret War of International Terrorism.* New York: Holt, Rinehart, and Winston.

Suárez-Orozco, Marcelo. 1992. "A Grammar of Terror: Psychocultural Responses to State Terrorism in Dirty War and Post-Dirty War Argentina." In Carolyn Nordstrom and Joann Martin, eds., *The Paths to Dominion, Resistance, and Terror.* Berkeley: University of California Press, pp. 219–59.

Talmud. 1978. *The Babylonian Talmud.* Translated into English with notes under the editorship of I. Epstein.

TAT. 1993. *Informe anual.* Bilbao, Spain: Torturaren Aurkako Taldea.

Taussig, Michael. 1987. *Shamanism, Colonialism, and the Wild Man: A Study in Terror and Healing*. Chicago: University of Chicago Press.

Taylor, Charles. 1971. "Interpretation and the Sciences of Man." *Review of Metaphysic*, 25 (97): 3–51.

Taylor, Maxwell, and Helen Ryan. 1988. "Fanaticism, Political Suicide and Terrorism." *Terrorism* 11 (2): 91–111.

Taylor, Meadows. 1839. *Confessions of a Thug*. London: R. Bentley.

no author. *The John Franklin Letters*. 1959 New York: Bookmailer.

Thomas, Pierre. 1995. "Our 'Subculture of Violence'." *Washington Post*, National Weekly Edition, March 20–26, p. 37.

Thornton, Thomas. 1964. "Terror as a Weapon of Political Agitation." In H. Eckstein, ed., *Internal War: Problems and Approaches*. New York: Free Press, pp. 71–99.

Time.

Timerman, Jacobo. 1982. *Prisoner without a Name, Cell without a Number*. New York: Vintage.

Tololyan, Katchig. 1988. "Cultural Narrative and the Motivation of the Terrorist." In D. Rapoport, ed., *Inside Terrorist Organizations*. New York: Frank Cass, pp. 217–33.

Trevanian. 1979. *Shibumi*. New York: Crown.

Trevor-Roper, Hugh R. 1956. *The European Witch-Craze of the Sixteenth and Seventeenth Centuries and Other Essays*. New York: Harper and Row.

Turner, Terence. 1977. "Transformation, Hierarchy and Transcendence: A Reformulation of Van Gennep's Model of the Structure of *Rites of Passage*." In S. F. Moore and B. G. Myerhoff, eds. *Secular Ritual*. Assen, Netherlands: Van Gorcum, pp. 53–70.

Turner, Victor. 1980. "Social Dramas and Stories about Them." *Critical Inquiry* 7: 141–68.

Tylor, Edward. 1958. *The Origins of Culture*. New York: Harper.

Urban, Greg. 1991. *A Discourse-Centered Approach to Culture*. Austin: University of Texas Press.

USA Today.

Van Creveld, Martin. 1991. *Transformation of War*. New York: Free Press.

Van Gennep, Arnold. 1960. *The Rites of Passage*. Chicago: The University of Chicago Press.

Vayda, Andrew. 1968. "Primitive Warfare." In D.L. Sills, ed., *International Encyclopedia of the Social Sciences*. Vol. 16. New York: Macmillan and Free Press, pp. 468–71.

Vercher, Antonio. 1992. *Terrorism in Europe: An International Comparative Legal Analysis*. Oxford: Clarendon Press.

Vico, Giambattista. 1968. *The New Science of Giambattista Vico*. Rev. trans. of 3d ed., T.G. Bergin and M.H. Fish. Ithaca, NY: Cornell University Press.

Wagner-Pacifici, Robin. 1986. *The Moro Morality Play: Terrorism as Social Drama*. Chicago: University of Chicago Press.

Wall Street Journal.

Walton, Kendall. 1978. "Fearing Fictions." *Journal of Philosophy* 75 (1): 5–27.

Washington Post.

Weber, Max. 1949. *The Methodology of the Social Sciences*. New York: Free Press.

Weinberg, Leonard, and William Eubank. 1993. "Political Terrorism and Political Development." In H. Han ed., *Terrorism and Political Violence: Limits & Possibilities of Legal Control*. New York: Oceania, pp. 29–39.

Wheeler, Edward. 1991. "Terrorism and Military Theory: An Historical Perspective." *Terrorism and Political Violence* 3: 6–33.

White, Hayden. 1973. *Metahistory: The Historical Imagination in Nineteenth-Century Europe.* Baltimore, MD: Johns Hopkins University Press.

———. 1978. *Tropics of Discourse: Essays in Cultural Criticism.* Baltimore, MD: John Hopkins University Press.

———. 1980. "The Value of Narrativity in the Representation of Reality." *Critical Inquiry* 7: 5-28.

Wieviorka, Michel. 1993. *The Making of Terrorism.* Chicago: The University of Chicago Press.

Wilkinson, Paul. 1974. *Political Terrorism.* New York: John Wiley and Sons.

———. 1977. *Terrorism and the Liberal State.* London: Macmillan.

———. 1986. "Trends in International Terrorism and the American Response." In L. Freedman, et al. eds., *Terrorism and International Order.* London: Routledge and Kegan Paul, pp. 37-55.

———. 1987. "Terrorism: An International Research Agenda?" In P. Wilkinson and A.M. Stewart, eds., *Contemporary Research on Terrorism.* Aberdeen: Aberdeen University Press, pp. xi-xx.

———. 1990. "Some Observations on the Relationships between Terrorism and Freedom." In M. Warner and R. Crisp, eds., *Terrorism, Protest and Power.* Brookfield, VT: Edward Elgar, pp. 44-53.

Wilson, Michele, and John Lynxwiler. 1988. "Abortion Clinic Violence as Terrorism." *Terrorism and Political Violence* 11: 263-73.

Winzeler, Robert. 1993. "Shaman, Priest and Spirit Medium: Religious Specialists, Tradition and Innovation in Borneo." In R. Winzeler, ed., *The Seen and the Unseen: Shamanism, Mediumship and Possession in Borneo.* Williamsburg, VA: Ashley, pp. xi-xxxiii.

Wittgenstein, Ludwig. 1971. "Remarks on Frazer's 'Golden Bough'." *The Human World* 3: 18-41.

Zulaika, Joseba. 1988. *Basque Violence: Metaphor and Sacrament.* Reno: University of Nevada Press.

———. 1991. "Terror, Totem, and Taboo: Reporting on a Report." *Terrorism and Political Violence*, vol. 3, no. 1: 34-49.

———. 1993a. "Further Encounters with the Wild Man: Of Cannibals, Dogs, and Terrorists." *Etnofoor* 6 (2): 21-39.

———. 1994. "El antropólogo como impostor." *Antropología* 7:115-30.

———. 1995. "The Anthropologist as Terrorist." In C. Nordstrom and A. Robben, eds., *Fieldwork under Fire.* Berkeley: University of California Press, pp. 206-222.

Index

Abraham: absurd transcendence of his faith, 124-127, 148; and the Innocent Killer, 123; as murderer or believer, 125-127; ritual substitution by, 226; willingness to sacrifice Isaac on Mount Moriah, 124; *See also* Kierkegaard; Religion

Academia: as cover, 62; disciplines best defined by their taboos in, 181; fashioning of terrorism discourse by, xi, 91-92; terrorism as growth industry in, 26, 32, 100; terrorism and curricula, 23; *See also* Anthropology; Experts

Achille Lauro, 175

Action: activism as quintessential to terrorism, 66, 75, 135; and narrative, 36; autonomy of, 76; as armed struggle, 57-58; as quintessential to terrorism, 34; as ordeal by fire and the real thing, 76. See also Ritual initiation; as propaganda by the deed, 33; as ritual performance, 76, 78. *See also* Ritual; collective, 56-59; context determines meaning of, 74; counterterrorist, ix; discontinuous, 75-78; "emplotted" in terrorism, 65; in front of TV cameras, 28; in ritual non-instrumental link between goal and, 25; McVeigh's, 76, 170; magic of, 75-78, 151; militants' credo, 33; modeled after an all-or-nothing game, 76; momentous versus cumulative process, 75; non-feedback type of, in chance election, 138-148; precedence of over belief in anthropology, 114, 117; rhetorics of as quintessential to terrorist, 4; semantic gap between and denotation, 17; sociological categories of, 58; statistics of, 8; types of in ritual, 77; versus writing, 34, *See also* Writing terrorism; *See also* Ritual

Adagiorum Collectanea, 160

Adams, Gerry, x, 236

Afghanistan, 178, 185, 23

Africa, 20, 46, 154, 157

African National Congress, 12, 73

Aizpurua, Joxe Domingo, 198, 200, 201, 206, 208

Algeria, 17, 36, 53, 157, 234

Allegories of terror: Abraham as ready to sacrifice Isaac, 124-127; analogy as Freud's approach to the unconscious, 106, 153; as an intellectual approach to terrorism discourse, 106-109; belief in

biblical Apocalypse, 161, 168; biblical parables as, 106. *See also* Abraham; Kierkegaard; Blake's "Marriage of Heaven and Hell" as, 196-197; Conrad's *agent provocateur* as, 137; cultural models and, 118; disciplinary, 116; ethnographic, 106-109, 113-115, 117-118. *See also* Totemism; Witchcraft.; fetishism as, 189; from religion, 110-111, 113-115. *See also* Religion; intellectual history of anthropology as providing, 113-116; historical, 106-109. *See also* Witchcraft; hysteria as, 94, 116; Jewish conspiracy, the witch craze, the Red Scare as, 183; madness as, 116. *See also* Psychology; moral and figurative content of, 109; mythology of language and, 117; out of context, 107, 111; premillennial "dispensationalism" as, 168-169; realist discourse averted by means of metaphors and, 186; ritual pollution and taboo as, 152. *See also* Taboo; ritual sacrifice as, 129-131; secularization of priest as parable for local history, 213-214; shamans, witches, prophets, madmen and the like as, 183; Shoenberg's theory of harmony as, 138, 143; *Totem and Taboo* as, 116; witchcraft as, 95-96, 98-100, 116, 154, 219, 238; *trompe l'oeil* school of painting as, 143; Vico's notion of allegory as true reality, 118; *See also* Discourse of terrorism; Fiction; Narrative; Rhetorics; Semantics of terrorism Wild Man

Ambassador at large for Counterterrorism, 55

Ambiguity: abjection is, 151. *See also* Semantics of terrorism; politics versus military action in relation to, 84; purpose and, 130; ritual form and unambiguity, 84. *See also* Ritual; ruled out in terrorism discourse, 180, 226; terrorist persona's fundamental, 152, 180, 182, 216; totalizing discourse and rejection of, 89; writing on terrorism and moral, 62; *See also* Semantics of terrorism

American politics: anarchism and, 17; as bipolar world, 18-19; its premises, 15; "paranoid style" in, 53; *See also* Counterterrorism; Discourse of terrorism

Ames, Aldrich, 178

Amnesty International, 200, 205

Amuriza, Xabier, 41, 42, 43